30

STREET JUSTICE

STREET JUSTICE

A History of Police Violence in New York City

Marilynn Johnson

BEACON
150

Beacon Press
Boston

Beacon Press
25 Beacon Street
Boston, Massachusetts 02108-2892
www.beacon.org

Beacon Press books
are published under the auspices of
the Unitarian Universalist Association of Congregations.

07 06 05 04 03 8 7 6 5 4 3 2 1

This book is printed on acid-free paper that meets
the uncoated paper ANSI/NISO specifications
for permanence as revised in 1992.

Text design by Sara Eisenman
Composition by Wilsted & Taylor Publishing Services

Library of Congress Cataloging-in-Publication Data
Johnson, Marilynn S.
    Street justice : a history of police violence in New York City /
Marilynn Johnson.
        p. cm.
Includes bibliographical references.
    ISBN 0-8070-5022-9 (cloth : alk. paper)
    1. Police brutality—New York (State)—New York—History. I. Title.
    HV8148.N52J63 2003
    363.2'32—dc21

                                    2003014312

FOR DAN, ROSA, AND JACOB

LIST OF ABBREVIATIONS

ABA	American Bar Association
ACLU	American Civil Liberties Union
ABCNY	Association of the Bar of the City of New York
CRC	Civil Rights Congress
CCRB	Civilian Complaint Review Board
CCAPB	Citizens' Committee Against Police Brutality
CPL	Citizens' Protective League
CCPL	Colored Citizens Protective League
CP	Communist Party (USA)
CORE	Congress of Racial Equality
CAS	Criminal Alien Squad
ESVL	East Side Vigilance League
FBI	Federal Bureau of Investigation
FAIR	Federated Associations for Impartial Review
FDRB	Firearms Discharge Review Board
ILD	International Labor Defense
LEG	Law Enforcement Group
MCU	Mayor's Committee on Unity
NAACP	National Association for the Advancement of Colored People
NNC	National Negro Congress
NYCLA	New York County Lawyers Association
NYCLU	New York Civil Liberties Union
NYPD	New York Police Department
PBA	Patrolmen's Benevolent Association
PPP	Police Practices Project
SPC	Society for the Prevention of Crime
SCU	Street Crime Unit
SDS	Students for a Democratic Society
TPF	Tactical Patrol Force
UC	Unemployed Councils
VDC	Voluntary Defenders Committee

CONTENTS

STREET JUSTICE

INTRODUCTION

Like many Americans, I watched in disbelief in April 1992 when a California jury acquitted four police officers in the beating of black motorist Rodney King. Having watched and rewatched the video-taped beating—in which the officers administered fifty-six blows to King as he lay on the ground—I found the jury's verdict unfath-omable and horrifying. My horror grew when Los Angeles erupted in five days of deadly rioting, as hundreds of black and Latino residents vented their outrage. Although Los Angeles was the epicenter of the police brutality crisis in the early 1990s, it soon spread to other cities. A few weeks later, New York entered into its own crisis as a drug scandal triggered a major investigation by the Mollen Commission into police corruption and brutality.

At the time, I was finishing a book about Oakland in the 1940s, another era when police misconduct was stirring black discontent. Yet despite more than four decades of civil rights agitation and re-form, police violence is as critical a problem today as it was then. After further research, I discovered that urban residents had begun complaining about police brutality in the mid nineteenth century and that New Yorkers had launched the first major investigation into police misconduct back in 1894. The Lexow Committee, as it was called, uncovered a litany of police abuses, including brutality, cor-ruption, and perjury—the very same problems the Mollen Com-mission investigated almost a century later. The recurring drama of public outrage over police violence has led some observers to con-clude that it is a timeless problem, an inevitable by-product of law enforcement in a violent and diverse urban world. Most scholars dis-agree, arguing that policing has become less violent over the years as police professionals have responded to new public demands for the protection of civil rights and civil liberties.[1]

In reality, the history of police violence is more complicated than either of these views would suggest. Police brutality is not a timeless, static phenomenon, nor has there been a linear progression toward more professional, less violent police behavior. Over the past 150 years, policing in the United States has undergone significant changes: The organizational and technological sophistication of police has increased, and the social makeup of urban police forces has shifted, as have the ethnic/racial identities of those targeted by law enforcement. Moreover, the problem of police brutality itself has been redefined, with public debate focusing on different types of abuse depending on the larger social, political, and economic context.

Legislative, judicial, and administrative reforms have modified and improved police practices over the past century, but they have also resulted in unintended problems and abuses. New weapons and tactics, for example, have minimized some forms of injury but led to an increase in others. In handling radicals and political dissidents, highly visible forms of police violence have frequently given way to more clandestine forms of policing that are equally repressive. Constrained by new laws and regulations, police have also found ways to conceal or justify misconduct. As a student in a federal law enforcement training program in the 1980s, I was struck by the amount of time and energy invested in teaching the proper "articulation" of probable cause, reasonable suspicion, and the use of deadly force—suggesting the objective circumstances of a police action could be reconstructed to fit legal requirements. Police brutality is less publicly acceptable than it was a century ago, but it has sometimes gone underground or found new legal pretexts and rationalizations.

To better understand this dilemma, *Street Justice* examines the history of police violence in New York City from the mid-nineteenth century to the present. The New York Police Department has attracted considerable historical attention over the years, and for good reason. Since its founding in 1845, the NYPD has been the nation's largest police department, one that has been a model for other cities. Like many urban departments in the nineteenth and early twentieth centuries, the NYPD had an unsavory reputation for corruption and close ties with the city's Democratic political machine, known as Tammany Hall. Beginning in the Progressive Era, however, periodic waves of reform made the department more centralized, bureaucratized, and highly regulated. Indeed, it sometimes pioneered efforts to reduce police violence, establishing the first regularly functioning police review board as well as the first panel to monitor police discharge of firearms. Compared with police agencies in Los Angeles, Chicago, and Miami, for example, New York has not been an especially abusive department. Moreover (and relatedly), New York has historically been the epicenter of antibrutality organizing. Both the American Civil Liberties Union and the National Association for the Advancement of Colored People, two organizations that led protracted campaigns against abusive police practices, had their national headquarters in New York and paid close attention to the local scene. As a case study, then, New York offers particularly rich documentation of police brutality in a city that was sometimes a pacesetter, though not always a successful one, in efforts to curb police violence.

New York's experience with police brutality dates back to the founding of the force and has taken many different forms. Urban residents in the late nineteenth century, for example, complained mainly about "clubbing"—the routine bludgeoning of citizens by patrolmen armed with nightsticks or blackjacks. With the rise of Prohibition and organized crime in the 1920s, reformers targeted the so-called "third degree," in which police detectives in the precincts used violent interrogation tactics to elicit confessions. During periods of social and political unrest such as the 1870s, the 1930s, and the 1960s, public attention centered on violent mass action policing—incidents in which the police used physical force to control or suppress strikes, demonstrations, or other public political events. In recent years, the emphasis has once again returned to cases of street brutality, though involving a wider range of police weapons and tactics.

While the definition of police brutality has continually shifted, the relationship between police perpetrators and their victims has

3

remained roughly the same. Like criminal suspects generally, victims of police brutality were mainly poor and working class, often immigrants or newcomers to the city. Jews and other southern and eastern Europeans were common complainants at the turn of the century, while African Americans and Latinos gradually replaced them by the mid-twentieth century. The overrepresentation of these groups was not just a result of economic and demographic trends; it was also aggravated by racial tensions and bias. With the NYPD drawn mainly from the upper ranks of the white working class (often Irish Americans), class and racial resentments made violent conflict more likely. Such conflicts were usually between police and lower class immigrants or African Americans, but on occasion— as in the clashes between police and antiwar demonstrators in the 1960s—they also flowed upward. Finally, gender has also been implicated in police violence, as notions of manhood and male prowess have contributed to numerous conflicts between predominantly male suspects and male officers. Even in the less common incidents involving female victims, sexual assaults and other forms of police violence against women have also reflected dominant gender relations.

Determining the actual level of police violence at any given time is virtually impossible. Prior to the creation of the Civilian Complaint Review Board in the 1950s, the city kept no systematic records of excessive force complaints. And as police experts point out, review board statistics themselves are notoriously unreliable indicators of police behavior, reflecting such factors as the changing size of the police force and public awareness of and confidence in the complaint system. Any study of police violence, therefore, must deal with public *perceptions* of the problem, paying particular attention to periods when protests over brutality were most intense and sustained.

Historically, public outcry against police brutality has followed a cyclical pattern that bears no simple or direct relationship to the crime rate. The episodic nature of this history is based on a constantly shifting balance between official efforts to ensure public order and safety on the one hand and public demands for the protection of civil rights and civil liberties on the other. City authorities have responded to outbreaks (or perceived outbreaks) of crime and disorder with stepped-up enforcement efforts—either through departmental orders to "muss up" the gangsters or through specialized units that used aggressive and violent tactics. Whether the strong-arm squads of the late nineteenth century, the prohibition and gun-men's squads of the 1920s, the Tactical Patrol Force of the 1960s, or the Street Crime Unit of the 1990s, these specialized anticrime and civil defense units repeatedly swept through the city's poor neighborhoods with a mandate to clear the streets and round up the thugs. In the process, they bred fear and resentment among local residents, some of whom ardently desired increased law enforcement but soon found their own safety and civil rights sacrificed in the process.

Since the 1890s, the city has seen numerous reform campaigns that have attempted to reduce the excessive use of force. Some of these efforts— including those that targeted the third degree, violent crowd-control tactics, and the misuse of deadly force—have been successful in reducing abuse. On the other hand, more common forms of street brutality have proven persistent and intractable. This study argues that the most successful reforms have been those that were justified not only on legal and moral grounds but on a pragmatic basis that spoke to the needs and effectiveness of law enforcement and criminal justice. As reformers persuasively argued, the third degree, violent crowd-control tactics, and certain uses of deadly force proved counterproductive by undermining public confidence in the police and the court system, generating public sympathy for protesters, and endangering police officers themselves. Reducing the more common and routine forms of street brutality has been a tougher sell, in part because the public and the police continue to believe that tough, aggressive street policing *is effective* and essential to ensuring public safety. They have come to this conclusion, however, without an adequate understanding of the adverse impact that such tactics have had on police-community relations and racial tensions, and how these deteriorating relationships ultimately affect the efficacy of law enforcement.

As police historians have noted, public scandals and investigations into police misconduct have recurred roughly every twenty years and have been followed by periods of reform. In succeeding decades, however, the reform impulse usually ebbed as new political and law enforcement priorities took hold. As abuses continued or mounted and police authorities became less responsive to citizen concerns, new scandals erupted and a new round of investigation, reform, and retrenchment ensued.

Although such exposés and investigations were sporadic and yielded only short-term benefits, they constituted the first crude forms of citizen oversight—a means of penetrating the closed and self-protective police bureaucracy and providing an outside citizens' perspective on police practices.[2] Initially, these exposés were provided by police reporters, reform-minded magistrates, and legislative investigations led by opposition political parties. In the twentieth century, new civil rights and civil liberties organizations practiced more consistent monitoring of police through legal defense and advocacy work. Ultimately, these groups helped build broader coalitions that waged a protracted struggle to create more permanent, institutionalized forms of citizen oversight—a struggle that continues to this day.

Interestingly, public outcry over brutality was often linked to scandals involving police corruption. Investigations by the Lexow Committee in the 1890s, the federal Wickersham Commission in the 1930s, and the Mollen Commission in the 1990s all made explicit connections between corruption and brutality. Other probes, including the Seabury investigation of 1930, the large-scale gambling investigation of 1950, and the Knapp Commission in the 1970s, revealed more subtle links. While the relationship between corruption and brutality is obvious and important, it is not a simple one, and efforts to remedy one problem have not always been effective in curbing the other.

On the one hand, there has been a clear and direct link between the two phenomena throughout the NYPD's history. Both the Lexow and Mollen commissions revealed numerous examples of corrupt cops who used violence and intimidation to further their nefarious activities. Moreover, both corruption and brutality thrived in the city's poorest neighborhoods, where vice and other criminal activity was concentrated and where poor immigrant and nonwhite residents had little power to resist. It was also well known that the NYPD transferred or "dumped" abusive officers in poor, high-crime neighborhoods as punishment for their misconduct— a practice that in reality punished the neighborhood more than the officer. For the city's poor and working-class residents, then, po- lice corruption and brutality went hand-in-hand, and they often lumped them together as examples of police lawlessness and im- morality. When granted a public platform, ordinary New Yorkers used corruption investigations as an opportunity to air their grievances about brutality as well. And because corruption scandals tended to reduce police credibility, allegations of brutality became more believable and more damaging.

In a more general sense, corruption and brutality are both forms of illegal misconduct that police officers—and often supervisors— have tried to conceal. By fostering perjury, a code of silence, and in- stitutional indifference, both phenomena have contributed to the development of an insular and secretive police subculture. Opening up police departments to public scrutiny and oversight and en- hancing police accountability and discipline have been logical steps toward reducing both types of misconduct. This has been the dom- inant strain of thought among police experts since the 1970s, but earlier reformers saw things differently.

In the late nineteenth and early twentieth centuries, reformers believed that corruption and brutality were both by-products of a crooked Tammany Hall political machine. Echoing the complaints of working-class residents, middle-class reformers added brutality to a list of police sins that included bribery, extortion, election tam- pering, drunkenness, and gross inefficiency. Their proposed reme- dies stressed honesty, bureaucratic efficiency and specialization, and a militaristic approach to law enforcement. Despite their antibru- tality rhetoric, reformers largely ignored the problem of police vio- lence. In fact, reform campaigns often encouraged aggressive and violent tactics in the interest of efficient crimefighting. For reform- ers, police use of violent force against the criminal class was fully justified. Prior to the 1930s, then, complaints about police brutality made by the immigrant poor, African Americans, and organized labor led to little if any effective reform. However, their efforts to

bring public attention to this problem—particularly following a series of turn-of-the-century racial and ethnic riots—laid the foundation for a new more legalistic understanding of police violence as a
civil rights issue, a view that would become dominant in the latter
half of the twentieth century.

As in other areas of social reform, the 1930s was a period of
sweeping change in the battle against police violence. The growing
role of the federal government in law enforcement and labor relations precipitated critical reforms designed to curb the use of the
third degree and of violent police tactics for suppressing strikes and
political demonstrations. In the 1940s federal intervention in police
brutality cases was further expanded to protect civil rights on the
basis of race. Federal initiatives in this area, however, were not
merely the result of elite reform efforts in Washington. They were
also the fruits of relentless grassroots agitation by Communist,
labor, and African-American activists in the 1930s and 1940s who
mobilized on behalf of working-class interests and civil rights.

For the remainder of the twentieth century, police brutality has
been understood largely as a racial issue, figuring prominently on
the civil rights agenda. Conflicts over police violence culminated in
powerful antibrutality campaigns in the 1960s and again in the
1990s as New Yorkers struggled to build effective public oversight
of the police through the Civilian Complaint Review Board. Their
efforts led the police department to implement some substantive reforms in this period, but as in the past, new practices led to new concerns and pitfalls. Moreover, public pressure for police to fight an
unprecedented increase in crime gave tacit approval to aggressive
policing that fostered a new cycle of brutality scandals and protests.
Most recently, the battle to curb police racism and violence has continued amid new challenges of subversion and terrorism in the
twenty-first century.

As this study makes clear, the problem of police violence developed not only in a changing urban environment but in an evolving
national and global context as well. Just as the foreign terrorist attacks have reshaped NYPD practices and priorities in the wake of
September 11, 2001, so too did earlier events and processes originat-

ing far outside city limits. Throughout New York's history, for instance, immigrants and newcomers have made up a significant portion of the city's poor and working class, those most vulnerable to police abuse. The social and political conditions in their homelands helped shape immigrants' responses to police brutality, sometimes heightening outrage as community leaders drew parallels to lynching in the South, pogroms in Russia, and political repression in the Third World. In a similar manner, a pervasive climate of antifascism during World War II, public sympathy for the southern civil rights movement of the 1960s, and anger over the carnage in Vietnam all helped fuel antibrutality sentiment at home. More recently, international human rights organizations have spoken out against police abuses in New York and other American cities, framing local brutality as part of a worldwide human rights problem. Unlike earlier histories of policing that focused almost exclusively on the local urban context, this study argues that police practices and public efforts to change them must be understood in this broader national and international context.

Historically, brutality opponents have tended to link police violence with other forms of oppression and have incorporated antibrutality messages into the larger political agendas of the labor movement, the Communist party, the civil rights movement, and other causes. Because political figures and movements have at times exploited the emotional value of police brutality incidents to further their agendas or careers, police advocates have generally dismissed them as demagogues who deliberately distort the police record. "*They* always cry police brutality," has been a familiar refrain intended to undercut the legitimacy of antibrutality protest. In reality, however, policing is part of a larger political, economic, and social system that treats some citizens, particularly those from poor, nonwhite, or socially stigmatized groups, more harshly than others. The recurring cycles of police reform and retrenchment have been determined in part by fluctuating political mobilizations that sought to defend the rights and interests of these groups. As this study shows, the mobilization of political will by an informed and vigilant public is essential to effecting change.

Before delving into the long history of police violence, I should say a few words about terminology and sources. I have used the term *police brutality* to mean the lawless and unnecessary or excessive use of force by police. I employ the term *police violence* as a more general term to encompass the police use of physical or deadly force that may or may not be justified under law. I use the term *police abuse* or *misconduct* to describe an array of illegal behaviors that includes brutality but also encompasses police corruption, as well as illegal searches, false arrest, coercion, perjury, etc. Although I have adopted a relatively narrow definition of brutality as physical abuse, it is important to note that there is and has long been a close correlation between physical brutality and other unlawful practices. Police regimes that encouraged aggressive tactics such as indiscriminate searches and arrests were more likely to be the subject of brutality complaints when citizens resisted such treatment. Similarly, police who were discourteous or who used ethnic or racial slurs were more likely to spark citizen defiance that escalated into violent confrontation. I have tried to highlight the important relationship between these different forms of misconduct, but I differ from those who use the term brutality to cover everything from the use of profanity to homicide and torture.

Writing about the history of policing poses difficult problems in terms of sources. Very few police departments maintain comprehensive records that are open to the public, and New York is no exception. Nineteenth-century police records were reportedly destroyed during the First World War, while most of the records of subsequent years are closed under privacy provisions. This includes most administrative records and reports that might shed light on important cases or policies. Fortunately, some of these documents are available in the correspondence between mayors and police commissioners, while others found their way into the files of civil rights and civil liberties groups. Newspapers have been an invaluable source for this study, as have the many reports, hearings, and investigations of police misconduct conducted by citizens groups over the years. While the voices of antibrutality activists are well documented in this study, the police perspective is more elusive, reflected primarily through the mayor's office and the press. The difficulties historians face in accessing police records and data have been characteristic of the secretive and defensive posture of the NYPD and most other police agencies. Historically, this closed culture has been one of the chief obstacles to those seeking effective citizen oversight of the police. By shedding more light on the problem of police brutality over the past one hundred and fifty years, I hope this study will contribute to that effort.

1. "THE CLUBBERS AND THE CLUBBED": POLICE VIOLENCE IN THE NINETEENTH CENTURY

Around midnight one summer evening in 1881, John McDonald and his wife sat down on the stoop of their home on Second Avenue. They had spent the last several hours caring for a sick child and decided to step outside to cool off. Before long, Officer Montgomery Ditmars of the Nineteenth Precinct strolled by and stopped in front of their house. With what the *New York Times* called "a pompous show of authority," he ordered the couple back inside. Tired and hot, John McDonald refused and told the officer to mind his own business. After further argument, Officer Ditmars drew his club and pummeled McDonald about the head and face until he begged for mercy. He then arrested both husband and wife for disorderly conduct and hauled them down to the station house, where the couple spent the night in a cell.

The next morning, the McDonalds were arraigned in the Yorkville Police Court before Justice Benjamin Wandell. Fortunately for the McDonalds, they had landed in the court of one of the city's best known judicial reformers and a vocal critic of police lawlessness. Seeing McDonald's bloody clothes, swollen eye, and numerous facial cuts and bruises, Wandell listened patiently to the suspect's story and then to the opposing account by Officer Ditmars. The judge was clearly skeptical of the officer's version and promptly dismissed the disorderly conduct charges. He then turned to the officer and issued a severe reprimand: "There is a society for the prevention of cruelty to children, and another to protect dumb animals," he said. "And there should be one to protect respectable people from clubs in the hands of officers such as you." He then suggested that the McDonalds file assault charges against the officer. The next day, a detailed account of the case appeared in the *New York Times* under the head-line, "A Brute in Police Uniform."[1]

The McDonalds' ordeal was just one of hundreds of press accounts of police violence that preoccupied New Yorkers in the late nineteenth century. Although citizens had complained of police brutality since the founding of the department in the 1840s, debates over the use of force emerged publicly in the wake of the Civil War as the city's political, ethnic, and class tensions intensified. Newspapers took the lead in exposing police violence, exploiting sensational cases for both their political and sales value. As the muckraker Lincoln Steffens would later explain, he and other police reporters were appalled at how baton-wielding police brutalized suspects while their supervisors sought to conceal the injured victims from public view.[2] Providing the first crude form of citizen oversight, police reporters used their access to New York Police Department headquarters, station houses, and courts to churn out numerous accounts of official violence that provide a unique record of the rough-and-tumble world of nineteenth-century policing.

As these articles reveal, young, working-class citizens from poorer ethnic neighborhoods were the primary targets of police violence, as they still are today. Despite a system that was stacked against them, working-class victims filed complaints against abusive officers, actively protesting the treatment they received. Middle-class journalists, judges, and reformers also became outspoken critics of police brutality and played a key role in shaping the public discourse. Despite substantial differences in their understanding of the problem, middle-class and working-class opponents of police misconduct sometimes joined forces against a brutal and corrupt police force. Ultimately, though, the more privileged and powerful reformers of the middle class would dominate the debate, articulating the problem in ways that reflected their specific class and political interests.

Violence in the Early New York Police

Founded under a state act in 1845, the New York Police Department was established as a bulwark against rising urban crime and disorder.

13

A growing metropolitan economy had attracted new immigrants, spurred the development of poor tenement districts, and fueled class and ethnic tensions that produced a wave of urban disorder in the 1830s and 1840s. Poor neighborhoods such as the predominantly Irish Five Points were plagued by high rates of property crime, violence, vice, and a series of street riots that convinced city officials to create a full-time professional police force along the lines of London's Metropolitan Police. Unlike the highly centralized British police, however, the NYPD reflected the American preference for local popular democracy. Initially, police were recruited locally on the recommendation of aldermen and other ward-level politicians, encouraging a neighborhood-oriented style of policing that ensured a degree of social and ethnic diversity on the force (as early as 1855, the proportion of Irish-born officers in the department equaled or exceeded the percentage of Irish in the general population).

Local recruitment, however, also involved patronage appointments that resulted in corruption and incompetence. Ward leaders invariably made appointments as rewards for partisan political service and expected appointees to do "favors" for their constituents. Precinct houses were thus effectively controlled by local party leaders, and police regularly overlooked illegal liquor sales and vice operations controlled by party supporters. To ensure protection, a lucrative system of graft developed that made police patronage appointments all the more valuable. Since police served as poll watchers at election time, officers were also expected to ignore ballot box stuffing, repeat voting, and other fraudulent practices by their political allies. Needless to say, professional qualifications counted for very little in this system, and critics rightly charged that the department was filled with unqualified and untrained political hacks who used their authority on behalf of their political patrons.[3]

As criticism of police corruption and inefficiency grew, elite reformers pressed for a number of measures in the 1850s designed to reduce political influence in the department. These reforms included physical and written examinations for applicants, a brief training program for new recruits, and the creation of a police commission to handle appointments and discipline. Most importantly, in a brazen attempt to wrest control of the force away from the local Democratic party, the Republican-dominated state legislature passed the Metropolitan Police Act of 1857. The act created an enlarged Metropolitan Police District (including Manhattan, Brooklyn, Staten Island, and Westchester) and established a seven-member police board appointed largely by the governor. Although hailed as a nonpartisan reform, in practice the act transferred control of the city's police from the Democrats to the Republicans, who controlled the governorship and the police commission for the next thirteen years. Although the Metropolitan police board instituted a number of new programs and reforms, patronage appointments continued under Republican auspices, and the police department remained a captive of partisan political interests.[4]

The close relationship between police and local politics in the nineteenth century tended to produce a self-perpetuating culture of violence. Revolutionary traditions of antiauthoritarianism and individual liberty had made Americans less responsive to police authority to begin with; political rivalries, patronage, and corruption further undercut public respect. As citizens flagrantly defied police authority, officers attempted to command respect through the use of coercion or force. Complaints of police violence date back to 1846, the NYPD's first full year of operation, when twenty-nine people filed complaints with the city clerk charging that they had been assaulted by police officers. Most of the early conflicts did not involve weapons, but growing public hostility would soon prompt officers to adopt tougher tactics, which in turn bred greater public hostility. This dynamic can be traced back to the 1850s, when gangs regularly attacked police who were affiliated with opposing political factions or who attempted to interfere with local criminal operations. In the Irish tenement districts of the Fourth and Eighteenth wards, for example, police officers were walking targets and would only patrol in groups of three or more. To reassert control of these areas, Capt. George W. Walling organized strong-arm squads in 1853 consisting of several plainclothes officers armed with clubs made of locust wood, an extremely hard wood that could crack skulls on impact. Squad members proceeded to "beat senseless" every known gang member in the area and allegedly dispersed the criminal element. As strong-arm tactics won praise from local business interests,

15

the department made nightsticks mandatory equipment for all officers, and patrolmen increasingly wielded their clubs as a means of preserving order and establishing authority. Many New Yorkers, however, resented this violent intrusion in their neighborhoods and would become even more antagonistic toward police.[5]

The highly politicized nature of the nineteenth-century criminal justice system also undermined confidence in the judiciary, encouraging officers to administer "curbside" justice. Like police officers, municipal judges were political appointees who served on the bench as a reward for party services. Before the 1870s, most magistrates had no prior legal training and administered justice in consultation with local party leaders. Graft was rampant, and many criminal offenders were released in return for payoffs or in response to political pressure. As former police captain and superintendent George Walling noted in his memoirs, "The police are by no means supported by the authorities in the enforcement of the law, and as a natural consequence, are sometimes dilatory in bringing culprits to justice, or, as has happened time and time again, mete out punishment themselves." Police also used discretionary violence to pay back political scores or to punish those who killed or injured fellow officers. Finally, if police believed the judicial system was ill-suited to handle certain offenders, they might execute their own style of justice. Domestic abuse cases are a good example. One nineteenth-century police officer explained how arresting wife beaters was ineffective since it robbed families of their breadwinners. Instead, he said, "I beat up the man myself and gave him a taste of his own medicine." Dispensing curbside justice, however, hardly promoted peaceful police-community relations. Police interference in such cases sometimes precipitated family or community brawls, while an officer's reputation for physical brutality encouraged some suspects to resist all the more.[6]

This cycle of violence intensified under the administration of the Republican-controlled Metropolitan police. During these years, political, cultural, and class conflicts converged in an explosive way as the city's predominantly ethnic and Democratic working class chafed under the control of a police force administered by elite, native-born Republicans intent on enforcing excise, Sabbatarian, and vagrancy laws. The new emphasis on policing morality fueled bitter resentments among the city's large Irish and German populations, which viewed the police as an alien and coercive force. Those resentments were evident in a series of ethnic riots in the summer of 1857, starting in the Irish enclave of the Five Points and spreading to the nearby German quarter. In both areas, neighborhood residents battled police, leaving more than a dozen people dead and scores injured, including several police. NYPD officers responded with calls for increased weaponry, and many officers began carrying revolvers at their own or their commander's initiative. By the 1860s, revolvers had become standard police equipment. Superior weaponry, however, did not reduce tensions between police and citizens and may in fact have aggravated them. Among much of the city's ethnic working class, an armed and aggressive Metropolitan police force was perceived as an occupying army—particularly during the strife-ridden era of the Civil War.[7] Popular hostility toward the Metropolitan police reached a bloody crescendo in the Draft Riots of 1863, when Irish immigrants lashed out against Republican attempts to enforce the federal conscription act. In four days of violence, Irish rioters battled police and torched a West Side station house while the Metropolitans counterattacked with clubs and revolvers. More than one hundred people were killed, including three policemen. A few years later, the NYPD ruthlessly suppressed the so-called Orange Riots of 1870–71 when Irish Catholics violently protested parades held by Irish Protestants commemorating the Battle of the Boyne. More than sixty people were killed and hundreds injured, including many women and children. After both the Draft and Orange riots, Republican leaders praised the police for their valiant service. Among some working-class citizens, however, the violent behavior of the police fueled greater resentment and more combative attitudes.[8]

The sudden visibility of police brutality cases in the late 1860s testifies to the poor state of police-community relations in the wake of the Civil War. During these years, the press began to cover police assault cases on a regular basis and to editorialize about "over-zealous policemen" and inadequate discipline by the commissioners. One contemporary observer described the weekly police disciplinary hearings as "humorous affairs" in which nine out of ten policemen were exonerated. Citizens who filed brutality complaints were questioned extensively about their moral character and behavior, a process that police jokingly referred to as "trying the complainant." Some citizens also reported threats and assaults by officers when they attempted to get badge numbers, while others charged that police had harassed them or offered them bribes in exchange for dropping complaints. Despite these obstacles, New Yorkers filed numerous complaints of brutality after 1865, and the press began to publicize these cases from a perspective that was pointedly critical of police. While the *New York Herald,* the *World,* and other newspapers sympathetic to the Democratic party were particularly vocal in condemning brutality, even the Republican *New York Times* regularly chastised the department for its weapons policies and its rough treatment of "respectable" citizens.[9]

Complaints of police violence continued to escalate after the Democrats recaptured the state legislature in 1870 and returned the department to municipal control the following year. As Tammany Hall Democrats increased their influence over the police, the *Times* and other Republican papers grew more strident in their denunciations of official violence and corruption.[10] Anti-Tammany forces also struck back through the judiciary, transforming police judgeships from elective offices controlled by Tammany to appointive positions controlled by the mayor. Under the Republican mayor, William Havemeyer, a group of elite appointees to the municipal bench launched a sweeping overhaul of the police courts in the early 1870s, demanding stricter standards of evidence and due process. Most importantly, they often initiated legal or administrative action against abusive officers or publicly reprimanded police for their unnecessary violence. Not surprisingly, the judges' courtroom diatribes against Tammany brutality—like Judge Wandell's rebuke of Officer Ditmars—were eagerly reprinted by the *Times* and other reform-oriented papers.[11]

Between 1865 and 1894, the *Times* alone published articles on more than 270 cases of alleged brutality, providing an invaluable historical source on police violence. Through these accounts, we can gain a better understanding of the brutality problem in the nineteenth century: the forms it took, the circumstances surrounding

the violence, and the social identity of the suspects and officers involved. Making allowances for the political and class biases of the
Times, we can explore the phenomenon of police violence as many
nineteenth-century New Yorkers saw it—through the press.[12]

The most common form of police violence in this period was
what the press referred to as "clubbing"—the bludgeoning of a suspect with a baton or nightstick. Fully three-quarters of all cases covered by the *Times* involved beatings of this sort, the majority of them
occurring between a uniformed officer and a single unarmed suspect (see Tables 1.1–1.3). Injuries and deaths resulting from such
beatings were common, with 9 percent of victims dying during or
soon after the encounter (see Table 1.2). Typically police used their
clubs when suspects posed a challenge to their authority. Insults,
snide remarks, rowdy or drunken behavior, or a failure to obey orders were common provocations. In the most frequent scenario, police officers ordered citizens to "move on" down the street; when
they "remonstrated" or refused to move, police wielded their clubs.
In such cases, the brutality complaint usually stemmed from a
minor incident rather than felonious criminal activity. In fact, more
than three-quarters of all brutality cases involved misdemeanors of
disorderly conduct and/or intoxication, while less than 3 percent involved major felonies (see Table 1.4). In a number of cases, there
were *no* charges filed against the suspects, suggesting that physical
violence was an accepted police practice that did not require an arrest or "cover charge" to legitimize it. The public nature of most of
these incidents likewise suggests that clubbing was a common and
accepted tactic among police.[13] Overall, nearly nine out of ten reported cases occurred in public settings, mainly in poor immigrant
neighborhoods such as the Tenderloin, the Lower East Side, the
Five Points, and the Gas House District (see Table 1.5). All of these
neighborhoods had large working-class populations, relatively high
levels of crime, and a boisterous and rowdy street life that encouraged aggressive police tactics. Officers' use of the club, then, was
chiefly a means of ensuring respect and compliance and maintaining public order in working-class neighborhoods.

Gender-related factors also shaped violent interactions between
police and citizens. Most brutality incidents involved young male

TABLE 1.1

Rank and Duty Status of Officers in Alleged Brutality Cases, 1865–1894

Rank of Officer	# of Cases	%
Patrolman	256	90
Captain	10	4
Detective	9	3
Sergeant	4	1
Other	6	2
Total	285	100

Duty Status of Officer		
Uniformed duty	148	77
Plainclothes duty	25	13
Off-duty	19	10
Total	192	100

suspects (the median age was twenty-one) who somehow challenged the authority of police officers in a public context (see Table 1.6). These challenges could potentially undermine the authority of police, but they also threatened an officer's sense of manhood and male prowess. The violent drubbing of a rebellious or disrespectful suspect, then, was one way of asserting one's manhood and dominance among men. Police attacks on women, however, were not uncommon. Women suspects were involved in 20 percent of all cases (see Table 1.6), and the circumstances in many of them reflected sex-

TABLE 1.2
Type of Brutality Case, 1865–1894

Type of Case*	# of Cases	%**
Clubbing	206	76
Wrongful shooting	20	7
Death of victim	25	9
Crowd control	13	5
Excise-related	11	4
Sexual assault	11	4
Medical neglect	7	3
Labor dispute	6	2
Domestic dispute	4	1

*Calculations are based on 272 total cases.

**Because some cases fit several of the above categories, the figures in this column do not add up to 100 percent.

and gender-related factors. The most obvious difference was the higher percentage of women's cases that occurred in private spaces—more than 20 percent compared to only 5 percent of the male cases (see Table 1.7). A number of these incidents involved domestic disputes within and between families in their homes. Police sometimes used violent tactics against squabbling couples and disagreeable female neighbors, both on duty and off. In other instances, wives, mothers, sisters, or daughters intervened in violent altercations between male family members and police. Most significantly, women were frequently the victims of sexual assault or harassment by po-

TABLE 1.3

Weapons Involved in Alleged Brutality Cases, 1865–1894

Weapons*	# of Cases	%**
Police/club	137	82
Police/gun	37	22
Police/other	3	2
Suspect/knife	4	2
Suspect/gun	1	1
Suspect/other	4	2

*Calculations are based on 167 cases in which weapons use was specified.

**Because suspects and officers sometimes used multiple weapons, the figures in this column do not add up to 100 percent.

lice, incidents that usually occurred out of public view. Sexual assault was alleged in 19 percent of cases involving women, while several others reported sexual harassment prior to other physical abuse. In many cases, police apparently believed the suspects to be prostitutes or promiscuous women who could be pressured into dispensing sexual favors. For working-class women—and for black women especially—merely being on the street at night made them morally and criminally suspect; their attempts to resist or to protest that stigma sometimes resulted in police beatings.

Among the 80 percent of cases involving men, the majority of alleged victims were white males from non-Anglo backgrounds. Sixty-four percent of suspects were of non-Anglo origins, with roughly half of those being of Irish or German descent (see Table 1.8). Jews (7 percent), Italians (2 percent), African Americans (4 percent), and other newer immigrant groups made up 17 percent of

TABLE 1.4
Charges Filed against Victims in Alleged Brutality Cases, 1865–1894

Charges Filed against Victim*	# of Cases	%**
Disorderly conduct	66	50
Intoxication	34	26
Assault	21	16
Assault of officer	11	8
Interfering	10	7
Assault & battery	7	5
Resisting arrest	4	3
Other	26	20
Murder	1	<1
Robbery	1	<1
Burglary	1	<1
Excise violation	4	3

*Calculations are based on 133 cases in which charges against the suspect were specified.

**Because suspects were frequently charged with more than one offense, the figures in this column do not add up to 100 percent.

TABLE 1.5
Precinct and Neighborhood of Police Officers in
Alleged Brutality Cases, 1865–1894

Officer Precinct	Location/Neighborhood*	# of Cases	%
Sixteenth	West Twentieth Street/Tenderloin	19	8
Twentieth	West Thirty-seventh Street/Hell's Kitchen	19	8
Fourth	Oak Street/Lower East Side	18	7
Nineteenth	East Thirty-fifth Street/Gas House District	18	7
Sixth	Franklin Street/Five Points	17	7
Ninth	Mercer Street/Greenwich Village	15	6
Fourteenth	East Fifth Street/Lower East Side	15	6
Seventh	Madison Street/Lower East Side	13	5
Twenty-ninth	West Thirtieth Street/Tenderloin	12	5
Eighth	South Village	10	4
Twenty-first	Murray Hill	10	4
Twenty-seventh	East Eighty-eighth Street/Yorkville	10	4
All Other Precincts		72	29
Total Cases in All Precincts		248	100

*Precinct locations refer to commonly recognized neighborhoods in the late nineteenth century. The precise boundaries of precincts changed repeatedly during this period and thus cannot be specified.

TABLE 1.6
Gender and Age of Victims in Alleged Brutality Cases, 1865–1894

Gender of Victim	# of Alleged Brutality Cases	% of Alleged Brutality Cases	% of All Arrestees*
Male	217	80	76
Female	53	20	24
Total	270	100	100

* The gender profile of all arrestees for this period is based on data from New York Police Department annual reports for 1871, 1872, 1887, 1888, 1890, and 1894.

Median age of alleged brutality victims**	21 years
Median age of all arrestees***	Upper 20s

**Based on 44 cases in which age was specified.

***Based on 255,164 cases from New York Police Department annual reports for 1871, 1887, and 1894.

all suspects. These percentages are roughly consistent with police department data on the nativity of all persons arrested during these years, suggesting that brutality affected a broad ethnic cross section of the city. The high rate of intergroup cases (more than three-quarters of all cases involved police and suspects from different ethnic groups) suggests that racial/ethnic conflict played a significant role in generating police violence (see Table 1.9). As for police, officers of Irish descent accounted for fully half of all those accused in brutality cases (see Table 1.10), though Irish-born police composed only 22 percent of the force in 1887. Irish officers were thus noticeably overrepresented as perpetrators in brutality cases.[14] One explanation is that racial/ethnic resentments figured more prominently in this struggling immigrant group that competed most directly with newer migrants in downtown neighborhoods and workplaces and whose "whiteness" was still in doubt in the nine-

TABLE 1.7

Location of Alleged Brutality Cases, 1865–1894

Location	Female victims		Male victims		All victims	
	# of Cases	%*	# of Cases	%*	# of Cases	%*
Street or Alley	25	48	123	59	149	57
Stoop or Entry	7	13	23	11	29	11
Bar or Saloon	5	10	23	11	28	11
Residence	9	17	7	3	17	7
Police Station	2	4	10	5	12	5
Transit Lines	1	2	9	4	10	4
Other	4	8	25	12	29	11
Total Cases in Public	39	75	191	92	231	89
Total Cases in Private	11	21	11	5	21	8
Total Cases Public/Private	2	4	6	3	8	3
All Cases	52	100	208	100	260	100

*Because many beatings occurred in more than one location, the total of the figures in the upper half of this column exceeds 100 percent.

TABLE 1.8
Ethnicity of Victims in Alleged Brutality Cases, 1865–1894

Ethnicity*	Brutality victims 1865–1894		All Arrestees
	#	%	%
English/Scottish/ Anglo-American	82	36	46
Irish	70	32	31
German	33	15	11
Jewish	15	7	–
African American	9	4	2
Italian	5	2	3
Other	9	4	7
Total	223	100	100

*Ethnicity of brutality victims was determined through analysis of surnames; ethnicity of arrestees was based on nativity data from the New York Police Department annual reports of 1871, 1887, and 1893.

teenth century. Such bias was clearly evident toward African-American suspects (all of whose cases involved Irish officers) and was likely directed toward other new immigrant groups as well. Racial and ethnic bias, however, was not limited to Irish police; officers from non-Irish backgrounds, though implicated in fewer brutality cases, were just as likely to assault those outside their own ethnic group (see Table 1.9).

Although the data suggests that gender and racial/ethnic conflict were important sources of police violence in this period, they were not prominent themes in the public discourse. Instead, gender, race, and ethnicity were subsumed in larger debates about class, morality, and politics that characterized New York in the late nineteenth century.

TABLE 1.9

Ethnicities of Officers and Victims in Alleged Brutality Cases, 1865–1895

	Irish/Irish American Police Officers		English/Scots/ Anglo-American Police Officers		German/ German American Police Officers		Other Police Officers		Total Police Officers	
	# of Cases	%	# of Cases	%	# of Cases	%	# of Cases	%	# of Cases	%
Officer/ victim of same ethnicity	35	32	33	36	3	30	1	5	72	31
Officer/ victim of different ethnicities	76	68	58	64	7	70	20	95	161	69
Total Cases	111	100	91	100	10	100	21	100	233	100

TABLE 1.10

Ethnicity of Officers Involved in Alleged Brutality Cases, 1865–1894

Ethnicity of officer*	# of brutality cases	%	% of total NYPD officers
Irish	130	50	28
English/Scottish/ Anglo-American	108	41	67
German	11	4	5
Jewish	11	4	–
Other	1	1	>1
Total	261	100	100

*Ethnicity of officers in brutality cases was determined through analysis of surnames; ethnicity of total NYPD officers was based on nativity data from the New York Police Department annual report of 1887.

Emerging Views of Police Brutality

As the primary targets of police violence, immigrant and working-class New Yorkers actively protested their treatment and were joined by middle-class journalists, judges, and reformers who also became outspoken critics of police brutality. Although the two groups shared a common moral framework and a general commitment to humanity and justice, they attached different meanings to these terms and employed them for different purposes. Even when their views seemed to agree, they differed substantially in their understandings of the brutality problem, their views of the role of the police and their relationship to the social order, and their proposed solutions to police abuse.

Although working-class New Yorkers filed hundreds of brutality complaints in this period, newspaper accounts of these incidents tell us very little about their attitudes toward police violence. We do know that blue-collar workers represented the vast majority of alleged brutality victims whose cases were publicized in the press. Skilled and semiskilled workers accounted for nearly two-thirds of the *Times* cases, while the unskilled and unemployed made up another 6 percent (see Table 1.11).[15] Working-class New Yorkers pursued these cases against great odds, since winning an assault case against a police officer was very difficult and even bringing a complaint could be risky. Officers sometimes intimidated complainants and witnesses or bribed them in exchange for dropping charges. In criminal and disciplinary proceedings, officers stuck together and corroborated each other's testimony; indeed, the contemporary practice of police perjury seems to have been a long-standing tradition. Commissioners and judges also protected brutal officers who shared their political interests. This was particularly true in the disciplinary proceedings of the police board, whose bipartisan structure resulted in countless split decisions and dismissals. Nevertheless, dozens of working-class people filed complaints each year, many of them bringing one or more witnesses to testify on their behalf (see Table 1.12). Most telling, perhaps, were the neighborhood crowds that often gathered around police clubbing incidents, yelling "shame, shame" at the officer or intervening to rescue a beaten suspect. Although such behavior probably only reinforced the tendency of police to use violence, it does suggest that working-class residents asserted a collective sense of identity in defense of the community's own moral order.[16]

Working-class attitudes toward police violence were most clearly manifested during strikes and labor protests in the strife-filled decades of the 1870s and 1890s. Charges of police brutality toward organized workers first surfaced in the Eight Hour strikes of 1872, when most of the city's skilled workers struck to force implementation of an eight-hour law passed by the state legislature in 1867. As the three-month strike dragged on, violence broke out when several hundred NYPD officers used clubs to forcibly disperse striking workers and reopen local workshops.[17] An even more serious police-labor confrontation occurred two years later with the outbreak of the Tompkins Square Riot on the Lower East Side. Battered by the hardships of the 1873 depression, a group of predominantly immigrant workers and Socialists formed the Committee of Public Safety

TABLE 1.11

Occupation of Victims in Alleged Brutality Cases, 1865–1894

	Occupation* of alleged brutality victims		Of all arrestees**	Difference
	#	%	%	
Services	51	37	27	+10
Skilled trades	38	27	16	+11
Clerical	30	22	10	+12
Professional	11	8	2	+6
Unskilled	5	4	25	−21
Unemployed	3	2	20	−18

*See appendix for the occupations making up each of the above categories.

**Figures on victims in brutality cases are based on 138 cases in which the person's occupation was identified; figures for all arrestees are based on occupational data on 244,132 arrestees listed in the New York Police Department annual reports from 1871, 1887, and 1894.

TABLE 1.12

Eyewitnesses Present in Alleged Brutality Cases, 1865–1894

Witnesses present	# of Cases	%
Cases with witnesses	123	45
For victim	73	27
For police	15	5
For both	35	13

*Calculations based on 272 total cases, of which 123 had reported witnesses.

31

and organized a mass meeting to demand public works and an end to evictions of the unemployed. The night before the meeting, city authorities revoked the permit, giving the organizers little or no advance notice. The next morning a crowd of more than seven thousand people gathered peacefully in the park, only to be driven off by more than sixteen hundred police using horses and clubs in what labor leader Samuel Gompers called "an orgy of brutality."[18] A similar onslaught occurred during a strike by Jewish cloakmakers in 1894. Led by the magnetic labor leader Joseph Barondess, eight thousand strikers and their supporters gathered in Rutgers Square for a march up to Union Square. Claiming that the march was unauthorized, police dispersed the crowd with clubs and warning shots, arresting Barondess and injuring several workers.[19] In all of these incidents, workers condemned police violence as unprovoked and unjustified. They held public protest meetings, filed petitions and complaints, and testified in disciplinary hearings before the police commission.

The language workers used provides important clues to working-class attitudes toward police violence. In describing the Tompkins Square Riot and other incidents, for example, labor leaders used the term "outrage" to describe the violent injuries inflicted by the police. Historically, the term was employed particularly in reference to abuses committed by soldiers, knights, and other martial forces representing power and authority. Working-class activists clearly intended this meaning, often labeling police as "despots" and "tyrants" who perpetrated a "reign of terror" upon defenseless workers. Shortly after the Tompkins Square Riot, *New York Sun* editor John Swinton, a noted defender of labor reform, delivered an impassioned appeal to the state legislature denouncing what he called "the Tompkins Square Outrage." His statement, later reproduced as a pamphlet, compared the New York police administration to "the operations of Pietri in Paris during the despotic regime of the Third Napoleon." Trade union leaders used similar analogies, equating police clubbing with "monarchical despotism" and calling police officials "Grand Bashaws" (a reference to the imperious Turkish pashas). Foreshadowing the use of such terms as "Cossackism" and "Gestapoism" by antibrutality activists in the twentieth cen-

tury, the equation of police violence with tyranny and foreign oppression would become a standard tactic among radicals and labor
leaders.[20]

Like other New Yorkers, working-class critics of police violence
tended to link brutality with corruption. Drawing on republican
ideology, labor and radical groups saw brutality as a by-product of a
morally and politically corrupt police system. Swinton argued that
the department's attack on starving workers was an attempt to curry
public favor in the wake of revelations of illegal jobbing and other
scandals in the street-cleaning division. Likewise, in a petition presented to a state committee investigating municipal corruption in
1890, the building trades section of the Central Labor Union accused the NYPD of political fraud, extortion, blackmail, and vice
protection as well as brutality and unfair treatment of strikers. Profits derived from such activities, the union argued, allowed police
officials to live "like nabobs" in lavish city mansions and country es-
tates. The petition also accused police of openly siding with and accepting favors from employers. Workers in the Eight Hour strikes
of 1872 expressed similar sentiments, arguing that "the police have
been too free with the cigars and etceteras furnished by the parties
whose manufactories they have been detailed to watch." Depicting
police as agents of employers, labor leaders called Chief James Kelso
"a tool of capitalists and political thieves" and accused him of ordering brutal attacks on workers while he "wines on fine cham-
pagne" with employers.[21] Working-class critics, then, defined police
corruption not only as political graft and vice protection but as the
immoral bargain struck between police and the city's employers.

Labor's charges of police-employer collusion were often justified.
During these years, police worked closely with employers to guarantee free access to workshops during strikes, and employers sometimes donated large sums to the police pension fund after receiving
such protection. Other factors also contributed to police-labor hostility. Although most police were drawn from the ranks of the working class, the stability and year-round nature of their work brought
their incomes well above those of most workers. Heavily enmeshed
in networks of partisan patronage, police showed little inclination
to unionize and were generally inhospitable to organizing efforts by

other workers. When strikes did occur, police officers were required to work shifts of sixteen hours or more with little sleep and minimal pay. As the *New York Herald* explained during the Eight Hour strikes of 1872, "The police look upon the laborers as the cause of an extra amount of duty they have been compelled to perform, and continually sigh for a time when they may at leisure draw upon their heads with their locust sticks." Given such competing interests and attitudes, there was little love lost between police and organized labor. Not surprisingly, workers tended to see police as the well-paid tools of the capitalist elite.[22]

For workers, the remedy for police corruption and brutality was a more democratic police administration and the protection of workers' rights. In the wake of the Tompkins Square Riot, trade unionists and Socialists circulated a petition calling for the abolition of the city's police board and the popular election of municipal police officials. Workers also advocated self-defensive measures against police violence and repression. At a Cooper Union meeting protesting police clubbing of strikers in 1872, hundreds of workers voted unanimously in favor of a resolution to "protect ourselves from any further unlawful attack" and to form a central committee composed of two members from each trade who would receive reports on any violations of workers' rights. There is no further evidence of this committee's activities, but its mere formation suggests a more proactive stance on the part of workers. Later, during the Jewish cloakmakers' strike, the union not only brought complaints against police who had clubbed workers in Rutgers Square but also filed a civil suit for ten thousand dollars in damages. The use of these self-defensive tactics indicates that working-class New Yorkers were now organizing to protect their group rights as workers and citizens.[23] In fact, nearly every labor-related complaint of police brutality made reference to workers' rights to strike or congregate free of police interference. Following the Tompkins Square Riot, for example, working-class leaders issued a handbill protesting "a violation of one of our fundamental rights" and filed a petition with the state legislature charging the police commissioners with "trampling upon the law and the privileges of the people."[24]

Lofty appeals to citizens' rights, however, did not prevent workers from exploiting incidents of police brutality for more practical ends. The Eight Hour strikes, the Tompkins Square Riot, and the Rutgers Square melee were followed by mass protest meetings designed to rally workers on behalf of their rights but also to build solidarity in the union and on the picket line. In the latter two conflicts, the victims of police violence were later exhibited on stage as martyrs to labor's cause and living examples of police repression (a tactic the Communist party would later use in its organizing campaigns in the 1920s and 1930s). That such abuses could occur, labor leaders argued, meant that workers had to organize in their own defense.

While police repression may have heightened working-class consciousness, workers' demands for recognition of their rights as citizens fell on deaf ears. In all three labor incidents, the NYPD dismissed workers' brutality complaints, claiming that police had used only necessary force to halt or prevent illegal strikes, marches, or meetings. Appeals to the courts and the state legislature also failed. Among the native-born middle and upper classes, immigrant workers had long been viewed as the source of urban riot and disorder. Fears of social upheaval ran high in post–Civil War New York, and ethnic and class anxieties were further heightened by the Paris Commune, a shot-lived revolutionary workers' government established in France in 1871. To the American elite, the specter of the Paris Commune was evident in the growing radical movements among labor and Socialists in U.S. cities. The *Times* and other elite newspapers thus generally condoned police clubbing of strikers and protesting workers in this period, portraying them as either drunken rioters or violent agitators. They likewise praised police for their discipline and effectiveness in preserving order. In the case of the Tompkins Square Riot, both the *Times* and the *Herald* denounced the Committee of Public Safety, comparing it to the Paris Commune and arguing that these agitators "understand nothing but brute force." In the case of a streetcar workers' strike in 1889, the *Times* even praised police clubbing of strikers, noting that "beneficial clubbing resulted." Even Lincoln Steffens, the muckraking reporter who exposed and condemned police clubbing in his autobiography, had little sympathy for striking Jewish workers who were beaten by police in the 1890s. After seeing these workers fight with scabs, Steffens admitted that he had come to sympathize with the police clubbers in their attempts to preserve the public peace.[25] To most middle-class journalists and reformers, then, public gatherings of working-class people on behalf of ethnic or labor interests were by definition disorderly and criminal and thus fair game for club-wielding police.

Police clubbing in other contexts, however, increasingly came under attack by these same journalists and reformers. Middle-class concern with police violence was part of a larger trend in Victorian culture toward a more humane sensibility. Prior to the eighteenth century, British and Anglo-American people feared pain but accepted it as an unavoidable misfortune or as punishment for sin. But a growing faith in human perfectibility, benevolence, and science tempered these feelings and, by the nineteenth century, produced a Victorian obsession with pain and suffering. At the same time, the competitiveness and individualism of an increasingly urban-industrial society contributed to a growing sense of social empathy that was manifested in a variety of humanitarian reform movements, including abolition, animal protection, and child protection.[26] Middle-class New Yorkers who denounced police brutality no doubt shared these sensibilities and frequently compared police violence to other forms of physical abuse, particularly animal cruelty. William Browne, the author of an 1887 tract titled *Stop That Clubbing!,* noted that "if a man outrageously ill-uses his horse, he is properly arrested and fined; but if a more cruel attack is made by one man dressed in a blue uniform on another man . . . the ununiformed man is arrested and fined, while the offender enjoys immunity and liberty." Browne also compared police brutality to the "indignities of slavery," describing it as "wantonly wicked" and a shock "to our common humanity." Like other middle-class commentators, Browne emphasized the "cruelty" of police clubbing and urged sympathy for its victims. Speaking out against police brutality was a moral duty, Browne claimed, since "the graphic pen of the reporter" made all New Yorkers into eyewitnesses.[27]

Unlike working-class critics who cast police as capitalist henchmen, middle-class reformers saw police as lower-class brutes allied with immigrant political machines. The term "police brutality," which first appeared in newspaper accounts in the 1860s, reflects some of these middle-class biases. The use of the term brutality— defined as the state or condition of brutes or animals—suggested that the infliction of pain on others turned man himself into a beast. "Police brutality" thus implied that police were inhumane beasts who cruelly and savagely abused citizens. Newspaper accounts, in fact, often described police as "brutes" or "ruffians" and highlighted the large physical stature of offending policemen versus the small frames of their victims. In highlighting the animal-like traits of policemen—most of whom came from working-class backgrounds —elite critics drew on popular ethnic and class stereotypes of lower-class people as bestial and subhuman. These derogatory characterizations would persist into the late twentieth century, with middle-class radicals of the 1960s casting police as "pigs" and "brutes."

The term brutality also implied other negative social attributes such as coarseness, incivility, and lack of intelligence. Newspaper editors and reformers actively promoted these lower-class images, attacking police officers as "ignorant," "rude," and "gruff," particularly in their dealings with "respectable" citizens. In the mid-1860s, for instance, the *Times* ran numerous editorials criticizing police for their rough handling of "gentlemen" and "respectable women" on the streets at night. Such men, the *Times* noted, had been mere passersby to sidewalk altercations or had been innocently awaiting streetcars, while unescorted women had been mistaken for "common bauds." Denouncing the officers' "ruffianism" and "impertinence," the *Times* called for the dismissal of such "idiots" from the force. Even more telling, however, was the middle-class obsession with the haughty and superior airs of policemen, allegedly due to their high pay:

Instead of civility, patience, and forbearing temper, we have arrogance, arbitrariness, and passion. The swagger and assumption of many members of the force are as offensive as they are ludicrous. . . . The high salary paid to young policemen—many of whom are barely of age, are drawn from the humblest walks of life, and have never handled more than five or six dollars a week before—has the effect of putting these men in an entirely wrong position, and inviting a style of life and degree of assumption entirely at variance with their station in life.

Such haughty attitudes, the *Times* warned, provoked resistance and violence on the part of otherwise inoffensive citizens. Clubbing critic William Browne echoed this sentiment, expressing outrage that police who were so "liberally paid" could be found "flaunting and flourishing their clubs in the faces of orderly citizens."[28]

The emphasis on protecting "orderly" and "inoffensive" citizens may have grown out of middle-class self-interest, but over time reformers and journalists came to define the victims of police brutality more broadly. While most of the editorials of the 1860s dealt with cases involving "respectable citizens," by the late 1870s the *Times* was vocally defending the rights of less fortunate and less affluent New Yorkers. The most infamous cases involved medical neglect of unconscious citizens in station house jail cells. In the spring of 1877, for instance, the local press offered extensive coverage of police negligence in the treatment of Edward Dierks, the secretary of a German benevolent society who had been the apparent victim of a robbery and assault. The unconscious and bleeding Dierks had been mistakenly arrested for drunkenness and taken to a nearby station house. Believing Dierks to be intoxicated, police offered no medical treatment until the following day; he was then sent to Bellevue Hospital, where he died of his injuries. The *Times* bitterly denounced police ignorance in this and other incidents involving sick or injured citizens, saying that to the average officer, "the word 'drunk' stands for every variety of condition which he does not readily understand." The *World* was even more vehement in its criticism, charging that "such stupidity, brutality, and neglect of duty ... is a monstrous satire upon our civilization."[29]

Unconscious individuals were just one example of the helpless victims abused by police; the press also assailed the clubbings of children, the elderly, the handicapped, and the insane. Perhaps most surprising was the condemnation of the common police practice of beating drunks and vagrants. In 1873, the *Times* chastised police for the unnecessary clubbing of drunks and insisted that officers be taught to "regard the club as a weapon of defense merely, not an instrument of offense and punishment." A few months later the *Times* published an angry letter from "A Taxpayer," describing a scene he had witnessed outside the window of his home on Fifth Avenue. To his horror, a police officer had ruthlessly clubbed a drunken vagrant who had ignored the officer's order to move on. "There could have been no necessity for the violence, as the man's feet were so sore he could scarcely walk. He had no shoes on—only old woolen stockings with rags in the soles." The letter writer's shock over this scene reflected growing middle-class concern not only with the abuse of police power but with its use against helpless and pre-sumably harmless victims, even those who might violate the norms of respectability.[30]

Finally, the press also defended New Yorkers who had been beaten by police in or around their homes without just cause. In March 1874 the *Times* denounced police for the near-fatal clubbing of a German man and his wife who had discovered two allegedly drunken officers in the hallway of their house. The officers claimed to be responding to a domestic dispute, but the editors were skepti-cal, charging the police with being "rather a danger than a protec-tion to society." The *Times* also criticized police for harassing and beating citizens who sat out on their stoops on summer evenings. "It is now as much as a man's liberty is worth, and almost as much as his life is worth, to sit on his front steps after sunset," the editors quipped in a tongue-in-cheek editorial titled "The Front Steps Crime." Such criticism reflected middle-class preoccupations with property rights and the sanctity of the home, but it also implicitly suggested a growing concern for the rights of ordinary citizens.[31] As we have seen, however, such concerns were narrowly circumscribed by class interests. Middle-class appeals for justice and citizens' rights were tempered by fears of social uprising and did not extend to or-ganized labor and dissident workers.

Among the city's reform-minded elite, citizens' rights were far less important than other moral and political considerations. From the beginning, middle-class critiques of police violence were cou-pled with calls for police reform and professionalization. This was especially true after 1870 when Democrats recaptured the state leg-islature and dismantled the state-controlled Metropolitan police, returning the NYPD to municipal control—and hence to Tammany Hall. Thereafter, the *New York Times* and other Republican and reform newspapers consistently linked their attacks on police violence with accusations of police corruption and the need for bureaucratic reform.

As the *Times* frequently reminded its readers, the "demoralization of the force" under Tammany was the key factor behind both police corruption and brutality. Partisan control of the police resulted in poor-quality recruits who preyed on and brutalized innocent citizens while "doing the dirtiest work of ward politicians." Reformers were of course referring to police protection of vice interests and fraudulent voting practices. As a result of these activities, reformers argued, police officers earned political protection from their superiors that shielded them from disciplinary action in all but the most heinous cases of abuse. Comparing the police to organized criminals gangs, journalists and reformers frequently emphasized the corruption and clannishness of police—from fellow officers who perjured themselves to protect each other, to police commissioners who refused to punish abusive officers because of their political connections.[32]

To remedy this endemic brutality and corruption, reformers called for a wholesale reorganization of the police force. The establishment of a nonpartisan police board that could make appointments, direct recruiting, and administer discipline free from political influence was frequently cited as the solution to police abuses. Improvements in recruiting and firm punishment or dismissal of officers who assaulted citizens, reformers argued, would help eliminate police brutality. By insulating the department from popular politics and centralizing authority, reform advocates hoped to make the police more professional and more like their counterparts in London and Paris, with whom the New York police were frequently and unfavorably compared.[33] For middle-class reformers, less democracy, not more, was the only way to eliminate police malfeasance.

While middle-class reformers and working-class dissidents both railed against police brutality, their understanding of the problem, its causes, and solutions were strikingly different. But there was some common ground. Both groups understood police violence as a moral problem, viewing brutality and corruption as mutual by-products of a debased political system that trampled on citizens' rights. Their perceptions of that system and the police who supported it, however, differed sharply. Middle-class reformers based their opposition to police brutality on notions of class privilege and Victorian empathy for the abused and helpless. Staunch advocates of civil service and police reform, they viewed police as lower-class thugs and saw brutality as a natural outgrowth of corrupt immigrant political machines. Working class critics of police brutality, on the other hand, argued that police were the paid agents of wealthy elites who used violence to repress the rights of labor and the poor. Rejecting reformist solutions of centralization and professionalization, they argued for a greater democratization of the force and increased public scrutiny. While both groups argued for the protection of citizens' rights, middle class critics defined those rights—and those who were entitled to them—more narrowly. These differing views and definitions of police violence would be incorporated in varying degrees into the public campaign against police violence that accelerated in the 1870s and 1880s and culminated in the Lexow investigation of 1894.

The Case of "Clubber" Williams

The convergence of middle-class and working-class views of police brutality is perhaps best illustrated in the public outcry over New York's most notorious tough cop, Alexander Williams. Known as "Clubber" Williams, this nationally famous policeman enjoyed a thirty-year career with the NYPD, rising from patrolman to inspector. During these years, he reigned over some of the city's most infamous crime and vice districts with a firm club-wielding hand. His dictum—"There is more law in the end of a nightstick than in a decision of the Supreme Court"—has become part of New York police lore. Even the *New York Times,* his most consistent defender, called him "the most notorious bully in the entire force."[34]

Born in Nova Scotia in 1839, Alexander Williams immigrated to New York with his parents, who were of English and Scottish descent. After working for several years as a ship's carpenter and excavator, he joined the police force in 1866 with the support of local Republican politicians. Because of his large size and athletic prowess, he was assigned to a dangerous post at Broadway and Houston streets, home to some of the city's toughest Irish street gangs. According to legend, Williams arrived and promptly picked a fight with two local gang members, knocked them unconscious with his club, and hurled them through the window of a nearby saloon. Over the next four years, Williams handled other gang members in similar fashion, earning him the nickname "Clubber." He won promotion quickly and served as captain in some of the city's high-crime precincts, including the Gas House District on the East Side and the Tenderloin on the West.

The Twenty-ninth Precinct, known as the Tenderloin, was a choice police assignment in 1876. Legend has it that Williams's remark upon being assigned to the precinct—"I have had chuck for a long time and now I am going to eat tenderloin"—gave the district its name. Extending from Fourteenth Street to Forty-second Street on the West Side, the Twenty-ninth Precinct encompassed an entertainment district that housed some of the city's best-known clubs, restaurants, hotels, and theaters as well as a thriving vice district. Williams's strong-arm approach to street crime won praise from local business interests, while his protection of gambling, prostitution, and liquor interests proved highly profitable. His ties to vice interests and control over polling places enhanced his political influence in the Republican party and fueled resentment among Tammany Democrats. But with the backing of his Republican supporters on the police board, Williams successfully fought off multiple charges of brutality brought against him.[35]

Public outcry over Williams's brutal practices in the Tenderloin came to a head in 1879. That year Williams became the subject of two major assault cases stemming from his alleged clubbing of spectators at public events. The first case involved Williams's alleged beating of a man at a public sports event. With the encouragement of one of Williams's political foes on the police commission, the victim filed an assault complaint. Claiming that the charges had been politically motivated, Williams maintained that the use of force was justified to prevent a riot. Sustained by the two Republican commissioners on the police board, Williams was exonerated.[36] The second and more sensational case occurred seven months later when Williams was accused of brutally clubbing a spectator at a military parade in Madison Square. Captain Williams and his officers were responsible for clearing a path for the parade and allegedly used their clubs freely to move the crowd back. According to several witnesses, Williams and his subordinate, Officer Thomas Fleming, clubbed twenty-six-year-old Charles W. Smith, who did not move out of the way quickly enough. As the police continued to beat the bloodied victim, the crowd grew increasingly volatile, and Williams summoned an ambulance to take Smith to the hospital. According to later courtroom testimony, Smith was taken to New York Hospital, where Williams barred doctors from treating Smith's head wound until he agreed not to press charges.[37]

Over the next few days, Smith's case was taken up by Samuel Whitechurch, an attorney who had witnessed the beating. Whitechurch was a reform-minded Republican and secretary of the Taxpayers' Association, a small group of businessmen based in an adjoining precinct. Insisting they would never get a fair hearing from the police commissioners, Whitechurch encouraged Smith to file criminal assault charges against the officers as well as a civil suit for ten thousand dollars.[38] The case quickly became front-page news and attracted a score of witnesses who volunteered to testify on Smith's behalf. Despite Smith's humble social standing—he was an unemployed city watchman—his case drew the sympathies of prominent merchants and businessmen, some of whom offered to donate funds to defray his legal expenses. These individuals expressed typical middle-class outrage over the base and brutal behavior of the police and the political influence that sanctioned it.[39] Public criticism of Williams's brutality was combined with allegations of corruption and mismanagement. The reform-minded *New York Sun,* for instance, was quick to point out that Williams was "very thrifty," having saved over one hundred thousand dollars from his two-thousand-dollar-a-year salary as captain of the Tenderloin. *Sun* readers seemed to agree; as one wrote in, "he has a fortune and

43

any one posted about his precinct knows how he got it." Howard Crosby, a prominent minister and antivice reformer with the Society for the Prevention of Crime, sent a letter to the police commissioners urging them to remove Williams, not only because of the clubbing incident but because of his long-standing practice of vice protection and blackmail. The two Democratic appointees to the police commission filed a motion to remove Williams, but the two Republican commissioners voted against it, effectively killing the motion. Like other politically influential police, Williams was protected by a bipartisan police commission that consistently defended its respective appointees.[40]

In both the police board hearing and subsequent criminal and civil trials, Williams maintained his innocence, claiming that Officer Fleming alone had administered the beating. As in past cases, Williams insisted that the assault charges were politically motivated and called the Taxpayers' Association "a political striking club." Although the exact nature of the Taxpayers' Association is unclear, it seems likely that it was a group of reformist businessmen that stood outside the mainstream Republican party. By contrast, Williams was supported by some of the city's most prominent Republican regulars, including his defense team of two former U.S. district attorneys, George Bliss and Elihu Root.[41] With the help of these powerful political allies, the jury acquitted him of all criminal charges, with the judge calling Williams's conduct "deserving of praise." He was also exonerated in a police board hearing and in a later civil trial. Williams was temporarily transferred out of the Tenderloin and made superintendent of the street-cleaning bureau, a well-known patronage refuge. He remained there for eighteen months and then returned to his command of the Tenderloin, where he resumed his old practices. Despite repeated charges of corruption and brutality, the police commissioners promoted him to inspector in 1887 and placed him in charge of the First District, which included all East Side precincts south of Harlem. [42]

Although successful in his police career, Williams continued to draw the wrath of both middle-class reformers and working people. By 1887 there had been more than 350 formal complaints filed against him, at least 100 more than anyone else in the department.

Over the course of his career he faced eighteen charges of assaulting citizens but was never found guilty. His years in the Tenderloin and as inspector on the East Side were marked by repeated campaigns by moral reformers to expose Williams's links to vice operations. These efforts culminated in an 1893 antiprostitution campaign on the Lower East Side led by Rev. Charles Parkhurst of the Society for the Prevention of Crime (SPC). During the campaign, Frank Moss and other SPC investigators testified against vice operators and their police allies in the Eleventh Precinct. Upon leaving the Essex Market Courthouse, they were attacked by an angry crowd that was clearly unsympathetic to their cause. Despite repeated appeals to police, they received no protection and later filed a complaint with the police commissioners. Inspector Williams, who was appointed to investigate the incident, defended the police and concluded that if any assault had occurred, the SPC agents had committed it. Needless to say, such experiences only hardened the reformers' antipolice attitudes and enhanced their sympathies for victims of police violence.[43]

Williams's outspoken nativism and antilabor attitudes also raised the ire of immigrant and working-class New Yorkers. His periodic slurs against Irish and Jews no doubt contributed to his unpopularity among ethnic New Yorkers. Speaking to a heavily working-class readership, the *Police Gazette* denounced Williams's insolence and violent tactics, calling him a "brutal British bully . . . who exerts the sway of a despot in our American city."[44] Working-class animus toward Williams intensified when he became inspector and was called upon to lead police antistrike activities. He played a prominent role in suppressing the 1889 streetcar strike led by the Knights of Labor and denounced the strike's Irish leader as "an ex-convict." Following the Jewish cloakmakers' strike in 1894, Williams investigated the incident and fully exonerated the police. According to the cloakmakers, Williams refused to take affidavits from the strikers, saying, "I shall not believe a Jew under oath." In the early 1890s Lincoln Steffens recalled a parade of "bandaged and bloodied prisoners" coming through Williams's office at headquarters, the bulk of whom were "strikers and foreigners." When the Central Labor Union filed a petition demanding a state investigation of the NYPD in 1890, its description of high-level police corruption, brutality, and strike-breaking fit Alexander Williams to a tee. For their part, middle-class reformers willingly led the legal crusade against Williams, presenting him as a symbol of police corruption and brutality in a department run by crooked political machines.[45]

The Crowley Rape Case

Another example of the convergence of working-class and middle-class attitudes toward police violence was the 1885 case of Sergeant David Crowley. In one of the most sensational trials of the late nineteenth century, Crowley was accused of sexually assaulting Maggie Morris, a sixteen-year-old factory worker, in the barroom of a Lower East Side fraternal hall. Like the campaign against "Clubber" Williams, the Crowley case highlights themes of class conflict and partisan politics, but it also illustrates how ideas about gender and sexuality shaped the debate as well.

According to testimony at the trial, Morris and several of her young friends were attending a dance to benefit a neighborhood boy who had recently lost his mother and his home in a tragic fire. Around midnight, one of Morris's friends introduced her to Crowley, an off-duty police officer who lived nearby. After declining to dance, Morris accompanied Crowley to a barroom downstairs where he ordered drinks and then instructed the bartender, William Blint, to leave and lock the doors. Brandishing his pistol, Crowley allegedly threatened to shoot Morris unless she cooperated and then raped her on the billiard table. In the meantime, Morris's friends came downstairs to check on her but were chased off by Blint. Crowley later escaped through the front entrance, while Morris fled upstairs and tearfully informed her friends that Crowley had "ruined" her. An officer from the local precinct arrived soon after and arrested Blint; Crowley was apprehended the following day after Morris filed a complaint against him.[46]

In the trial that followed, both Morris and Crowley became symbols in a melodramatic morality play that pitted working-class female virtue against corrupt and predatory police authority. The

prosecution and the press emphasized Morris's youth and innocence as well as her vulnerability as a fatherless child, factory worker,
and sole support of her widowed mother. Crowley, by contrast, was
portrayed as a dastardly villain who used his political influence and
police authority to violate innocent young girls. Crowley's background made him ideal for the part: He was a prosperous and politically connected police sergeant who owed his position to
powerful Republican friends. He was particularly close to Col.
George Bliss, the Republican party leader who had defended "Clubber" Williams against brutality charges six years earlier. According
to press reports, Crowley had used his political influence to escape
several charges of brutality and misconduct during his nine years on
the force. Recently, however, he had been fined and transferred out
of his local precinct on charges of drunkenness and firing his pistol
at a fellow officer in the station house. Commanders of the Seventh
Precinct apparently disliked Crowley and claimed that he was in
league with members of the notorious border gang who worked for
the Republicans at election time.[47]

Crowley's trial quickly became a popular spectacle that drew both
well-known political figures and large crowds of working-class onlookers. According to press reports, no trial in recent years had attracted such intense public interest. Forming what the *Herald* called
a "roaring, shabby, down-at-the-heels crowd," hundreds of working-class men, women, and children thronged the courthouse to
cheer at Morris and heckle Crowley. Eager spectators reportedly
offered as much as five dollars for seats inside the courtroom, and on
several occasions, the police used their clubs to control the unruly
gathering. Inside the courtroom, prominent Republican party
figures rallied around Crowley while several high-level police
officials and city aldermen were also in attendance.[48]

The prosecution's case had a dual emphasis; it sought to highlight
Morris's innocence and vulnerability as a "poor working girl" while
presenting Crowley as an immoral authority figure who betrayed
the public trust. As the working daughter of a poor widow, Morris
was emblematic of the precarious existence of many working-class
families who were forced to send their children into the labor force.

Fears of female sexual vulnerability grew as young working women pressed for greater social freedom at work and in their leisure hours. Not surprisingly, one of the central issues of the case was the propriety of Morris's attending a late-night public dance without a male escort. The prosecution defended Morris's right to attend the dance—a community event to aid a local orphan—and to enjoy herself "in innocent and natural ways." The fault, they argued, lay with Sgt. Crowley, whose immoral character led him to take advantage of a poor innocent girl. Abandoning his wife and three children at home, Crowley had gone on a drunken spree that ended with his assault on Morris. Since he was a police officer who should have been a protector of vulnerable young women, Crowley's act was particularly heinous. His attack on Morris was not so much a violation of her rights as an individual as a betrayal of public trust and an assault on the "virtue of the working classes."

In his defense, Crowley's attorney argued that although it was "very improper" for the sergeant to invite Morris to the barroom, he had not assaulted her. In a scheme hatched by Crowley's "enemies in the Seventh Precinct," the bartender had locked the door in an attempt to create a scandal and drive Crowley off the police force. The defense also attacked Morris's moral character by presenting her as an impulsive and unsupervised young woman who went to dance halls unescorted. Although she willingly accompanied Crowley for a drink downstairs, they argued, she soon found herself in a compromising position and therefore claimed that she had been attacked. Crowley's enemies then convinced her to file false charges against him. Citing the inconclusive medical examiner's report (which indicated a physical struggle but was unclear about rape), the defense claimed that no assault had occurred and that Morris's virtue was "unsullied."[49]

Interestingly, the defense's case hinged on a police conspiracy theory that played on popular notions of police corruption and political intrigue. This was a familiar refrain among New York Republicans whose political careers were built on anti-Tammany rhetoric, but it was not a winning strategy. Crowley was himself a highly partisan figure and a former enforcer for the state Republican party. He was hardly a convincing poster boy for police reform.

Even Republican papers like the *Times* denounced him, wistfully hoping that recent civil service regulations would prevent future Crowleys from joining the force.

The prosecution, by contrast, portrayed Crowley as a rogue cop who had disgraced the department. According to the *Herald,* the prosecuting attorney called Crowley "a wolf in sheep's clothing" and declared that "the policemen of New York are against Crowley and want to see him punished." In their view, the corruption in the case was of a moral and personal nature—not an attribute of the police administration or political system. Crowley's corruption was also linked to his privileged social position. "He has friends and money and had every chance to succeed in life," the prosecutor explained, yet he would "rob a working girl of her only jewel—her virtue." In this statement and others, the prosecution portrayed Crowley not only as a privileged exploiter, but as a coward whose manhood was in question. Notions of gender and sexual propriety were thus linked with class resentments, discrediting Crowley as a greedy and dastardly thug who preyed on the daughters of the poor.[50]

The judge and the jury were apparently persuaded by the prosecution's case. Crowley was found guilty of sexual assault and sentenced to seventeen and a half years in Sing Sing, the most severe sentence given in any police brutality case between 1865 and 1894. Thousands of spectators gathered at the courthouse to hear the verdict, which was received with wild cheers and jubilation. A few days later, large crowds again turned out to heckle Crowley as he was transported from the Tombs Prison to Grand Central Station, and groups of spectators gathered at the Yonkers and Tarrytown stations to jeer at his passing train. Several New York journalists even accompanied him to Sing Sing to report approvingly on the spartan conditions of his cell and meals.[51]

Crowley's conviction, however, could not repair Maggie Morris's damaged virtue. Though the popular heroine of the courthouse crowd, the stigma of her "ruin" at the hands of Crowley was impossible to erase. During the trial her friends had surrounded her and shrouded her in a veil when passing through the crowds on her way to the police van. Ironically, the judge had ordered that she be se-

49

cluded in the Women's House of Detention to prevent any further intimidation by Crowley, who was free on bail provided by his political friends. After the verdict, the *Herald* reported that Morris had been advised to leave the city and had accepted a job as a companion to an elderly woman in the countryside. Throughout the ordeal, she had been treated as a child in need of protection and a symbol of the "outraged virtue of the working classes." Her tragedy as an unescorted woman would serve as a cautionary tale of female vulnerability—even (and perhaps especially) at the hands of police.[52]

As the Crowley and Williams cases show, incidents of police violence in the late nineteenth century generated intense public outcry among a broad spectrum of the citizenry and could even result in criminal convictions. Working-class New Yorkers enthusiastically followed these trials and generally supported middle-class reformers' efforts to curb police brutality and corruption. In these cases, prosecutors presented Williams and Crowley as evil and corrupt villains who preyed on innocent young workingmen and women in an attempt to satisfy their own greed and lust. They represented the forces of moral decay in the department and highlighted the corrupt relationship between police and partisan politics. Such cases, however, were rare and involved mainly Republican regulars opposed by both municipal reformers and Tammany Democrats. Finding cover through influential police officials, politicians, and judges, the department's numerous Tammany appointees successfully dodged conviction or serious disciplinary sanctions in most assault cases. Republican regulars such as Williams and Crowley thus became convenient targets for police reformers whose campaign against brutality and corruption culminated in a state legislative investigation in 1894.

The Lexow Investigation

On the morning of October 2, 1894, more than a hundred New York City police turned up in uniform before a state committee investigating police corruption and misconduct. The Lexow Committee, as it was called, had subpoenaed these officers, all of whom had been convicted of assaults on citizens within the last three years. Dubbed the "Clubbers Brigade" by the press, the assembled police became the symbol of a brutal and corrupt police force that was, in the words of committee counsel John Goff, "exempted from and above the operation of the law of the land."[53]

Subsequent testimony revealed that these officers had been collectively convicted of fifty-six charges of assault in the third degree, forty-five counts of assault in the second degree, and assorted other charges of criminal neglect, oppression, and attempted rape. Of the assault cases, only four of the convicted officers had been dismissed; the remainder was let off with fines or suspensions. Of the four dismissals, three involved assaults on fellow police officers. In only one instance, then, was an officer dismissed for assaulting a citizen during the last three years. As Goff explained to the committee, "a police officer of this city can brain a citizen with a club, and he may reasonably expect that all the penalty he will have to pay for that is about . . . $30."[54]

The exhibition of the clubbers brigade followed months of testimony by New York residents who claimed to have been victims of or witnesses to police clubbings, shootings, and other physical abuse. Over the course of the ten-month investigation, a steady stream of alleged victims appeared before the committee, some with bloodied bandages, facial disfigurement, bruises, and other injuries. The victims came from a wide range of social backgrounds, from immigrant bootblacks and prostitutes to well-known lawyers and journalists. As with earlier clubbing cases, the press faithfully covered these accounts and frequently editorialized about the scourge of police clubbing that plagued the city. As the first major investigation of police violence in American history, the Lexow Committee was the culmination of years of public criticism of the NYPD and marked the emergence of police brutality as a serious public policy issue.

When the Lexow Committee convened in early 1894, Alexander Williams was exhibit number one. As a walking example of police corruption, brutality, and political influence, he and other high-ranking police officials seemed to symbolize the overall demoralization of the department under Tammany control. While both working-class and middle-class New Yorkers expressed concern over these issues, it was middle-class reformers and politicians who launched the 1894 investigation. Once underway, however, the hearings offered an opportunity for working people to air their concerns about police violence, prompting reformers and politicians to take a somewhat broader view of the problem.

The Lexow investigation came about through the combined efforts of urban moral reformers and Republican party regulars. Reverend Charles Parkhurst, attorney Frank Moss, and other members of the Society for the Prevention of Crime had long attacked police for their complicity in prostitution, gambling, and other vice operations. Though generally unsympathetic to such reformers, Republican regulars sought to expand their political influence in the NYPD as Tammany Democrats had increased their control of the department over the past two decades. They thus joined reformers in calling for a state investigation of the department that would serve to discredit Tammany leadership (but also sacrifice Alexander Williams and a few other corrupt Republican officials in the process). After the GOP won control of the legislature in 1893, the senate appointed an investigating committee led by Sen. Clarence Lexow of Rockland County and dominated by upstate Republicans.

Meeting intermittently from February through December 1894, the committee conducted an extensive and damning inquiry of the NYPD. Issuing more than three hundred subpoenas and questioning some six hundred witnesses, the Lexow Committee produced more than ten thousand pages of testimony that detailed multiple cases of police graft, vice protection, racketeering, and election fraud.[55] Moral reformers, who themselves had been targets of police threats and intimidation, also highlighted the issue of police brutality. The infamous Clubbers Brigade was in fact the brainchild of Frank Moss, an attorney for the Society for the Prevention of Crime and a former leader of the Owners and Business Men's Association, a group that crusaded against vice in the Nineteenth Precinct and led a campaign for the removal of Inspector Alexander Williams in the mid-1880s. Moss conducted a survey of police trials between 1891 and 1894 that yielded the grim statistics on police assaults and punishments cited above. The presentation of these statistics was accompanied by the procession of the Clubbers Brigade along with detailed accounts of the clubbing careers of Alexander Williams and other top offenders.[56]

The Lexow Committee's treatment of this issue reflected typical middle-class attitudes toward police violence that saw brutality as a by-product of corruption. Many cases, for example, involved citizens who had become targets of violence when they became entangled in police corruption schemes. Frank Prince, a brothel owner on East Ninety-eighth Street, testified that police arrested and brutally beat him after he refused to make his monthly ten-dollar protection payment to the local precinct. Placido Galindo, a Cuban boarding house owner on West Third Street, claimed that a local police captain wanted his house for a well-known madam to use as a brothel. When he refused, three police officers entered his house, clubbed and robbed the residents, and took him to the Mercer Street station house, where he was again beaten in his cell. Portraying police as brutal enforcers, these cases stressed the direct links between corruption and violence. Moreover, the poor quality of police recruits generally and the lenient treatment of clubbers by their superiors served as prima facie evidence of the corrupt political influence of a Tammany-controlled department.[57]

Like earlier journalistic accounts of police violence, the Lexow investigation highlighted cases of police abuse toward "respectable" citizens. One of the more dramatic moments of the Clubbers Brigade came when Thomas Mason Knox, a Columbia College student, testified about a recent incident in which fifty police violently attacked a group of Columbia students attending a bonfire on East Sixty-eighth Street. Although the group had an approved permit for the event, police dispersed the gathering with their nightsticks, leaving several students badly injured. In another highly touted case, a journalist named August E. Costello testified (reluctantly under subpoena) that he was severely beaten by a police captain in a dispute over a book-writing deal. Costello had agreed to write a laudatory history of the department (later published as *Our Police Protectors*) in exchange for donating a percentage of the profits to the police pension fund. But when the book proved highly profitable, the department attempted to renegotiate the deal, which the author

53

refused to do. Costello maintained that he was then arrested on trumped-up charges and beaten until "You could hardly recognize me as a human being." Stories like these emphasized the brutal behavior of insolent police against respectable middle-class citizens.[58]

The Clubbers Brigade, however, also featured victims from less elite backgrounds. Some of these victims—young children, mothers, residents sitting out on their stoops, etc.—were the kind of "inoffensive" citizens that middle-class critics of police brutality had long defended. But other working-class witnesses, like the brothel owner Frank Prince, were less savory characters. Indeed, one of the unintended consequences of the Clubbers Brigade was that it served as an invitation to working-class New Yorkers to come forward with their own accounts of police violence without fear of intimidation. A few days after the presentation of the Clubbers Brigade, SPC representative Frank Moss noted, "There are a great many people in this city who are in terror of the police, who have felt their club. . . . These people [have begun] to realize that they can come here and be protected in telling their story." Thereafter, the committee regularly introduced new witnesses—some of them bandaged and bruised —who had voluntarily come forward to testify about police beatings. According to Moss, there was such an influx of these volunteers that "We could occupy nearly every day with them."[59]

The infusion of working-class voices into the investigation prompted the committee to expand its definition of what constituted police brutality. Many of the witnesses were poor or foreign-born and openly admitted that they had been drinking, quarreling, or engaging in other disorderly behavior at the time. In one case, a truckman and rigger named Thomas Lucas testified that a police officer stole some money from him one night while he was asleep on a doorstep. When Lucas later confronted the patrolman, he was allegedly clubbed and arrested for interfering with an officer and was then beaten again in his cell. When discussion ensued as to Lucas's possible guilt in the matter, chairman Lexow replied that "even if a man is guilty of a crime he ought not to be punished that way." Lexow likewise came to the defense of Rose Smith, the purported victim of a violent assault in a liquor store by Officer George Lair. When Lair attempted to defend his actions by noting that Smith was a prostitute, Lexow insisted that prostitutes "are entitled to the same amount of protection that anybody else is."[60]

The chairman's forthright defense of these disorderly individuals suggests an emerging definition of police brutality based on a broader notion of citizens' rights. Unlike earlier middle-class critiques of police brutality based on empathy and class privilege, reformers in the 1890s acknowledged that police violence disproportionately affected poor and working-class New Yorkers and that they as citizens were entitled to protection, regardless of their guilt or innocence. As committee counsel John Goff explained in his introduction to the Lexow report:

Those in the humbler walks of life were subjected to appalling outrages.... They were abused, clubbed and imprisoned, and even convicted of crime on false testimony by police and their accomplices.... The poor, ignorant foreigner residing on the great East Side of the city has been especially subjected to a brutal and infamous rule by the police....

Goff concluded that the fault lay with those who controlled departmental discipline who have "managed it with utter disregard of the plain constitutional rights of the people."[61]

While acknowledging certain working-class perspectives on police violence, the committee was conspicuously silent about others. There is no mention, for instance, of police abuse of African Americans and no evidence that any black witnesses appeared before the committee.[62] Even more noticeable was the complete absence of labor representatives, who for years had criticized police violence during strikes. In fact, labor and Socialist organizations had been calling for a state investigation of police practices since the Tompkins Square Riot of 1874. The Lexow investigation not only disregarded antilabor violence but pointedly denounced police brutality against the foreign-born because of its potential for discrediting government and encouraging radicalism.[63] Not surprisingly, middle-class reformers eschewed labor's more radical vision of group rights for a more bourgeois conception of individual rights that could be achieved through political and institutional reform of the current system.

For all the fanfare and publicity, the actual results of the investigation were disappointing. Revelations of police corruption and brutality helped Fusion party (an alliance of reformist Republicans and anti-Tammany Democrats) candidate William L. Strong win the mayoralty away from Tammany in 1894, but his attempts at removing high-level police officials generally failed. On the state level, Republican regulars used the investigation's findings to promote a bill establishing a bipartisan four-member police commission. The bill passed in 1895, and Mayor Strong appointed a new commission headed by reform advocate Theodore Roosevelt. Roosevelt implemented stricter recruiting and disciplinary practices and engineered the retirement of Alexander Williams in 1895. Echoing earlier middle-class reformers, he also insisted on courteous behavior and more restrained use of the club on "respectable" citizens. Ultimately, however, Tammany maintained its grip on the department, and the continuing political influence of both parties on the police commission hampered further reform.[64]

Although police violence continued to flourish under such conditions, growing public recognition of the problem meant that it would hereafter become a serious issue addressed by progressive mayors, chiefs of police, and national police organizations. As we shall see, the public linking of corruption and brutality that first occurred in the late nineteenth century would characterize and complicate efforts to combat police violence for the next forty years. Moreover, the contacts established between middle-class reformers and working-class victims during the Lexow investigation resulted in a new definition of police brutality based on a broader, but still limited, notion of citizens' rights. This new understanding laid the groundwork for the more diverse antibrutality movement that would develop in the Progressive Era and the 1920s, one that would include African Americans, labor activists, and legal reformers who would fashion still newer understandings of police violence in the twentieth century.

2. RIOTS AND THE RACIALIZATION OF POLICE BRUTALITY, 1900-1911

Since the early days of Alexander "Clubber" Williams, the Tender-loin had been one of New York's most notorious vice districts. Stretching from Twenty-third Street to Forty-second Street on the West Side, the area housed a strip of saloons, brothels, and dance halls along Sixth Avenue that moral reformers had dubbed "Satan's Circus" in the late nineteenth century. More recently, the neighborhood had also become home to the city's growing black population. Forced out of their older downtown neighborhoods, African Americans lived in residential clusters in the Tenderloin interspersed among an even larger population of working-class Irish immigrants, with whom they competed for jobs, housing, and other resources. This competition grew during the 1890s as a new wave of southern black migrants settled there. During the course of the decade, New York's black population grew from 23,600 to more than 60,000, with the largest concentrations in the Tenderloin and surrounding neighborhoods. Racial tensions in the area grew accordingly, and patterns of segregation and discrimination hardened. One manifestation of these tensions was the Tenderloin Riot in the summer of 1900.[1]

Around 2 A.M. on August 12, Arthur Harris was leaving Mc-Bride's Saloon on Eighth Avenue, where he had spent the evening. A black newcomer from the South, Harris was supposed to meet his girlfriend, May Eno, out front at closing time. When he came out the door, he saw a white man accosting Eno. As it turned out, the man was Robert Thorpe, a plainclothes officer from the Twentieth Precinct who was arresting Eno for soliciting, a charge commonly used against black women on the streets at night. Harris intervened in the conflict and was clubbed by Officer Thorpe; Harris then pulled a knife, stabbed Thorpe, and fled. The officer died in the hospital the next day. As word of Thorpe's death spread, racial tensions in the neighborhood intensified. A few nights later, a fight broke out between a white man and a black passerby outside the house where Thorpe's wake was taking place. Before long dozens of white onlookers had joined the fray, and a full-scale riot was underway.[2]

Newspapers estimated that more than ten thousand people took part in the rioting that night. Nearly all the violence was initiated by whites who chased and beat unsuspecting blacks, dragging them off the Eighth Avenue streetcar and out of nearby hotels and saloons. As white crowds rampaged through the West Twenties and Thirties, they attacked black pedestrians stranded on the streets and threatened to lynch them. The police department called out nearly six hundred reserves from eleven precincts to help quell the violence. The rioting continued for several hours until a torrential downpour drove most people off the street around 2 A.M. Although there were no reliable estimates of the number of people injured, dozens of black residents later testified to the beatings they received during the riot. The local press described the West 37th Street police station as "a battlefield hospital" filled with black prisoners with "battered faces, broken heads, and crimson-hued tattered garments."[3]

Not all the injuries, however, were caused by street mobs. As several newspapers reported, police officers were frequently the perpetrators of violence, joining in or looking the other way when white crowds attacked blacks. In many cases, the *Tribune* reported, "a crowd of hoodlums would make a dash at some Negro . . . and then policemen would join in the chase of the frightened colored man, catch him, club him if he resisted, and then drag him away to a police station." The *Evening Post* was even more blunt, saying police "clubbed and misused colored folk wherever they could find them. . . ." In a series of affidavits taken after the riot, eight black witnesses described how police either handed them over to the crowd, looked on while whites beat them, or joined in the collective attack.

One of the more chilling accounts came from Chester Smith, a young black man who was attacked by a group of white youths as he returned home from work. When Smith tried to flee, a police officer grabbed him and struck him with his club. Stunned by the blow,

Smith fled into a nearby saloon, followed by another police officer. After a few minutes, the patrolman told him that the crowd had dispersed and that he should go home. Smith looked out the door, however, and saw the youths still waiting outside. When he refused to leave, the officer picked him up and hurled him through the swinging doors on to the sidewalk. The mob pounced on him and beat him, with the enthusiastic assistance of several police.[4]

At least three other witnesses claimed they had appealed to police officers for protection but were clubbed in response. Two of the alleged victims were female, and witnesses testified that police clubbed at least three other women as well. Moreover, since some black residents were afraid to testify and since many of the reserves were dressed in civilian clothes, the number of police assaults was no doubt higher than reported. Indeed, some witnesses believed that the police did more harm to blacks than did civilian rioters.[5]

As it turned out, the riot was merely the opening round in a series of racial/ethnic disturbances in which a predominantly Irish-American police force openly sided with violent white crowds who attacked blacks, Jews, and other new migrants. At least three such disturbances—in the Tenderloin, the Lower East Side, and San Juan Hill—took place in the first decade of the twentieth century, some of the peak years of urban migration. As record numbers of southern blacks and new immigrants streamed into New York's old ethnic neighborhoods, the Irish, Germans, and other older immigrant groups came to resent the newcomers who competed with them for jobs, housing, public space, and political power. Perhaps equally important, however, was the old-stock immigrants' desire for social acceptability as "white" Americans. As historians have shown, European working-class immigrants embraced whiteness as a means of distinguishing themselves from African Americans, whom they associated with slavery and dependency, and from newer immigrants, whom they perceived as strange and inferior races. This was particularly true for the Irish, a group that had long occupied the bottom ranks of the social hierarchy and whose own whiteness was often called into question. The Democratic party eagerly appealed to Irish whiteness by opposing the expansion of black civil rights and defending Irish residents who attempted to drive blacks, Jews, and other racial outsiders from their neighborhoods. Because the Irish were so well represented in the police department, many officers were sympathetic to or at least tolerant of the racial offensives led by their countrymen.[6]

While police largely ignored the whites who initiated the Tenderloin Riot, most of the black victims were arrested and jailed at the West 37th Street station house. A subsequent police investigation of the riot indicates that out of nineteen arrests on the night of August 15–16, sixteen were African Americans. At least five of those arrested later testified that police beat them in the station house. One of these was William Elliott, a hotel bellman who was arrested on a weapons charge when he appealed to police for protection from an angry crowd. Once inside the station house, Elliott testified, police escorted him into the muster room, turned off the lights, and proceeded to punch, kick, and club him until acting captain John Cooney ordered them to stop. As it turned out, several reporters were present in the next room who heard Elliott's cries and later testified to his bloodied and beaten condition.[7]

Elliott and other black men who attempted to defend themselves from street mobs by carrying revolvers, knives, or other weapons were special targets of police attention and abuse. At least five beating victims were arrested on weapons charges, although only one of them actually drew a knife. Police also zeroed in on black residents who expressed their displeasure by hurling stones, bottles, or other debris from windows and rooftops. Officers responded by randomly firing their pistols at tenement windows and, in some cases, invading homes and beating the alleged perpetrators. John Haines, a black longshoreman who was asleep in his apartment, was clubbed in his bed by police who accused him of shooting at them. They arrested him for possession of an illegal firearm and took him to the police station dressed only in his undershirt. There he was beaten again in front of the sergeant's desk and several witnesses. Two of these witnesses later testified about Haines's beating, and his bloody bedclothes were retained as evidence.[8] In Haines's case and others, police interpreted black attempts at self-defense as a challenge to their authority and retaliated with acts of violence.

Police assaults on African Americans in the Tenderloin, the press argued, were carried out to avenge the killing of Officer Thorpe by a black man a few days earlier. A *Herald* reporter claimed that during Thorpe's funeral, he had overheard police making threats against blacks over the officer's body. Susie White, a woman whose building was stormed by police during the riot, testified that police threatened to "make it hot for you niggers" for killing Thorpe. A few days after the riot, the *Commercial Advertiser* reported that despite their earlier disagreements, the force had closed ranks behind Chief William Devery because "He gave the men 'a night off' to 'teach the niggers a lesson.' The men appreciate it." All of the press accounts stressed how well liked Thorpe was in the Twentieth Precinct, and the *Tribune* intimated that Thorpe was to have been the future son-in-law of Captain Cooney. In light of these issues and the widespread and extreme nature of police violence during the riot, the revenge motive seems plausible.[9]

Police vengeance, the press noted, occurred in the context of deep-seated corruption, immorality, and lax discipline on the part of the police administration. Echoing reformers' long-standing views of the force as a corrupt tool of Tammany Hall, newspaper editors claimed that officially sanctioned vice and corruption fostered disorder among the "criminal classes." The *Herald* blamed Chief Devery for allowing black and white criminals to thrive in the Tenderloin, claiming that "the open flourishing of vice draws the vicious—whites and blacks—from all parts of the country to this city and creates the conditions out of which disorder and crime arise." Tolerance of vice, the editor added, resulted in a "morally crippled police force" that encouraged criminals and police alike to engage in illegal and disorderly activities. The effectiveness of the police in suppressing disorder, the *Tribune* said, was undercut as "a police mob in uniform incited a mob without uniform to break the laws." Without proper supervision or discipline, police officers could do as they pleased, and "the ambition to club the life out of a nigger is cherished among the Tammany pets who wield the locust." The *Herald* concurred, calling the Tenderloin outbreak a "police riot."[10]

As in the past, journalists and reformers blamed police misconduct not on individual officers but on poor administration at the highest levels of the department. Chief Devery's corrupt leadership came in for particularly harsh criticism, as did the spinelessness of the police commissioners who appointed and supported him. Reformers and editors agreed that the only way to stop police corruption and brutality was to throw out the bosses, "overhaul the system," and "take the police out of politics." Any attempt by the current Tammany-dominated police department to investigate itself, they argued, was doomed to failure.[11]

The reformers' cynical assessment of the department was borne out over the next two weeks as police officials refused to admit any wrongdoing and failed to undertake disciplinary action. Police officials uniformly blamed the black residents of the Tenderloin for inciting the riot, particularly recent migrants from the South. Chief Devery claimed that "the colored people who live in this precinct are a bad class. . . . Most of them are from the South, and they came here with very peculiar ideas as to freedom of action." Referring to blacks in the Tenderloin as "savages," Captain Cooney argued that police had been outnumbered and used only the amount of force necessary to suppress the riot. In his report to Chief Devery, Inspector Walter Thompson said that all of the black clubbing victims incarcerated at the Twentieth Precinct had been armed and had committed assaults or resisted arrest. With the exception of William Powers, an unpopular off-duty officer who was fined ten dollars for drunkenness and inciting a riot, the department took no disciplinary action against any officer. Responding to a barrage of brutality complaints stemming from the riot, Police Commissioner Bernard York told the *Evening Post* that he did not believe the complainants' stories. "If a man gets clubbed, it's proof that he's where he has no business," York argued in an astounding piece of circular logic. "If the negro doesn't want to get clubbed, let him keep out of disorderly crowds." For twelve days following the riot, the police showed no inclination to investigate brutality charges despite a strongly worded request to do so from the acting mayor, Randolph Guggenheimer (Mayor Robert Van Wyck was out of town at the time).[12]

In requesting official hearings on police misconduct, Guggenheimer was no doubt responding to growing political pressure by the city's black elite. In the days immediately following the riot, black leaders including T. Thomas Fortune, editor of the black-owned *New York Age,* and at least four prominent black ministers denounced the violence and police involvement in it. Black Democrats from the United Colored Democracy also condemned police brutality in the riot and dispatched the group's leader, Edward E. Lee, to visit the mayor's office to demand an investigation. The most significant protest, however, came in a sermon delivered on August 26 by Rev. W. H. Brooks of St. Mark's Methodist Episcopal Church on West 37th Street, the largest and wealthiest black congregation in the city. Recounting a litany of police assaults on innocent black citizens during the riot, Brooks vowed to pursue formal charges against the police and urged aggrieved victims to come forward and testify.[13]

Over the next two weeks, Brooks and several prominent black ministers, doctors, lawyers, and businesspeople organized the Citizens' Protective League (CPL) to press their claims against the department. They retained Frank Moss, a white attorney and former police commissioner, to represent black victims. The counsel for the Lexow police investigation of 1895, Moss was also a leading member of the Society for the Prevention of Crime, which now joined the CPL in condemning police brutality and investigating police activities during the riot. On August 30, Moss ran ads in the morning newspapers urging victims and witnesses of police violence to come forward and swear out complaints. Moss eventually collected more than eighty affidavits, later published under the title *Story of the Riot.* The CPL also retained another attorney, Israel Ludlow, to handle civil suits against the police totaling $250,000. At its peak, the organization boasted more than five thousand members and turned out some thirty-five hundred people for a protest meeting at Carnegie Hall in September.[14]

The popularity of the CPL was based on a complex array of class, racial, and gender-based appeals. Like their white middle-class allies, black elites of the CPL understood police brutality in moral and political terms, viewing it as a by-product of vice and political corruption. "The recent riot had its origin . . . in bad whiskey, bad women, and corrupt police officers," Brooks asserted in his August 26 sermon. But while Brooks condemned black lawlessness in the Tenderloin, he insisted that no black crime could "justify the policemen in their savage and indiscriminate attack upon innocent and helpless people." Those clubbed by the police were all "decent, honest, hard-working people" including honorable businessmen and respectable women. Frank Moss offered a similar description of the victims, noting that there were no black criminals among them. "The gamblers and inmates of disorderly houses were not molested," Moss maintained. "They have been standing in with the police for years and undoubtedly do yet. They knew in advance what was coming and kept out of the way."[15]

Moss, Brooks, and other CPL leaders claimed that police knew and approved of the mob's actions in advance, and they blamed Tammany officials for police complicity in the violence. Arguing that the police commissioners were more responsible for the violence than the officers who wielded the clubs, Brooks identified Tammany as the main culprit. Rev. P. Butler Tompkins, pastor of St. James Presbyterian Church in the Tenderloin and a member of the CPL executive committee, denounced Tammany Hall in biblical terms as "the breeder of evil, the feeder of sin and crime," and urged his followers to "crush the head of this hellish serpent." Other black ministers in the CPL assailed Tammany Hall from the pulpit and warned black men against voting with the machine on election day.[16] Building on old abolitionist networks and decades of black alienation from the Democratic party, CPL leaders made common cause with Frank Moss and other white Republicans who had been battling police corruption for the past twenty years. Like these reformers and much of the city's white press, the black leadership of the CPL viewed police brutality as a moral problem that required a reformist political solution.

But why did middle-class blacks suddenly rally in support of the victims of police brutality? For decades, police had harassed and beaten African-American suspects with little or no vocal protest from black elites. Since most of the victims were poor and without political influence, black leaders had generally been unwilling to risk their reputations in defending such individuals. The riot, however, presented a different scenario in which police violence was more blatant and widely dispersed. Although the majority of victims were working class—longshoremen, bellhops, janitors, etc.—they also included a few elite or educated individuals such as John B. Mallory, a mechanical engineering student, and Headley Johnson and Richard Taylor, two Pullman porters (a high-status occupation in the black community). Complaints by such respectable persons lent credibility to the claims of others and showed that no one with dark skin was immune from attack. Moreover, the riot itself was one manifestation of the increasing segregation and discrimination that characterized black life in New York around the turn of the century, changes that acutely affected middle-class blacks. As racial boundaries solidified, these "respectable" black citizens increasingly felt the impact of white racism in their daily lives. Finally, CPL leaders reached out to defend working-class blacks because they feared losing credibility as community leaders at a time when black political power was diminishing. "If we sit idly and allow the iron heal of oppression to grind us into powder," CPL leader D. Mason Webster told his colleagues, "then we will lose the respect and sympathy of all good people and merit the wrath of the lawless and criminal classes."[17]

Although black elites shared a common moral and political framework with white middle-class reformers, they reached out to working-class African Americans through explicitly racial appeals. Most significantly, CPL leaders repeatedly compared the Tenderloin Riot to lynching in the South. The riot, said Rev. P. L. Culyer of the downtown Zion Methodist Church, was even worse than a southern lynching because in New York "the guardians of the peace appear to have participated in the cruelty." Furthermore, "there was no pretense of seeking out the guilty ones, if there were any," Culyer said. "It was sufficient to find a man with a black face, pounce on him, and endeavor to hang him from a lamp post."[18] Like nineteenth-century workers who compared police violence to European tyranny and monarchial despotism, black leaders appealed to their followers' past experience with authority and the abuse of power—in this case in the American South. Their appeals, however, were racial rather than class-based. As Brooks plainly put it, "our people were beaten because of the color of their skins." For the first time, then, opponents of police brutality articulated the problem as a racial one and appealed to their brethren on the basis of racial dignity and justice.

Appeals to racial dignity, however, were distinctly gendered. In his momentous sermon of August 26, Reverend Brooks drew particular attention to police attacks on "respectable helpless women." Describing how police beat and threatened women who appealed for help, fired at innocent mothers and children in tenement windows, and dragged women from their beds "in nude condition," Brooks called on his male followers to defend black womanhood. He went on to attack Tammany Hall and its black supporters in similarly gendered terms, saying, "I can't understand how a self-respecting colored man can support an organization that has no respect for his wife or daughter." Other CPL leaders echoed these themes as they implored followers to wage "a dignified and manly protest" against police brutality and for the Negro to "rise up in his manhood" against Tammany Hall. Highlighting black female vulnerability, such appeals drew on nineteenth-century ideals of manhood (bravery, honor, dignity, independence, etc.) to validate political protest among black men. The conceptual linkage between manhood and racial dignity, so evident in the suffrage struggles of the Reconstruction South, were now deployed in an increasingly racialized battle against police brutality in the urban North.[19]

At the same time, CPL appeals also presented brutality as a universal problem, invoking the more legalistic principles of human rights and due process. While acknowledging that blacks were beaten because of their skin color, Reverend Brooks wrote to Mayor Van Wyck, "what was done to our race by the wholesale occurs constantly in separate instances to white persons." Frank Moss seconded this view, noting that the police commissioners' failure to take action against abusive officers during the riot was typical of their general handling of all citizens' complaints. CPL leader D. Mason Webster made the most sweeping appeal of all:

When the humblest citizen is not safe the most exalted is in danger. This wanton outrage is the affair of every person in the state of New York and of every person in the nation. It appeals as much to the residents of Fifth Avenue as it does to those of the Twentieth Precinct. When your life and your property can be taken without due process of law, anarchy is not far off, and anarchy is the death of law.

At a time when the white middle class lived in fear of bomb-throwing anarchists, Webster depicted brutal policemen as the moral equivalent of foreign revolutionaries intent on destroying American liberty.[20]

Sustained protests by the CPL eventually forced the police commissioners to hold public hearings on several riot-related complaints. On September 7, the commissioners began hearing evidence in the alleged beatings of William Elliott and seven other black suspects. From the beginning, Commissioner Bernard York presented himself as a defender of the department rather than an impartial judge of police behavior. According to CPL attorney Frank Moss, York examined William Elliott and other black witnesses as though they were hostile parties, while police "were carefully nursed and led by him." The *Herald* and the *Evening Post* also condemned York's conduct, noting that he grilled Elliott for an hour and a half, treating him "as though [he] had brutally assaulted a police officer." When another witness, Edward S. Corbin, testified to Elliott's beating, police disputed Corbin's claim and York threatened him with perjury. Even more galling to CPL attorneys was York's refusal to issue subpoenas for additional witnesses or to allow cross-examination of police officers, despite numerous "inconsistencies and contradictions in their testimony." In defending his actions, York said he did not want to furnish evidence that would bolster the complainants' civil suits against the city nor provide "opportunities for professional reformers to air their eloquence for the benefit of newspapers."[21]

While York's procedural decisions seriously handicapped CPL lawyers, his insistence on trying individual policemen—rather than their supervising officers—made conviction virtually impossible. In the case of William Elliott, for example, several witnesses (including three white journalists) testified on the victim's behalf, but they were unable to identify particular officers among the fifty to sixty who participated in or observed the beating in the muster room that night. Since Captain Cooney and several of his subordinates denied that the beating took place, York concluded that the evidence was contradictory and that no conviction could be sustained. Frank Moss then filed a complaint against Chief Devery, Inspector Thompson, and Captain Cooney charging them with neglect of duty and failure to maintain discipline. Commissioner York refused to accept the complaint. Outraged, Ludlow denounced the hearing as "a premeditated whitewash," a judgment widely echoed in the press. As the *New York Herald* put it, the hearing was "a one-sided affair that was neither a judicial inquiry nor a serious investigation . . . It [was] a farce."[22]

While the remaining complainants faced a similar fate at the hands of the police commissioners, Moss turned to the magistrate's court in an attempt to bring criminal charges of assault against two officers. Earlier efforts to bring criminal indictments had failed when the grand jury found that victims and witnesses could not identify individual policemen. In the cases of officers Herman Ohm and John J. Cleary, however, there were several complainants and witnesses who were willing to testify and identify the perpetrators. William Johnson and John Haines (the longshoreman who was beaten in his bed) both testified that Ohm assaulted them without cause during the riot; William Hopson and George Myers (along with eight other black eyewitnesses) testified that Cleary brutally beat them during a subsequent racial outbreak on August 26. A number of police and local white residents then offered testimony in defense of the officers. Magistrate Henry A. Brann ruled that the officers' actions were justifiable and discounted the testimony of black witnesses who he described as "vindictive" and "bitter." The police commissioners' final report on the riot echoed this view, arguing that "the bias of the complainant is so apparent that the fact of the clubbing would not . . . justify a conviction." Accordingly, no charges were ever preferred against any officer (other than the drunken William Powers) in connection with the riot.[23]

The police department's only concession to its critics came on September 21 when Chief Devery issued a special order instructing policemen to be "courteous" to citizens. Warning officers against indifferent, rough, and insolent behavior, Devery noted that violations would result in formal complaints and investigation. Although the chief disavowed any connection between the special order and the Tenderloin Riot, the press insisted it was "a tacit admission that policemen have been guilty of unwarranted violence."[24] The courtesy order, however, was small consolation for the CPL's many months of organizing, collecting evidence, and preparing cases. By the time the police commission released its final report in December, several months had passed since the riot, and the CPL was unable to regain its former momentum. After fruitless appeals to the mayor and Gov. Theodore Roosevelt, the organization quietly disbanded.

Tammany's shameful behavior in the affair, however, would not be forgotten. As the mayoral election of 1901 approached, black political leaders made the candidates' position on police brutality a litmus test for their support. At a meeting of the United Colored Republicans in October 1901, state committee member Charles Anderson announced that he was supporting the Fusion candidate, Seth Low, because of Tammany's role in the Tenderloin Riot. "We are not so much voting for Low as we are voting against Devery . . . our battle cry is 'Remember the Riot.' " The following week, a delegation representing black organizations throughout the city met with Low to discuss their concerns about racial violence and voice their support for his candidacy. Low went on to win the election by a slim margin, with the pro-Fusion votes of black and Jewish New Yorkers playing a key role. Reformers' hopes that a new administration would clean up the police department, however, were quickly dashed. By the summer of 1902, the department was once again at the center of a political maelstrom growing out of the worst anti-Semitic police riot in the nation's history.[25]

The Hoe Riot

Like the Tenderloin, the Lower East Side was undergoing significant ethnic transition around the turn of the century. From 1900–1910, millions of Jews, Italians, Chinese, and other new immigrants entered the country, making it the peak decade in the history of American immigration. More than 176,000 Jews alone arrived between 1900 and 1902, the largest influx for any consecutive three-year period up to that time. More than three-quarters of them settled on the Lower East Side. With the influx of Jews and other new immigrants, tensions developed between these groups and the older established residents, particularly the Irish. Irish-American gangs attacked Jews and other newcomers, creating a climate of fear on Cherry Street, the east end of Grand Street, and other Irish strongholds. One particular trouble spot was in front of the printing factory owned by Robert Hoe and Company on Grand Street. On several occasions in 1901 and 1902, young Irish apprentices employed by Hoe had assaulted local Jews who passed by the factory. The Irish-dominated police force rarely intervened in these incidents and had a well-earned reputation for harassing and beating pushcart peddlers, striking workers, and other poor immigrants who posed a challenge to police authority. Although Jewish residents periodically complained about the abuse, most realized that appeals to the police were futile.[26]

The problem reached a bloody crescendo on July 30, 1902. On that day, thousands of Jews lined the streets of the Lower East Side to pay their respects to Chief Rabbi Jacob Joseph, the head of a federation of orthodox synagogues on the Lower East Side. The procession began at the Rabbi's home at 263 Henry Street and wound its way past five East Side synagogues en route to the Grand Street ferry and the cemetery in Brooklyn. Anticipating a crowd of about twenty thousand mourners, the funeral organizers had requested an escort of twenty to twenty-five police. The night before the event, however, a reporter from a local Yiddish newspaper called the department to say there would be a tremendous turnout and that more police were needed. The warning was ignored.

When crowds of fifty thousand to a hundred thousand people gathered the next morning, the level of police protection was woefully inadequate. Police on duty at the rabbi's home had a difficult time containing the crowd. The *Evening Post* reported that officers used considerable roughness in clearing the street before the funeral, forcibly removing hundreds of women and old men who may not have understood police orders. "Men were flung down, women were dragged out by arms and shoulders and pushed headlong down the street . . . one might have thought the police were putting down a riot from the way they handled many of the unfortunate men and women who happened to be in front." This encounter, the *Post* maintained, aroused the indignation of the Jews and prompted police to request reinforcements. More requests followed, and by 11 A.M. more than a hundred officers had been dispatched. The level of protection was still insufficient; as a later investigation revealed, events of this magnitude normally warranted an escort of at least four hundred officers.[27]

Nevertheless, the procession moved peacefully through the East Side until it reached the Hoe factory at the corner of Grand and Sheriff streets. As the hearse approached the plant around 1 P.M., Hoe employees on the upper floors began to jeer and hurl debris at the marchers. Screws, wood blocks, oil-soaked rags, buckets of water, and other objects rained down on the mourners and the casket. Disturbed by this disrespectful treatment, several groups of Jews entered the Hoe building to protest to the management. While the first delegation was received respectfully, a second group of protesters—highly agitated and speaking in Yiddish—was forcefully ejected from the premises after a struggle. Around this time, the Hoe management called the police station for more help. It also ordered its employees to use fire hoses to repel intruders, drenching dozens of mourners and spectators out on the street. Although the exact sequence of events is unclear, a number of Jews thrust their umbrellas through ground floor windows and hurled back the debris being thrown at them. Additional police reserves arrived soon after, and the water hoses were turned off. By 1:20 P.M., the officers had secured the area in front of the factory and calm was restored.

Soon after, however, a contingent of two hundred police under Inspector Adam Cross arrived on the scene and, without warning, used their clubs to clear the remaining crowd. According to the *Times,* the police attacked the crowd indiscriminately, "slashing this way and that with their sticks, shouting as they waded through the dense gathering, and shoving roughly against men and women alike." A few Hoe employees came out and joined the police in forcefully dispersing the crowd. Eyewitnesses later testified that police pursued and clubbed several people who tried to move away, and at least two suspects claimed that officers choked them in the patrol wagon. In the half hour it took to disperse the crowd, eleven Jews were arrested and scores injured. More than a hundred people required medical attention, and doctors worked at the scene for over an hour. Nine of the Jews who had been arrested were fined five or ten dollars for disorderly conduct, vandalism, or assault; two others were held on a thousand dollars bail for inciting a riot. As for the Hoe workers who had initiated the disturbance, only one was charged—a man who had sprayed a police officer with the company's fire hose.[28]

In the immediate aftermath of the riot, the police department defended its actions on Grand Street as a tactical necessity against a disorderly Jewish crowd. The factory owner, Robert Hoe, agreed, claiming that the funeral marchers had been combative and disorderly even before they arrived at his plant. After conducting a brief investigation in which he interviewed only police and Hoe employees, Inspector Cross charged that Jewish marchers had carried paving stones and iron bolts with them to the factory. Their attack on the building, he concluded, had been premeditated. Sparking widespread outrage in the Jewish community, the claim was so patently absurd and inflammatory that Police Commissioner John Partridge immediately transferred Cross out of the Lower East Side to a distant post in the Bronx.[29]

Not satisfied with this mild rebuke, Jewish leaders demanded a thorough investigation of the incident. Over the next week, they organized several protest meetings and at least five different committees to look into the Hoe incident. These groups raised funds, secured legal representation, collected evidence, offered rewards for information relating to the riot, and met with the mayor and other city officials to demand an investigation. Like the Citizens' Protective League in the Tenderloin, most of the committees were headed by doctors, lawyers, and other professionals. The most prominent group was the East Side Vigilance League (ESVL), an invitation-only committee of some three hundred professionals affiliated with the downtown Hebrew Institute of Doctors and Lawyers. Led by the attorney Abraham H. Sarasohn and physicians Julius Halpern and Joseph Balsky, the ESVL took depositions from riot victims and witnesses, provided legal representation for those filing brutality complaints, and met with Mayor Low to demand official action. Other groups such as the Committee of the United Hebrew Community, the East Side Hebrew Association, and the American Hebrew League represented Zionists and religious leaders who also participated in these activities.[30]

The ESVL and other Jewish groups viewed police brutality in the riot as part of a long-standing pattern of anti-Semitic police behavior. As P. Epstein of the East Side Hebrew Association put it, "For years I have known that the police had no use for the Jews of the East Side, but their dislike never was evidenced as brutally as in this riot." The Yiddish daily *Forward* accused police of a "blood thirsty anti-Semitism" and claimed that officers at the riot scene were "beating up anybody who looked Jewish." Most significantly, Jewish leaders appealed to collective memories of ethnic and religious persecution by comparing the riot to a Russian pogrom. Just as blacks had claimed that the Tenderloin Riot was worse than a southern lynching, Jews insisted that even Russian police would not have attacked innocent funeral mourners. Describing the police beatings of women and children, Dr. Paul Kaplan of the ESVL insisted "such murderous behavior would not have happened even in Russia." Ironically, Russian Jews had come to America to escape the pogroms, *Forward* editor Abraham Cahan told a crowd assembled at Cooper Union, but now "they receive similar treatment from the anti-Semitic police" in America. Virtually every mass meeting included speeches equating the New York police with Russian Cossacks, and the Yiddish press regularly referred to the Hoe Riot as a "police pogrom."[31]

Although appeals to racial identity were the most common organizing tactic, some Jews also presented police brutality as a class-based political problem. Dubbing police the "protectors of the rich," labor and Socialist leaders blamed police behavior in the Hoe Riot on capitalist political control that permeated machine and reform administrations alike. The day after the riot, the Socialist *Forward* attacked prominent religious Jews and Jewish politicians for supporting those who controlled the police. "The crowd of Jewish citizens who got their heads split yesterday, themselves put the clubs in the hands of these anti-Semitic, anti-working class goons," the *Forward* editorialized. "They teach the Jewish masses to give up their power to bands of anti-Semites." In a mass meeting at Cooper Union sponsored by the *Forward*, Abraham Cahan argued that, "the police force was reared by Tammany and controlled by the reformers. One party is as responsible as the other." Another speaker, Joseph Barondess, seconded this view and urged Jews to abandon the major parties in favor of the Socialists.[32]

As a longtime leader in the needle trades, Barondess was no newcomer to the brutality issue. He had led the Jewish cloakmakers' protest against police violence in 1894 and claimed that detectives beat him while in custody. Barondess's emphasis on the class dimension of police brutality, however, was more muted in 1902 than it had been in the 1890s. Barondess, Cahan, Meyer London, and other Socialists who denounced police violence in the Hoe Riot emphasized police anti-Semitism more than class struggle. In fact, their initial criticism of upper-class Jews quickly disappeared as the *Forward* lent increasing support to the work of the elite East Side Vigilance League. Their concern with anti-Semitism and Jewish identity was nothing new; Jewish labor leaders had long organized on ethnic as well as class lines, and Barondess himself had recently embraced Zionism. But the specific circumstances of the Hoe Riot also made a class-based analysis of police brutality less compelling. After all, police had not only intervened on behalf of the Hoe management but had also overlooked the violent provocations of an unruly group of Irish factory workers. Moreover, in the melee that followed, Jews of all social levels became targets of police clubbing. Under such circumstances, older notions of police repression of the working class seemed less appropriate than a racially based argument of anti-Semitism.

Cahan, Barondess, and other Socialist leaders were also shrewd politicians who hoped to exploit Jewish anger over police anti-Semitism to strengthen the Socialist party. By condemning both of the major parties—"the silk-stockinged reformers" and Tammany alike—the Socialists hoped to win a greater number of votes from Jews in the next election.[33] Building on the Jewish community's legitimate anger over the riot, the Socialists appropriated the antipolice rhetoric long used by reformers fighting Tammany and deployed it against Mayor Low and the current reform administration. On the East Side, at least, appeals to Jewish identity and the critical importance of the Jewish vote offered a potentially effective means of winning support for the Socialists.

The mainstream parties were equally anxious to exploit the riot for political advantage. In the days following the riot, both the Democrats and Republicans denounced police brutality in hopes of winning East Side votes. Leading the attack was Florrie Sullivan, Democratic leader of the Lower East Side's Eighth Assembly District. Sullivan appeared at the police commissioner's chambers on August 2 to demand punishment of abusive officers. A few days later, Sullivan and other Tammany leaders were pressuring the board of aldermen to hold hearings investigating police misconduct in the riot. Seeing it as a prime opportunity to woo Jewish voters back to the Tammany fold, the Democrats eagerly attacked the Low administration as inept and incapable of maintaining police discipline. A local Jewish Republican leader, Mayer Schoenfeld, refuted this view and suggested that Tammany-backed police officers had used the riot as a pretext for punishing Jews for their political independence in the last election. Hoping to prevent a highly partisan political spectacle, Republicans called for an independent investigation headed by the mayor. Municipal reformers no doubt preferred this approach to a Tammany-led investigation designed to discredit the Low administration. Veteran anti-Tammany reformer Frank Moss even wrote to the East Side Vigilance League offering his support and investigative services. Perhaps remembering his defeat as counsel for the Citizens' Protective League the previous year, the ESVL declined his offer, preferring to use its own attorneys.[34] The league thus positioned itself as a politically independent ethnic organization, but one that was continuously courted by the Democrats, Republicans, and reform groups.

With the major parties vying for influence in the Jewish community, the ESVL and other groups used Jewish votes as a bargaining chip in gaining redress for police brutality. Claiming to speak for 350,000 East Side residents, the *Jewish World* published an open letter to Mayor Low on August 2 demanding the dismissal of the abusive officers as the price of Jewish electoral support. Noting that Jews had helped put Low in office, the *World* vowed that they would use their votes to elect those who would provide "the protection guaranteed by the constitution and the law."[35] Threats of ethnic voting blocs, however, were tempered by appeals to citizenship and Americanism. Jewish leaders issued protests in "the spirit of Americanism" and proudly affirmed their rights as American citizens. During the mass meeting at Cooper Union, for example, Paul Kaplan of the ESVL emphasized the dual identity of his listeners as Jews and American citizens. "We pay our taxes. We do our duty. Our young men have fought for our country, and we have as much right to live in peace as any other citizens."[36]

Initially, Jewish groups concentrated on legal and administrative remedies for police brutality. Representing Harris Rosenbloom and several other alleged victims, the ESVL filed complaints with the police commissioner against five officers involved in the riot. None of the clubbing complaints were sustained, however, and ESVL attorney Abraham Sarasohn complained that the trials were marred by long adjournments, false testimony by police, and lax discipline by the police commissioner. In the meantime, Jewish groups were also meeting with Mayor Low and District Attorney William Jerome to press for a grand jury investigation into possible criminal charges. While voicing concern over police misconduct, Jerome adopted a wait-and-see attitude in referring cases to the grand jury. To many Jews, his action appeared to be a deliberate delaying tactic.[37]

Responding to growing Jewish pressure for an independent inquiry, Mayor Low announced on August 6 that he was establishing a special citizens' committee to investigate the riot. Selecting prominent New Yorkers known for their public service, Low appointed five members to the committee that included both Republicans and Democrats as well as those of Irish and Jewish descent. Unlike the Lexow Committee, which had concentrated on police corruption, the 1902 committee was a far less partisan affair and adopted police brutality as its central line of investigation. Though lacking subpoena power, the committee was highly regarded by East Side Jews who were eager to volunteer their testimony. Moreover, it was the first citizens' committee established to investigate a racial/ethnic riot in American history.[38]

The hearings opened on August 12 at the University Settlement House on Rivington Street. The committee heard testimony from dozens of Jewish mourners and other eyewitnesses describing unprovoked attacks by Hoe workers and police. Inspector Cross contradicted these accounts, reiterating his view that Jews had planned the attack in advance and that the police were justified in using force to suppress the disorder. A number of Hoe workers and supervisors supported this version of events, claiming that the Jews had initiated attacks on police. They also sought to vindicate themselves by stating that the iron bolts used as ammunition in the riot had not come from the Hoe plant. A later tour of the factory by committee members, however, turned up hundreds of such bolts. The committee also inquired into the police department's prior knowledge of and planning for the funeral procession as well as their handling of earlier incidents of antagonism between Hoe workers and local Jews.[39]

As in the Lexow hearings, the committee's inquiries into police-citizen relations precipitated an outpouring of accumulated grievances. Once the committee indicated that it would hear testimony on incidents of police brutality other than the Hoe affair, "Jews of every sex, age, and station" came forward, the *Times* said, "all with stories of bitter experiences." East Side residents told of how police once roughed up a Jewish family sitting peacefully in front of their building, clubbed a young boy reciting poetry in the park, regularly shook down pushcart peddlers, and turned a blind eye when young thugs attacked local Jews. Others complained that they could not get a fair hearing in the magistrate's court; even some police officers testified that judges often dismissed suspects arrested for assaulting Jews. The complaints came not only from poor Russian immigrants, but from prominent German-Jewish elites and "impartial" Christian observers as well.[40]

When the committee issued its report on September 15, it fully exonerated the Jewish funeral marchers. The primary responsibility for the outbreak, the committee said, lay with the Hoe workers whose "insults to the procession and bystanders led to all that followed."

The report dismissed Inspector Cross's theory that the Jews' attack on the factory was premeditated, saying it was "entirely unsupported by the evidence." Having established that Jews were not the aggressors, the committee found considerable fault with the police department's handling of the riot. To begin with, there was "gross negligence" in the department's planning for the funeral. In stipulating the size of the escort, the committee argued, police had accepted the judgment of an unskilled civilian and had failed to reconsider this plan even after warnings of a potentially large turnout. The committee likewise condemned the brutal behavior of officers assigned to disperse the crowd in front of the Hoe factory and the "marked incivility and roughness" that characterized police behavior toward the mourners throughout the day. Although it refrained from judging the actions of specific officers, the report encouraged further investigation by the police commissioner and the criminal prosecution of officers involved in the beatings.[41]

The committee also commented on the long-standing and generally hostile relations between the police and local Jewish residents. Noting that "instances of uncivil and even rough treatment toward the people of this district by individual policemen are inexcusably common," the report identified lax disciplinary measures as a possible cause. Committee members also suggested that the police department "exercise more discrimination in the selection of the men assigned to duty in this quarter." In general, however, the committee believed that the brutality problem was beyond the scope of its investigation; its remedies were therefore limited.[42] Nevertheless, the committee was the first official body to link police brutality with racial/ethnic conflict and civil disorder, a connection that would be echoed by virtually every riot commission of the twentieth century.

The committee's report was widely hailed in both the mainstream and Jewish press. Praising the report's findings, the *Times* excoriated the police department for its long-standing abuse of the Jews, its poor planning for the funeral, and its failure to protect the mourners during the riot. The *Evening Post* issued a scathing denunciation of the brutality and "race prejudice" of the police, blaming it on Tammany control of the department that continued even under a reform administration. "The police force of Colonel Partridge is the police force of Devery," the *Post* asserted, "Colonel Partridge has thus far merely disturbed the surface of things." The committee's report, the *Post* continued, would hopefully "open the Mayor's eyes to the dangerous condition of the police force" under Partridge's leadership.[43]

Mayor Low's response was prompt and deliberate. Less than a week after the release of the report, Low directed Partridge to bring charges against police officials responsible for mishandling the riot. Partridge subsequently filed departmental charges against three officers: Inspector Adam Cross, Capt. John D. Herlihy, and Capt. Charles Albertson. Two other officers, Sgt. John Brady and Captain William Thompson, were also implicated but avoided charges by retiring (with pensions) prior to the hearings. Among those officers accused of beating Jewish mourners, officers James Jackson and Henry Doupe were facing criminal charges of second degree assault after District Attorney Jerome succeeded in bringing grand jury indictments against them in late August.[44]

For East Side Jews and other police critics, the results of these cases were deeply disappointing. First, juries in the trials of Jackson and Doupe acquitted both officers on grounds of self-defense despite damning testimony by several Jewish witnesses. Then on December 24, Commissioner Partridge announced that he was dismissing all charges against Inspector Cross and captains Herlihy and Albertson because of insufficient evidence. Partridge's unwillingness to issue even a mild rebuke must be seen in the context of his waning career. Under fire for both his handling of the Hoe Riot and his tolerance of vice and corruption, Partridge had submitted his resignation to the mayor two weeks earlier and was due to leave office at the end of the year. Whether his role in the Hoe affair alone would have forced his resignation is unclear; the combination of corruption *and* brutality, however, enabled reformers to build a devastating case against him. Although Partridge's departure pleased his critics, it had little impact on the department's policy concerning brutality. Low's new police commissioner, Francis V. Greene, waged a concerted campaign against vice and corruption but issued no new directives on police use of force. As in the Lexow investigation, the combination of corruption and brutality had served to bring down a police administration, but the social and occupational sources of the brutality problem remained unaddressed. As the Yiddish daily *Forward* put it, "the police can now, as always, beat up Jews and no one will punish them."[45]

In retrospect, however, the ESVL and other Jewish defense organizations had scored a significant public relations victory. Relying on the financial resources of the German-Jewish elite and exploiting their political influence with the Low administration, Jewish groups had launched a blistering attack on the NYPD and successfully pressured the city to hold public hearings on the Hoe Riot. A citizens' committee publicly exonerated Jewish mourners, denounced police behavior in the disturbance, and called attention to the long-standing and systemic abuse of East Side ghetto residents by local police. Key Jewish figures in the Hoe episode went on to play significant roles in later civil rights organizing. In 1906 Louis Marshall, a member of the citizens' committee investigating the riot, helped found the American Jewish Committee, the oldest permanent Jewish defense organization in the United States. A few years later, he and ESVL supporter Jacob Schiff became founders and financial supporters of the National Association for the Advancement of Colored People (NAACP).[46] The common abuse of Jews and African Americans at the hands of police during these years thus laid the groundwork for the black-Jewish alliance that would become particularly important in the 1930s and 1940s. Among their other responsibilities, these new civil rights groups would monitor incidents of police brutality, reflecting the new racial/ethnic understanding of the problem that had grown out of the riots.

The "Battle of San Juan Hill"

In the meantime, however, tensions between the all-white, Irish-dominated police force and the city's new migrant communities continued to fester. The newest locus of conflict was San Juan Hill, a growing black enclave on the Upper West Side. During these years, the city's black community was moving uptown from its old center in the Tenderloin to this new settlement in the West Fifties and Sixties. Known as San Juan Hill because of the large number of black

Spanish-American War veterans who settled there, the formerly Irish neighborhood was home to approximately twelve thousand blacks by 1905. Along with this new population came a number of black-owned businesses, saloons, clubs, and theaters that had relocated from the now-decaying Tenderloin. Much to the dismay of local black residents, Capt. John Cooney—notorious commander of the Twentieth Precinct during the Tenderloin Riot—was also dispatched uptown to the West 68th Street station house as part of a campaign to clean up the area's growing vice operations.

Not surprisingly, tensions between black and Irish residents and the police grew precipitously. Trouble was evident as early as July 1903, when a group of black youth on West 62nd Street between Amsterdam and West End Avenues battled police following an alleged attack on the son of a local Irish politician. Problems on the block resumed the following year when patrolman Frank McLaughlin of the Twenty-sixth Precinct shot and killed John W. Patterson, a black night watchman, during a failed arrest attempt. At his trial, McLaughlin testified that he had shot in self-defense after Patterson had resisted arrest by hurling bricks at him. Patterson, however, had been shot in the back, and several black witnesses testified that McLaughlin had fired several shots at Patterson as he lay lifeless on the ground. Based on this testimony, McLaughlin was found guilty of murder in January 1905, one of the earliest successful prosecutions of police brutality involving an African-American suspect.[47]

According to local black residents, the police of the Twenty-sixth Precinct were determined to seek revenge on behalf of McLaughlin. Whether a direct consequence of the McLaughlin case or the culmination of a series of racially charged incidents, a series of minor riots broke out on West 62nd Street the following summer. According to the New York Age, the trouble started on July 16 when an Irish youth taunted a Jewish pushcart peddler passing through the neighborhood. A local black man, William Preice, came to the peddler's defense and was set upon by a white crowd. Black onlookers then joined the fray in an attempt to rescue Preice, and a major brawl ensued. Police dispatched reserves from eighteen precincts under the personal command of Commissioner William McAdoo and made around forty arrests. As in past racial disorders, African Americans

81

made up a disproportionate number of those arrested. Over the next few days, police reserves patrolled San Juan Hill ordering all blacks off the streets and staking out local pawn shops to arrest black customers attempting to buy or redeem weapons. Similar activities by whites were ignored.

Despite (or perhaps because of) the increased police pressure on the black community, violence broke out again the following night. The conflict began when someone on a rooftop threw a brick at officers trying to clear the street in front of a saloon on West 62nd Street. Police then rushed into the bar, clubbing the black patrons and firing their pistols. The officers also raided the billiard room across the street and placed all its occupants under arrest for suspicion. During the raids, police shot and seriously injured Robert Christopher, a black carpenter who was climbing a fence to escape the riot area. They also allegedly shot and beat another black man, Arthur Moody, while arresting him for the earlier brick-throwing incident. He later died from his wounds at Bellevue Hospital. Contrary to police accounts, witnesses to the incident insisted that Moody was innocent and that another man had thrown the brick.

In the meantime, police had transported the men arrested at the billiard hall to the West 68th Street station house, where more violence ensued. According to a later report in the *New York Age,* the men had to "run the gauntlet" through a darkened muster room while police beat them with clubs across their heads and bodies. Dating back to medieval Europe, running the gauntlet was a communal and ritualized form of punishment commonly practiced in the military and later adopted by some police. Walter Frazier, the owner of the billiard hall, later described his experience in a sworn affidavit:

[Each prisoner] was led to the back room, through which he had to pass to get to the cells. The lights were out in this room and it was filled with policemen with drawn clubs. Before it was my turn to go in, I heard the sound of clubs on the heads of other prisoners and heard them crying for mercy. I was frightened sick. When it came my turn I think I was struck about a dozen blows. I am sore and black and blue all over yet. Several of the blows were on my head.

Frazier's description of the station house gauntlet was remarkably similar to William Elliott's account of his experience in the Twentieth Precinct during the Tenderloin Riot five years earlier. As black leaders pointed out, Capt. John Cooney had been the commanding officer on both occasions.[48]

With the events of 1900 still fresh in their memories, black community leaders immediately rallied on behalf of some sixty black men imprisoned during the riots. Gilchrist Stewart, a black attorney and member of the Nineteenth Assembly District Republican Club, contacted several white colleagues and formed a committee to provide bail and legal representation. Stewart and two other attorneys subsequently represented the black suspects in magistrate's court and won dismissals for nearly all of them. Together with former Citizens' Protective League chairman W. H. Brooks, Stewart also established a committee to meet with Police Commissioner McAdoo. Accompanied by the wife of Robert Christopher (the black carpenter who had been shot by police), a committee of three prominent black ministers met with McAdoo and District Attorney William Jerome to protest police bias and mistreatment of black suspects. Following the meeting, McAdoo instructed all commanding officers to avoid unwarranted arrests of black citizens, and Jerome opened investigations into the beating of Robert Christopher and the killing of Arthur Moody. Most significantly, McAdoo announced that he was transferring Captain Cooney out of the San Juan Hill precinct, a move the *Times* interpreted as "an admission of mismanagement."[49]

Encouraged by these initial responses, Stewart, Brooks, and other black leaders approached the local chapter of the National Negro Business League about establishing a permanent civil rights committee. The group would monitor cases of police misconduct and other civil rights violations against black New Yorkers, taking the recent riot cases as their first assignment. At a meeting of the National Negro Business League on August 3, a group of "representative colored men" founded the Colored Citizens' Protective League (CCPL), headed by businessmen Phillip A. Payton, Jr., and Samuel R. Scottron. The executive committee included Reverend Brooks, T. Thomas Fortune, and several other veterans of the earlier CPL. Like its predecessor, the group was nonpartisan and attracted prominent members from both the Democratic and Republican parties.

83

While there were obvious continuities with the CPL, the CCPL was distinctly more race conscious. As its roots in Booker T. Washington's National Negro Business League and the addition of the word *colored* in its name suggest, the CCPL was committed to black self-defense and self-reliance. Unlike the earlier CPL, which relied on white lawyers and reformers, the CCPL appointed its own black attorneys and formed a network with other black business and political organizations. CCPL lawyers investigated cases, collected evidence, and sought to confront white police officers directly in the courts. Moreover, the CCPL downplayed the moral aspects of police vice and corruption that had been so evident in the clergy-led movement of 1900 in favor of a more legalistic discussion of racial bias and police lawlessness. In particular, the city's whitewash of police abuses in the Tenderloin Riot, CCPL leaders argued, encouraged "the lawless of one race to insult, harass, maltreat, and incite the lawless of the other race to revenge, retaliation, and violations." Knowing the police would side with local whites, the CCPL maintained, blacks were taking up arms and attempting to defend themselves. This cycle of lawlessness would produce an endless round of race riots that would harm the criminal and respectable alike.[50]

Although the CCPL's analysis of police brutality was more sophisticated than its predecessor's, the results were equally disappointing. There is no evidence that the district attorney ever filed any charges against officers in either the Christopher or Moody cases, nor is there any record of successful civil prosecution or police disciplinary action. In fact, none of the cases arising from the infamous "Battle of San Juan Hill," as African Americans called it, received any media coverage at all after mid-August. The CCPL also disappeared from public view. Although incidents of racial tension between police and black New Yorkers occurred regularly on the West Side and in Harlem over the next decade, the organization does not seem to have played a role in monitoring these cases. Exactly what became of the group is unclear.

The CCPL did, however, establish an important precedent in the history of antibrutality organizing. As the first major African-American defense league in the city, the CCPL articulated the problem of police brutality in explicitly racial terms and linked it to other civil rights struggles over segregation and discrimination. The fight against police violence, then, was a key issue in the rise of black civil rights activism in the Progressive Era. W. H. Brooks, Gilchrist Stewart, and other veterans of the CCPL would go on to join the New York branch of the NAACP in 1911. The NAACP immediately took up several cases of police misconduct and organized the New York Vigilance Committee, under the direction of Gilchrist Stewart, to investigate and pursue incidents of police brutality and other civil rights violations. Around the same time, other black community leaders were beginning to make the connection between police violence against African Americans and the absence of black officers on the force. Beginning in 1907, Rev. Reverdy C. Ransom, pastor of the Bethel African Methodist Episcopal Church in the Tenderloin, led a campaign calling for the hiring of black officers to the all-white NYPD. African-American officers, Ransom maintained, would be better able to handle black lawbreakers and would avoid unnecessary violence against black citizens. In 1911, the department hired its first black officer, Samuel Battle. Over time, Battle and other black officers would become important fixtures in Harlem, San Juan Hill, and other black communities, helping—in limited ways—to reduce tensions between the department and the black community.[51] The linking of police violence with other black civil rights struggles, an approach pioneered by the CCPL, would become an important characteristic of antibrutality organizing in the twentieth century.

Between 1900 and 1911, the fight against police brutality in New York was redefined in important ways. The racial upheavals of 1900–1905 led to the formation of citywide defense leagues that mobilized their communities across class and political lines, making race/ethnicity the defining feature of their struggle. Using gendered appeals rooted in their group's collective experiences of persecution, the defense leagues helped foster a new understanding of police brutality that saw it as a product of racial/ethnic bias. The earliest of these groups had close ties with the anti-Tammany reformers of the 1890s and shared their understanding of police misconduct linking brutality with moral and political corruption. The later organizations, however, took a more independent and legalistic approach that emphasized civil rights and due process. As self-defense groups led exclusively by blacks and Jews, they became increasingly suspicious of reformers and bosses alike and demanded that the major parties protect their constituents in exchange for their votes.[52] Though short-lived, the defense leagues were the crucibles of permanent civil rights organizations such as the American Jewish Committee and the New York NAACP. These groups would take up antibrutality organizing in the twentieth century and would forcefully reassert the significance of race in the public discussion of police violence, particularly in the years following World War II.

At the time, however, the success of the defense leagues was limited. Among the officers charged with misconduct in the three riots, there were virtually no successful criminal or civil prosecutions and only one minor disciplinary action. It is notable, however, that after 1905 there were no similar incidents of mass ethnic or racially-motivated riots in the city until World War I—and even then police action would be less blatantly biased and gratuitous. The African-American and Jewish defense leagues had successfully exposed the racial violence of an all-white police force and had helped discredit it through appeals to Americanism and democracy. Their demands for a more enlightened and neutral police force were picked up by Progressive reformers, who would develop their own priorities in a series of campaigns to reform the New York police.

3. BRUTALITY AND REFORM IN THE PROGRESSIVE ERA

As the defense leagues succeeded in curtailing police riots in racial and ethnic communities, the more common forms of police clubbing and street brutality continued to plague the city. While the typical problems and victims remained much the same, a new wave of Progressive reform swept New York in the wake of the Lexow investigation. Between 1895 and World War I, a succession of reform-minded mayors and police commissioners set out to make the NYPD more honest, efficient, and professional. For at least one of these reformers, police brutality was a pressing issue. For most of them, however, it became a necessary consequence of a more crucial effort to combat crime. Under both Democrats and Republicans alike, the seeming contradictions between efficient crime-fighting and antibrutality policies made the police reform movement a problematic vehicle for reducing police violence.

The Roosevelt Era

The earliest group of police reformers had close ties to the elite anti-Tammany coalition that spearheaded the Lexow investigation of 1895. Comprised of prominent Republicans, anti-Tammany Democrats, and various moral and municipal reform leaders, these conservative reformers decried police corruption, inefficiency, and political influence. During the Lexow investigation, they also presented a compelling critique of police brutality, viewing it as a by-product of moral and political corruption. The police scandal uncovered by the Lexow Committee helped elect a reform administration in 1894, and Mayor William Strong appointed Theodore Roosevelt as head of the police commission. Unlike Frank Moss and other police reformers connected to the Lexow investigation, however, Roosevelt expressed little interest in the brutality problem. In fact, as Roosevelt launched his campaign to suppress crime and vice, allegations of police violence became a serious obstacle to his reform efforts.

From the beginning, Roosevelt's primary concerns were police corruption, inefficiency, and the illicit ties between the department and the city's political machines. To stem corruption, he advocated rigorous excise enforcement and vice suppression in hopes of curtailing police blackmail of brothel owners and saloonkeepers. To reduce Tammany influence and improve the quality of the force, he implemented stricter recruiting and disciplinary practices and was known to prowl the streets at night in pursuit of officers who were drinking or loafing on duty. In 1895 he engineered the retirement of Inspector Alexander Williams and Superintendent Thomas Byrnes, two top police officials whose corruption, brutality, and close ties with political machines had been prominently featured in the Lexow hearings. Although Roosevelt temporarily improved police service and won public acclaim for his reforms, his achievements were in fact limited. His campaign to close saloons on Sundays proved unpopular and difficult to enforce. Moreover, political influence in the department was deeply entrenched, and Tammany managed to maintain its grip despite his efforts.

Police brutality was at best a minor concern for Roosevelt. The ouster of Williams and Byrnes, for example, stemmed from their participation in graft and machine politics; their violent treatment of the citizenry was never at issue. Like middle-class reformers, Roosevelt did insist on courteous behavior and more restrained use of the club on "respectable" and "inoffensive" citizens. But when it came to criminals and other "vicious" characters, he advocated aggressive and forceful tactics.[1] Viewing the police as a military organization, Roosevelt declared "war" against crime and corruption and insisted on improving "the fighting efficiency of the police." Under his leadership, the commission increased the amount and power of police weaponry and gave officers more license to use it. His handling of the nightstick controversy of the 1890s illustrates

Roosevelt's approach to the use of force and some of the dilemmas inherent in it.

Back in 1892, the police commission had passed a resolution banning the use of batons except in cases of "disorder, riots, and other emergencies." Following the example of the club-free police force established to patrol the Columbian Exposition in Chicago, Superintendent Byrnes had recommended that the heavy duty eighteen-inch nightstick be abolished and replaced with a lighter weight, fourteen-inch "pocket bludgeon." The new baton would be worn in a sheath on the pant leg and drawn only in cases of emergency or self-defense or by order of the superintendent. In signaling for backup, officers were to use whistles rather than the traditional method of rapping nightsticks on the sidewalk. Henceforth police would use batons only in emergency or life-threatening circumstances and were not to twirl, brandish, or otherwise deploy them while on duty.[2]

Many police officers believed the new policy endangered their personal safety and reduced their power and effectiveness on the street. While some officers quietly criticized the ban, others tried to circumvent it. Patrolman John Hickey, for example, explained in his memoirs how he improvised his own weaponry in place of the baton:

I manned myself with a piece of rubber hose, about eighteen inches long, a piece that had been well used in the cellar or behind the bar of the saloon of that day. Yes and you can believe me it was better than a night stick, for when it was not in use I would carry it up the sleeve of my coat, ever ready for any emergency, and when the tough fellow would come up to me to give me an argument . . . I would lead off with my left and soak him with the rubber hose with my right, and he would fly for his life, saying to himself, gee what the h—l did he hit me with?[3]

Presumably, other officers followed Hickey's example and found new ways to intimidate suspects and recalcitrant citizens in lieu of clubbing. It is possible, then, that the department's ban on clubs may have merely changed the form of police violence rather than reducing it.

Although the *New York Times* claimed that the number of clubbing complaints fell dramatically after the implementation of the ban, there is no data to confirm this assertion. Nor did the *Times'* own coverage suggest that much had changed. The number of alleged clubbing cases reported in the paper remained roughly the same in the three years before the ban and in the three years following it (ten before, nine after). Significantly, however, there were no reported fatalities stemming from police clubbing cases during the three years the ban was in effect. Conceivably, the elimination of the heavier locust clubs may have reduced the severity of clubbing injuries and saved civilian lives.[4]

When Roosevelt took over in 1895, he quickly came out in opposition to the anticlub policy. A few weeks after joining the police commission, he publicly praised Edward Burke, an officer accused of clubbing a prominent Tammany politician and saloon owner during an excise arrest. Three months later, when another excise officer was fatally beaten in the line of duty, Roosevelt ordered police to carry nightsticks again during evening hours. The night batons "ought never to have been taken away," he argued. "Any individual who mishandles them will be held to a strict accountability by the board." Roosevelt believed officers should draw their batons only in serious cases, but when necessary he wanted them "to have the most efficient club there is." Under his leadership, police were to walk softly and courteously among respectable citizens but carry a big stick to deal with criminals and thugs.[5]

Although reasonable on its face, Roosevelt's approach ignored a number of thorny issues. Exactly what constituted a serious situation and who was considered a criminal was determined by individual officers, men who were not particularly well trained and not always knowledgeable about the neighborhoods they patrolled. Under Roosevelt's aggressive style of crime fighting, officers might be tempted to use their clubs against relatively minor offenders, as long as police believed they posed a threat to public safety. Although Roosevelt maintained that officers would be held accountable for abusing their clubs, disciplinary action in police assault cases did not substantially improve. Although the number of fines and dismissals issued by the Roosevelt board rose significantly over previous years, the change was due to increased surveillance of patrolmen by roundsmen and other police officials. These spot inspections revealed obvious cases of drunkenness, negligence, and failure to patrol, but they were less likely to uncover assault cases. Moreover, brutality was very difficult to prove. Even in well-substantiated cases, police officers generally supported each other's accounts and contradicted the suspects' testimony. Anxious to defend the department and protect their political allies, the commissioners tended to exonerate the officers or censure them with small fines or departmental rebukes. Officers might be held accountable for their brutal actions but not necessarily deterred from repeating them. Finally, Roosevelt's assumption that "efficient" weapons would lead to "efficient" policing was also open to question. As police deployed more substantial weaponry and more violent tactics, New Yorkers responded in kind, escalating the cycle of violence on the streets. Instead of defusing violence, Roosevelt's big stick approach probably helped perpetuate it, requiring greater police resources than before.

Following Roosevelt's departure for Washington, his successors on the police commission continued to support use of the nightstick. The only dissenter was Frank Moss, the noted police critic and former counsel to the Lexow Committee whom Mayor William Strong appointed to fill out Roosevelt's term. In December 1897, Moss called on the commission to discontinue use of the locust nightstick, calling it a "barbarous weapon." The three other commissioners opposed his motion, but a compromise was reached when Chief John McCullagh agreed to instruct officers to wear the locust batons on their belts and to avoid twirling them in a threatening fashion. The warning apparently went unheeded. For the next several years the press repeatedly denounced epidemics of police clubbing and noted that the commissioners were "generally club-blind." In the conservative reform ethos, aggressive crime fighting took precedence over police civility.[6]

The use of firearms was also standardized and legitimized under the Roosevelt administration. Although the New York police had been carrying firearms since the 1850s and 1860s, they sported a bewildering array of revolvers, some of notably poor quality. (In defending themselves from wrongful shooting charges, officers sometimes claimed that their weapons could not shoot farther than fifteen or twenty feet.) In 1895 the board required all officers to carry a standard .32 caliber Colt that could be purchased from the department. The standardization of weaponry was accompanied by a new emphasis on firearms training. Noting that most police were poor and inexperienced marksmen, the department established a School of Pistol Practice in 1896 and required eight hours of training per year for all officers. The program provided an opportunity for target practice while training police in the care and handling of revolvers and the principles of aiming and firing. One of the first firearms training programs in the country, the school was a significant innovation that helped improve police marksmanship. It did not, however, teach officers when and under what circumstances to use their weapons, issues that were at the heart of most wrongful shootings. Firearms training thus made police more accurate and more deadly in their use of force, but it did not train them to know when—and when not—to use it.[7]

The inadequacy of this training became evident over the next few years as several police officers were implicated in questionable shooting cases. In 1896, Officer Michael J. Carey shot and killed an alleged thief, John O'Brien, after firing what was supposed to have been a "maiming shot" at his legs. Although Roosevelt defended Carey's actions, eyewitnesses claimed that the shooting was unnecessary and that Carey could easily have apprehended the suspect without using his weapon. The following year, Officer John J. Hannigan shot seventeen-year-old Charles McNally on a Harlem street after he refused the officer's order to stop playing football. Hannigan apparently drew his weapon to fire a warning shot when he stumbled and hit McNally. Hannigan was later convicted of second-degree assault and sentenced to two years in prison.[8] These cases revealed police officers' ignorance of department rules that forbid the use of warning or maiming shots. It would take another decade before the department would seriously address these issues.

The Bingham Era

While historians generally agree that Roosevelt's reforms improved police service and standards, his tough-minded approach to crime fighting raised serious and unresolved problems around the use of force. His reform-minded successors—Francis V. Green, William McAdoo, and Theodore Bingham—attempted to advance Roosevelt's agenda and confronted many of the same dilemmas. This was particularly true of Bingham, who served as police commissioner from 1906 to 1909 under a Democratic reform mayor, George B. McClellan, Jr. A former military aide to Roosevelt, Bingham was an ex-Army general and engineer known for his strong organizational skills and strict discipline. He was also a stern figure with an irascible personality that alienated his friends as well as his enemies. Although working for a Democratic administration, he was an outspoken Republican reformer who sought to suppress crime, clean up the department, and sever its political ties with Tammany Hall.[9]

Fortunately for Bingham, he did not have to contend with the political gridlock that had characterized the old bipartisan police board. In 1901 control of the department had been centralized under a single commissioner, allowing Bingham to weed out dishonest or incompetent officers and pursue a vigorous campaign of crime fighting and vice enforcement. He encouraged officers to use their weapons against criminal and disorderly persons and ordered patrolmen to discard their belts and carry their nightsticks in hand at all times. He also adopted a repressive approach toward the Socialist party and other radical groups, using the police to prevent or break up public political meetings. His combative style and his periodic shake-ups of the department won enthusiastic praise from the City Club, the Citizens' Union, and other municipal reform groups.[10]

Opponents of Bingham's administration, however, were equally vociferous. Disturbed by his transfers and demotions, his severe disciplinary style, and a general disruption of power relations in the department, many police officers and their representatives in the police associations bitterly denounced Bingham's policies. Leaders of Tammany Hall and other Democratic machines were similarly distressed as they watched their political influence in the department diminish under Bingham's reorganization. His get-tough approach to crime and vice control also alienated a variety of citizens' groups and individuals. Beginning in this period, police efficiency in suppressing crime would be measured largely by arrest statistics, a tendency that encouraged more aggressive policing and the potential abuse of power. Similarly, vigorous vice enforcement and political repression aroused strong antipathy among the city's ethnic working class and fueled growing resentment of police for their "autocratic" methods. Criticism of Bingham's administration thus came from many quarters. While his opponents inside the department denounced his personnel policies and centralization of power, a number of disgruntled citizens accused police of violating their civil rights. The city's Democrats seized on this latter issue and maintained a steady drumbeat of criticism in hopes of forcing Mayor McClellan to replace Bingham with a more congenial appointee.

The first major accusation of police brutality grew out of a melee that occurred at an outdoor meeting of the unemployed in Union Square on March 28, 1908. Sponsored by the Socialist Conference of the Unemployed, the meeting called on the city to provide public works employment for the thousands of city residents left jobless by the panic of 1907. As in the Tompkins Square Riot of 1874, the police initially issued a permit for the meeting but later revoked it. The Socialists denounced the revocation of the permit as a "direct and open violation of the constitutional guarantee of free speech and assembly" and were determined to proceed with the meeting. Squads of patrolmen, however, descended on the gathering—estimated to be around twenty-five thousand—and attempted to clear the area by charging the protesters with their horses and clubs, just as their predecessors had done in 1874.

If the initial police action was reminiscent of Tompkins Square, what happened next was more like the 1886 Haymarket Riot in Chicago. After the police cleared the area of all but a few stragglers, one of the remaining men attempted to throw a bomb at a group of officers. The device detonated prematurely, killing a civilian bystander and injuring the bomber himself, a young tailor who claimed to be seeking revenge against police for beating him a week earlier. The explosion set off further disorder, and according to the Socialists, "the police seized the opportunity, not to attempt to restore order and prevent further injury, but to charge upon the crowds, riding down and clubbing the people indiscriminately while they were attempting to disperse."[11]

The Socialists immediately issued statements denouncing the brutality of police, making the now familiar comparisons to Russian "Cossacks." They accused Inspector Max Schmittberger, who commanded the Union Square forces, of violating their constitutional rights and inciting a riot. Calling attention to Schmittberger's "malodorous record," they linked his brutal behavior toward the Socialists with his confessed involvement in graft and extortion rackets before the Lexow Committee thirteen years earlier. They likewise condemned the violence of the bomb thrower but described it as an "act of an irresponsible person, rendered desperate and mad by police repression." A week later, the Socialists sponsored a mass meeting at Grand Central Palace to protest police brutality and repression. Attended by some three thousand people, the meeting resulted in resolutions condemning police actions and the formation of a committee to investigate the incident and collect affidavits from eyewitnesses. Although the committee interviewed at least twenty four witnesses and vowed to publish the testimony, there is no indication that the documents were ever released or used in legal or disciplinary proceedings. On April 12, the Central Federated Trades Union failed to adopt a resolution supporting legal action against the department, and the antibrutality campaign fizzled.[12]

Although Socialists found little explicit support for their campaign against police brutality, other New Yorkers were also filing complaints against police clubbing and harassment under Bingham's regime. In July 1906 T. B. Connery, an avowed supporter of police reform, wrote a letter to the editor of the *New York Times* complaining of police use of the club in minor cases of disorderly conduct. Connery argued that police continued to use their clubs indiscriminately, just as they had in the days of Tammany. Other New Yorkers shared Connery's view and complained of unwarranted attacks by police armed with blackjacks, a small but deadly weapon that was gaining popularity among detectives and plain-clothes officers. In 1909 "Big Tim" Sullivan, a prominent and col-orful Tammany leader from the Lower East Side, sponsored a state legislative bill banning police use of blackjacks, brass knuckles, and other unorthodox weapons. Although opponents claimed the bill was designed to protect gangsters allied with Tammany Hall, Sulli-van insisted that the law was necessary to prevent police from estab-lishing "a rule of armed terrorism" in his district. Attuned to the needs of his working-class constituents (he also supported housing reform, labor legislation, and gun control), Sullivan sought to tap popular outrage over police brutality and harassment in his district. Commissioner Bingham, however, vigorously denounced the bill and helped ensure its defeat. Police, he argued, needed the most effective weapons available in their battle against crime.[13]

Perhaps the most intriguing critique of police brutality during Bingham's administration came from G. M. Jurgenson, a paper box manufacturer in south Brooklyn. Police from the Butler Street sta-tion house arrested him on his stoop one evening in April 1909 and allegedly roughed him up. Incensed at this treatment, Jurgenson led his own personal crusade against the precinct by publishing the *So-cial Mirror,* a magazine devoted to exposing police abuse in the But-ler Street station house. The first (and perhaps only) issue featured a fictionalized account of a wealthy couple who had fallen on hard times. Although never involved with the police before, the impov-erished couple now became targets of police abuse. The wife, "a per-fect lady" and teetotaler, was falsely arrested for intoxication and confined to a dark and dismal cell. When her husband came to se-cure her release, he was attacked by a dozen "burly bluecoats" with nightsticks. Dressed in common workingman's clothes, his body was later discovered floating in the Gowanus Bay—evidence of what happens to poor citizens who challenge the police. Steeped in Vic-torian melodrama, Jurgenson's story dramatized the perils of police brutality and the particular vulnerability of the poor, even under a reform administration.[14]

Jurgenson was not the only critic of the Brooklyn police. Since the beginning of his administration, Bingham had been a thorn in the side of the local Democratic machine led by state senator Pat McCarran, who resented Bingham's dismissive treatment of key Democratic allies in the police department. McCarran was also upset by Bingham's continued shake-ups and vice raids in Brooklyn and asked Mayor McClellan to remove him.[15]

Although McClellan initially stood by his commissioner, the infamous "Duffy affair" of 1909 changed his mind. The case, involving police harassment of a young milk deliveryman named George Duffy, was first brought to the mayor's attention by William J. Gaynor, a New York State Supreme Court judge and a customer on Duffy's delivery route in Brooklyn. During his fifteen years on the bench, Gaynor had been an outspoken critic of police abuses and an ardent defender of citizen's rights and civil liberties. On many occasions he had ruled in favor of those whom police had arrested or detained unlawfully or otherwise mistreated. He had also spoken out publicly on the "autocratic methods" of police before the Committee of Nine, a group of reformers who sought to clean up the department during McClellan's first term. His interest in the Duffy case, then, was consistent with his past record, but his efforts on the young man's behalf would have unprecedented and far-reaching results.[16]

Duffy's problems with the police began in June 1907, when he was arrested on suspicion of breaking a window in a Brooklyn saloon. Duffy, who was seventeen at the time, denied any role in the affair, and the saloon owner confirmed that Duffy was not responsible. The arresting officers, however, had been aware of Duffy for some time because of his alleged association with "thieves and felons." Consequently, they took the opportunity to arrest, strip search, and photograph him for the so-called Rogues' Gallery, a police archive of known criminals. Duffy was released without charges the following day, but his picture remained in the Rogues' Gallery. Afterward, police watched Duffy closely and arrested him several more times for minor infractions or suspicious behavior. As a result of this treatment, Duffy said, he was afraid to walk the streets and lived in fear of losing his job. Angered and frustrated by police harassment of his son, Duffy's father enlisted Judge Gaynor's help.

Gaynor fired off a letter to Commissioner Bingham complaining of the illegal use of photographs by police and urging them to cease harassing the boy. Bingham denied the allegations, and police pressure on Duffy intensified. On one occasion, Duffy claimed, he was hauled into the local station house on a false charge of vagrancy and surrounded by more than a dozen detectives who yelled and shoved him around, ridiculing his failed attempts to have his picture removed. Outraged at this incident, Gaynor took Duffy's case directly to Mayor McClellan and released copies of his complaint to the press.[17]

McClellan, who had no doubt grown tired of defending Bingham from his many critics, launched a personal investigation into the case. For the next several weeks, the mayor examined George Duffy, the police officers who arrested him, Duffy's parents, and a host of character witnesses. McClellan's willingness to take the Duffy case seriously unleashed a torrent of criticism against the police. As in previous outbreaks of public concern with police misconduct, New Yorkers seized the opportunity to relate their own stories of brutality and harassment. For the next month, both McClellan and Gaynor received dozens of letters and visits from aggrieved citizens, one coming from as far away as Philadelphia.[18]

With evidence mounting against the department, McClellan became convinced of Duffy's innocence and believed that police were actively obstructing his investigation. The mayor later charged that certain police were protecting the officers involved in the case by suborning witnesses, having them in some cases "spirited out of the state." He was also angered by an earlier letter he had received from Bingham's personal secretary, Daniel Slattery, responding to the mayor's inquiry about the Duffy case. Rather than justifying police actions, Slattery launched a personal attack on Judge Gaynor, claiming he was a drunkard and a wife-beater who had had unpleasant dealings with police in the past. The story may well have been true— Gaynor was a heavy drinker with a hot temper—but it had no bearing on the validity of Duffy's case.

On July 31, the mayor issued a sixty-page report criticizing the department for its mistreatment of Duffy and other questionable practices. In a clear rebuke of Bingham, the mayor condemned the misuse of Duffy's photograph and ordered it returned to him.

He also ordered the demotion, transfer, or dismissal of four police officials involved in the case. In an attempt to address the systemic problems that led to Duffy's abuse, McClellan criticized Bingham's policy of promotions and demotions based on the officer's number of arrests, a system he believed encouraged overzealous policing. Moreover, he commanded the commissioner to issue new general orders establishing a special inspector-at-large to investigate all citizen complaints and requiring all such complaints to be forwarded to the mayor's office along with a report detailing subsequent police actions.

Bingham reluctantly complied with most but not all of the mayor's orders. He returned Duffy's picture and demoted two of the officials involved. He flatly refused, however, to dismiss the other two, whom he insisted bore no direct responsibility for the treatment of Duffy. As for the new general orders, he issued them reluctantly, noting that they would "ruin discipline in the department" by encouraging police to back away from difficult arrests or influential suspects. Denouncing Bingham's actions as insubordination, the mayor removed him and appointed Deputy Commissioner William F. Baker to take his place.[19]

Judge Gaynor—riding a crest of popular support from his role in the Duffy affair—ran for mayor on the Democratic ticket that November. Long a critic of police misconduct, the judge also knew a good political issue when he saw one. With Tammany's support, he tapped popular resentment of police harassment and brutality to capture the mayoralty. His success marked an important turning point in the history of the antibrutality movement. Since its emergence as a political issue after the Civil War, police violence had been mainly the concern of Republicans and reformers battling a Tammany-dominated police department. After 1900, however, Tammany bosses came to understand the importance of police brutality. Like other liberal reform initiatives, efforts to curb police misconduct proved highly popular among the city's ethnic working class—those who had been the victims of the Tenderloin and Hoe riots and the aggressive tactics and weaponry introduced by Roosevelt and Bingham. "Big Tim" Sullivan's attempt to ban police use of blackjacks in early 1909 was one indication of the Democrats' growing awareness. Tammany's support for William Gaynor, an independent Democrat known for his impassioned defense of ordinary citizens, marked the party's tentative embrace of the antibrutality issue. How Gaynor and his fellow Democrats would fulfill this mission once in office, however, remained to be seen.

The Gaynor Revolution

Within days of moving into city hall, Mayor Gaynor embarked on a police reform campaign that was markedly different from those of his predecessors. Building on the efforts of judicial reformers in the state and municipal courts, the former judge used his power as mayor to overhaul police practices. Although retaining McClellan's police commissioner, William F. Baker, Gaynor made it clear that he would play a strong role in running the department. Like previous reform administrations, the mayor sought to improve efficiency and reduce corruption, but his most cherished goal was curbing police lawlessness. In keeping with his earlier pronouncements from the bench, Gaynor held civil liberties paramount and insisted that police officers treat citizens with respect and uphold the legal rights of suspects. Most importantly, he sought to eliminate arbitrary arrests and the excessive use of force.

Gaynor's first priority was stopping police brutality. Thirteen days after taking office, the mayor met with a Brooklyn man named Oscar Gregory who claimed that he had been brutally clubbed by Officer James Devon. According to Gregory, he and his wife had been waiting for the streetcar when he saw the officer beating up two suspects. When he protested, Officer Devon arrested and beat him as well. The mayor quickly fired off a letter to Commissioner Baker ordering an immediate stop to police clubbing. "The sight of the young man is shocking," wrote Gaynor. It is time that "the police be fully informed that to commit a battery on a citizen, or make a false or unnecessary arrest, or unlawfully enter a house, is a far graver offense than to let a criminal escape." The mayor ordered Baker to bring Devon up on disciplinary charges and to dismiss him if found guilty. He also wrote to the Brooklyn district attorney urging him to prosecute Devon on charges of assault and battery. In a police disciplinary hearing two weeks later, Devon was found guilty and dismissed from the force.[20]

Gaynor's firm stand in the Devon case encouraged other aggrieved citizens to come forward, and the resulting parade of brutality victims prompted him to formulate a new policy on the use of force. Over the next week, at least ten alleged victims descended on city hall to air their complaints. Determined to stop police clubbings, Gaynor considered reinstituting the nightstick ban of 1892. Press reaction was overwhelmingly negative, however, and he discarded the idea. Instead, he instructed Commissioner Baker to issue a new general order requiring the lieutenant or captain on duty to hear all assault complaints and forward a report of any incident to headquarters by the end of the shift. Failure to do so would result in dismissal. General Order Number Seven, as it was called, precipitated a blizzard of brutality complaints, including more than thirty cases reported in the press during the first two months of Gaynor's administration. The alleged victims included men and women, young and old, immigrant and native born; they came from all five boroughs and all walks of life. The alleged offenses ranged in severity from minor cases of arm twisting to brutal incidents of sexual assault and homicide. Under the mayor's direct oversight, the department preferred charges in many of these cases, and at least ten of the accused officers were eventually dismissed from the force.[21]

Gaynor also instructed police to refrain from using violent tactics against peaceful protesters. Beginning in December 1909, the Women's Trade Union League charged that police had been openly siding with employers and beating and harassing striking women workers at the Triangle Shirtwaist factory in Washington Square. Responding to these complaints, the mayor met repeatedly with police inspectors to remind them that the force was to remain neutral in industrial disputes and to respect the rights of strikers. He took a similar position with the Socialist party, instructing the police to issue permits for public meetings as long as the applicants agreed to comply with municipal regulations. Gaynor, it should be noted, was not always sympathetic to organized labor and considered the Socialists hopelessly idealistic and wrongheaded. His tolerance of dissent and defense of free speech, however, was a dramatic departure from the policies of former commissioner Bingham.[22]

The mayor's emphasis on protecting civil liberties affected other aspects of police administration as well. In an effort to eliminate unwarranted arrests, he ordered police to issue summonses for petty offenses in lieu of arrest. This policy helped to reduce the total number of arrests from 220,334 in 1909 to 170,681 in 1910, a 22 percent decrease. Gaynor also ordered police to refrain from entering homes illegally and to remove the photographs of all nonconvicted persons from the Rogues' Gallery. Because of their reputation for brutality and corruption, he eliminated the so-called strong-arm squads of plainclothes police designed to target gangs, vice operations, and other forms of organized crime. His most controversial new initiatives were in the areas of excise and vice enforcement. Rejecting the aggressive style of enforcement favored by Roosevelt and Bingham, Gaynor attempted to break up police graft by eliminating direct contact between officers and saloon owners. Henceforth, police could no longer enter offending establishments but would instead report obvious liquor violations to the district attorney's office, which would prosecute the offenders. The new policy successfully reduced liquor graft and flagrant Sunday drinking, but the backroom business continued to thrive. Gaynor accepted this state of affairs, noting that workingmen were merely doing what the wealthy did in their own private clubs. The mayor took a more direct approach in suppressing gambling and prostitution, but even in these areas he settled for the appearance of "outward order." No amount of policing, he admitted, could completely suppress vice in the city.[23]

Gaynor's liberal policies soon came under bitter attack by moral reformers and other conservative opponents. While Protestant reformers denounced the mayor's tolerance of backroom drinking and vice, City Magistrate Joseph E. Corrigan and other leaders of the Fusion party blamed him for an incipient crime wave and a rising tide of gang warfare. The press reported a number of incidents in which criminals allegedly taunted police by threatening to "tell the mayor." The most serious incidents occurred in the summer of 1910 when the notorious Car Barn gang drew a chalk mark outside its East Harlem headquarters, labeling it, "Dead line for cops, by order of Mayor Gaynor." They proceeded to wage a series of assaults on local police, injuring several officers. Under such conditions, critics maintained, the police were becoming demoralized and intimidated. "The criminal classes of the city 'had the drop' on the police," Judge Corrigan wrote, "and commercial crime and vice flourished in New York as it had not done for years." Criminals were thus flocking to the city, he said, seeing it as a "wide open" town.[24]

Many police officers apparently seconded this view. Soon after Gaynor's new policies were implemented, the deputy police commissioner, Frederick Bugher, claimed that citizens were losing respect for the police and that it was no longer safe for officers to patrol alone in rough areas. After the confrontation with the Car Barn gang, some police argued that Gaynor's General Order Number Seven was responsible for dozens of officer injuries and deaths. There were also reports that police were afraid to use their nightsticks and were neglecting to make arrests in order to avoid possible investigation and disciplinary action. While on trial for neglect of duty charges, patrolman William Sherry accused the police commissioner of demoralizing the force and "making cowards" of the police. "We are told we must not do this and we must not do that; we must not use our nightsticks in making arrests and such things," Sherry charged. "Some day we'll have to wear white gloves in making arrests. That's what it's coming to."[25]

The implementation of the new policies was in fact confusing for many police. After years of conservative reform stressing aggressive crime-fighting tactics, Gaynor's policies ran counter to the on-the-job practices of veteran officers. Barred from using their clubs freely and lacking formal training in alternate defensive tactics, some officers chose to back away from volatile arrest situations. Police attempts to avoid investigation and disciplinary action were understandable. Such proceedings not only threatened an officer's livelihood but were routinely performed during off-duty hours without compensation. Police, then, were facing potentially longer hours and a greater likelihood of disciplinary action on the one hand, while enduring growing criticism of crime waves and ineffective policing on the other. Many tended to concur with the conservatives, blaming the mayor for "tying the hands of the police."[26]

Gaynor sharply rebuked his critics for fabricating phony crime waves and insisted that police had always been free to use force against violent criminals and gangs. The police department released statistics showing that while total arrests had decreased under the new policies, the elimination of arbitrary and unnecessary arrests accounted for the bulk of the reduction. Coming to Gaynor's defense, Chief Magistrate William McAdoo and twelve other city magistrates wrote an open letter censuring their colleague, Judge Corrigan, for what they saw as an inappropriate attack on the mayor and suggesting that the magistrate's accusations were made in retaliation after the mayor had passed him over for the position of chief magistrate.

Corrigan's criticisms, however ill-founded, hit a popular nerve. He reportedly received dozens of sympathetic letters from ministers, businessmen, police, and other respected citizens supporting his views. The local press, always anxious to cover sensational crime news, joined in the chorus of police criticism. This was particularly true of the Hearst papers, the *New York Journal* and *American,* which were longtime foes of the mayor. The *Times,* which had previously supported the mayor's police reforms, now editorialized that he had "gone too far," and several other papers followed suit.[27]

With anti-Gaynor sentiment growing, Corrigan and his allies on the board of aldermen stepped up their offensive and succeeded in launching grand jury investigations into the alleged crime problem in Manhattan and Brooklyn. In many ways, the proceedings resembled the familiar anti-Tammany police investigations of the past. Republicans, Fusion Democrats, and leading members of the City Club, the Society for Prevention of Crime, and other moral and municipal reform groups joined forces to orchestrate the proceedings. Veteran police investigator Frank Moss, now an assistant district attorney in Manhattan, was selected to help conduct the inquiry. Subpoenaing the mayor, the police commissioner, and numerous civilian witnesses, the attorneys attempted to solicit testimony about police corruption and inefficiency. In a noticeable departure from past investigations, however, Moss and the reformers no longer queried witnesses about incidents of police harassment and brutality. Instead they interrogated the mayor and the commissioner about their attempts to limit police power and solicited citizen accounts of police negligence and incapacity in the face of rampant crime. Stopping brutality was no longer on the reformers' agenda.[28]

The results of the probe were mixed. Far from being a wholesale condemnation of the department, the grand jury presentment downplayed the alleged crime wave and found little evidence of police corruption. A grand jury investigating the crime problem in Brooklyn around the same time reached a similar conclusion. The Manhattan jury did, however, acknowledge a growing problem of gang-related crime in some neighborhoods and urged police to use tougher methods to fight it. "In some parts of the city policemen should have a freer use of their clubs without having to worry about vengeful charges by criminals and the expense and uncertainty of trial on charges," the report stated. "It is not well that policemen properly performing their duties should submit to the insults and contempt of criminals and disorderly persons." The report also recommended the reinstitution of plainclothes police units—or "strong-arm squads"—to help suppress criminal gangs. Many of Gaynor's most cherished antibrutality measures thus came under attack by the grand jury.[29]

The resignation of Gaynor's police commissioner, James C. Cropsey, a few days after the grand jury presentment only compounded the mayor's problems. Although the stated reason for Cropsey's resignation was his violation of civil service hiring procedures, there had been rumors of tension between Cropsey and Gaynor for some time. The bad publicity accompanying the grand jury investigations no doubt aggravated these problems. Moreover, Cropsey was already Gaynor's second police commissioner in less than eighteen months; the first commissioner, William Baker, had resigned in October 1910 under charges of lax vice enforcement. Gaynor's desire to have a tough disciplinarian in charge of the force, coupled with his tendency to micromanage the police department, placed his commissioners in an untenable position. Perhaps recognizing this problem, the mayor selected his loyal and pliant fire commissioner, Rhinelander Waldo, to succeed Cropsey. Thereafter, Gaynor virtually ran the department himself. The repeated turn-over at the top, however, only increased the perception of chaos and mismanagement in the department.[30]

Although Gaynor remained publicly committed to his liberal policies, the combination of public criticism and internal dissension prompted him to retreat from some of his more sweeping reform measures. In the wake of the grand jury investigation, the depart-ment seems to have adopted a more restrained disciplinary ap-proach. Judging by the contents of the mayor's police files, citizens continued to file brutality complaints throughout Gaynor's term, but the percentage of cases in which the department preferred charges dropped noticeably after mid-1911. During the first sixteen months of his administration, fully half of the assault complaints re-sulted in departmental charges against the officers involved. After the release of the grand jury presentment in May 1911, however, less than 15 percent of cases resulted in disciplinary charges. Even in rel-atively well-substantiated cases with multiple witnesses, police officers were rarely held accountable. In dealing with brutality cases, the department apparently retreated from its rigid disciplinary stan-dards and fell back into a more traditional approach that favored po-lice officers over civilians.[31]

Another concession to the crime critics was the reinstitution of strong-arm squads. In the summer of 1911, Commissioner Waldo announced the formation of a new plainclothes squad under Lt. Charles Becker to combat gang activity and other forms of street crime. Comprised of twenty officers known for their fighting abili-ties, the group included such legendary characters as M. B. Conlon, the "strong-arm dude of Broadway"; Nathan Waxman, the "Yiddish Irishman"; and Joseph "Eat 'em up alive" McLaughlin. These husky police were used to break up gangs, disperse loafers, roust ferryboat and streetcar rowdies, and even arrest "undraped bathers" at Coney Island. According to one journalist, Commissioner Waldo in-structed his men to arrest such individuals and to give them "a strong dose of their particular brand of medicine." Becker's squad took this mandate seriously, making 345 arrests in July and 237 in the first two weeks of August. Several arrestees complained to magistrates about brutal treatment at the hands of squad members, but few took their complaints to the police commission. As departmental discipline relaxed, proactive policing became more prevalent, and additional strong-arm squads were created to help suppress gambling and prostitution. Beginning in 1912 the arrest rate would climb again, from a low of 153,768 in 1911 to 170,375 in 1912 and to 182,011 in 1913. Gaynor's goals of reducing arrests and eliminating brutality were thus abandoned in an effort to crack down on crime and vice.[32]

During his brief campaign to curb police lawlessness, however, Gaynor became the first mayor to address the problem of police brutality in a committed fashion. He insisted that even criminals had rights and argued that lawless police were potentially more dangerous to American liberty than individual criminals. This radical position and Gaynor's strict antibrutality measures sparked fierce opposition from conservative reformers who viewed crime and vice suppression as the number one priority. Their belief that effective crime fighting required specialized anticrime squads, violent tactics, and high-volume arrests, however, was open to question. Such methods inevitably trampled on individual liberties, resulted in increased complaints of police harassment and brutality, and fed public resentment of the police that fueled further conflict. Gaynor, however, was unable to make an effective case for his more liberal approach. Portrayed as being soft on crime and hostile to police, Gaynor retreated from his antibrutality campaign and sowed the seeds of his own political demise. Sadly, his commitment to curbing police violence would not be seen again at city hall for at least another twenty years.

Arthur Woods and Modern Police Reform

Among reformers, John Purroy Mitchel was the youngest and most idealistic mayor of New York in the Progressive Era. His police commissioner, Arthur Woods, likewise became the police department's best-known reformer and modernizer. Like Roosevelt, Bingham, and other reform commissioners, Woods worked to create an honest, efficient, and nonpoliticized department. But he did not completely share his predecessors' militaristic approach toward crime fighting. Rather he pioneered a modern, sociological brand of police reform that emphasized crime prevention through public contact and cooperation with philanthropic organizations, particularly those dealing with young people. He also promoted scientific expertise and professionalism in police work that resulted in improved training programs for both new recruits and veteran officers. Such changes helped to professionalize police work and temporarily banished the image of the corrupt and brutal Tammany cop. Although New Yorkers continued to file assault complaints against police, public debate about brutality virtually disappeared during these years. The sociological approach, however, did not apply to everyone. From the beginning, Woods made it clear that gangsters and other known criminals would be dealt with severely and that earlier antibrutality policies would be abandoned.

In actuality, this get-tough policy with gangs and criminals predated Woods's administration. Gaynor had been moving in this direction since mid-1911, and Mitchel merely accelerated these efforts. Within days of taking office, Mitchel's interim police commissioner announced the formation of an enlarged and centralized strong-arm squad and the "restoration of nightstick rule." Hereafter, he said, "patrolmen need fear no pressing of charges against them if they used their clubs on young men with no apparent means of support and evil reputations." Effectively eviscerating General Order Number Seven, he instructed inspectors to investigate the character and reputation of anyone alleging assault by a police officer and to disregard those complaints filed by criminals. When he took over the department a few months later, Arthur Woods enthusiastically supported this policy, as did Mayor Mitchel himself. "I hope the police will use their clubs on every gunman on whom they can lay their hands," Mitchel said.[33]

Many police officers, however, continued to press for official repeal of the anticlubbing order. With General Order Number Seven still on the books, some police feared that they would still be subject to costly and time-consuming investigations by inspectors. The decision to forward a complaint, they argued, should remain with precinct supervisors who were most familiar with local conditions.

The counsel for the police fraternal organizations voiced this demand explicitly in January 1915, together with calls to give police wider latitude in making arrests and conducting searches. These demands were seconded by a new anticrime group, the Citizens' Protective League, headed by Frank Moss and other moral reform leaders. Borrowing its name from the black antibrutality group founded in the wake of the Tenderloin Riot, this elite white group did not seek to stop police violence but rather promoted it. The gang evil had grown under Mitchel's administration, they argued, because police were still hamstrung by excessive regulations. Attempts to control graft and brutality had been made at the expense of efficient crimefighting.

Mitchel and Woods dismissed these criticisms as absurd and warned police against such insubordinate statements. Woods confirmed that General Order Number Seven was no longer being enforced and that officers could and did use their clubs and revolvers against criminals. The commissioner maintained this stance throughout his administration, citing gang suppression as his highest priority. The department did in fact arrest several major crime figures and broke up a number of gangs. It did this through strong-arm squads that conducted wholesale sweeps of working-class neighborhoods, clubbing and arresting hundreds of suspected gang members. As Woods bragged in his final report to Mitchel, "There is no longer a deadline for police. They go anywhere and everywhere in pursuit of criminals and suppression of crime." While police under Woods were trained to recognize and understand social problems and act as "big brothers" to wayward youth, there was no such consideration given to hardened criminals. Use of the nightstick and revolver were encouraged, and brutality complaints by real or suspected criminals were ignored.[34]

Despite the escalation of force inherent in such an approach, Commissioner Woods insisted that police discipline was better than ever. Like his predecessors, he recognized the problem of police perjury and sought to persuade officers to tell the truth and to confess their violations. To this end, he successfully campaigned for a state bill allowing local departments to give probation instead of fines, suspensions, or dismissals as penalties in disciplinary hearings. This more lenient sentencing, Woods claimed, resulted in a higher conviction rate and an overall drop in the number of complaints filed. Under the new system, the number of complaints against officers fell from 3,648 in 1915 to 2,100 in 1917, and approximately 80 percent of the accused officers pled guilty. Only 126 of these cases resulted in the officer's dismissal from the force, a noticeable drop from the number of dismissals during the Gaynor years. According to Woods, "the greatest factor in our success in getting better discipline with less punishment has been the feeling of the men that they were sure of fair treatment, so it was safe to tell the truth." As in his sociological approach to crime prevention among youth, Woods sought to reach out to errant police officers and offer them rehabilitation in lieu of more punitive measures.[35]

The commissioner's claims of improved discipline are open to question, however, particularly as they applied to brutality. Critics of police brutality had long argued that officers faced little risk in beating suspects and that weak penalties were a key factor contributing to the problem. More lenient sentencing may have encouraged more officers to plead guilty, but it also ensured that abusive officers would have a longer tenure on the force. For civilian complainants, some of whom were understandably afraid of their police assailants, the new system may have discouraged them from filing complaints at all. Moreover, the department's decision to disregard assault complaints filed by "criminals" no doubt served to reduce the overall number of disciplinary cases. Although there is no specific data on brutality cases, it seems likely that a decline in the number of assault charges (assuming it followed the general disciplinary trend) was not due to improved discipline but to a greater reluctance or inability of citizens to file complaints.

In other areas, however, the potential for police violence was reduced. Following William Gaynor's example, Mitchel and Woods maintained a policy of tolerance toward labor unions, Socialists, anarchists, and other radical groups. During the transit and garment industry strikes of 1916, Mitchel took an active role in mediating the disputes and insisted on police neutrality on the picket lines. Public protest meetings by Socialists and anarchists, though closely monitored by police, were likewise permitted. The price for this official tolerance was high: In place of overt political repression, police developed covert tactics designed to disrupt and discredit radical groups. Police spied on political meetings, intimidated private hall owners, and tapped the telephones of dozens of labor unions and political organizations. The police Bomb Squad, established in August 1914, infiltrated the Industrial Workers of the World and various anarchist groups with the intent of stirring up violence and internal dissension. The Industrial Squad, founded in 1917, played a similar role in the labor movement, using plainclothes detectives to keep tabs on racketeers, Communists, and other "subversives." For a while, these new covert forms of police repression largely replaced the traditional approach of directly and violently suppressing political meetings. The Mitchel administration thus maintained police pressure on radicals while avoiding any mass incidents of police violence.[36]

Woods's pioneering efforts in police training probably also helped to reduce the excessive use of force. In 1915 the NYPD opened its Training School for Police, featuring a rigorous twelve-week training program for new recruits as well as special courses for veteran officers. The introductory program significantly expanded upon the existing four-week course and included legal instruction at Columbia University to teach recruits the rules of arrest, search, and seizure. Firearms training was also improved, incorporating educational work "to prevent reckless shooting." As the department stated in its 1917 report, "Our aim has been to train the men never to shoot unless they have to; but if they have to, to hit the mark they aim at and nothing else." The military-style marksmanship approach of Theodore Roosevelt was thus expanded to address both the use and *misuse* of firearms. Given the departmental pressure to get tough on criminals, it is hard to know just how much impact this new training had on actual police performance. It was, however, a step in the right direction.[37]

Whether incidents of police brutality declined under Woods's administration is impossible to say, but the public debate about it clearly diminished. Indeed, the quiescence of the years 1914–1917 stands in stark contrast to the uproar over police clubbing during the Bingham and Gaynor administrations. Woods's expansion of officer training programs probably reduced unnecessary shootings, and the administration's tolerance of political dissent no doubt undercut the potential for open police violence against labor and radicals. Similarly, in the absence of any mass ethnic or racial rioting in these years, there were no community-based mobilizations against police misconduct as there had been at the turn of the century. Moreover, the administration's indifference to brutality complaints—particularly by those it considered criminals—likely reduced the number of disciplinary cases and the publicity that accompanied them. The political identity and sympathies of the Mitchel administration also help explain the public silence on this issue. The mayor's close ties to the Fusion reform community and his attempts to advance its agenda served to placate most of the anti-Tammany police critics. Those reformers who did challenge the department, such as Frank Moss and the new Citizens' Protective League, pressed for even *more* aggressive anticrime measures. Moss's opposition to police brutality, so prominent a part of his earlier reform agenda, had been cast aside in the quest for efficiency and crime suppression.

In many ways the Woods administration continued the conservative reform tradition of Roosevelt and Bingham, but there were also important differences. Like his conservative predecessors, Woods's top priorities were efficiency and crime suppression, while police brutality was generally ignored. On the other hand, new sociological techniques of crime prevention, improved officer training, tolerance of public political dissent, and more restrained methods of excise enforcement were all positive steps in limiting opportunities for police use and misuse of force. In terms of the police brutality problem, the more sophisticated modern style of reform advocated by Woods was no doubt an improvement over the conservative militaristic approach of Roosevelt and Bingham.

Given the diverse array of philosophies and initiatives, the impact of Progressive Era police reform on the brutality problem was ambiguous. The most far-reaching antibrutality measures promoted by William Gaynor came under intense political fire and were effectively scuttled. The dominant group of reformers, who had led the battle against police brutality since the Lexow investigation, subsequently abandoned the issue as incompatible with efficient crime-fighting. Their successors, the modernizers like Arthur Woods, like-wise rejected explicit antibrutality measures and put their faith in professionalization, assuming that improved training and community relations were sufficient remedies. While some of Woods's reform measures helped reduce the potential for violence between police and citizens, others served to increase it. Whatever progress reformers had made, however, would be largely lost when Tammany Democrats recaptured city hall in 1917 and would preside over a host of new problems spurred by Prohibition, corruption, and organized crime.

4. PROHIBITION, THE WAR ON CRIME, AND THE FIGHT AGAINST THE THIRD DEGREE

In the 1929 film *Alibi,* two police arrest a small-time hood and usher him into the police inspector's office. The hood, who is suspected of driving the getaway car in a recent robbery and murder, refuses to give up his accomplices, so the officers decide to "give him the works." As the police inspector opens the window, the detective dons a pair of gloves, grabs a gun, and tells the suspect that he will be shot while attempting to escape. He shoots the gun at the floor and then presses it to the suspect's temple. Following a dizzying swirl of the camera, the young hood confesses and gives up his accomplice, the notorious gangster Chester Morris.[1]

In movies like *Alibi,* Hollywood popularized "the third degree" and other violent police tactics for generations of American filmgoers. Exploiting the public's fascination with gangsters, these films also reflected the country's growing concern over a surge in organized crime and gang warfare that had occurred as a result of national Prohibition in the 1920s. Like their real-life counterparts, police in these gangster films used the third degree and other violent or coercive tactics to ferret out criminals and elicit confessions. In the real world, though, such methods provoked a growing chorus of protests from journalists, lawyers, and civil liberties groups. In particular, these activists targeted the notorious third degree, effectively redefining the problem of police brutality. No longer was brutality equated with random street clubbings or racial/ethnic animosity; in this period, its predominant image was one of officially sanctioned torture of criminal suspects within the confines of police station houses.

Prohibition and the War on Crime

The third degree was one of several violent and invasive tactics developed by police in what they would soon describe as a "war" against Prohibition-induced crime. The passage of the Eighteenth Amendment in 1919 produced an explosion of bootlegging, vice, and racketeering operations, as well as a pervasive climate of police laxity and corruption. With the passage of the Mullen-Gage prohibition law in New York in 1921, the NYPD inherited the thankless task of raiding and shutting down the city's fast-growing crop of speakeasies and bootleggers. Within two weeks of the law's passage, prohibition cases on local court dockets increased tenfold, and local prosecutors complained they could not find enough jurors to hear the flood of new cases. In Manhattan alone, the grand jury heard more than sixty-nine hundred prohibition cases over the next two years. Although the legislature repealed the Mullen-Gage Act in 1923, the NYPD continued to make periodic liquor raids under the public nuisance laws, particularly during the administration of Commissioner Grover A. Whalen (1928–1930). A special prohibition enforcement unit known as "Whalen's Wackers" reportedly raided as many as sixty speakeasies per night in 1928.[2]

Police enforcement of Prohibition resulted in a rash of citizen complaints of harassment and brutality. The first major scandal occurred in July 1921, when Detective Charles Tighe allegedly went on a rampage during a raid on Coen's Restaurant, a former saloon in Hell's Kitchen that police suspected of gambling and liquor violations. According to numerous witnesses, Tighe "went berzerk," beating and arresting twenty-seven patrons, including several women and children, a one-legged bootblack, and an elderly man. Tighe was later convicted on second degree assault charges and sentenced to two to four years in prison. Tighe's case was only the beginning, however. At least six more cases of alleged brutality occurred over the next month, and a steady stream of new prohibition-related cases continued to surface in 1922. The situation clearly alarmed City Magistrate Joseph Corrigan, who declared in March 1922 that he had "never seen conditions so bad among policemen as in the past few months. . . . Raid after raid is being brought into these courts despite the fact that magistrates have been declaring them illegal. The police are running roughshod over the rights of the people." Citizen complaints of police brutality during liquor raids continued, however, even after the NYPD turned over most prohibition enforcement activities to federal authorities in 1923.[3]

Civil rights violations were not the only problem; prohibition enforcement also offered ample opportunities for graft. Such opportunities would be eagerly exploited by police under Tammany Democrats who had recaptured city hall in 1918. Speakeasy operators paid protection money to police to ignore liquor violations and to tip them off about raids. Some officers took a more active role, steering customers to local speakeasies, becoming partners in bootlegging operations, or selling confiscated liquor. While police extorted untold amounts of payoff money, they sometimes encountered violators who resisted the shakedowns. In such cases, police threats could escalate into physical violence. In March 1924, for example, off-duty patrolman Daniel Bruns shot two managers of a Manhattan nightclub after they allegedly refused to comply with his demands for a two-hundred-dollar bribe. In his 1932 investigation of New York City government, a former state supreme court judge, Samuel Seabury, recounted the case of a widow who sold liquor to friends in her home to earn extra money. In the summer of 1930, two vice officers came to her apartment to purchase drinks. When she asked them to leave an hour later, they revealed their identity and demanded a five-hundred-dollar bribe. When the widow refused to pay, the police assaulted her and a female friend and took them both into custody. Shocked by the battered condition of the women, the arraigning magistrate dismissed all charges against them; the two officers were later convicted of second degree assault. Other allegations of police brutality stemming from failed shakedowns surfaced periodically until the repeal of the Eighteenth Amendment in 1933.[4]

Violent encounters between police and speakeasy operators also occurred when the latter refused to serve alcohol to officers who wanted it. In October 1927 two uniformed Brooklyn patrolmen coming off their evening shift shot and injured a Fulton Street cabaret owner, allegedly because he refused to serve them drinks. In a similar case in March 1931, Bronx patrolman James Russell was charged with felonious assault for beating two restaurant managers with a blackjack after they allegedly refused to serve him after closing time. Restaurant operators were thus placed in an awkward position: If they served liquor to police officers, they risked shakedowns or prosecution under prohibition laws; if they refused, they might incur the wrath of police who viewed after-hours tippling as a professional perk.[5]

Police consumption of alcohol could also result in outbursts of violence against innocent bystanders. Although drunken rampages by police were hardly a new phenomenon in the 1920s, the criminalization of the liquor trade under Prohibition made such incidents appear more transgressive. In the past, drunken police officers that abused citizens were often disciplined internally on charges of intoxication. In many cases, the officer's intoxicated condition served as a pretext for his erratic behavior. During Prohibition, however, drunkenness implied police association with lawbreakers and official complicity in illegal liquor trafficking. Violence committed by an intoxicated officer thus bore the stamp of police corruption. A 1922 case involving David Owens, an officer with the Marine Division, is a good example. After the end of his shift on August 6, an obviously intoxicated Owens was refused entry into a restaurant on West Fifty-fifth Street. Enraged, Owens became abusive to bystanders on the street, chasing them, firing his service revolver, and seriously wounding an elderly resident and another police officer who tried to disarm him. Interestingly, publicity surrounding the case focused on Owens's role in raiding a rum-runner's boat earlier that day. Although marine police had seized a hundred cases of liquor, only thirty-five had been turned over to federal authorities, who were now investigating the incident. The possibility that the purloined alcohol had fueled Owens's deadly rampage made his actions seem all the more heinous.[6]

The case of Officer John J. Brennan was an even more telling example of the relationship between Prohibition-era brutality and corruption. In January 1926, police charged Brennan, a patrolman from the Clymer Street station house in Brooklyn, with first-degree murder in the shooting death of shopkeeper Samuel Kranin. The previous evening, an intoxicated Brennan had entered Kranin's store and ordered the storekeeper to give him two dollars. When he refused, Brennan struck him over the head with his billy club, fired his revolver into the floor, and fled. A few hours later, Brennan was summoned to a lineup, where Kranin identified him as the assailant. Before he could be booked, Brennan pulled out his service revolver and fired three shots at Kranin, shouting, "You won't squeal against anyone again." Kranin later died of his wounds—a shocking reminder of the risks faced by citizens who filed complaints against police.

In the ensuing trial, the defense argued that Brennan's drunkenness and police department complicity in the liquor trade were to blame for Kranin's tragic death. According to his attorney, Brennan shot Kranin because he was crazed with liquor after two days of drinking in speakeasies near the station house. For Brennan, "the uniform was simply a means of getting booze. . . . It shows how speakeasies are covered up and made the source of police graft and booze for policemen." The defense's argument did not persuade the jury to exonerate him; in fact, it may have done just the opposite. After a short deliberation, the jury convicted Brennan of first-degree murder and sentenced him to death. For its part, the NYPD pointedly denounced Brennan, portraying him as a rogue cop with a history of drunkenness, violence, and insubordination. For the press and the public, however, the image of violent drunken cops was consistent with the climate of official corruption that pervaded Prohibition-era New York.[7]

As in the 1890s, political opponents of the Tammany-controlled police linked brutality and corruption in their efforts to discredit the department. State Assemblyman Louis Cuvillier, an independent Democrat from East Harlem who led an ongoing crusade against police corruption under Prohibition, emerged as a defender of brutality victims in mid-1923. Cuvillier's campaign began in June when he took up the case of Thaddeus Lynch, a Harlem carpenter who was beaten by a police officer on strike duty outside a construction site. Lynch was arrested and jailed in the East 126th Street station house despite major head injuries. He later collapsed in his cell and was taken to Bellevue, where he died a few hours later. Following his funeral, two police detectives raided the local VFW post and allegedly attacked five of Lynch's friends—all World War I veterans who were planning to testify against Lynch's assailant. Cuvillier interceded in both cases, pressuring the district attorney to bring indictments. His involvement in these high-profile cases precipitated an outpouring of brutality complaints from other veterans around the city. Soon the assemblyman was monitoring more than a dozen brutality cases and won convictions in at least two of them. Because the alleged victims were mostly war veterans, public sympathy and publicity was abundant. Cuvillier seized the opportunity to write open letters to Tammany Mayor John Hylan lambasting the police as corrupt thugs and attacking his administration. Like the Republican architects of the Lexow investigation, Cuvillier bolstered his attacks on Tammany police corruption with emotionally charged cases of brutality against upstanding citizens.[8]

Prohibition not only facilitated police corruption; it also led to the rapid expansion of organized crime and open gang warfare on city streets. As other historians have shown, bootlegging became big business in New York, where gangsters such as Arnold Rothstein, "Legs" Diamond, "Dutch" Schultz, Owney Madden, "Lucky" Luciano, Vincent Coll, and Frankie Yale quickly cornered the liquor market. Using the highly profitable liquor trade as a base, these underworld figures built extensive crime syndicates that dominated the speakeasy and nightclub business, as well as moving into gambling, prostitution, racketeering, and other activities formally controlled by local gangs. The consolidation of large-scale crime organizations, however, was the result of a protracted and deadly gang warfare in the late 1920s and early 1930s that contributed to the highest homicide rates in the city's history (rates that would not occur again until the 1960s). Armed with newly acquired automobiles and Thompson machine guns, the gangsters established a reign of terror on New York streets that prompted city officials to launch their own "war on crime" well before the FBI did so in the 1930s.[9]

Targeting the growing criminal population, the NYPD instituted a number of get-tough measures in the late 1920s, including the use of dragnets and strong-arm squads. Although police had occasionally relied on such measures in the past, the use of them in the 1920s and 1930s was more visible and widespread than at any prior time in the department's history. Beginning in March 1925, Commissioner Richard Enright ordered a series of police roundups of "thieves and criminals" at a number of well-known speakeasies, arresting as many as one hundred suspects per night. Building on this record, Commissioner Grover Whalen launched the most concerted anti-crime campaign of the decade. Shortly after his appointment as commissioner in December 1928, Whalen ordered a series of Saturday night dragnets in Manhattan and Brooklyn that typically netted around two hundred people. The suspects were taken to headquarters, booked on vagrancy charges, and held until after the Monday morning police lineup in hopes of catching wanted felons. In the arraignments that followed, however, the overwhelming majority was released without charges. At the same time, Whalen announced the formation of six new strong-arm units called "Gunmen's Squads" that would patrol notorious street corners, speakeasies, and poolrooms looking for gangsters. Recruited for their ability to use their fists, squad members were instructed to use "nightstick law" to prevent New York from "becoming another Chicago." In defending such tactics, Whalen insisted that crooks and gangsters must be treated "on the assumption that they have no constitutional rights. . . . Any man with a previous record is public property."[10]

Whalen's tactics and pronouncements sparked a flurry of protest from judges and civil libertarians. Writing on behalf of the American Civil Liberties Union in February 1929, Arthur Garfield Hays criticized Whalen's use of roundups, raids, and police clubbing in both organized crime and prohibition cases. "We hold no brief for gangsters or speakeasies," wrote Hays, but such practices "may easily be turned tomorrow against any group with which the police find it difficult to deal lawfully." Two months later, a New York state supreme court justice, Selah B. Strong, and a Kings County judge, George Martin, also denounced Whalen's methods, calling them "un-American, illegal and unjust." Whalen quickly dismissed the judges' statements, saying they were "giving encouragement to criminals." His successor, Commissioner Edward P. Mulrooney (1930–1933), essentially continued Whalen's aggressive anticrime measures, ordering frequent roundups and instructing police to "shoot above the waist" when encountering known criminals or racketeers.[11]

Although the repeal of Prohibition put an end to the bootlegging business, organized crime continued to flourish after 1933, and the NYPD maintained its commitment to tough anticrime tactics. While playing a key role in reducing police repression of labor and radicals (see chapter 5), the Fusion reform mayor, Fiorello La Guardia, and his police commissioner, Lewis Valentine, continued to take a hard line against the city's criminal element. In November 1934, in the wake of three unsolved shootings of local merchants, Valentine urged police to "muss up" the gangsters. Referring to a dapper murder suspect in the morning lineup, he told a gathering of two hundred detectives that "A fellow like him ought to come in here well marked up. His type ought to be mussed up. I don't want them coming in looking like fashion plates." Treating criminals roughly, the commissioner argued, would soon drive them out of the city.

Valentine's muss-up order suggested a different relationship between corruption and brutality than the one underlying earlier criticism of police prohibition raids or Cuvillier's 1923 protests. Rather than seeing corruption and violence as mutually reinforcing, the reform-minded Valentine believed that a Tammany-dominated police department had grown accustomed to treating politically connected gangsters with kid gloves. Like his Progressive Era predecessor, Arthur Woods, Valentine promoted anticorruption efforts in the department in tandem with tough policing of criminals. Through a series of internal shake-ups and the formation of a new Confidential Squad to root out police corruption, the commissioner hoped to free honest cops to "take their gloves off" and urged them to pursue criminals in a no-holds-barred fashion.[12] For reformers like Valentine, police violence was only a problem if used against innocent civilians or political dissidents; when directed against hardened criminals, rough tactics were essential to efficient and effective law enforcement. The acceptability of such tactics among legal and law enforcement professionals nationwide, however, was called into question by the mid-1930s as a result of a prolonged battle over the third degree.

The Third Degree

By far the most controversial crime-fighting tactic of the 1920s was what came to be known as "the third degree." A highly elastic term, the third degree encompassed a variety of questionable police interrogation practices including physical violence and torture, prolonged grilling, food and sleep deprivation, and psychological coercion. Although public interest in the third degree was a new development, police use of violence to elicit confessions was a long-standing practice. According to police lore, violent interrogation of suspects by urban law enforcement dates back at least to the late nineteenth century. Richard Sylvester, president of the International Association of Police Chiefs from 1901 to 1915, claimed that third-degree tactics originated in post–Civil War cities as escalating crime and violence prompted police and military authorities to use extraordinary interrogation measures. Among these techniques was the "sweat box," a superheated jail cell (adjacent to the furnace) designed to "sweat" confessions and other information from uncooperative suspects. In New York, police sources date the practice to the early 1880s, when Inspector Thomas Byrnes organized a citywide detective bureau to help solve high-profile felony cases. Before long, Byrnes's detectives won acclaim for their hard-boiled interrogation tactics, including the grueling and violent sessions that were soon dubbed the third degree.[13]

The term itself seems to be derived from nineteenth-century Freemasonry. During this period, prospective Masons underwent elaborate initiation rituals into each of the society's successive orders, known as degrees. The highest order of Master Masons—the third degree—had the most grueling initiation rites, involving long and secretive examinations of Masonic beliefs and rituals. Afterward, inductees were strictly forbidden to speak of their ordeal to others.[14] The parallels with old-style police interrogations were obvious: Police subjected suspects to grueling and protracted rounds of questioning (often accompanied by police "rituals" of beating and intimidation), during which the subjects tried to demonstrate loyalty to a secret brotherhood (the criminal underworld). Afterward, few suspects dared speak of their ordeal for fear of police retribution.

For the most part, police in the nineteenth century were successful in keeping suspects quiet about their ordeal. For many young working-class suspects, male pride and bravado kept them from "squealing" about their treatment at the hands of police. Indeed, members of street gangs took it as a point of pride to "take their lumps" rather than divulge information about their associates. (In the 1920s, a group of robbery suspects who based their defense on police use of the third degree were quickly dubbed "the Cry Baby Gang" by the popular press.) Moreover, public indifference over police treatment of "hardened criminals" and victims' fear of police retribution further discouraged most suspects from bringing complaints.

There is no doubt, however, that such practices were in use. New York writers and journalists have long credited Superintendent Thomas Byrnes with "inventing the third degree" and making it a routine part of late nineteenth-century detective work. Retired police inspector Daniel Costigan confirmed this point in a 1930 interview, describing how the third degree flourished in the 1890s:

There was a man named "Chew Tobacco Mike," a missing link sort of person with huge hands who would go down to the cells at 300 Mulberry Street in his red flannel undershirt and would beat the prisoner with a nightstick and the prisoner would then be in a talkative mood. The prisoners would come to the Magistrate's Court pretty badly bandaged up and no questions would be asked.[15]

Unlike the controversial clubbing cases of this period, third-degree beatings seemed to elicit little judicial comment.

Judicial silence on this issue was partly the result of an important change in New York criminal procedure in 1881 that gave the state more leeway in the use of confession evidence. For much of the nineteenth century, New York had adhered to the common law rule against self-incrimination, requiring that confessions be voluntary and that they proceed "from the spontaneous suggestion of the party's own mind." Confessions made under duress or violence were unreliable, the court held in 1857, and could thus be excluded by the judge. In 1881, however, critics of the common law rule—who believed it unduly favored defendants—convinced the legislature to adopt a new provision in the state's Code of Criminal Procedure. Under Section 395, all confessions except those "made under the influence of fear produced by threats" were admissible. Judges could exclude confessions only when both parties agreed that abuse or coercion had occurred (something that almost never happened). In the vast majority of cases where police and defendants disputed the facts, confessions were submitted to the jury to determine their credibility in light of the totality of evidence. Thus, even as a more professionalized judiciary was taking issue with police clubbing, Section 395 effectively prohibited magistrates from excluding confession evidence in most potential third-degree cases. It thus opened the door for police to procure confessions by any means necessary.[16] It is no coincidence that Superintendent Byrnes "invented" the third degree shortly after this provision appeared on the books.

The first significant criticism of police interrogation tactics came during Mayor Gaynor's antibrutality crusade of 1910. Sanctioned by the mayor's official pledge to fight police abuses, a growing number of magistrates and judges openly condemned police violence, including an alleged police beating of a murder suspect, Stephen Boehm, in April 1910. In this case, Boehm confessed to murdering the victim but later retracted his statement, claiming police beat him and withheld food to force a confession. Although Boehm was convicted on collateral evidence gleaned from the confession, Judge Crain of the Court of General Sessions pointedly denounced police methods as "dangerous" and "demoralizing." The *New York Times* and other newspapers agreed with the judge in editorials denouncing the third degree. Calling it an "invention" of the press, Commissioner William Baker and former Commissioner Theodore Bingham denied police use of violent interrogation methods, and the International Association of Police Chiefs passed a resolution denouncing such "unjust accusations" that blighted the professional image of the police.[17] In later years, police sources acknowledged that the third degree had existed under the administration of Commissioner Arthur Woods (1914–1917), but there was virtually no discussion of it in the press during those years.[18] Public alarm over the issue in the Progressive Era thus proved fleeting and ineffective.

In the 1920s, however, public debate over the third degree reemerged with a vengeance. A number of factors converged to produce this newfound concern. As noted above, Prohibition expanded opportunities for criminal activity and encouraged the growth of organized crime. Fattened on the profits of bootlegging, criminal syndicates bought protection from a growing number of politicians, judges, and police and hired expensive criminal defense lawyers to win their release from those who could not be bought. Given such resources, police found it more and more difficult to secure convictions. Honest cops may well have resorted to rougher tactics as a means of obtaining evidence—or failing that—punishing offenders. Administrative sanction for such tactics also grew as the public clamored for more aggressive law enforcement to curb the open gang warfare and violence that periodically exploded on city streets. Declaring a "war on crime," police responded with proactive measures such as mass roundups, detentions, and high-pressure interrogation tactics designed to root out criminal elements.[19]

Before long defense lawyers and other members of the legal profession were openly challenging the use of third-degree tactics. Top criminal defense lawyers like Samuel Liebowitz exploited the battered condition of their clients to discredit confession statements and win acquittals. Prison physicians, parole officers, and other penal authorities often provided testimony in such cases, and the American Prison Association publicly condemned the third degree as early as 1922. More importantly, new legal defense organizations established during and after World War I played a critical role in raising public consciousness. The most well known was the American Civil Liberties Union (ACLU), founded in 1920 to defend civil liberties in the wake of government repression during the war and amid the growing abuse of radicals during the Red Scare. Quickly expanding its mandate to include due process issues under the Fourteenth Amendment, the ACLU began monitoring third-degree cases in the early 1920s and lobbied actively against the practice over the next two decades.[20]

The most important local critics, however, came from the ranks of the legal aid community that had developed in the 1910s to provide criminal defense services for the poor. Hoping to encourage respect for American law among the immigrant poor and to drive out unethical "shysters," a group of prominent New York attorneys organized the Voluntary Defenders Committee (VDC) in 1917. Led by former Manhattan prosecutors William Dean Embree and Timothy N. Pfeiffer, the VDC assembled a crew of private practice attorneys to do pro-bono work in felony cases involving indigent defendants. Embree, Pfeiffer, and a small staff operated out of an office in the criminal courts building provided by the city and worked with judges in the Court of General Sessions, who referred defendants to them. By the mid-1920s, the VDC was handling roughly five hundred cases per year in New York County, a significant proportion of which involved allegations of police brutality—most notably the third degree.[21] Although the VDC did not dare endanger its relationship with local government by openly criticizing police methods, its attorneys worked through local and national bar associations to encourage reform.

The first organized protest against the third degree in New York occurred in the spring of 1926 around police treatment of four robbery suspects, reputed members of a gang run by "English Harry" Wallon. Apprehended in the act of robbing a crowded nightclub, the four suspects were taken to the station house, where police allegedly "worked them over" in hopes of getting them to implicate their leader. According to the suspects, detectives beat them until they collapsed and then jumped on them from a table as they lay on the floor. Three of the suspects sustained serious injuries, including fractured ribs and arms, head and leg lacerations, and extensive body bruises. As it happened, two of the gang members were on parole and were obliged to meet with their parole officer before arraignment. The officer was so shocked by their condition that he notified the Society for Penal Information, which sent in a representative to certify the prisoners' injuries. The two penal officials then consulted with VDC attorney Louis Fabricant, who took the case before the Criminal Courts and Procedures Committee of the New York County Lawyers Association (NYCLA), a reform-oriented bar association whose members specialized in charitable and educational work.

Seeing the case as a clear-cut and egregious example of the third degree, the committee appointed a delegation led by former New York District Attorney Robert H. Elder and the VDC's Louis Fabricant to meet with Police Commissioner George McLaughlin. According to Fabricant, the commissioner gave them a brief and discourteous hearing in which he defended the arresting officer's use of force to protect himself and patrons of the nightclub. Following the meeting, McLaughlin fired off an open letter to the NYCLA accusing it of "creating false propaganda" and "discouraging members of the police force from performing their duty and giving aid and comfort to the criminal element in the city."[22]

Developments in the subsequent trial, however, made a mockery of McLaughlin's statements. Patrolman Green, the arresting officer, testified that the four suspects had thrown down their weapons and submitted peacefully to arrest. In addition, one of the nightclub patrons, whom police had summoned to the station house to identify the suspects, testified that he found a squad of detectives "fixing them up nicely with reddish pipes." Following the trial—which resulted in convictions of the four gang members—VDC chairman William Embree issued a follow-up report on behalf of the NYCLA condemning police use of the third degree and the commissioner's attempts to justify it.[23]

Soon after, the VDC began collecting data on allegations of the third degree and other police brutality incidents reported by their clients. Timothy Pfeiffer and other VDC attorneys were also instrumental in convincing the nation's oldest and most elite legal organization, the Association of the Bar of the City of New York, to address third-degree abuses. In May 1928 the association's Committee on Criminal Courts, which included Pfeiffer as well as three former U.S. attorneys and three former Manhattan district attorneys, issued a twenty-page report asserting that many accusations of third-degree brutality were "well founded." Declaring these practices illegal and counterproductive, the committee urged the New York State Crime Commission to conduct an investigation. Such an investigation, the committee argued, would be advantageous to "those district attorneys (and we believe there are many of them) who neither take part in nor permit such invasion of the rights of defendants, but who are liable to be made to share in the public mind the blame that is incurred." Although the bar association's report was a significant breakthrough, the new police commissioner, Grover Whalen, quickly issued a statement denying the department's use of violent third-degree tactics, and the State Crime Commission declined to conduct an investigation.[24]

Although stymied on the local level, criminal attorneys continued their campaign against the third degree and joined with the ACLU and other civil rights groups to bring the problem to national attention. They succeeded in 1929 when the American Bar Association (ABA) formed a Committee on Lawless Enforcement of the Law and commissioned a study of third-degree cases in federal and state appellate courts during the 1920s. Finding the third degree to be "in use almost everywhere" in the United States, the report condemned the practice as obnoxious, arbitrary, and dangerous. The committee urged the ABA and its state and local affiliates to "shame their own members, the prosecuting attorneys, from longer participating in these inquisitions." Although the ABA report did not result in any official resolutions condemning the third degree, it indicated a significant and growing concern with the problem among legal professionals.[25]

While some attorneys opposed the third degree on constitutional or humanitarian grounds, most prosecutors and bar associations spoke out against its adverse impact on the *effectiveness* of the criminal justice system. Most obviously, third-degree tactics sometimes produced false confessions that wasted prosecutors' time and left the guilty parties at large. More critically, however, accusations of the third degree were becoming a standardized defense that was undermining prosecutorial efforts. During the 1920s, numerous felony cases ended in acquittal after defense lawyers convinced juries that police had beaten suspects to extract confessions. Jurors were becoming distrustful of police testimony, and attorneys even screened potential jurors with the question, "If the sole witness for the prosecution were a police officer, would you believe him?" Jurors' antipathy toward the NYPD was vividly dramatized in the Oberst case of 1926. During the trial, a gang of young robbery suspects claimed they confessed because Bronx detectives repeatedly beat them with fists, kicks, and a rubber hose. Their description of the ordeal prompted one outraged juror to jump up and cry, "This is too revolting. I demand the right to be relieved of this trial." His passionate protest resulted in a mistrial and a flurry of bad publicity for the police.[26] Once an asset, the liberal admissibility of evidence in third-degree cases was now becoming a liability.

Defense attorneys eagerly exploited jurors' growing skepticism of confession evidence. Reporter Charles J. V. Murphy wrote that some lawyers advised their criminal clients who were wanted by police to have themselves photographed before surrendering. By being uncooperative thereafter, suspects might invite a beating, and the attorney would then have the suspects rephotographed to document the injuries. In other instances, suspects confessed immediately to "avoid the pounding" but then recanted their statement in court, claiming police intimidation. Third-degree opponents denounced these ploys but insisted that they worked precisely because such incidents had a real basis in fact. As one reformer put it, "Lawyers make trade upon the third degree, but its existence creates their opportunity."[27]

New York judges contributed to the growing wave of anti-third-degree sentiment by denouncing the practice from the bench. As early as 1922, Judge Franklin Taylor of the Brooklyn County Court condemned alleged third-degree methods used against two recently acquitted defendants and ordered a grand jury investigation of the officers involved. Other judges took similar actions, including General Sessions Judge Charles C. Nott and Magistrate Joseph E. Corrigan. The outspokenness of the latter, who became chief city magistrate in 1930, was particularly surprising, since he had long advocated police toughness with criminals and had been the most vocal opponent of Mayor Gaynor's anticlubbing campaign. Third-degree confessions, however, were unreliable evidence, Corrigan maintained, and were undermining public faith in the criminal justice system. In a 1930 interview, Corrigan admitted that he himself would not believe a police officer's account of a suspect's confession unless corroborated by other evidence.[28]

Judicial criticism of police interrogation tactics also came from the state's highest court, led by Chief Justice Benjamin Cardozo. In *People* v. *Doran* (1927), the court of appeals upheld a murder conviction but acknowledged that Doran had been held incommunicado, without arraignment, and had been urged to confess by a police officer wearing a boxing glove. In a blistering dissent, Judge William Lehman attacked the admissibility of the confession: "We have long ago abolished the rack and thumbscrew as a means of extorting confession; the courts cannot sanction the introduction of the boxing glove in their place." One year later, the judges joined unanimously in reversing a murder conviction against Robert Weiner, who charged police had beaten him prior to confessing. Testimony by an assistant district attorney and several prison officials confirmed Weiner's injuries, prompting the court to rule his confession inadmissible.[29]

Perhaps the most important judicial criticism of the third degree came as a result of the case against Joseph Barbato. An Italian farmworker in upstate New York, Barbato was accused of killing a female acquaintance in the Bronx in September 1929. Police brought Barbato back to the Fifty-second Precinct house, where they subjected him to fifteen hours of questioning and a severe beating until he scrawled a four-word confession. On the basis of that confession, he was convicted of first-degree murder and sentenced to death. Fortunately for Barbato, his son was a practicing attorney who had been able to convince the arraigning judge to transfer the obviously battered suspect out of police custody to a county jail facility. There Barbato's son arranged for his father to be photographed and examined by a physician who documented numerous injuries including a black eye, lash marks and abrasions, and extensive bruising of the face, chest, arms, legs, and buttocks. Based on the doctor's testimony and photographs, a New York state court of appeals judge, Cuthbert Pound, later ruled the confession inadmissible and set aside the verdict. "If we are going to use torture," Pound said scathingly, "it is best to admit it frankly and no longer hypocritically pretend that we have abandoned the medieval inquisition or the witch tortures of early modern times."[30]

In the wake of the Barbato case, New York judges played an increasingly active role in ferreting out third-degree abuses. In December 1930, Judge Max Levine of the Court of General Sessions ordered a photographer and Tombs prison physician to examine William Sutton, a robbery suspect who accused police of beating him until he confessed to a jewelry store heist. A few months later a federal judge personally inspected and documented the injuries of two suspected counterfeiters in his courtroom who claimed that NYPD detectives had beaten them during interrogation.[31] Such dramatic judicial actions were eagerly publicized by the press, which used headlines of "police torture" to attract readers.

Just as they had exposed clubbing and other forms of street brutality in the nineteenth century, journalists also played a key role in uncovering and combating the third degree. In the 1920s and 1930s, New York dailies provided extensive coverage of third-degree cases and frequently editorialized against such practices. The after-the-fact condemnation by editors, judges, and lawyers, however, paled in comparison to the grisly accounts of police beat reporters who witnessed the third degree at close range. Spending long hours in police headquarters and precinct houses, reporters were often privy to the inner workings of the department. They routinely saw suspects enter the station in good condition, heard their screams from police interrogation rooms, and watched as their battered bodies were carted off to court. Nor was it unusual to hear detectives boast about how they "made a suspect talk." A few select reporters gained the confidence of police officials and were even permitted to sit in on interrogation sessions. Such privileges were based on professional discretion and cooperation. Police offered access to trusted reporters who could dramatize the department's crime-fighting accomplishments; reporters knew that their privileged access depended on their discretion. As one journalist explained, "these reporters, whose livelihood depends upon cordial relations with the police, found it wise to close their eyes and say nothing, even when they saw suspects cold on the floor in squad rooms just under the Commissioner's office."[32]

In the late 1920s, however, this tacit understanding began to break down. Between 1927 and 1930, at least three reporters from major New York dailies broke their silence and published detailed exposés of the third degree. A. C. Sedgewick, a police reporter for the *New York Times,* was the first to go public when he published a 1927 article in the *Nation* describing and condemning violent police interrogations. Two years later, reporter Charles J. V. Murphy published a lengthy account of third-degree practices in the *Outlook and Independent,* culling his material from "ten fat envelopes" of clippings from the library of the *New York World*. Most shocking, however, was the 1930 publication of *The Third Degree: A Detailed and Appalling Exposé of Police Brutality,* a book-length account of police violence and corruption by Emanuel H. Lavine, a veteran police reporter with the *New York American*. Drawing on events he claimed to have witnessed, Lavine recounted numerous horror stories of police torture. In one case, for example, police repeatedly pounded a suspect's Adam's apple until blood spurted out of his mouth; in another, detectives summoned a "dentist" who drilled a suspect's healthy molars with a rough burr until he agreed to talk. While claiming to be sympathetic to police and their crime-fighting efforts, he concluded with a blistering attack on third-degree methods:

The third degree is much more than merely an occasional or a secondary weapon in the hands of the police; it is actually the main reliance of the police in obtaining information from stubborn prisoners. In its use the law is candidly, cheerfully and consistently violated by those who are sworn—and paid— to uphold it....

Under such conditions, Lavine argued, the police station had become a center of lawlessness. "Once you pass its green lights you are beyond the law." Lavine's book drew strong criticism from Commissioner Mulrooney, who like previous commissioners denied that the NYPD used third-degree methods.[33] Among the public, however, the book created an immediate sensation, and in the coming year federal investigators would draw on Lavine's work and others' as part of an historic nationwide study of law enforcement.

The Wickersham Commission

Modeled after Progressive Era crime commissions established by the states, the National Commission on Law Observance and Enforcement was created by President Herbert Hoover in 1929 in response to law enforcement problems created by Prohibition and to growing public fear of crime. Headed by former federal judge George Wickersham, the Wickersham Commission—as it came to be known—issued fourteen reports in 1931 providing a comprehensive national survey of such topics as the causes of crime, criminal prosecution, policing, and penal institutions. Interestingly, the report that had the greatest impact was Number 11, *Lawlessness in Law Enforcement,* a devastating indictment of police brutality and the third degree. For months, ACLU director Roger Baldwin had lobbied the commission to conduct a study of police practices, an issue that was consuming a growing amount of the union's energy and resources. The commission eventually agreed and, at Baldwin's suggestion, appointed ACLU-affiliated attorneys Walter Pollak, Zachariah Chafee, and Carl Stern to author the report. The authors then hired San Francisco journalist Ernest Jerome Hopkins as a field investigator to conduct a coast-to-coast survey of local law enforcement. Hopkins, who was chief editorial writer at the *San Francisco Examiner,* was a top investigative journalist who had exposed conditions at San Quentin Penitentiary in the 1910s. Using materials collected for the Wickersham Commission, Hopkins went on to publish his own scathing account of police practices, *Our Lawless Police,* in 1931.[34]

Hopkins and the commission surveyed various forms of police harassment and brutality, but they devoted most of their energies to the third degree. They did so because, unlike street brutality, third-degree violence was clearly unconstitutional under the Fifth Amendment and was thus considered more amenable to legal and administrative remedies. In its attention to systemic legal reform, the Wickersham inquiry was a distinct departure from the Lexow Committee and other earlier police investigations. While the Lexow Committee embodied the moralistic nineteenth-century view of police brutality as a by-product of corruption, the Wickersham report reflected the more modern view of brutality as a civil liberties issue that was important in its own right. In keeping with Progressive-style scientific standards, the Wickersham report (and Hopkins's later book) provided a wealth of scientific data and analysis on the third degree, forcing the issue to the center of criminal justice debates.

Canvassing the country from Boston to Los Angeles, the Wickersham investigation provided a survey of police interrogation tactics in fifteen cities. Using statistics from the Voluntary Defenders Committee, the report ranked the NYPD as one of the nation's worst third-degree offenders. According to figures from 1930, 23.4 percent of the VDC's 1,235 clients reported brutal treatment at the hands of police. Roughly two-thirds of these cases involved alleged third-degree methods that produced injuries ranging from black eyes to broken limbs.[35] While police most often relied on punching and kicking, they frequently resorted to the rubber hose and the blackjack—weapons that rarely left marks on the victim (blackjacks were reportedly soaked in water to reduce the likelihood of abrasions). Other more unusual methods of physical abuse included choking with a necktie, dragging by the hair, squeezing the testicles, and hanging a suspect out an upper-story window. The report also cited widespread use of "mental third degree tactics"—prolonged grilling, food and sleep deprivation, threats of physical violence, etc.

Some of the most chilling accounts combined physical and psychological torture. In one case reported by Emanuel Lavine, police assured a suspect they would not beat him, then hit him from behind with a club. When he came to, police sympathized with him and reassured him—only to have the same thing happen again and again until the suspect confessed. In another method, known as "Taps," a suspect was tied to a chair and beaten with a rubber hose every thirty seconds, causing both pain and fear. Such beatings could be quite severe. A former district attorney told the commission of one case in which a police surgeon was called into a third-degree session to monitor the victim's pulse and advise police as to whether he could stand more blows.[36]

The Wickersham investigators also provided a demographic profile of alleged victims. First, police used violent interrogation tactics almost exclusively on male suspects. Of 106 appellate cases across the nation involving the third degree in the 1920s, only 6 had female defendants—most of whom claimed psychological coercion, protracted grilling, or food and sleep deprivation. In New York, Emanuel Lavine claimed that the police rarely used the third degree against women, and when they did, it usually took the form of shouting, hair pulling, or spitting tobacco juice. All of the VDC's 166 third-degree cases in 1930 involved male suspects, more than three-quarters of whom were under the age of thirty.[37] The youthfulness of this sample is not surprising given that young men in their teens and twenties committed a large proportion of felony crime. The reluctance of police to apply the third degree to female suspects is more perplexing, since women accounted for a small but significant proportion of street brutality victims. Most likely, the violent treatment of female suspects already in custody would have violated police notions of manhood and professional respectability. More importantly, most juries would not have tolerated police abuse of women suspects, who did not fit gendered stereotypes of the "hardened criminal" deserving of such treatment.

The data on the class background of suspects is more problematic. Because the VDC represented indigent clients, the sample is obviously skewed toward the lower end of the economic spectrum. Thus it is not surprising that brutality complainants represented by the VDC uniformly ended their schooling on or before graduation from grammar school. The VDC sample, however, may not be atypical. Based on a wider range of sources, Emanuel Lavine, Ernest Hopkins, and the Wickersham Commission all argued that the third degree was used especially against "the poor and uninfluential." More affluent suspects were less likely to be detained by the police and were more likely to be in contact with an attorney shortly after arrest. Also immune were most gang members and organized crime figures that had both political friends and high-paid defense lawyers looking out for their interests. The same was true for Communists, union members, and other political dissidents, whose organizations kept tabs on their members that were taken into custody. Typical third-degree victims, then, were as Lavine put it, "the poor, the ignorant, and the friendless."[38]

The VDC data on race is particularly telling. Among VDC clients reporting third-degree abuse in 1930, 36 percent were African-American men. This figure far exceeds the black share of the city's population in that year, which was just below 5 percent. Clearly, African-American men—often poor, without influence, and at the mercy of an all-white detective force—were disproportionately subject to third-degree abuse. What is surprising is that no one at the time seemed to notice. Although Ernest Hopkins wrote eloquently about the discriminatory use of the third degree against immigrants and police terror against black suspects in the South, he failed to note the racial disparity in third-degree cases in New York and other northern cities.[39] The Wickersham report and other brutality exposés were likewise silent in this regard. The pervasive racism that inspired such abuses by police, it seems, also blinded white reformers to the obvious racial dimensions of the problem. In the absence of a powerful civil rights movement, these connections remained unexplored.

In defending the third degree, police insisted it was an important tool used only against hardened criminals. Most VDC clients reporting third-degree abuse were in fact charged with "felonies of medium importance," including robbery (48 percent), assault (45 percent), burglary (44 percent), and grand larceny (41 percent). There were only two cases of homicide, presumably manslaughter, since New York State law provided for paid counsel in all capital cases (in state appellate courts, however, several murder defendants claimed third-degree abuse during the 1920s). The conviction rate in the VDC felony cases was 70 percent, a very high figure that seemed to prove the "efficiency" of using third-degree methods. However, since some of these defendants confessed and pled guilty under physical duress, the validity of those pleas is questionable. Moreover, VDC data indicates that only 17 percent of defendants reporting third-degree treatment had prior felony convictions, and 45 percent had no prior record whatsoever. These figures are, as Ernest Hopkins wrote, "a staggering refutation to the usual claim that only hardened criminals are abused."[40]

Police in fact used the third degree against different types of subjects for different reasons. In most cases, police used violent tactics to elicit confessions from those whom they knew or had reason to believe were guilty. Such confessions not only implicated the suspect but could also provide other important information or material evidence, such as the identity of accomplices or the location of stolen property or abducted persons. In the context of early twentieth-century policing, these confessions and evidence were vital for successful prosecution. Because forensic science was still in its infancy and witnesses were often afraid to testify, police relied heavily on tips from informers. Since many of these tips were hearsay or made by informants who were unwilling to testify in court, police needed additional evidence to win convictions. Oftentimes, late in the day, they arrested individuals "on suspicion" (a vague charge of suspicious behavior) or brought them in for "voluntary" questioning. Since the City Magistrate's Court was closed until morning, detectives could hold suspects incommunicado and grill them for hours prior to arraignment. During this time, they might use whatever means necessary to elicit confessions or other incriminating information. On isolated occasions, police might subject reluctant witnesses to the same sort of treatment, particularly if they had prior criminal records.[41]

Two retired NYPD commanders confirmed the use of such methods in books published in the early 1930s. Michael Fiaschetti, the former head of the Italian squad and author of the book *You Gotta Be Rough* (1930), described cases in which he himself administered beatings and argued that the use of informers and the third degree was the best way to deal with organized crime. In his book, *Behind the Green Lights* (1931), a former police captain, Cornelius Willemse, argued that third-degree tactics were even more effective against "ordinary stick-up mobs." Informers usually tipped off the police about these small-time crooks, "and when you treat them rough they can't take the gaff. . . . Under the blackjack or the hose, they squeal loud and long." The concrete evidence and confessions that resulted, police argued, would hold up even in New York's highly politicized and often corrupt court system.[42]

In other third-degree cases, vengeance was a more important motive than procuring evidence. This was particularly true in cases where suspects were accused of killing police officers. Ernest Hopkins discussed several such incidents in his book, and Emanuel Lavine maintained that New York police regularly beat up suspects who had killed or wounded fellow officers. Newspapers refused to cover such incidents, he said, for fear of encouraging cop killers. In 1932, however, a particularly egregious case of revenge-motivated violence on Long Island made front-page headlines in the New York press. Hyman Stark, a suspect in a robbery and assault of an elderly woman, died of a fractured larynx and a cerebral hemorrhage following eight hours of police interrogation. As it turned out, one of the detectives who was left alone to question Stark was the son of the elderly victim. Stark's death provoked a public furor and was held up as an example of the third degree run amok. "Justice is not torture," fumed the *World-Telegram*. "Justice is not vengeance entrusted to police officers for the purpose of satisfying their desire of seeing a thug 'get what's coming to him' while they try to force a confession."[43]

Revenge beatings by police occurred in other circumstances as well. Suspects in heinous crimes, particularly those against children, were sometimes beaten as an act of police vigilance. In *You Gotta Be Rough,* Michael Fiaschetti described his involvement in beating up suspects in the Varotta kidnapping case of 1921. Following the abduction of a five-year-old boy, Fiaschetti and his squad apprehended the kidnappers as they picked up the ransom. The Varotta boy was later found dead, killed by an accomplice still at large. Unable to comfort the grieving parents, Fiaschetti "went down to the Tombs and got myself a sawed-off baseball bat. . . . I wasn't taking any chances of their beating the case." Emanuel Lavine described a different type of revenge beating in his book. In an early 1920s case, a detective brutalized a suspect as punishment for "squealing" in court about an earlier third-degree beating he had received.[44] Finally, in cases where police "haven't got the goods to put these boys away," Michael Fiaschetti explained, officers "will give it to them just as punishment."

According to the Wickersham Commission, police detectives in local station houses were responsible for most of the third-degree beatings in New York. As a rule, the arresting detective did not administer the beating so that he could later testify in court that he did not use force. Police typically attributed obvious physical injuries or hospitalization to accidents, claiming the suspect fell down the stairs, rolled out of his bunk, or was beaten by his cellmates (who might be induced to corroborate the story). Police supervisors sustained these flimsy explanations and occasionally sanctioned or participated in the beatings. One case, involving a suspect accused of murdering a Tombs prison warden in 1927, reportedly occurred in the basement of police headquarters. According to Emanuel Lavine, the police commissioner himself had been present on several occasions to hear the screams of interrogation victims. Some district attorneys and judges were also implicated. In his book, Cornelius Willemse described how detectives induced prosecutors to leave the room so police could strong arm their suspects. Retired judges and attorneys interviewed by the Wickersham Commission admitted that some prosecutors and magistrates "winked at the practice" or would "make allowance if they know the arresting officer concerned is a person of discretion and the crime warrants it."[45]

When on the record, however, standing police officials and district attorneys vehemently denied the existence of the third degree. Following the release of the Wickersham report in August 1931, Commissioner Mulrooney and the district attorneys of all five boroughs released a statement denying that the NYPD used violent third-degree tactics. Mulrooney admitted that detectives sometimes interrogated felony suspects for prolonged periods, but defended the practice as a useful crime-fighting tool. Noting that no reports of third-degree violence had been filed with their offices, the five prosecutors said that unscrupulous defense lawyers encouraged their clients to make such allegations in hopes of winning acquittals. As in the past, most police and other city officials dismissed criticism of excessive force and charged the critics themselves with aiding and abetting criminals.

While police officially denied charges of third-degree abuse, they warned strongly against any efforts to curb the use of force against criminal suspects. Retired New York police interviewed by the Wickersham Commission referred ominously to the Gaynor years, claiming that the mayor's anticlubbing policies had emboldened gangsters and set off a major crime wave. In the current climate of

Prohibition and gang warfare, they argued, police needed every means available to contain criminals, who were now better organized, better financed, and better able to manipulate the city's corrupt criminal justice system. The so-called "war on crime" thus became the civilian equivalent of martial law, in which police needed emergency powers to combat emergency conditions. To illustrate this point, Manhattan district attorney Thomas F. Kane referred to a pending case in which police allegedly used third-degree methods against a witness in a gangland shooting in Harlem. The witness, a rival gang member and the target of the gunmen, survived the assault, but four young children were injured in the fray, one fatally. Kane defended the rough treatment of the witness, saying, "What are we to do—give our baby killers ice cream?" In this case and others, police maintained, they used violent tactics only against hardened criminals and in cases where such measures were absolutely essential. Attempts to limit the use of force would invite civil lawsuits, make police reluctant to take on criminals, and irreparably damage the department's efficiency and morale.[46]

The Wickersham Commission and other brutality opponents rejected these views, arguing that the third degree was a poor crimefighting tactic that actually encouraged lawlessness. Ernest Hopkins and Harry Elmer Barnes, a Columbia University history professor and ACLU board member, argued that the "war theory of crime" was a poor justification for the third degree since it did little to stop organized crime. Big-time gangsters were never subjected to the third degree; it was reserved for "the little fellows . . . the scum and bums of the underworld," said Barnes. Police violence against petty criminals was thus not a useful crime deterrent. Rather, it inspired vengeance and could turn "a boy bandit into a gunman and a 'cop killer.'" Citing the case of Luther Boddy, reformers described how a nineteen-year-old bootblack in Harlem had been repeatedly harassed and beaten by local police. When Boddy was arrested in January 1922 on suspicion of killing a police officer, he reportedly became so fearful of the beating he would get that he pulled a gun on the steps of the station house and shot and killed the two arresting detectives. In this case and others, reformers argued, police violence helped create the hardened criminals it was supposed to suppress. This police lawlessness, Hopkins said, was particularly detrimental to the immigrant poor who were likely to lose respect for American law. "Men will respect the law only when law is respectable," explained commission chair George Wickersham. "The method of administering justice is often more important than justice itself."[47]

Most importantly, reformers also argued that the third degree fostered public distrust of police, thus undercutting the effectiveness of the criminal justice system. Third-degree violence and the police perjury that accompanied it undermined the department's credibility with the public. Defense lawyers exploited that distrust, allowing guilty felons to be acquitted or convicted of lesser charges than they deserved. "The result," said Emanuel Lavine, "is that the reputation the police have won militates against their own efforts." Public distrust of the police also made potential witnesses afraid to cooperate with them. The police in turn become frustrated and resort to still more violence. "So lawlessness begets more lawlessness, and the situation shows a vicious circle," Hopkins explained.[48]

Finally, reformers insisted that police reliance on the informer system and the third degree resulted in poor investigative work. Informers—often criminals themselves—were not always credible sources. They sometimes passed along false rumors or, acting out of revenge or jealousy, might deliberately frame a competitor. Thereafter, police often did not bother investigating those individuals named by informers but simply pounded them into making a confession. This lazy approach, reformers argued, undercut the search for physical evidence and discouraged the development of good detective work. The infamous Leopold and Loeb case in Chicago was a case in point. Following the abduction of young Bobby Franks in May 1924, Chicago police arrested a local schoolteacher and beat him until he falsely confessed. While doing so, they overlooked important physical evidence that later implicated Nathan Leopold in the crime. In this case and others, reformers claimed, police relied on the third degree to the detriment of good scientific methods of investigation.[49]

Reformers frequently held up Chicago as an example of the debilitating effects of police lawlessness. Chicago police were infamous for their third-degree tactics, yet the gangland violence directed by Al Capone and other underworld figures had only escalated. Some of this violence was directed against police. In 1930 alone, thirteen Chicago police were murdered and several others captured and beaten—some in retaliation for police beatings of friends or fellow gang members. Rumors circulated that officers should be more cautious in using the third degree, and incidents of it seem to have diminished thereafter. The moral, however, was clear: Third-degree violence had not solved Chicago's crime problem but had in fact aggravated it.[50]

By contrast, reformers cited Boston, Philadelphia, and Cincinnati as proof that policing could be effective and efficient without resorting to the third degree. These three departments, run by reform-minded police chiefs, had virtually eliminated the third degree in favor of prearrest investigation and evidence collection, prompt interrogation, and clever questioning techniques. The superiority of these practices was evident in Philadelphia, where police had gone from being one of the worst third-degree offenders to among the best. The department's efficiency as a crime-fighting unit had not suffered, Ernest Hopkins claimed, but had noticeably improved.[51]

Remedies

Drawing on the examples of Boston, Philadelphia, and Cincinnati, reformers urged police officials to eliminate unlawful arrest and detention practices that facilitated the third degree. Mass roundups and ill-defined arrests "on suspicion" enabled police to detain and interrogate suspects in what Ernest Hopkins called a "pre-trial inquisition." Long detentions, in which the prisoner was held incommunicado, likewise provided police with prime opportunities for prolonged grilling and abuse. To eliminate this practice, reformers called for immediate arraignment before a magistrate, at which point suspects could make voluntary confessions if they so desired. Thereafter prisoners would be turned over to county (or other) penal authorities that would detain them in separate facilities where they would be less vulnerable to police abuse. During interrogations, an official stenographer should record all proceedings, including confessions. Throughout the arrest, arraignment, and detention process, reformers argued, police and penal authorities should keep timed and dated records of the location and physical condition of all prisoners. Such measures would reduce opportunities for the third degree and would build accountability into the system if abuse did occur.[52]

Reformers also called for judicial reforms to eliminate the third degree. Most importantly, judges should condemn illegal police practices in no uncertain terms. Questionable arrests or detentions should not be tolerated, and coerced confessions should be excluded as evidence—as they were under federal rules of evidence. Fifteen states had laws requiring their courts to follow the federal rule barring the introduction of evidence that was unlawfully obtained, but most, including New York, did not. Under Section 395 of the New York Code of Criminal Procedure, juries could decide on the validity of confessions unless those confessions were "made under the influence of fear produced by threats." It was, however, up to the defense to prove—against the denials of police—that such confessions were indeed coerced. In the overwhelming majority of cases, then, confessions induced by third-degree methods were admissible (even if the defendant recanted), and juries based their decisions on the likely truthfulness of the defendant's initial statement along with other corroborating evidence. The validity of confession evidence, not the suspect's right against self-incrimination, was the guiding principle. Appalled by this violation of due process and the license it granted police to use third-degree methods, reformers urged states to adopt the federal rule and called on jurists to be more aggressive in suppressing coerced confessions.[53]

Third-degree opponents also put forth other legal remedies. To protect the rights of the accused, Ernest Hopkins proposed extending the nascent public defender system to all criminal suspects, while the ACLU insisted that all suspects be informed of their right to silence and their right to consult an attorney (as the Miranda decision affirmed many years later). Finally, the ACLU called for third-degree victims to file civil and criminal lawsuits against offending police. Although many alleged victims did appeal to the ACLU in the early 1930s, it found these cases difficult to prove. As of 1935, none of the ACLU cases had resulted in the recovery of damages or the prosecution of police officers. Nevertheless, the ACLU maintained that the threat of such suits and the bad publicity accompanying them had "a restraining effect on police departments."[54]

The time and difficulty involved in pursuing those cases prompted the ACLU to propose a new organizational mechanism for monitoring police practices. In 1932, ACLU staff members discussed the establishment of a third-degree complaint bureau in New York consisting of distinguished attorneys and penologists that would investigate cases, file disciplinary complaints against police, and conduct a larger probe of police practices. Acting as a watchdog agency, the bureau would be independent and nonpartisan and would *not* act as attorney for those who lodged complaints. It was, in effect, an early version of what would eventually become a civilian review board. At the time, however, there was little public support or funding available for such a proposal, but it did plant the seeds for later police monitoring activities by the ACLU.[55]

Finally, the ACLU and other reformers called for the passage of anti-third-degree legislation by the states. Because the criminal justice system was slow to respond to reform initiatives, they proposed legislation mandating such practices as immediate arraignment, separate detention facilities, official record keeping of prisoners' whereabouts and condition, and the right of suspects to consult legal counsel. Reformers also proposed more punitive measures including the imposition of fines and/or imprisonment for police convicted of third-degree abuses and the exclusion of confession evidence obtained through such methods. Reformers recognized that legislation was no panacea—use of the third degree had continued in states that had such laws—but it did officially discourage such practices and made it easier to prosecute offending police.[56] In 1936 the ACLU crafted a statute that became a model for anti-third-degree bills introduced in the New York State legislature at least four times between 1936 and 1940. The bill provided for the immediate arraignment of all suspects, detention in facilities controlled by the state Department of Corrections, and written records documenting the condition and whereabouts of all prisoners. After an initial defeat in 1936, the bill was reintroduced the following April and became the subject of a heated and emotional debate.

Sponsored by Democratic Assemblyman Ira Holley of Manhattan, the bill was supported by the ACLU and other legal and penal reform groups. The NYPD, however, vigorously opposed the bill, claiming it would tie the hands of police officers while giving more power to criminals. Mayor Fiorello La Guardia, who had won praise from the ACLU for ordering an end to police beatings of Communists and other street demonstrators, sided with police against the Holley bill. To dramatize his concern about crime, the mayor denounced the bill as he departed the funeral of a police detective who had been shot and killed in a gun battle with two robbery suspects. Arguing that the Holley bill would cripple police in their battle against gangsters, La Guardia called it "a Magna Carta for the punks, pimps, crooks, gangsters, racketeers and the shyster lawyers in the magistrates courts." The bill's supporters in the legislature in turn accused the mayor of "grandstanding" to police and "electioneering at the casket of a slain policeman." At the same time, however, they too appealed to public outrage by invoking the Veronica Gedeon case, a 1937 murder investigation in which the victim's aggrieved father was falsely accused and beaten by police during interrogation. But these impassioned appeals were not enough; the bill passed the assembly but was killed in the senate a few days later.[57] Amended versions of the bill were introduced again in 1938 and 1939, but they too were defeated.[58]

The continuing threat of such legislation, however, was a powerful incentive for administrative reform within police circles. At a 1938 meeting of the New York State Police Chiefs Association, Federal Bureau of Investigation (FBI) inspector W. H. Drane Lester urged local chiefs to take every action necessary to eliminate the third degree in their jurisdictions. By doing so, Lester maintained, they would make unnecessary the odious anti-third-degree legislation pending in the legislature. Ultimately, the Wickersham report strengthened the position of reform-minded police chiefs and reinforced trends toward police professionalism. As head of the newly invigorated FBI, J. Edgar Hoover denounced brutal third-degree methods in favor of scientific investigation and interrogation, and

FBI agents did their best to disseminate this message to local law enforcement. In a 1936 issue of the FBI journal, *The Investigator,* Special Agent E. J. Chayfitz called the third degree a "barbarity" that "constitutes an admission of failure." The FBI's National Police Academy, founded in 1934, also discouraged brutal practices and promoted police professionalism to its own agents and selected local officers. Police training manuals reflected this new approach. One of the most popular works, W. R. Kidd's *Police Interrogation,* published in 1940, strongly discouraged third-degree methods and urged police to use their wits instead of their fists. Prescribing a variety of emotional appeals, bluffs, and other interrogation tricks, Kidd assured police that such refined methods would not endanger their masculinity. "Shunning the third degree does not make us sissies. It takes more guts to control yourself and fight it out brain to brain than it does to slug it out," said Kidd. "If you resort to torture, you admit your victim is the better man." Couched in the language of male pride and police professionalism, such appeals were probably effective inducements to change.[59]

One indication of changing police attitudes was the reaction to Commissioner Lewis Valentine's 1934 order to "muss up the gangsters." While earlier calls to rough up the criminal element had generally been well received, Valentine's order provoked a storm of criticism from police officials and prosecutors around the country. Querying law enforcement experts in several U.S. cities, the *New York Times* found at least six who disagreed with Valentine's statements. Such an approach, they argued, could lead to abuse, indiscriminate brutality, and the acquittal of criminal defendants who bore the marks of such treatment. The ACLU, which led the protest against Valentine's order, now had support from within the ranks of police professionals.[60]

Pressure from the federal judiciary also helped to reduce violent police interrogation tactics. Although federal courts had followed the common law rule on the admissibility of confessions (requiring that they be free and voluntary) since 1884, they had made no effort to extend this rule to the states. In the landmark *Brown* v. *Mississippi* case in 1936, however, the Supreme Court excluded the confessions of three black murder suspects who had been tortured by Mississippi police. In a horrific case of racist southern justice, police openly admitted whipping the defendants and stringing up one of them on a lynch rope to force a confession. Shocked by this brutal treatment, the justices were even more outraged that the Mississippi high court had condoned such police torture. In ruling the confessions inadmissible, the court extended the common law rule to state and local cases under the due process clause of the Fourteenth Amendment. In the 1940s, the Supreme Court expanded this precedent to cases involving prolonged police grilling and psychological coercion as well.[61]

The Brown decision was a clear deterrent to the overt use of violent third-degree methods and helped transform police interrogation practices. During the 1940s and 1950s, most interrogation cases coming before federal and state appellate courts involved psychological rather than physical coercion. Moreover, those cases involving allegations of physical abuse were rarely as clear-cut as Brown and usually involved a "swearing contest" between defendants who claimed abuse and police who denied it. In New York, the state's Code of Criminal Procedure still required that such disputed confessions be admitted in evidence to a jury. The prejudicial nature of this procedure, however, came under increasing criticism in the 1950s and was finally rejected by the Supreme Court in 1964. In *Jackson* v. *Denno,* the court ruled that the New York procedure "did not afford a reliable determination of the voluntariness of the confession" and thus found it a violation of due process. In response, the New York Court of Appeals stipulated a new procedure the following year in *People* v. *Huntley,* requiring a pretrial hearing on disputed confessions. "The Judge must find voluntariness beyond a reasonable doubt before the confession can be submitted to the trial jury," the court ruled. "The burden of proof as to voluntariness *is on the People*" (emphasis mine).[62] The ruling thus encouraged New York police and prosecutors to develop systematic procedures and safeguards to prevent violence and ensure "clean" admissible confessions.

The Supreme Court also continued to expand due process protections with its watershed *Miranda* v. *Arizona* decision in 1966. To ensure Fifth Amendment protection against self-incrimination, the court required police to advise suspects of their right to remain silent, that any statements may be used as evidence against them, and that they have a right to have an attorney present during questioning. As legal scholars have pointed out, *Miranda* has not been a foolproof solution; defendants who waive their rights continue to fall victim to psychological and even physical abuse at the hands of police. But most legal experts agree that the violent third degree is now relatively rare. As police interrogation policy increasingly discouraged physical intimidation, psychological coercion and trickery have become the more crucial problems. Although allegations of third-degree violence by the NYPD (particularly against African Americans) would periodically surface over the next several decades, most cases of physical abuse occurring in police station houses would generally be administered as punishment rather than as a means for procuring confessions.

In retrospect, the 1930s campaign against the third degree was largely successful. Significantly, this campaign occurred in a context of widespread criminality and corruption. Prohibition-era bootlegging and organized crime fueled police graft as well as aggressive anticrime measures. As in the Lexow investigation of the 1890s, attacks on corruption and brutality reinforced one another, damaging the credibility of the department and opening the door to complaints of police misconduct of all types. Although antibrutality reformers were unsuccessful in pressuring police to abandon dragnets, roundups, strong-arm squads, and other repressive tactics, they effectively curtailed the third degree through pragmatic arguments about public distrust of police, skeptical juries, and increasing acquittal rates. This approach, together with growing pressure from the federal judiciary, strengthened the hand of reform-minded police professionals and prosecutors who discouraged violent interrogation practices as counterproductive to effective law enforcement. The same type of pragmatic reasoning would be used to combat another form of police brutality in the 1930s—the violent repression of Communists and labor radicals who took to the streets by the thousands during the Great Depression.

5. POLICE, LABOR, AND RADICALS IN THE GREAT DEPRESSION

In the realm of mass action policing, the early 1930s stand as the bloodiest era in the city's history. Battered by the economic hardships of the Great Depression, a growing number of communists, labor radicals, and unemployed New Yorkers took to the streets to vent their grievances and encountered violent repression at the hands of police. This rough treatment was consistent with the department's long-standing tradition of strikebreaking and antiradicalism. But it would also prove to be a watershed in NYPD history, as reform-minded city leaders decided that tolerance and restraint were a more appropriate and effective means of maintaining public order in a new political climate. The transition from the old-style mass policing to the new, however, was filled with obstacles and would take nearly a decade to complete.

As we saw in earlier chapters, police repression of labor and radicalism has a long history in New York. Beginning in the 1870s, the NYPD aligned itself with the city's employers and business interests in suppressing strikes and breaking up political meetings and protests. This violent, repressive approach later gave way to a more tolerant attitude under Progressive mayors William Gaynor and John Purroy Mitchel in the 1910s. During World War I, however, police repression escalated as the NYPD once again began requiring permits, suppressing radical meetings, and spying on dissident groups. Although there was little direct violence, police used the newly formed Bomb Squad to infiltrate radical groups and sometimes stood by as patriotic vigilantes attacked left-wing or antiwar speakers. This growing popular reaction during the war ultimately fueled official repression on a larger scale in the postwar era.[1] The Russian Revolution of 1917 intensified political passions on all sides. As Socialists and other left-wing activists expressed enthusiasm for the new Soviet experiment, both federal and local authorities grew apprehensive. In 1918 Mayor John Hylan ordered a ban on displaying red flags and instructed police to suppress any political meeting that threatened disorder or promoted hostility toward the government. Following a series of bombings around the country in the spring of 1919, the Bomb Squad used Hylan's order to justify raiding the offices of radical groups and disbanding their meetings, sometimes with violence.[2]

Allegations of violent beatings surfaced that fall in connection with a series of raids by the Bomb Squad. The National Civil Liberties Bureau (forerunner of the ACLU) collected affidavits from ten witnesses who claimed they were violently interrogated or beaten when police swept the offices of two radical organizations. During a raid on the Textile Workers Industrial Union on November 7, police allegedly beat four occupants with blackjacks, leaving two of them unconscious. Ten days later the Bomb Squad raided the Manhattan office of the Industrial Workers of the World. After searching the occupants, police ordered them to leave by a side door, outside of which two lines of officers flailed them with blackjacks, table legs, and baseball bats. According to at least eight witnesses, police forced them to run the gauntlet, and several sustained injuries requiring hospitalization. The use of the gauntlet ritual—like the one used on black men during the San Juan Hill riot of 1905—suggests that police had developed a visceral dislike of radicals and were engaging in some patriotic vigilance activity of their own. No one on the Bomb Squad was ever disciplined for these abuses.[3]

Police repression of political dissidents continued in the early 1920s but gradually abated as the Red Scare effectively decimated the left. Except for a 1927 Sacco and Vanzetti protest, in which police used clubs to disperse a peaceful crowd at city hall, there were no major incidents of official antiradical violence between 1922 and 1928. At the same time, however, the NYPD became increasingly repressive toward organized labor. The first sign of changing police policy came in March 1919, when eighteen striking members of the Dress and Waistmakers Union filed brutality complaints against police who had broken up the women's picket line. Although the department found no grounds for disciplinary action, a growing chorus of labor complaints in the 1920s suggests that police were taking a more aggressive antilabor stance.[4]

The rise of a strong probusiness climate set the stage for this new policy. With the weakening of organized labor following a wave of unsuccessful strikes in 1919, employers launched the open shop drive in an attempt to roll back labor gains made during the war. Increasingly, employers won antipicketing injunctions and demanded police protection of their premises and personnel. In the New York needle trades, employers became especially vigilant as Communist organizers began their policy of "boring from within" established unions. Responding to these developments, the NYPD deployed the Industrial Squad, a plainclothes unit established during World War I to suppress violence and sabotage during strikes. Reorganized in 1926, the Industrial Squad was combined with the Gangster Squad and retooled to deal with the growing influence of organized crime and racketeering in labor disputes. The unit was headed by the legendary tough cop, John J. Broderick, who like Clubber Williams before him, grew up on the rough-and-tumble streets of the Gas House District and was known for his physical prowess. A former bodyguard for American Federation of Labor (AFL) president Samuel Gompers, Broderick had little patience with labor militants and led the Industrial Squad in a series of violent melees with the Communist-led Fur Workers and the insurgent Consolidated Railway Workers during strikes in 1926–27.

Police violence, however, was also directed at more conservative unions. In 1921 and again in 1925, the AFL Teamsters charged police strong-arm squads with beating striking drivers and conducting "guerilla warfare" against labor. In December 1926, the ACLU and the Women's Trade Union League appealed to the mayor on behalf of striking paper-box makers and charged police with brutality against fourteen male and female pickets. The NYPD, however, consistently dismissed such complaints, arguing that strikers had perpetrated violence, violated antipicketing injunctions, or were unable to identify the officers who beat them. Anti-Tammany reformers disagreed. As Fusion candidate for mayor in 1929, Fiorello La Guardia accused the Industrial Squad of extorting payoffs from both labor and employers and claimed that "Instead of preserving order, this agency has done more to create disorder than anything else."[5]

Police hostility and violence toward labor and the left clearly escalated in the post–World War I era. The use of the NYPD as a strike-breaking force in the 1920s created tensions that would explode during the Great Depression, making the years 1929–1934 a time of unprecedented violence and repression.

Blood in the Streets

Several factors converged in the late 1920s to produce a highly volatile political and social climate in New York City. First, the Communist party (CP) entered a new militant and combative phase known as the Third Period. Beginning in 1928, the CP proclaimed a new ultrarevolutionary stance that included militant street demonstrations, dual unionism, interracial organizing, and vigorous denunciations of the Socialist party and other left-wing rivals. Although such tactics and rhetoric had little popular appeal, the onset of the Depression made the CP's revolutionary approach seem more compelling. As the economic crisis deepened, the party's vigorous and uncompromising organizing efforts on behalf of labor and the unemployed attracted a growing number of sympathizers. Hoping to placate alarmed business owners, city leaders adopted a repressive approach toward Communist and labor protests and charged police with maintaining order—by force if necessary. A string of Tammany police commissioners (four served over a six-year period between 1929 and 1934) futilely battled radicals on the streets, creating a mutual and self-perpetuating cycle of violence and hostility.

The individual who bore much of the responsibility for this strife was Police Commissioner Grover A. Whalen (1929–30). A former contractor and businessman, Whalen had close ties to the Hylan administration, serving as the mayor's personal secretary and later as commissioner of the Department of Plant and Structures. In 1925 he returned to the private sector to work as chief of security at Wanamaker's department store. Impressed with his performance at Wan-

152

amaker's and the strong support Whalen enjoyed in the city's business community, Mayor James Walker tapped him for the police commissioner's post in 1929. Once in office, Whalen pleased his political and business sponsors by reinvigorating the Radical Squad (the former Bomb Squad) and launching a concerted offensive against the "red menace."[6]

Whalen's antiradical crusade began in early 1929 in response to the CP's new union organizing drives. Rejecting AFL leadership, the new Communist-led affiliates of the Trade Union Unity League established separate industrial unions and launched strikes among workers in the needle trades and food service industry. In February, following the arrest of some thirteen hundred striking dressmakers, two hundred members of the Needle Trades Workers Industrial Union staged a protest at city hall charging police with strikebreaking and brutality toward peaceful pickets. Filing their protest with Mayor Walker, the predominantly Jewish needle trades workers denounced police terror by "Tammany Cossacks," thus combining traditional ethnic appeals against anti-Semitism with Progressive anti–political machine slogans.

Similar rhetoric characterized another antibrutality outcry in May protesting police beatings of striking cafeteria workers with the Communist-led Amalgamated Food Workers Union. Angered over police clubbings of two pickets outside a midtown cafeteria and the shooting of a truckman who violated an antipicketing injunction, fifteen hundred union supporters rallied in Union Square on May 11 to denounce police violence against labor. A week later, during the city's annual police parade up Broadway, Communists unfurled a forty-foot long banner reading "Down with Walker's Police Brutality" outside CP headquarters in Union Square. Given the reverential tone of the police procession, it was a provocative action. Not surprisingly, officers began to tear down the banner, saying the party had no permit to display such a sign. They were blocked, however, by a group of Communist youth singing the *Internationale* and carrying placards reading "Down with Mayor Walker's Cossacks." A street brawl ensued in which police were pelted with "missiles" and twenty-seven Communists were arrested and one injured.[7]

The Union Square fracas marked the beginning of a mutually reinforcing pattern of hostility and violence, setting the tone for police-Communist relations for the next several years. Instead of cautiously tolerating radical protests and theatrics (as police often do today), Whalen's repressive tactics angered strikers and demonstrators and served to escalate the level of violence. And police brutality, the CP soon discovered, was a resonant issue for many working-class New Yorkers—one that could be deployed on behalf of the revolution. Although the party increasingly relied on police brutality as an organizing issue, it steadfastly refused to file official complaints or seek disciplinary action against abusive officers. During the cafeteria workers strike, for example, the ACLU filed a brutality complaint on behalf of Albert Rescigne, one of the pickets severely beaten by police. Much to the ACLU's surprise, Rescigne failed to appear at the departmental hearing on the advice of a lawyer with the International Labor Defense (ILD), a legal organization affiliated with the Communist party. Insisting there could be no justice for workers in capitalist courts (a not unreasonable claim given the history of antibrutality efforts), the party preferred mass protests in which brutality was used to heighten outrage over capitalist oppression of labor and the city's corrupt probusiness rule. Only a Soviet-style workers' state, the CP maintained, could eliminate police brutality.[8]

Communist organizers soon discovered that police brutality was an even more explosive issue in the African-American community. Following a new party mandate to organize black workers, the CP launched a municipal elections campaign in the summer of 1929 in which black and white Communist candidates addressed a series of Harlem street meetings. Predictably, the NYPD broke up the "unauthorized" meetings—sometimes with violence. This ongoing conflict culminated in a violent melee at a meeting on September 15 when police arrested thirteen people, firing several shots and leaving several people injured. The violent attacks on Communist speakers and their scathing denunciations of police brutality against the black community raised the CP's profile and credibility in Harlem. In fact, in the wake of the September 15 violence, black attendance at Communist street meetings grew, with crowds of a thousand or more turning out to boo and hiss at police. Although Communists interpreted police violence as a class issue rather than a racial one, the party's recognition of the problem and its more general embrace of black leaders and issues attracted new African-American members.[9]

Liberal commentators pointed out the irony of the situation—that a police policy designed to eradicate the Communist party was helping to strengthen it. In his column in the *New York Telegram* Socialist leader Heywood Broun argued that "idiotic reactionaries" like Grover Whalen—not Communists—were the real threat to capitalism. "It is this kind of misguided zeal which overturned the governments of France and Germany and Russia," the *Telegram* editorialized. Like those who criticized the third degree as counterproductive, liberal critics of anti-Communist police violence made their case on pragmatic grounds, arguing that more tolerant police practices would undercut the party's appeal and strengthen the democratic capitalist system. Whalen and the NYPD, though, ignored such advice and continued to suppress Communist-led meetings that winter.[10]

CP organizing around police brutality intensified in January 1930 in response to the death of Steve Katovis, a worker shot by police during a Food Clerks Union strike. The shooting occurred as Katovis and other union members were leaving a Communist strike support meeting in the Bronx. When police ordered the lingering crowd to disperse, a scuffle broke out and one of the union men struck an officer and grabbed his nightstick. The officer drew his gun and fired two shots, hitting Katovis in the back. Charged with felonious assault, Katovis died a few days later in the prison ward at Lincoln Hospital. As the CP began organizing protests against the shooting, the NYPD attempted to ban its meetings by withholding permits and closing down halls. Meeting privately, the party defied police orders and organized a midday protest at city hall on Saturday, January 25.[11]

The Katovis protest proved the most violent clash yet between police and Communists, putting Whalen's tactics on display before thousands of homebound office workers. Even before the protesters arrived, more than a hundred patrolmen and twenty-five mounted police were installed around City Hall Park, and by 12:30 P.M., some three hundred to four hundred Communist protesters had gathered in front of the building. As the first CP speaker ascended the steps and began to address the crowd, police officers moved in and began dispersing the crowd with fists, clubs, and blackjacks. The protesters scattered in all directions, pursued by mounted police who chased them out of the park. Some of the Communists fought back against police and reassembled in smaller groups on surrounding streets. As officers moved to break up these clusters, they also pummeled a number of onlookers, including some of the office workers who were leaving nearby buildings. All told, five protesters were arrested for disorderly conduct, and at least twelve people were hurt. Among the injured were six Communists, four police officers, a Brooklyn businessman, and a *New York World* reporter.[12]

In the wake of the city hall incident, public reaction to police behavior grew increasingly negative. The more liberal New York dailies, though hardly sympathetic to the Communist party, denounced Whalen's repressive approach and demanded a formal investigation. Both the *Telegram* and the *World* criticized the Communists' ideology and provocative tactics but blamed the police for playing right into their hands. In an editorial titled "Silly and Brutal," the *Telegram* condemned police repression of free speech, saying they "did exactly what the communists wanted them to do, namely, give them a righteous sense of martyrdom." The *World* agreed, arguing that brutal police tactics "disgraced the city" and gave radicals "an opportunity to associate the police with the Cossacks and their hateful methods."[13]

For its part, the ACLU sent letters of protest to the mayor and police commissioner defending the CP's right to free speech. The group also offered its legal services to Communist victims of police violence, an offer that was flatly rejected. As in earlier cases, the party refused to participate in capitalist legal or administrative proceedings and branded ACLU director Roger Baldwin "a sanctimonious petty-bourgeois liberal" who served as "an agent of the police." The party leadership was equally vitriolic toward rival Socialist party leader Norman Thomas, who also sent a protest telegram to Mayor Walker. Hurling the familiar Communist epithet "social fascist," the CP repudiated any cooperation with "right-wing Socialists" or "petit-bourgeois liberals."[14]

To many of the party's critics, the CP appeared to be uninterested in seeking justice for brutality victims or ending police repression. The party, however, had a larger revolutionary agenda and saw antibrutality agitation as a useful organizing tool. Because police violence was a powerful issue that tapped a deep vein of working-class resentment, the CP won new adherents by organizing around it. High-profile violence against Communists served to vilify capitalist police and government and could help build sympathy for the Communist cause. For these reasons, the CP spurned reformist solutions—which it saw as short-sighted remedies that merely propped up the capitalist system—and sought to martyr fallen comrades like Steve Katovis. Shortly after the city hall protest, in fact, the party constructed an elaborate shrine at CP headquarters where Katovis's body was laid in state under a portrait of Lenin and a banner admonishing workers to "Answer the Murder of Steve Katovis by Police." Hundreds of workers came to pay their respects and march in a mass funeral procession, and the Bronx section of the party was renamed the Katovis branch in his honor. Party members, however, played no role in legal or disciplinary proceedings against the officer who shot Katovis. Confirming the CP's cynicism with the legal system, the coroner's jury exonerated the officer on grounds of self-defense, and a Bronx grand jury even commended him for his bravery under attack.[15]

In addition to vilifying capitalist police, the party was also busy fusing the brutality issue to what was the most pressing concern of most Americans in 1930: unemployment. Beginning in February 1930, the CP and the Trade Union Unity League staged a number of small demonstrations at city hall protesting unemployment, all of which were dispersed by police. These events, however, were merely preparing the ground for a much larger, nationwide protest against unemployment slated for March 6—including a mass meeting in New York's Union Square.

On the morning of the demonstration, police arrived in Union Square with two riot squad trucks armed with tear-gas bombs, machine guns, and sawed-off shotguns. Over the next few hours, the

NYPD deployed more than a thousand officers to the scene under the command of Commissioner Whalen, who was overseeing operations from a temporary command post in the Union Square Garden House. By noon, somewhere between thirty-five thousand and sixty thousand people had gathered to view the event, which lasted for several hours.

The meeting proceeded peacefully until the very end. At that point, Communist leader William Z. Foster announced that the NYPD had refused a permit for a planned march by the unemployed to city hall and urged the crowd to defy the ban. As loyal party cadres began moving toward Broadway singing the *Internationale,* Whalen ordered police into action. Descending on the square from all sides, hundreds of police waded into the crowd using horses, fists, clubs, and fire hoses to clear the area. Protesters who attempted to march were forcibly repelled, and some engaged in pitched battle with police. In the confusion, the officers did not discriminate between marchers and onlookers. As the ACLU later described it, police made "a general attack on anybody in the square. . . . Scores of persons were injured; some were pursued and beaten up by frenzied officers." When the riot was over, thirteen protesters had been arrested, twelve people were seriously injured, and more than a hundred sustained minor injuries.[16]

Police actions in the aftermath of the demonstration were equally harsh. The CP speakers at Union Square were later arrested on charges of inciting to riot. When a magistrate released them on bail, police rearrested them for felonious assault—an obviously trumped up charge—and held them incommunicado under prohibitively high bail. Perhaps most tellingly, Commissioner Whalen personally appealed to film companies and theater chains to suppress a controversial newsreel showing NYPD officers brutally beating demonstrators in Union Square. In the most shocking scene, one officer was shown holding down a youth while another beat him repeatedly with his nightstick. As in the 1991 Rodney King case, a newly available film medium lent extraordinary power and legitimacy to familiar claims of police brutality.[17]

The public reacted to the events of March 6 with both shock and confusion. Most of the New York press, including the more liberal dailies, condemned the CP's provocative behavior and attacked CP leaders as "cowardly" and "irresponsible." The same newspapers, however, were also critical of police behavior. Both the *Telegram* and the *Herald-Tribune* censured those police officers that behaved like "bloodthirsty lunatics" and demanded that they be brought up on disciplinary charges. Most press accounts, then, sought to distinguish Whalen's leadership in this incident from the reckless behavior of individual cops whose patience had been worn thin by months of confrontation with overzealous Communists. A few papers even offered outright praise for Whalen's leadership, and the Kings County Grand Jurors' Association commended him for "the brave, patriotic, and businesslike way in which you promptly halted the Communists."[18]

Sensing that the tide of public opinion was turning, Whalen stepped up his attacks on the Communists. On March 8, he delivered a public address, boasting of his recent victory in Union Square and describing the behind-the-scenes activities of the Radical Squad. Police operatives, he explained, had thoroughly infiltrated the local Communist party. They knew who the members were, how many there were, and what demonstrations and other activities they were planning. Undercover officers had been among the honor guard protecting Steve Katovis's casket, Whalen said, and had been enthusiastic participants at the March 6 protest:

I thought I would crack my sides laughing at some of the undercover men who figured in the Union Square demonstration last Thursday . . . They carried placards and banners demanding the overthrow of the government and made as much noise as the genuine Reds. But the fun started when one of the undercover men started to razz a cop. He got a terrific punch in the eye and was knocked down before the cop was pulled off.

Whalen's frank comments on the role of police as agent provocateurs were followed by an even more shocking revelation. The Radical Squad, he announced, had a detailed card file on more than ninety-seven hundred Communists in New York City and had turned some of this information over to local corporations, government departments, and schools that were being "infiltrated" by the party. With the encouragement of the New York Chamber of Commerce,

Whalen then met with corporate and city leaders who vowed to fire the alleged Communists in their employ.[19]

The commissioner's revelations of espionage and blacklisting put an end to his brief moment in the sun. Liberals and radicals alike joined in attacking Whalen's anti-Communist crusade and wholesale violations of civil liberties. On March 11, eighteen professors at Columbia University Law School sent an open letter to Whalen protesting the government-sponsored blacklisting of Communists. A few days later, Socialist party leader Norman Thomas presented a petition to Mayor Walker calling for Whalen's dismissal, citing his blacklisting campaign, his use of agent provocateurs, and the brutal handling of the March 6 demonstration. Ninety-six prominent non-Communist leaders signed the petition, including John Dewey, Henry Sloane Coffin, John Haynes Holmes, Charles and Mary Beard, Rexford Tugwell, Roy Stryker, and Mary Ware Dennett.[20]

Although disavowing the Communists and their tactics, the ACLU likewise protested Whalen's "Czarist methods." The union filed an injunction to stop Whalen's blacklisting activities and offered legal services to the victims of police brutality on March 6. The Union Square demonstration, the ACLU pointed out, had been the most violent in the country. Similar Communist demonstrations that day in Philadelphia, Baltimore, San Francisco, and Chicago had no police interference and had proceeded peacefully. Joining the call for Whalen's removal, the ACLU held a luncheon for two hundred civil liberties supporters at which they screened the suppressed film clips of the Union Square police assault and adopted a resolution calling for the commissioner's dismissal. By the next day, rumors were circulating that Mayor Walker would remove Whalen. When the mayor took no action, the ACLU appealed directly to New York governor Franklin Roosevelt and issued a twelve-page pamphlet titled *Police Lawlessness Against Communists,* detailing all of Whalen's abuses. The *Nation* also condemned Whalen in a full page editorial on March 26, linking the recent attacks on Communists with a more general disregard for the Constitution apparent in his use of raids, dragnets, gunmen's squads, and the third degree.[21]

Although Whalen hung on for two more months, the mounting

criticism took its toll. On May 20, at the behest of the mayor and the governor, Whalen announced that he was resigning and returning to his previous position at Wanamaker's. Just what role Whalen's anti-Communist policies played in forcing his resignation is not clear. But his bloody street battles with Communists and his blatantly unconstitutional methods of political repression put Whalen's tough style of policing squarely in the public spotlight and prompted powerful legal arguments against it.

The Interregnum

Police Commissioner Edward Mulrooney (1930–1933) took up his post with hopes of defusing the tensions between police and radicals that had grown up under his predecessor. Once set in motion, however, the cycle of ill will and violence proved difficult to break. Recognizing the utility of police brutality as an organizing issue, the Communist party measured workers' militancy by their ability to withstand police repression and urged increasingly aggressive action toward these "Tammany Cossacks." Many party members, angry over the months of abuse under Whalen's administration, were eager to oblige. Giving official sanction to this new assertiveness, the party announced the formation of a Workers Defense Corps that would physically protect strikers and demonstrators from police attacks.[22]

At the same time, many police officers had developed their own reservoir of resentment toward Communist protesters. Like their predecessors, police in the 1930s were generally unsympathetic to organized labor and hostile toward radicals. As many CP supporters were Jewish, ethnic rivalries also continued to fuel tensions with a predominantly Irish Catholic police force. During the Depression, however, these tensions became more acute as Irish Americans fell victim to unemployment in the construction and waterfront trades, while Jews—with growing numbers in professional, entrepreneurial, and government employment—fared somewhat better. These economic resentments toward Jews converged with a growing wave of Catholic anti-Communism spurred by recent papal appeals to combat the Communist menace. Among African

Americans, long-standing racist practices by police likewise found new legitimacy when victims could be tarred with the brush of Communism. As ACLU director Roger Baldwin pointed out, "The police have come to regard Communists as their natural enemy and treat them as such."[23]

Not surprisingly, police violence was soon back in the headlines with the killing of two Communist organizers in Harlem. On June 27, an African-American party member named Alfred Luro was fatally injured while attending an antilynching protest sponsored by the Young Communist League. Party sources claimed he had been critically wounded by police officers during a fight that broke out between the Communist protesters and a group of Marcus Garvey supporters—political adversaries that the police had herded together. Just two days later, another death occurred during a procession up Lenox Avenue by Communists en route to Luro's memorial service. Patrolman Edmund O'Brien attempted to stop the procession, led by the party's Negro and Latin American sections, because of their failure to secure a parade permit. The angry crowd pounced on him, took his nightstick, and began hitting him. O'Brien then pulled out his revolver and fired at one of his assailants, a Mexican national named Gonzalo Gonzales. When the crowd fled, O'Brien hailed a cab and took Gonzales to the hospital, where he was dead on arrival.

The party immediately denounced "the consistent policy of bloody brutality" by city officials and added Luro and Gonzales to the pantheon of working-class martyrs buried alongside Steve Katovis. Their mass funerals cast them as martyrs and celebrated the growing militancy of the working class in resisting police repression. Both incidents, the *Labor News* pointed out, "brought into play new Communist tactics of self defense against the police. Police in the act of clubbing workers were surrounded and beaten with fists, their sticks torn away and broken and their badges seized." The provocative actions of Communist protesters help explain why the ACLU did not file complaints against the officers' specific acts of violence, but rather against general police policy in handling demonstrations. Forcing rival Communists and Garveyites to share the same street corner and demanding parade permits for informal sidewalk processions were foolish and unnecessary policies that helped incite violence, the ACLU argued. The NYPD disagreed, fully exonerating Officer O'Brien and his superiors.[24]

Violent clashes between police and radicals continued through the summer and fall. During this time, police used violence to disperse Communists at anti-imperialism protests at the British and French consulates and were accused of brutality by striking dressmakers with the International Ladies Garment Workers Union. Even more controversial was an incident that occurred on August 1, following an otherwise peaceful Communist antiwar protest in Union Square. Coming to the aid of an officer involved in a scuffle with lingering protesters, police reserves moved in and began clubbing the crowd indiscriminately, injuring a half dozen people. While the ACLU unsuccessfully ushered the case through the usual disciplinary channels, the CP devised its own "Labor Jury" where working-class witnesses could recount their own side of the story. The victims' testimony, complete with descriptions of their plight as oppressed or unemployed workers, was later issued as a party pamphlet and distributed around the country. Exploiting the emotionally charged issue of police brutality, the CP used the Labor Jury as a propaganda weapon in the fight against capitalist oppression of workers and the unemployed.[25]

The Labor Jury was one of the party's attempts to link the issues of police brutality and unemployment. That summer, the CP created the Unemployed Councils (UC), which began planning fall protests explicitly connecting the two issues. During an October 16 meeting of the Board of Estimate to consider a seven-million-dollar allocation to increase police salaries, the UC sponsored a rally on unemployment outside city hall and dispatched a delegation to present its demands to the board. Protesting salary increases for police who waged a "reign of terror" against the city's workers, the four UC delegates insisted the money be reallocated for relief. The mayor ruled the protesters' demands out of order, but the Communist delegates continued their protests. When UC secretary Sam Nessin called Mayor Walker "a grafting Tammany politician," the mayor threatened to give him "a good thrashing" and had the delegates ejected. According to a *Times* reporter at the scene, the police then threw

Nessin down the stairs and beat him relentlessly. Pandemonium also erupted outside city hall as mounted police dispersed the protesters, some of whom aggressively fought back. By the time the park was clear, seventeen people had been arrested and scores injured. Several windows of the Woolworth Building lay shattered, and blood stains lined a staircase and landing inside city hall.[26]

Progressive forces immediately denounced the brutality of the staircase beating and Mayor Walker's role in it. While pointedly denouncing the disruptive tactics of the Communists, Socialist party leaders Norman Thomas and Heywood Broun condemned the violent attack on Nessin and accused Walker of inciting the violence. The ACLU also sent letters to the mayor and police commissioner protesting police violence at city hall and urging an investigation. While acknowledging the Communists' disruptive behavior at the Board of Estimate meeting, the ACLU maintained that "It is the Communists' business to be provocative, and it is the business of the police not to be provoked." In a subsequent investigation, the police department cleared its officers of any misconduct, prompting another complaint letter from the ACLU. In it, the ACLU noted that the NYPD had not disciplined even a single officer in the scores of political beatings cases that had occurred over the past year.[27]

Police repression of political dissent had no doubt kept the ACLU busy in 1930, but the bloody street battles between Communists and the NYPD were in fact winding down. From 1931 to 1933, there was a noticeable drop in the number of CP-led mass protests and an accompanying decline in police repression. The reduction of hostilities was due in part to changing Communist priorities, which shifted from mass strikes and unemployment protests in 1929–30 to neighborhood-based organizing through the Unemployed Councils. Anti-eviction protests and sit-ins at relief bureaus sparked several skirmishes with police in 1932 and 1933, but with organizing still at an early stage, the overall level of protest and repression was clearly down. One sign of the apparent détente was the NYPD's decision to abolish the notorious Industrial Squad in 1933.[28] Fast-changing political currents in both city hall and on the streets, however, meant that the détente was exceedingly fragile.

The La Guardia Experiment

Civil libertarians and organized labor watched the 1934 inauguration of Mayor Fiorello La Guardia with high hopes. His first day in office, La Guardia met with police officials to remind them of the importance of patience, courtesy, and restraint in dealing with the public, particularly at large gatherings and meetings. He also ordered police to remain neutral in all strikes and labor disputes. The mayor's more tolerant attitude toward labor and the left was not surprising given his background. The son of an Italian-American father and Jewish mother, La Guardia had worked as a labor lawyer and won election to Congress representing working-class districts in lower Manhattan and East Harlem. He became well known for his sympathies for organized labor and was cosponsor of the Norris-La Guardia Act, a 1932 bill that prohibited "yellow-dog" contracts and the use of court injunctions in labor disputes. A key part of La Guardia's appeal, then, was his reputation as a friend of the working class.[29]

For political reasons, however, La Guardia found himself saddled with a new police commissioner who did not share his prolabor views. Commissioner John O'Ryan was first and foremost a military man—a former commander of the New York State National Guard and major general of the Twenty-seventh Army Division in World War I. Like other police commissioners from military backgrounds, O'Ryan had little tolerance for political dissenters, seeing them as a threat to civic order. "My background has been military and my training hasn't much to do with liberalism," he once explained, "I don't believe in times of emergency in letting crowds collect." In the crisis conditions of the early 1930s, O'Ryan was not well suited to uphold La Guardia's pledge of tolerance and neutrality.[30]

Admittedly, 1934 was not an easy year to be police commissioner. In Toledo, Minneapolis, and San Francisco, a growing wave of labor militancy led to general strikes that ended in bloodshed and raised widespread fears of class warfare. At the same time, a rising tide of fascism in Europe fueled strong antifascist sentiments on the left and raucous demonstrations by the city's Communist and Socialist parties. Moreover, CP agitation around the Scottsboro Boys case in Alabama sparked a mass demonstration by African Americans in Harlem. Among the unemployed, Communist-led organizing through the Unemployed Councils began to bear fruit in a series of militant protests against the New York City welfare department. Police repression of these protests ended the short-lived détente between radicals and the NYPD and made 1934 one of the most contentious years in the city's history.

The first confrontation between police and radicals came in February in response to antifascist protests against the Dolfuss regime in Austria. On February 14, some four thousand Communists, Socialists, and other antifascist protesters gathered outside the Austrian consulate near the corner of Forty-second Street and Fifth Avenue while CP and SP delegations met with the Austrian consul inside. By rush hour the crowd had become larger and began to block traffic on Fifth Avenue. Scuffles broke out between demonstrators and police who tried to disperse them, and mounted police charged up the steps of the Public Library, where an overflow crowd had collected. In the ensuing tumult, police swung their clubs freely and charged the crowd on horses in what several newspapers described as a "riot" spreading down several blocks of Fifth Avenue.

Blaming police for triggering the violence, both Communist and Socialist party representatives met with Mayor La Guardia the following day. The Communists accused La Guardia of "fascist methods," claiming that the police attack on demonstrators at the consulate "places the present Fusion administration definitely on the side of the Austrian fascists." Although the Socialists avoided such vitriolic attacks, the equation of brutality with fascism would become an increasingly common metaphor in the fight against police repression. In a letter to La Guardia the next day, for example, the ACLU protested police methods at the consulate, asking "Can it be that New York's finest are learning their lessons from Hitler and Dolfuss?" Such accusations enraged the mayor, who blamed the Communists for inciting the disorder. Police brutality, he insisted, would not be tolerated by his administration, and he pledged that the NYPD would not interfere with demonstrations if political groups policed their own events and maintained order. Although the feuding Socialists and Communists had a difficult time meeting this challenge, the mayor kept the police at a safe distance from several raucous antifascist meetings later that week.[31]

A month later, however, La Guardia's noninterference policy faltered again. The occasion was a street rally in Harlem to honor Ada Wright, mother of two of the nine black boys falsely convicted of rape in Scottsboro, Alabama. Ever since the International Labor Defense had first become involved in the case in 1931, the Communist party had worked tirelessly to stir public protest, particularly in black communities like Harlem. Two earlier protest marches led by the ILD in Harlem in 1931 and 1933 had been violently dispersed by police. ILD activists may thus have anticipated more trouble from police this time, and they soon got it. Following a march across 125th Street by Wright and some five hundred supporters—mainly women and children—the crowd convened at a reviewing stand at Lenox Avenue and 126th Street. As the marchers crossed the street and blocked traffic, several police officers were dispatched to help clear the roadway. The officers ordered protesters off the street and sidewalk, and when that failed, drove a patrol car into the crowd, knocking people down and blocking the reviewing stand. Angry onlookers then started pelting police with bottles, fruit, and vegetables. The officers responded with tear gas and smoke bombs and used their nightsticks to disperse the remaining crowd. Four people were arrested and several (including police) received minor injuries.[32]

Representatives of the ILD and ACLU met with Mayor La Guardia the next day to complain about police violence and the use of tear gas against the Scottsboro demonstrators. No doubt unhappy over the failure of his tolerance policy, La Guardia ordered an investigation of the event headed by his most trusted ally in the department, Chief Inspector Lewis Valentine. The subsequent investigation, which featured more than thirty eyewitnesses, was an open and judicious proceeding. Valentine allowed full press coverage of the hearing and invited lawyers from the ACLU and ILD to cross-examine witnesses. After two days of testimony, Valentine concluded that initial police actions were "responsible for much of the subsequent disorder" and that police use of tear gas was inappropriate. He then preferred disciplinary charges against three patrolmen, two detectives, and one sergeant. The ACLU promptly praised La Guardia's administration for its fair and open handling of the investigation.[33]

The Communist party, however, was less sanguine and organized a mass march and meeting protesting police brutality on March 25. Under the banner "Down with Fascist Police Brutality," Ada Wright and other speakers recounted their experiences at the Scottsboro march and linked "police terror" in New York with southern racist justice in Scottsboro and capitalist oppression around the world. The meeting attracted about a thousand spectators, more than double the number who had come to the first rally. Once again, the CP tapped black outrage over police violence to try to recruit a following for its larger anticapitalist agenda. This time, however, the police did not take the bait. La Guardia ordered a low-key police detail to accompany the march, and advised CP leaders to maintain "proletarian discipline" in their own ranks. The event proceeded without disturbance.[34]

That same week, however, a violent labor dispute sparked another outcry against La Guardia's policing tactics, this time from the right. A month-old strike by taxi drivers seeking union recognition had become increasingly bitter and contentious. The mayor, who was openly sympathetic to the drivers' cause, insisted that police remain neutral and not interfere with union picketing around fleet garages. To reinforce the point, La Guardia ordered police on strike duty to report without their nightsticks. In their disarmed state, police were not prepared to deal with the wave of arson and violence that broke out during a labor demonstration on March 22. Going from city hall to Columbus Circle, more than a thousand striking drivers paraded up Broadway and Lafayette Streets, attacking nonunion taxis along the way. Strikers smashed windows, slashed tires, and overturned taxicabs and set them on fire. Scab drivers were assaulted and beaten, resulting in more than twenty injuries. Initially, the unarmed police escort stood by while the violence spread; only after strikers began attacking drivers did La Guardia order a full-scale police response. The damage, however, was done, and the taxi companies and their allies in the business community were irate. The next day a "Committee of 100" concerned citizens publicly condemned La Guardia's leniency toward strikers and protesters and called on the governor to remove him from office.

The conservative attack on La Guardia continued in a later grand jury investigation into the riot. In a presentment issued on April 12, the grand jury accused the mayor of being "overly sympathetic" to labor and of disarming the police and leaving them defenseless against rioters. They demanded that police immediately disperse all assemblages threatening disorder and that no group be allowed to meet or march in public without a permit. Permits for "workers' assemblages," the grand jury said, should be confined to particular areas, with marching (except to and from such localities) prohibited. Defending his policy of free speech and assembly, the mayor pointedly rejected the grand jury's proposals, calling them discriminatory and "provocative of disorder." A few days earlier, however, he had quietly reversed the order banning nightsticks on strike duty, an implicit acknowledgement that labor disputes sometimes required police to use force to maintain order.[35]

While La Guardia was busy fending off attacks from the right, Communist organizers in the Unemployed Councils launched a new round of militant protests against the city welfare bureaucracy. For the past two years, the UCs had been mobilizing local neighborhood residents to stage protests and demand relief at city welfare bureaus around the city. More recently, social workers and other employees in the welfare department began organizing unions to obtain better working conditions for employees as well as increased relief budgets and improved grievance procedures for clients. With growing support for welfare rights among both clients and employees, the UCs and relief workers' unions forged a coalition called the United Action Committee (UAC) and planned a demonstration for May 26. Mobilizing six hundred demonstrators in front of the city welfare department offices on Lafayette Street, the UAC demanded a meeting with the welfare commissioner, and when he refused, proceeded to enter the building. The police, who were unarmed, then attempted to disperse the crowd but were attacked by angry protesters wielding banner staves. Police emergency units were called in, and the melee spread, resulting in ten arrests and fifteen injuries. Among the injured were eight police, four protesters, and three spectators. Violence resumed the next day during the arraignment of the demonstrators at the Tombs Court. While ejecting a boisterous crowd of UAC supporters from the courtroom, police and protesters came to blows as frustrated officers repelled UAC supporters who tried to reenter the courthouse.[36]

Police actions in these incidents drew immediate protests from the UAC, the ACLU, and several public employees' unions. Charging police with excessive force and brutality, these groups insisted that the unemployed had a right to meet and demonstrate without police interference. When police behaved properly, they insisted, demonstrations remained peaceful and orderly. Moreover, they demanded that police be removed from relief bureaus (where they had been stationed to prevent disruptions by protesters) and that complaint bureaus be established at all relief stations. As in earlier Communist protests, the UAC drew direct links between police brutality and unemployment. During a June 1 meeting between the UAC, the ACLU, and Mayor La Guardia, some fifteen hundred protesters rallied outside city hall carrying placards saying "Blackjacks or Relief?" and "We Want Jobs, Not Police Clubs." Once again, the police brutality issue served as an organizing vehicle for a more radical economic agenda.[37]

The city administration, of course, saw things differently. The Communists, La Guardia said, were exploiting the plight of the unemployed and inciting them to disorder by forcibly occupying relief bureaus and disrupting services. Presenting himself as the true friend of the unemployed, the mayor insisted that such disorder hindered genuine administrative and political reform of the relief system. La Guardia's hostility toward the radicals was revealed most vividly during the June 1 meeting when he called UAC leader James Gaynor "a yellow dog" who incites people to riot then "runs away while others get hurt." As for the police, he said, they had shown great restraint in the face of deliberate and repeated provocations. Shortly afterward, La Guardia met privately with the city press corps and implored editors not to criticize the police for violence against the unemployed, warning that it would play into the hands of "red agitators." Police Commissioner John O'Ryan, heartened by the mayor's show of support for tougher policing, dashed off a letter to the welfare commissioner pledging firm police protection of the Home Relief Bureaus and swift disciplinary action against officers who failed to use sufficient force to suppress violence.[38]

The La Guardia administration's heightened vigilance came amid a growing wave of class warfare around the country that summer. The month of July was particularly bloody, as strike-related violence in Minneapolis and San Francisco left four people dead and dozens wounded. In response, NYPD commissioner O'Ryan organized a military-style "Rifle Squad" of twelve hundred officers designed to quell potential labor disturbances and riots. The department also called on "responsible unions" to submit credentials and photographs for their legally authorized representatives, so that the NYPD could distinguish them from "irresponsible persons, racketeers and gunmen" (among whom Communist agitators were no doubt included). At the same time, the NYPD's Criminal Alien Squad had stepped up its surveillance and harassment of labor radicals in the needle trades and food service industry, using third-degree tactics to try to drive organizers out of town or into jail.[39] Taken together, these measures constituted a wholesale assault on the rights of labor and precipitated a firestorm of protest from the left.

When news of O'Ryan's rifle squad and photo/credential system leaked out in late July and early August, liberals and radicals alike called for O'Ryan's resignation. Accusing him of militarizing the police force and violating the rights of labor, the Socialist party denounced his policies as "utterly at variance with the boasted attitude of the present administration and in line with militaristic and Fascist trends abhorrent to the democratic spirit." The Communist *Daily Worker*, which had been calling for the commissioner's head since June, repeated its demand to sack the "fascist" police commissioner. Labor unions and liberals now also joined in denouncing O'Ryan. In a *Nation* article titled, "Commissioner O'Ryan: Terrorist," Walter Wilson examined the commissioner's military background and his role in whitewashing army brutalities during World War I. Warning that his militarization of the NYPD would lead to disaster, Wilson concluded that O'Ryan was not an appropriate commissioner for a liberal administration. As the tone of public criticism suggests, O'Ryan's violent tactics and militarization of the police were becoming highly objectionable in an international climate of fascist repression and war.[40]

With public outrage against O'Ryan at an all-time high, La Guardia moved to end his long and cantankerous relationship with the commissioner. Deliberately circumventing O'Ryan in discussing police preparations for the upcoming primary elections, La Guardia relied increasingly on his ally, Chief Inspector Lewis Valentine, to direct the daily operations of the department. The exasperated commissioner got the message and tendered his resignation on September 13.[41]

The Valentine Era

A thirty-year veteran of the NYPD, Lewis Valentine was an obvious choice to replace O'Ryan as police commissioner in the La Guardia administration. A key player on the department's various confidential squads—the forerunners of internal affairs—he was known as a zealous corruption fighter who had served under reform administrations since the days of John Purroy Mitchel. As a committed anti-Tammany crusader, Valentine promised to sanitize and professionalize the department through high standards, firm discipline, and improved public relations. Like other reform administrations, however, Valentine's professionalism helped reduce corruption but did not necessarily address the problem of excessive force. In fact, as we saw in the last chapter, in his quest to combat crime Valentine encouraged police to "muss up the gangsters"—a bare-knuckled approach that La Guardia also favored. But when it came to handling labor and political dissenters, Valentine affirmed the mayor's commitment to tolerance. The era of police red-baiting and political favoritism was over, the new commissioner announced; henceforth, the NYPD would be tolerant of all but "thugs, gorillas, and assassins."[42]

Within a year of Valentine's appointment, two critical events would help to make La Guardia's policy of political tolerance more feasible. First, in July 1935, President Franklin Roosevelt signed the National Labor Relations Act, guaranteeing workers the right to organize and providing federal oversight through the newly created National Labor Relations Board (NLRB). The Wagner Act, as it became known, explicitly protected workers' right to free speech in advocating unions and the right to protest unfair labor practices. Although it would take some time for the courts to affirm these rights, the act empowered the NLRB—rather than local police authorities—to determine the legitimate representatives of labor and to protect their right to strike and picket. Around the same time, the CP was undergoing a major shift in party line with its international call for a united front against fascism. By the fall of 1935, Communists had abandoned the strident and isolationist stand of the Third Period and began to build alliances with Socialists, New Deal Democrats, and other progressive forces. The Popular Front, as these alliances came to be known, was also a response to the leftward shift of the New Deal, evident in such measures as the Wagner Act. Communists would now work alongside other progressives to build strong unions inside the new Congress of Industrial Organizations (CIO) and to fight for workers' rights within New Deal agencies. Most critically, the Popular Front helped improve the party's credibility on the left while its coalition politics provided cover for Communist organizers within a broad-based left-liberal movement.[43] Together, these measures helped defuse some of the long-standing hostilities between the NYPD and the city's Communist-led organizations.

Although it would take two more years to fully implement the tolerance policy, the ACLU found Commissioner Valentine to be a more cooperative figure than O'Ryan. Shortly after taking office, the Civil Liberties Union met with Valentine to discuss police policy on picketing, permits, and other key issues. Believing Valentine would give them a respectful hearing, the New York ACLU went on to establish a committee on police administration to study police regulations and make recommendations for handling outdoor meetings and parades. Although policing problems continued, the ACLU reported in 1935 that Valentine's regime was "a great improvement over recent administrations. Mass picketing is generally permitted; the police have orders not to interfere with peaceful picketing in nonlabor disputes; permits for parades are not unduly restricted; police lawlessness is discouraged." Police cooperation, the

ACLU noted, was especially good when political groups consulted with the department in advance of strikes or demonstrations, suggesting that supervisors could effectively manage the police by establishing well-understood ground rules and procedures for both sides.[44]

Although police relations with labor and radicals clearly improved during 1935 and 1936, certain trouble spots remained. Strikes involving unorthodox tactics or clashes between picketers and strikebreakers sometimes led to charges of police brutality. In strikes by retail department store workers at May's and Orhbach's in 1935–36, for example, police used their clubs to disperse workers who attempted to chain themselves to pillars near store entrances or enter stores to accost strikebreakers. On the Chelsea waterfront, where striking seamen engaged in heated exchanges with strikebreakers exiting ships, police violently dispersed picketers on two occasions in the spring of 1936. After complaints by the International Seamen's Union and other labor organizations, however, the police backed off, leaving a similar strike in the fall of 1936 "practically undisturbed." Police violence toward the unemployed at Home Relief Bureaus also declined. Although there were numerous clashes between police and the UCs in 1934–35, improved grievance procedures at relief bureaus and more conciliatory tactics by the Communist-led councils resulted in a drop in brutality complaints after 1935.[45]

The shift from cash relief to work relief after 1935 also helped to refocus radical activism around the Works Progress Administration, making WPA protests a more likely occasion for policing problems. The most serious conflict occurred on February 15, 1936, when fifteen thousand demonstrators gathered at Madison Square to protest recent cutbacks in the WPA budget. The Workers Alliance, a Popular Front group representing WPA workers, had requested a parade permit but was turned down by police. When the crowd began to march anyway, police arrested Congressman Vito Marcantonio and thirteen other protest leaders and then dispersed the crowd using blackjacks. Labor and left-wing groups immediately registered their protests over police brutality and the use of "protective custody" arrests (the leaders were released without charge shortly after the demonstration). Although Commissioner Valentine denied using the term, a report by a "citizens' jury" that investigated the conflict called protective custody a Nazi tactic and roundly condemned police for denying a permit. As in past conflicts, police violence was equated with fascism and exploited for its propaganda value in organizing relief workers ("Let Them Eat Clubs!" one handbill declared).[46]

Given the administration's sincere efforts to promote tolerance, why did such violent conflicts continue? In the case of the WPA march, the denial of the permit was probably a result of the administration's animosity toward public-sector unions. The Wagner Act did not cover public employees, and La Guardia regarded relief worker organizing as a direct affront to his efforts to aid the unemployed. In this case, then, the mayor's tolerance policy simply did not extend far enough. The problems arising from private-sector labor disputes, on the other hand, were more complicated. Police sometimes found it difficult to distinguish lawful picketing from dangerous and disorderly behavior, particularly in large strikes. Was blocking traffic illegal? Obstructing entrances? Loud chanting or accosting of strikebreakers? Sit-down strikes within plants? In time, the courts would rule on many of these issues (often to labor's detriment), but in the meantime officers relied on their own discretion in policing strike scenes. Moreover, racism, anti-Semitism, and anti-Communism continued to thrive among rank and file police, most of whom were Catholic and some of whom proved receptive to proto-fascist groups like the Christian Front. At a police Holy Name Society breakfast in 1937, for instance, the mayor got a tepid reception when he appealed for sympathy and forbearance for the unemployed. But when Patrick Scanlon, the red-baiting editor of the *Catholic Tablet,* said it was shameful that police were forced to endure insults from agitators at relief offices, he got a thundering ovation.[47] The political and ethnic identities of the department's rank and file thus worked against the diffusion of the administration's policy down to the street level.

Commissioner Valentine worked to overcome these problems through tighter supervision and the development of explicit procedures and regulations for handling crowds. In early 1937, the New

York ACLU submitted its report on police procedures, which featured twenty-five recommendations, including equal treatment in issuing permits, advance consultation between police and sponsoring organizations, a low-key uniformed police presence at public events, disregard of provocative language, and explicit guidelines for the permissible use of force and weapons.[48] Although there is no concrete evidence that the NYPD accepted these proposals, the transformation in department policy from 1935 to 1937 reflects their influence. Two articles on crowd control in the NYPD magazine, *Spring 3100,* illustrate just how much department policy changed under Valentine.

In a 1935 article titled, "Mobs, Riots and Disorders," Lt. William J. McMahon presented the classic view of the irrational mob and its dangerous collective psychology. Viewing crowds as collective entities that overwhelmed individual intelligence and rationality, he argued that such mobs "are quick to act" and "are only powerful for destruction." Curiosity seekers and respectable citizens thus got caught up in the frenzy and later complained of false arrest or police brutality. To control this "contagion," McMahon went on to outline steps for policing gatherings that became or threatened to become disorderly. Calling for a heavy police presence, he recommended that patrolmen be deployed on both sides of the speaker (to deter him from inflaming the crowd) and at five-foot intervals around the outside perimeter. This formation would allow officers to contain the crowd, discourage curiosity seekers, and if necessary, allow them to disperse the crowd by driving a wedge through its center. He also explained how to use mounted squads to perform a frontal assault on illegal or potentially disorderly marches. Displaying hostility toward all radical political gatherings, McMahon's procedures reflected the old-style public-order policing that led to so many incidents of violent repression under commissioners Grover Whalen and John O'Ryan.[49]

Two years later, Lewis Valentine presented a very different scenario in his article about policing labor disputes. Reiterating La Guardia's policy of tolerance and neutrality, Valentine emphasized advance consultation, careful planning, and close supervision via the department's new Bureau of Operations. Under this new system, precinct commanders would no longer handle strikes and demonstrations on their own, but would consult with the bureau in advance to determine acceptable conditions for picketing, parading, and other activities. In dealing with labor disputes, Valentine ordered police to act with "vigilance, good judgment, tact, diplomacy, restraint, self-control, fairness and a liberal, flexible policy." The use of "warnings and sympathetic advice," he noted, was preferable to arrest or the use of "oppressive methods." Unlike many of his predecessors, Valentine recognized the propaganda value of police repression for radical groups. "Brutal measures or contact with police stations and courts do no good," he insisted, "They only tend to further intensify an already serious situation by sometimes making martyrs of professional agitators and trouble-makers." Although the commissioner had little sympathy for Communists and other "agitators" in the CIO unions, he expressed a firm belief in the New Deal labor formula, predicting that in time, "capital and labor will march side by side to heights of success and prosperity never before seen."[50] Like the liberal brutality critics of the ACLU, Valentine had come to believe that a more restrained brand of mass action policing was more effective in containing radicalism and preserving public order.

The administration's determination to implement this policy had been reinforced by a tragic event in South Chicago in the spring of 1937. In what became known as the "Memorial Day Massacre," Chicago police opened fire on the backs of pickets at the Republic Steel plant, killing ten strikers and wounding thirty others. When the firing ended, police moved in on the demonstrators—many of who were still huddling on the ground—and beat them with billies and ax handles. This horrifying scene was captured on newsreel, which became key evidence in the subsequent hearings of the LaFollette Committee, a U.S. Senate committee investigating the violation of civil liberties in labor relations. The Memorial Day Massacre shocked the American public and prompted Mayor La Guardia to reassert his tolerance policy more forcefully. Addressing a police awards ceremony three days after the massacre, the mayor declared that "economic issues cannot be settled with a policeman's nightstick." "So long as I am mayor of New York," he continued, "I shall protect the constitutional rights of every citizen, whether I agree with him or not, and whether I like him or not." He repeated this message a month later at the annual convention of the New York State Police Chiefs Association. Commissioner Valentine then showed the newsreel of the Chicago massacre, calling it "a pictoral indictment of a great police department."[51]

Both Valentine and La Guardia maintained that labor disputes should be settled not by police nightsticks but by "tribunals set up by the federal government." And indeed by 1937 the NLRB and the federal courts were actively defining the parameters of acceptable labor-management relations. The Supreme Court upheld the Wagner Act in 1937 and then proceeded to rule on several cases affirming the rights of labor, including the right to picket. The Supreme Court also handed down two significant decisions in 1937 upholding the rights of Communists and other political dissenters. In *Dejong* v. *Oregon* and *Herndon* v. *Georgia,* the Court affirmed the First Amendment rights of Communist organizers, thus increasing pressure on local government and police to exercise tolerance.[52]

Federal intervention, coupled with local administrative reform efforts, resulted in a dramatic improvement in the NYPD's record of mass-action policing. The New York ACLU noted in its 1937–1938 annual report that "The Committee rarely has occasion to criticize the conduct of police in strikes." Police repression of Communist political activities also dropped dramatically in 1937, both in New York and around the country. The NYPD's improved record is evident from the reports of the Criminal Alien Squad. These reports, filed by members of the squad assigned to hundreds of radical meetings from 1939 to 1941, contain few comments other than "no disorder or arrests." The most telling evidence of the department's change in policy, though, comes from a 1941 Civil Liberties Union report on police action at street meetings. Based on reports by local Civil Liberties Union observers at more than thirty strikes and street meetings that summer, the report found that "police follow a general hands-off policy toward the speakers, and generally try to make themselves fairly unobtrusive." Although most police were unsympathetic to labor and considered radicals to be "crackpots," the report said, their biases were passive and did not generally affect their work. In fact, police often took extra measures to protect the rights of speakers by dealing aggressively with hecklers and temporarily stopping traffic to allow pedestrians to pass around sidewalk crowds.[53] As these reports indicate, the transformation in public order policing in New York was truly significant. But the new style of policing also had some drawbacks. As evidenced by the extensive Criminal Alien Squad (CAS) reports, the NYPD came to rely increasingly on surveillance and intelligence by plainclothes detectives. In the late 1930s and 1940s, the CAS usually acted as a passive surveillance unit and took little or no action against demonstrators. In isolated cases, however, detectives from the CAS and other units made arrests and used third-degree tactics against suspects out of public view. The ACLU reported several such cases, including the beatings of two union members in a Brooklyn shipyard strike in 1937 and a teachers' union leader protesting WPA cuts in 1941. No disciplinary action was taken by police in either case.[54]

These incidents point to a larger trend in the policing of radical groups, away from violent street confrontations and toward more clandestine forms of surveillance and repression. At the same time that La Guardia and Valentine liberalized police policy toward public strikes and demonstrations, they increased reliance on the undercover red squad. Although behind-the-scenes repression was relatively rare during this period, the beatings of these labor radicals suggest that detectives sometimes resorted to old-fashioned red bashing in the confines of the station house. As in the Progressive Era, greater police tolerance of public protest was accompanied by more invasive and sophisticated forms of covert surveillance. When radicalism resurfaced in the 1960s, the red squad would develop an elaborate array of intelligence-gathering and countersubversive tactics that would be far more devastating to the left than police batons and tear gas. The liberalization of public order policing, then, came at a price for the city's radicals—one that would not become clear until thirty years later.

Nevertheless, the transformation of mass action policing in the 1930s stands as a watershed in the history of police-community relations. By the 1940s, the NYPD generally respected the First Amendment rights of all New Yorkers, and the use of police violence at public political events declined dramatically. This transformation demonstrated that with sufficient political will — on both the federal and local levels — even the most entrenched and conservative of police departments could be made to change its ways. Moreover, for the next two decades the department's more permissive policy served to uphold the political status quo by allowing New Yorkers to vent their protests freely, making political rallies and demonstrations a routine and unremarkable feature of city life.

Finally, the events of the 1930s also introduced Communists and other progressives to the gravity of the police problem in the African-American community. As we shall see in the next chapter, left-wing organizing around this issue in the 1930s and 1940s literally caught fire in Harlem and other black communities. In the process, the problem of police brutality was transformed from a class issue into a racial dilemma that would preoccupy the city for the rest of the twentieth century.

6. THE RESURGENCE OF RACE

As recently as the 1970s, New Yorkers who criticized police brutality were routinely branded as "Communists" by the police and their supporters. Although this red-baiting enraged civil rights activists who had no love for the Communist party, such epithets grew out of a long history of Communist and left-wing activism around racially motivated police violence. Beginning in the 1930s and 1940s, African Americans, Communists, and other progressive forces in Harlem and Bedford-Stuyvesant joined together in the Popular Front to combat police brutality and abuse. Like other left-wing causes, the success of their efforts rose and fell in response to an international climate of depression, war, and a postwar anti-Communist crusade. Despite mixed results, the antibrutality campaign of this period once again redefined police violence as a racial issue, one that would become part of the larger civil rights struggle of the late twentieth century.

Although black New Yorkers had cast police violence as a racial concern since the beginning of the century, antibrutality activism among African Americans was largely dormant in the 1910s and 1920s. As we saw in chapter 2, the Tenderloin and San Juan Hill riots of the early 1900s were the crucibles of black activism around police misconduct and civil rights. Following the riots, however, the NAACP and other black organizations concentrated on integrating the NYPD and pressured the department to hire the city's first black police officer, Samuel Battle, in 1911. Thereafter the department hired a small but growing number of black officers, particularly after World War I as black population gains increased African-American political influence.

Most of the black recruits were sent to precincts in Harlem, which had become the city's largest African-American community by 1920. The bitter racial climate in the old West Side neighborhoods following the riots, the opening of the Lenox Avenue subway line in 1904, and the influx of black southerners during World War I all fueled Harlem's growth. During the 1910s, in fact, the black population of Harlem nearly doubled, exceeding one hundred thousand by 1920. As in the earlier Tenderloin, city authorities funneled vice operations into Harlem, where poverty fueled an underground economy and police earned payoffs from speakeasies, prostitution, and gambling. The flowering of jazz in the 1920s also brought a nocturnal influx of white "slummers" into the neighborhood in search of chic new nightspots like the Cotton Club and Small's Paradise. The flood of affluent white voyeurs stirred some discontent among black locals who were barred from the most fashionable clubs; others resented the takeover of Harlem by vice dens catering to whites and police dispatched to protect them. Police protection of vice, combined with aggressive enforcement tactics designed to protect white tourists and businesses, made for poor relations between the NYPD and the black community.

The hiring of more African-American officers was one way to address this deteriorating relationship. By 1926 the NYPD had forty-nine black officers, and that same year Samuel Battle was promoted to sergeant, making him the department's first black supervisory officer. By the early 1930s, the NYPD had more than a hundred black officers, most of whom were assigned to Harlem and other black neighborhoods. The hiring of African-American officers was a major victory in the fight for equal employment, and it also helped ease tensions between police and the African-American community. As Harlem's pioneer black cop, Samuel Battle won widespread respect from both police and black leaders for his ability to mediate between the department and the community. In 1919, for example, he successfully warded off an angry Harlem mob that had surrounded a white officer after he fatally shot a local black man during the so-called "Straw Hat Riot." In general, Battle's contacts with Harlem leaders enhanced communications between police and the community during times of racial tension. But despite these accomplishments, Battle and other black officers faced persistent discrimination in work assignments and promotions and were limited to posts in Harlem and other black precincts.[1]

Although they helped mediate between the department and the African-American community, the hiring of black officers was no panacea. Violence between police and black suspects seemed to escalate during and after World War I, culminating in a minor riot in Harlem in 1928. The July riot, precipitated by a white officer's attempt to arrest a black assault suspect, attracted a hostile crowd that grew to 2,500 or more. After an hour-long battle by 150 police reinforcements, order was restored. Police rescued the white officer and three other patrolmen who had come to his assistance, including one black officer. Unlike Samuel Battle's role in the 1919 outbreak, however, the black officer's presence in this conflict did little to mollify the crowd.[2]

Black officers, in fact, were increasingly implicated in cases of police brutality in Harlem. As racial pioneers in the department, black rookies were anxious to prove themselves and often adopted the tough and aggressive style of policing that characterized the Prohibition-era NYPD. In 1928 the department hired Benjamin Wallace, the legendary "terror of Harlem" who killed five black suspects and wounded dozens of others over the course of his career. Although Wallace's gun-slinging style was extreme, it was consistent with the NYPD's "muss em up" approach and was emulated by other officers, black and white. Moreover, some of Harlem's black businesspeople and professionals supported the use of tough crime-fighting tactics to preserve order in their rapidly growing community.[3]

The increased profile of black police in African-American neighborhoods and the conflicting pressures on these officers to be both peacemakers and crime fighters probably discouraged the NAACP from pursuing police brutality cases. Nor was the conservative political climate of the 1920s conducive to black activism. Nationally, NAACP membership fell from ninety thousand in 1920 to twenty thousand in 1929, and the New York branch—which tended to defer to the nearby national office—was particularly weak. As businesspeople and professionals who had worked to open police and other civil service occupations to blacks, raising the issue of police violence threatened to sever the personal and political contacts with white elites that made such breakthroughs possible. Preoccupied with lynching in the South and the battle against racial segregation, the NAACP pursued only a handful of brutality cases, most involving middle-class black victims in predominantly white or mixed-race public settings. Limiting its work to the courtroom and elite political channels, the NAACP's approach to police misconduct in these years had little resonance with poor and working-class African Americans who faced police abuses in their neighborhoods on a daily basis.[4]

The Communist Connection

In the 1920s the fledgling Communist party was in no better position to organize against police violence than the NAACP. The small number of black cadre, the party's minuscule presence in Harlem, and a Soviet-crafted ideology of Marxist revolution meant that the CP's appeal among African Americans was extremely limited. In the conservative 1920s, black urbanites were far more likely to respond to Marcus Garvey's appeals to race pride and black self-determination than they were to Communist visions of a color-blind class struggle.

In 1928, however, the CP passed a new resolution that made organizing the "black masses" a top priority and provided black party leaders with an opportunity to mobilize around the struggle for Negro rights.[5] Soon after, the onset of the Great Depression wreaked havoc in black communities around the country, making them more amenable to radical appeals. In New York, unemployment ranged from 25 to 50 percent among black workers, running two to three times the rate for whites. Long lines of black men waited for hours outside Harlem shelters and soup kitchens, while crowds of black women gathered each morning at the street corner "slave markets" to barter their domestic services to the highest bidder. Many Harlem families lost their homes and savings. In 1931 the local Urban League received appeals from ten to twenty families every day who faced eviction. Requests for relief, however, quickly outpaced the supply of government and charitable funds. Even after the establishment of

New Deal work relief programs, black New Yorkers faced persistent discrimination in hiring and work assignments.

Responding to these crises, Communist organizers in Harlem led mass protest movements around unemployment and racial justice that attracted thousands of African-American supporters. As we saw earlier, the NYPD frequently attacked Communist-led protests by radical unions and the Unemployed Councils. Party leaders quickly realized that police repression actually reinforced black support for party-led organizing efforts and that "police terror" could be rhetorically linked to the larger racial and class struggle. Perhaps the most glaring examples of "police terror" in Harlem were the repeated clashes around the Communist-organized Scottsboro demonstrations. The violence surrounding the March 17, 1934 protest march and the police inquiry (described in chapter 5) provided an opportunity for Communists to draw parallels between police terror in Alabama and Harlem.[6]

Although the party's use of the brutality issue was driven in part by political opportunism, black Communists also experienced police repression firsthand. Prior to La Guardia's tolerance policy, police regularly harassed black CP leaders both in public and in private. Furthermore, the party's firm commitment to interracial organizing and social life resulted in hostile police action designed to discourage race mixing, particularly between black men and white women (the justification being that prostitution was involved). In 1933 party members reported numerous cases of Harlem police forcibly separating interracial couples on the street and noted that police were especially vigilant in breaking up mixed-race CP meetings and socials. That summer Cyril Briggs, the light-skinned editor of the *Harlem Liberator*, was arrested on a disorderly conduct charge while accompanying a black woman on the street. When police realized that Briggs was "colored," they dropped the charges. Undeterred, Briggs pledged to fight police discrimination and "rally the masses of Harlem for mass violation of all Jim-Crow laws and practices."[7] For Briggs and other black Communists, then, the battle against police misconduct was personal as well as political.

As Communists became more sensitive to problems of policing

in the black community, the scope of their activism expanded. Agitation around police brutality had initially focused on Communist martyrs such as Steve Katovis and Alfred Luro, but by the mid-1930s the party was defending a broader array of victims. Unlike the NAACP and other middle-class black organizations, the CP did not handpick cases of model black citizens—even the most destitute merited the party's support. In 1933 for example, the Young Communist League publicly condemned the police "murder" of twenty-three-year-old Ira Wallace, a homeless and unemployed Harlem man who was killed in a hail of bullets on a fire escape during a burglary attempt. It was the young man's hunger and desperation, the league claimed, that drove him to break into an apartment and steal food from the icebox. Linking Wallace's killing to the city's refusal to provide relief and shelter to unemployed youth, YCL leaders used popular anger over a local police shooting to try to build support for the Communist program. Wallace's status as a lawbreaker did not prevent the CP from defending him, while his impoverished and homeless state became prima facie evidence of police terror against the unemployed.

Nor did the party balk at the fact that one of the accused officers was African American. Viewing police repression as a class issue, Communists attacked the NYPD for its violent attempts to sunder the growing unity of black and white workers. Although most Harlem residents did not embrace this heroic vision of interracial class struggle, many were impressed with Communist efforts to defend poor and working-class Harlemites from police abuse and sympathized with CP calls to restrain the police—black as well as white.[8]

The biggest catalyst for antibrutality organizing, however, was the Harlem Riot of March 19, 1935. Fueled by festering resentments over unemployment, racial discrimination, and police misconduct, the disorder was sparked by the arrest of Lino Rivera, an Afro–Puerto Rican boy caught shoplifting a penknife in the Kress store on 125th Street. A store guard and manager tried to stop him, and a scuffle broke out. Once Rivera had been subdued, the manager turned him over to a police officer who took the boy to a rear basement exit and released him. In the meantime, however, a black female customer shouted that police had taken the boy to the basement to beat him up. As rumors of the beating spread, shoppers began to overturn counters and toss merchandise on to the floor. Police reinforcements were unable to convince the crowd of the boy's safety and eventually ejected everyone and closed the store.

By this time, however, rumors of the incident had spread around the neighborhood, and a large crowd had gathered out front. Soon organizers from the Young Liberators (a Communist-led black youth organization) had set up a picket line and were handing out pamphlets saying, "CHILD BRUTALLY BEATEN...NEAR DEATH." Calling the incident a "lynch attack," the Young Liberators urged black and white workers to "Stop Police Brutality in Negro Harlem." When someone in the crowd threw a rock through the Kress window, police pulled the speakers from their platform and began to disperse the crowd. A full-scale street battle ensued that intensified when a hearse pulled up behind the store, fueling rumors that Rivera was dead. The rioting spread over several blocks as the crowd battled police and looted hundreds of stores. By the end of the night, one person was dead, sixty-four injured, and seventy-five under arrest.[9]

Police officials and District Attorney William Dodge immediately charged that Communists were responsible for inciting the riot. The Hearst press echoed these accusations, as did some black conservatives in Harlem. Mayor La Guardia reacted more cautiously and appointed an eleven-member biracial commission to study conditions in Harlem. Anxious to defend themselves, Communists joined with other black community leaders in a campaign to expose the racial discrimination and dire social and economic conditions that led to the riot. While hardly sympathetic to the Communist cause, many black religious and community leaders strongly resented the dismissive attitude of city officials who willfully ignored poverty and racism in favor of red-baiting.[10]

The CP channeled the efforts of its best organizers into marshalling data and presenting evidence to the five subcommittees established by the Mayor's Commission on Conditions in Harlem. Communist activity was especially evident during hearings by the subcommittee on crime and police, chaired by ACLU attorney Arthur Garfield Hays. Working with Adam Clayton Powell, Jr.—a young minister from Harlem's Abyssinian Baptist Church— James Ford and other party organizers mobilized a large and vocal audience and presented a litany of police abuses. Speakers criticized police behavior during the riot, noting the mishandling of Rivera, the failure to dispel inflammatory rumors, and the fatal shooting of a young looter. As in past riot investigations, though, the bulk of the testimony concerned the accumulated grievances of Harlem residents over illegal searches, false arrests, and excessive force. Powell and his Communist allies also seized the opportunity to present several recent cases of alleged brutality, including that of Thomas Aiken, an unemployed man who was blinded by blows from a police officer while standing in a Harlem bread line. Others complained of police tolerance of vice operations and the unwarranted harassment of mixed-race couples. Perhaps the most explosive moment came when Charles Romney, a local civic leader, accused police of intimidating several witnesses slated to testify at the hearings. The next time a policeman "interferes with me, my relatives or my witnesses," he warned, "I am going to take the law into my own hands." Nearly everyone in the room jumped to their feet to cheer Romney's defiant statement. At this and other points, the audience became so emotional that the chair had to temporarily adjourn the hearings to restore order.[11]

The public's impassioned testimony during the hearings had a profound impact on the committee. In a subsequent report, the commission stated that "the insecurity of the individual in Harlem against police aggression is one of the most potent causes for the existing hostility to authority.... Police aggressions and brutalities more than any other factor weld the people together for mass action." The commission went on to make several recommendations including the development of police procedures for rumor control, tougher discipline in misconduct cases, the closing of vice dens, and noninterference with mixed-race groups or couples. Most critically, the commission called on the police commissioner to establish a biracial committee of Harlem citizens who would hear civilian complaints and act as a liaison with the department.[12]

The report of the mayor's commission—which also included scathing exposés of Harlem housing, health care, education, recreation, employment, and relief—elicited sharp criticism from city officials and local business interests. Responding to the report on crime and policing, Commissioner Valentine systematically refuted the commission's criticisms and insisted that the hearings were biased and dominated by Communist agitators. He denied that Harlem residents resented the police and claimed that "any resentment which does exist is borne by the lawless element because of the police activity directed against them." The Uptown Chamber of Commerce echoed these sentiments, insisting that extreme police measures were required to combat Harlem's high crime rate. Bowing to such pressures and unwilling to jeopardize his relations with Valentine and the police department, La Guardia suppressed the report.[13]

Although the scuttling of the commission's report angered and disheartened black leaders, the community organizing and network-building that came about as a result of the hearings led to the rise of a broad-based left-wing movement in Harlem. After working with Communists at the hearings, many of Harlem's civic and religious leaders were impressed with their commitment and effectiveness (which stood in stark contrast to the silence and inactivity of the NAACP). Soon after, the CP's new mandate for a Popular Front against fascism allowed Harlem Communists to solidify and expand these riot-spawned networks. Abandoning the war against "Negro reformism," Communists leaders in the late 1930s joined Adam Clayton Powell, Jr., A. Philip Randolph, and other black labor and religious leaders in a united front against racial and economic injustice. In this way, Communist protest activities—including those around police violence—spread to the mainstream Harlem community.[14]

The collaboration between the Communist left and other black community leaders began with ongoing defense work on behalf of Thomas Aiken and four other brutality complainants whose cases had been aired at the hearings. While there is no indication that these cases were successful, the ILD continued to solicit and represent complainants in the months following the riot. This type of defense work was a clear departure from the party's earlier refusal to cooperate with the capitalist legal system. As part of the Popular Front, Communists now functioned as critical supporters of American democracy and vowed to work within the legal system to stave off the more serious threat of fascism. The campaign against police brutality culminated with the founding of the United Civil Rights Committee in Harlem in April 1936. Forged around the case of John McNeill, a Harlem man who was severely beaten by a police officer in front of dozens of witnesses, the committee was a coalition effort of the ILD, the ACLU, the NAACP, and other labor and progressive organizations. Before long, the group was representing several other brutality complainants and conducting meetings with the mayor and top police officials regarding police practices in Harlem.[15]

A similar effort emerged in Brooklyn's Bedford-Stuyvesant neighborhood, where growing black population and increasing white resentment were fueling racial tensions. With the opening of the Fulton Street subway line in 1936, the old Bedford and Stuyvesant Heights neighborhoods in north central Brooklyn became home to a growing number of working-class immigrants and African Americans. By the late 1930s, the combined Bedford-Stuyvesant area had a black population of around sixty thousand, making it the city's second largest African-American settlement. Old-time white residents, many of them Jews who had settled there after World War I, worried about declining property values and growing vice and street crime that they associated with blacks. The Midtown Civic League, a white business and homeowner's association, lobbied Mayor La Guardia for greater police protection and even threatened to lead a vigilante movement against criminals in the neighborhood in 1936. White demands for increased law enforcement encouraged a more aggressive style of policing that led to numerous complaints by black citizens.

The case of Alton Dunne, a black motorist arrested in July 1936, sparked the first major antibrutality campaign in Bedford-Stuyvesant. Brought to the Atlantic Avenue station house for questioning about a hit-and-run case, Dunne was allegedly beaten by three officers who resented his insistence on proper legal procedures. After spending the night in jail and receiving six stitches for head wounds, he was cleared and released. Dunne's case became one of the first orders of business of the newly formed Brooklyn branch of the National Negro Congress (NNC), a Popular Front organization established a few months earlier to fight racial discrimination and promote black participation in the labor movement. As in Harlem, Communists joined with an array of labor and community leaders in Brooklyn to represent Dunne and other black complainants in criminal and civil cases against the NYPD.[16] NNC chapters in Chicago, Philadelphia, Buffalo, and Washington, D.C., also led antibrutality drives in the late 1930s. As in the Brooklyn NNC, black Communists in these cities worked closely with non-Communist leaders to try to reduce police harassment and violence in their communities.[17]

Unfortunately, these campaigns made little headway against the entrenched power of municipal police departments in the 1930s. In New York neither the Brooklyn nor Harlem antibrutality campaigns won any significant victories, and both fizzled out in 1937. Police violence in the black community, however, did not disappear—nor did the left-wing reform networks spawned by the riot and the Popular Front. Before long, a new set of social and international conditions would produce a dramatic resurgence of antibrutality activity that would play an important role in black urban politics for more than a decade.

World War II and the New Black Militancy

The United States' entry into World War II introduced a whole new set of social, economic, and ideological forces that fueled racial militancy around the country. Mass mobilization of the military and civilian defense sector, a new wave of black migration, and a powerful antifascist sentiment created a domestic context that heightened black expectations and tested the nation's commitment to democracy. Civil rights activists pressed the country to make good on its claims of racial equality by protesting discrimination in the armed forces, employment, housing, and other areas. Law enforcement was no exception; in Harlem and other black communities, police violence became one of the most sensitive and symbolically loaded issues of the war era.

The renewed fight against police brutality took place amid a climate of mass mobilization and social upheaval. An estimated one million black men and women served in the U.S. military during the war, while an even greater number of black civilians migrated across state lines, mainly to northern and western defense centers. In New York, increased labor demands boosted migration, pushing the city's black population up from 458,000 in 1940 to an estimated 547,000 by 1945.[18] Although the war's demographic impact on the city was less dramatic than in Detroit or Los Angeles, the conflict nevertheless had profound effects on the city's African-American community. Thousands of black newcomers settled in or passed through New York via the military or in search of civilian employment. As a port of embarkation in proximity to numerous Army and Navy installations, New York hosted a constantly churning military population, and Harlem became a magnet for black servicemen on furlough or awaiting departure overseas. Civilian migrants were also drawn to existing black neighborhoods such as Harlem and Bedford-Stuyvesant because of chain migration networks as well as racially discriminatory housing practices elsewhere in the city. Located near the bustling Brooklyn Navy Yard, Bedford-Stuyvesant saw particularly explosive growth. Nicknamed "Little Harlem," Bedford-Stuyvesant was transformed from a mixed-race area to a predominantly black neighborhood by the late 1940s. In both Harlem and Bedford-Stuyvesant, racial transition sparked numerous conflicts, including those involving rival youth gangs. With many parents working overtime shifts and childcare and recreation in short supply, youth were often left unsupervised and at risk for delinquency. In white and black neighborhoods alike, the influx of large numbers of single war workers and servicemen fueled the entertainment and vice industries, leading to a rise in drunk and disorderly behavior. These new forms of wartime behavior, coupled with the shortage of police personnel due to military induction, led many observers to conclude that a major crime wave had broken out in the city's black neighborhoods.[19]

While migration brought social upheaval to New York's black communities, the departure of thousands of young African-American men into the military was equally significant. Black inductees faced a rigidly segregated armed forces in which Negro divisions were relegated to second-class status and treatment. The discrepancies were especially evident to black northerners stationed at military bases in the South. Throughout the war, the black press ran regular reports on the mistreatment of black servicemen on southern bases and the violence directed against them by civilian authorities in surrounding communities. In 1942–43 alone, white military and civilian police killed young black soldiers stationed in Virginia, Louisiana, Texas, Arkansas, Alabama, and South Carolina. Black outrage peaked in 1943 when the 369th Coast Artillery—New York's own Negro outfit—was transferred to Camp Stewart in Georgia, where white commanders were determined to put "the pride of Harlem" back in its place. Letters from the troops describing their poor treatment and humiliation poured into New York newspapers. Their unit, they reported, was being billeted in a garage and fed only cold sandwiches; their black officers had been transferred and replaced with white ones; and those who ventured into nearby Savannah were subjected to exclusion, harassment, and beatings by white police and business owners. In response, the NAACP organized a protest meeting in New York that drew several thousand people. Racial indignities, though, were not limited to the South. Incidents of racial discrimination and violence were also reported at nearby Fort Dix, New Jersey; Hempstead, Long Island; and the Fox Hills army base in Staten Island. For African Americans, the shoddy treatment of patriotic black men, who were risking their lives in a war against fascism, was a vile and hypocritical insult.[20]

The antifascist rhetoric that flourished during the war was a critical tool for civil rights advocates who sought to challenge racial inequality. Labor leader A. Philip Randolph was among the first to exploit the discrepancy between rhetoric and reality with his proposed march on Washington in 1941, which led to Executive Order 8802 barring discrimination in defense employment. Others elaborated on this theme, proclaiming a "Double V" campaign for victory against racism at home and against fascism abroad. Those working to curb police violence adopted these arguments as well, equating abusive New York cops with racist southern police and "Hitler's Gestapo." Of course Communists and Popular Front activists had been using antifascist rhetoric for years, but the changing ideological climate of the war made such appeals more powerful and resonant.

The resurgence of antibrutality organizing was centered around Adam Clayton Powell, Jr., pastor of the Abyssinian Baptist Church in Harlem. One of the city's oldest and most influential African-American churches, Abyssinian Baptist had been headed by Powell's father for thirty years until the younger Powell took over in 1938. A gifted orator, Powell also brought to the pastorate a broad network of political contacts in the Harlem community. During the 1935 Harlem Riot investigation, Powell had forged alliances with Communists, labor, and other progressive forces to work for fair employment and housing. In 1941 Powell rekindled his ties with the left and called on the Harlem CP and the American Labor Party (a left-wing alternative to the more conservative Tammany-controlled New York Democratic party) to support his candidacy for city council. Incorporating them into his "People's Committee" campaign, Powell won his seat with a strong showing. Though always fiercely independent, he would continue to work closely with Communists and left-wing unions whenever their political interests coincided.

As a city councilman, Powell adopted the Communist organizing approach combining legal defense with mass action to advance racial causes. He thus reorganized his People's Committee to act as an advocacy group for his constituents and to mobilize community action around pressing racial issues. Almost immediately, the People's Committee was deluged with Harlem citizens complaining of police harassment and brutality. The committee offered legal representation to the victims and published stirring accounts of their cases in Powell's weekly newspaper, the *People's Voice*. In the first four months of 1942, the People's Committee handled at least five cases of alleged brutality but failed to win any indictments. In May 1942, however, the *People's Voice* reported a new case, which would soon attract citywide attention.

On the evening of May 12, Harlem resident Lindsay Armstrong called police to report that his thirty-year-old son, Wallace, was mentally unstable and requested that he be committed to Bellevue

Hospital. When Officer Harold Reidman arrived with an ambulance, Wallace Armstrong proceeded to leave the building, ignoring Reidman's orders to halt. When the officer moved to stop him, Armstrong hit Reidman and then drew a knife. Reidman immediately drew his service revolver and told Armstrong to drop the knife. The deranged man then turned away and wandered off down 128th Street where he soon encountered another officer, Patrick Smith. There were conflicting accounts of what happened next. The police maintained that Armstrong attacked Smith with his knife and that Reidman shot Armstrong in defense. Other eyewitnesses, however, insisted that Armstrong made no attempt to use the knife and that Smith beat him severely about the head and arms with his nightstick and then shot him when he tried to escape the blows. The incident attracted a crowd, many of whom followed the ambulance to Harlem Hospital, where Armstrong was dead on arrival. When news of his death circulated, the angry crowd surrounded the hospital and pushed into the lobby shouting abuse at Reidman. Fearing a possible riot, the NYPD dispatched forty-six officers and mounted units to disperse the volatile gathering.

The killing of Wallace Armstrong was a classic example of poor police handling of a mentally ill individual. Armstrong's impaired condition and the plight of his aggrieved father generated widespread public sympathy and intensified the antipolice sentiment that had been festering for months. Representing the Armstrong family, Powell's Committee sought to inflame passions around the case with a front-page headline in the *People's Voice* that read: "Demented Man, Half-Conscious, Slain by HARLEM GESTAPO." Powell also called a community protest meeting the following week with handbills reading "One More Negro Brutally Beaten and Killed! Shot Down like a Dog by the Police." The intemperate tone of these appeals angered Mayor La Guardia, who refused Powell's requests for a meeting. He also ordered Powell to cancel the scheduled protest for fear that it might spark further disorder. Powell, however, pointedly refused and presided over a gathering of more than four thousand people at the Golden Gate Ballroom on May 17. During the meeting—which was monitored by the NYPD's Criminal Alien Squad—local black community leaders repeatedly equated the abusive behavior of the New York police with "Gestapo methods" and southern racism.[21]

Despite the vocal protest, the NYPD steadfastly defended the officers' actions and a grand jury refused to indict. The grand jury's action was consistent with its refusals to indict in earlier police assault cases that year. In the months that followed, the People's Committee, the NAACP, and other civil rights organizations would take up additional brutality cases against black citizens in Manhattan and Queens. In all of the cases pursued by the district attorney, all-white juries accepted police explanations and cleared the officers involved.[22]

Outraged by this "whitewashing," Powell called a protest meeting in Harlem on December 7 (the one-year anniversary of Pearl Harbor) where he outlined a list of wartime priorities to the roughly five thousand people in attendance. Dubbing it the "Harlem Charter," Powell called for an array of civil rights measures from fair employment practices in defense industries to desegregation of the military. Most dramatically, he demanded an end to police violence and killing of black civilians and servicemen, free legal aid for brutality victims, and increased black participation on grand juries. Just as the Atlantic Charter had laid the ideological groundwork for U.S. cooperation with the Allies, Powell attempted to lay out the terms of black cooperation with the American war effort.[23]

The Harlem Charter also denounced the so-called "crime smears"—efforts by the white press and police to paint Harlem as a zone of rampant criminality. Shrill headlines warning of Negro crime sprees had appeared sporadically in the late 1930s but became a frequent affair during the war years. Beginning in 1942, the *Times,* the *Daily News,* and the *World-Telegram* joined the Hearst-owned tabloids in serving up sensational front-page stories of blacks stabbing, raping, and mugging whites in Harlem and other black neighborhoods. Indeed, the term "mugging"—meaning robbery with violence—originated in New York in this period, nearly always with reference to black-on-white crime. The press campaign peaked in the spring of 1943 when a so-called mugging outbreak prompted police to pull a thousand officers from clerical duty and assign them to special plainclothes details in Harlem and Bedford-Stuyvesant. The NYPD also ordered the closing of the Savoy Ballroom, a popular Harlem nightspot run by one of Powell's partners at the *People's Voice*. While police and military authorities condemned the Savoy as a danger spot for prostitution and venereal disease, many Harlemites believed the dance hall was targeted because it catered to a racially mixed clientele. Like the crime wave headlines, the closing of the Savoy was intended to keep white visitors away from Harlem by stigmatizing the neighborhood as a dangerous lair of Negro crime and vice.

Black community leaders reacted bitterly to this stigma. Benjamin Davis, Jr., head of the Harlem CP, enlisted the support of Powell and State Assemblyman William T. Andrews to combat the crime smear campaigns. Brandishing arrest statistics that showed most major crimes had actually declined in 1942, Powell and Davis called for a boycott of newspapers that used lurid Negro crime headlines to sell more papers. They also demanded that the press discontinue use of the term "mugging" and the practice of racially identifying only black suspects. Such irresponsible reporting slandered the black community, they argued, and promoted police practices that fueled brutality. The increased police presence in Harlem served to reinforce notions that police were—as local Communists put it—"an occupying army" sent to protect whites, keep blacks in their place, and discourage racial mixing.[24]

The NYPD also targeted several transient hotels in the neighborhood in an attempt to suppress prostitution and the spread of venereal disease among servicemen. The Hotel Braddock on West 126th Street was among the suspect establishments. The site of several prostitution arrests, the Braddock was declared a "raided premises" in 1943, and a police officer was stationed in the lobby to deter sex violations. Locals reported that the hotel refused to rent rooms to mixed race couples, and that the officer sometimes raided rooms and physically separated those who managed to slip by the front desk. According to one investigator, the police crackdown on mixed race couples, both in the Braddock and on nearby Harlem streets, had aroused considerable ill feeling in the neighborhood. Here again, selective enforcement practices suggested that the NYPD tolerated vice in Harlem, taking action only when white people were affected.

Black distrust of the police was magnified by the shocking events in Detroit in June 1943. Following a series of racial clashes over housing, employment, and other issues, the nation's "arsenal of democracy" exploded in a mass race riot that lasted four days and left thirty-four people dead. Although both whites and blacks initiated the violence, the majority of the fatalities were among African Americans, most of whom were killed by police. As the young NAACP lawyer Thurgood Marshall pointed out in a *Crisis* article titled, "The Gestapo in Detroit," police clubbed and shot at black looters and bystanders while they took little or no action in white neighborhoods, even when white mobs were attacking blacks. Speaking before the city council in New York, Adam Clayton Powell drew parallels between the black citizens killed by Detroit police and the victims of NYPD brutality whose assailants had never been punished. Powell then called on Mayor La Guardia to meet with him and a biracial committee to discuss racial tensions in the city. In the wake of the Armstrong case, however, La Guardia had developed a deep distrust of Powell and ignored his entreaties. The mayor's failure to address pressing racial concerns in the city would soon lead to catastrophe.

The volatility of race relations in New York became painfully clear on August 1 when an incident of alleged police brutality at the Braddock Hotel sparked another racial uprising in Harlem. The altercation began when a white police officer stationed in the lobby arrested a young black woman for disorderly conduct (she had reportedly become abusive during a dispute with the elevator operator). In the midst of the arrest a second woman, Florine Roberts, intervened in the dispute. Roberts was a domestic from Connecticut who had come to Harlem to see her son, Robert Bandy, a twenty-six-year-old black MP on leave from the Army's 703d Battalion in Jersey City. Returning to retrieve her luggage at the hotel, Roberts witnessed the arrest and demanded that the officer release the young woman. Before long, Roberts's son also intervened, and a violent struggle ensued in which Bandy seized Collins's nightstick and hit him with it while Collins responded by shooting Bandy in the shoulder. Both men were taken to Sydenham Hospital, but none of the injuries proved life-threatening.[25]

Nevertheless, Harlem was soon abuzz with rumors that "a white cop killed a black soldier." Over the next few hours, angry black crowds gathered outside the hospital, the hotel, and the Twenty-eighth Precinct house. After police moved Collins from the hospital to the police station, over three thousand people surrounded the building and threatened to seize the officer. Before long, angry mobs began throwing bricks and bottles, overturning cars, fighting with police, smashing windows, and looting stores. The rioting continued through the night, resulting in 6 deaths, 185 injuries, 550 arrests, and at least a quarter of a million dollars in property damage.[26]

Although the origins of the riot were multifaceted and deeply rooted, the issue of police brutality was the most visible cause and was emblematic of a whole range of black grievances. Adam Clayton Powell, Sr., explained, "When Bandy hit Collins over the head with that club. . . he was mad with every white policeman throughout the United States who had constantly beaten, wounded, and often killed colored men and women without provocation." Given the community outrage over the mistreatment of black servicemen, Bandy's identity as a soldier was particularly important. The tragic and heroic figure of the young soldier reinforced notions of black patriotism and helped crystallize racial resentments. A Harlem newspaper described him as "a symbol of all the injustices our boys in uniform suffer," while NAACP secretary Walter White maintained that "Had it been a Negro civilian, however prominent, who was shot, there would have been no riot." The power of the rumor, he argued, was based on "the fury born of repeated unchecked, unpunished, and often unreported shooting, maiming, and insulting of Negro troops." As these comments suggest, the larger national context—especially the plight of black servicemen down South—played a critical role in perceptions of police brutality in New York and their potential to spark violence.[27]

The presence of Bandy's mother in the precipitating incident was also important. Rumors emphasized that Bandy had been shot trying to "protect his mother" and had been killed "in the presence of his mother." Like Wallace Armstrong's father, Florine Roberts had been witness to the shooting of her son over a relatively minor incident that had somehow escalated to the use of deadly force. The rumors, then, enlisted the listener's empathy with the aggrieved parent whose noble (or feeble) son had been needlessly sacrificed. The false rumors of Bandy's death also echoed those surrounding the Lino Rivera incident that sparked the 1935 Harlem Riot. In both versions, an innocent black youth was killed by a repressive white police system designed to protect whites or white business interests in Harlem. The symbolic significance of the victims, then, was key to the unleashing of violence.

In response to the riot, civil rights leaders condemned the U.S. government's failure to protect black servicemen and chided Mayor La Guardia for ignoring the recommendations of the 1935 riot commission. Arthur Garfield Hays, who had chaired the 1935 committee on crime and police, noted that none of the committee's recommendations had been implemented and suggested that the city do so immediately. La Guardia's handling of riot control, however, was widely praised. Dispatching thousands of police to the area, the mayor had instructed them to use force only when necessary and to shoot or use tear gas only as a last resort. La Guardia also called on Walter White and other black community leaders to join him in touring the riot area, using sound trucks to dispel rumors and urge calm. Most importantly, the city summoned squads of black MPs and deputized more than a thousand black men and women to help patrol Harlem streets in the wake of the disturbance. When they arrived on the scene, looters reportedly ceased their pillaging to cheer the black deputies. Moreover, the relatively small number of casualties was a stark contrast to the mayhem in Detroit.[28]

But not everyone was happy with the mayor's performance. Conservatives charged that police had been "handcuffed" in dealing with rioters and that police leniency had caused the riots in the first place. Westbrook Pegler, the acerbic columnist for the *World-Telegram,* articulated this viewpoint a few days after the riot when he blamed La Guardia for coddling Negro criminals and systematically undermining the authority of police. Referring to the mayor's tolerance of labor and political dissidents, Pegler argued that Harlem Communists had stirred up unrest and irreparably damaged police morale by turning every altercation with police into "a case of Cossack persecution."[29] Although Pegler's dim view of La Guardia was not widely shared in the wake of the riots, the political and racial resentments that underlay it would resurface a few months later.

Shortly after the Harlem Riot, the Midtown Civic League in Brooklyn launched a campaign to get the Kings County grand jury to investigate the crime problem in Bedford-Stuyvesant. Beginning its probe in late August, the all-white grand jury interviewed more than a hundred people and issued its presentment two months later. The grand jury report denounced the growing wave of vice and crime that made it "dangerous and unsafe to traverse the streets of this area before and particularly after dark. . . . Innocent and law-abiding citizens have been assaulted, robbed, murdered, and insulted both on public streets and on public conveyances." While denying there was a "race problem," the grand jury emphasized the recent influx of black migrants, the deterioration of the neighborhood, and the maladjustment and misbehavior of black newcomers. The most scathing criticism, however, was directed at Mayor La Guardia for assigning "an appallingly insufficient number of patrolmen" to the area and for failing to adopt "the 'muss em up' attitude that this kind of lawlessness deserves and requires."[30]

The grand jury presentment echoed the racist themes that characterized the earlier Harlem "crime wave" as well as similar crime scares in defense centers around the country in 1943. From Brooklyn, New York, to Oakland, California, black migrants were used as scapegoats to explain wartime racial tensions and social disorder in communities undergoing rapid social and demographic change. Black community leaders in New York immediately condemned the presentment as "a severe indictment of the Negro community" that failed to address the underlying social and economic factors giving rise to such conditions. Building on the Popular Front alliances developed in the late 1930s, the Brooklyn National Negro Congress, the CIO Community Council, and Peter Cacchione, the Communist city councilman from Brooklyn, held mass meetings protesting the presentment and the racist motivations of the Midtown Civic League.[31]

Acutely aware of the volatility of race relations in the city, Mayor La Guardia dismissed the grand jury report as the work of "crackpots and publicity seekers" and launched his own survey of local crime conditions. In late November, the mayor issued a set of corrected crime statistics for the neighborhood that contradicted the grand jury's dire scenario. At the same time, however, he acknowledged a growing juvenile delinquency problem by establishing a new juvenile-aid unit in Bedford-Stuyvesant to focus on crime prevention. Fearful of sparking another racial conflagration, La Guardia resisted demands for a stepped-up police presence and specifically warned officers against using the "muss em up" tactics proposed in the presentment. He thus renounced the rough-and-tough crime-fighting tactics that his own administration had so strongly promoted in the late 1930s.[32]

Following the advice of the Mayor's Committee on Unity (MCU), a newly formed municipal commission on race relations, La Guardia and Valentine also moved to increase recruitment of African-American officers. In 1943, there were only 155 black officers out of a force of 16,000 — only 22 more than a decade earlier. Moreover, the number of black detectives in Harlem had fallen precipitously—from 10 in the late 1930s to only 5 in 1943. La Guardia correctly noted that wartime shortages of manpower and funding had hampered recruitment efforts. But as black leaders also pointed out, racially biased promotion practices as well as strong antipolice sentiments in black communities lowered morale among black officers and made recruitment more difficult. The New York Urban League and the Harlem YMCA tried to counter these trends by establishing training courses for potential black recruits in late 1943. The following spring, the NYPD acknowledged such efforts when Commissioner Valentine announced a new campaign to recruit black officers: "I say to colored boys throughout the city, come join us. We need you!"[33]

Over the next decade the number of black officers increased from 155 to more than 600, raising black representation in the NYPD from less than 1 percent to a little more than 3 percent. Although civil rights groups had hoped for more, they supported the NYPD's effort to diversify its ranks. But how such diversification might affect police-community relations was unclear. The vast majority of the NYPD's new black recruits were dispatched to Harlem and other black precincts where they served as low-level beat cops or as detectives for the vice or Criminal Alien Squads (where they were used to spy on black vice operators and radicals). Barred from the upper echelons of the command structure, black officers had neither the opportunity nor the power to reshape the police culture. And those who managed to break into the mid-level command ranks did so by demonstrating their loyalty to the police fraternity and culture, defining themselves as "blue" rather than black. The pressure to maintain police solidarity was so strong that attempts to form a black police association during the war failed due to fear of management recrimination. In the late 1940s, a group of black police began meeting secretly at the Harlem YMCA and formed the Guardians Association, a fraternal organization of African-American officers. After a long struggle, the NYPD acknowledged its charter in 1949, but it was not until the 1960s that the Guardians would become a vocal force in challenging police practices in black communities.

For the most part, the NYPD viewed black police as "riot insurance"—a political concession to angry black communities which would hopefully help prevent and/or control future outbreaks of racial violence, just as the black deputies had done during the 1943 riot. There was no intention, however, of changing police procedures or of addressing the larger context of racial animosity in the city. Without such changes, the problem of police violence in the black community would continue to fester.[34]

The Postwar Era

In the postwar period, neither the local or national climate bode well for improved race relations. In New York and other northern cities, the urban economy and population was in flux. Many older manufacturing operations shut down, relocating to the suburbs or the Sunbelt and displacing thousands of blue collar workers. White workers followed these jobs into the suburbs and, with the help of the GI Bill, settled in the new affordable (and all-white) subdivisions in Levittown and other communities in Long Island and New Jersey. Beginning in the late 1940s, then, the city's white population began to decline, replaced by a continuing influx of migrants from the South and the Caribbean. As these newcomers overspilled the boundaries of existing racial/ethnic enclaves, social tensions grew, often in the form of youth gang rivalries and street violence. Growing competition for stable jobs in the city's dwindling manufacturing sector, combined with daily struggles over neighborhood turf, schools, and services, made postwar urban life increasingly volatile. Black and Puerto Rican residents were the most disadvantaged in these struggles, but also became scapegoats for more generalized fears of crime and disorder in the postwar city.

Racial tensions were even greater in the South, where white mobs and local law enforcement used violence and intimidation to enforce black subordination. The late 1940s saw a bitter backlash designed to reassert traditional racial hierarchies disrupted by the war. The year 1946 proved to be especially volatile. In Columbia, Tennessee, a black serviceman's efforts to defend his mother from insults and abuse at the hands of a white shopkeeper precipitated a mob attack on the city's black district that left two dead and more than a hundred in custody. More violence ensued that summer when white vigilantes fatally shot a black veteran, his wife, and another couple in Monroe, Georgia, and lynched Maceo Snipes, a young black man who had dared to vote in that state's primary election. Alarmed at the growing violence and the inaction of southern authorities, black civil rights activists mobilized black voters in the North to press for federal intervention to punish the perpetrators.[35]

For New Yorkers, however, the most shocking incident of racial violence was a southern police officer's assault on Bronx native Isaac Woodard, a recently discharged Army sergeant. Within hours of release from his post in South Carolina, Woodard boarded a bus for home and soon became involved in a verbal dispute with the white driver. When the bus stopped in nearby Batesburg, the driver summoned the local police chief, who removed Woodard from the bus and savagely beat him with a nightstick, permanently blinding him in both eyes. The police chief, who was indicted for assault, was later acquitted before a cheering South Carolina courtroom. In New

York, the NAACP pressured the U.S. Justice Department to launch an investigation while a coalition of civil rights groups sponsored a mass protest rally and benefit at Lewisohn Stadium in the Bronx that attracted more than twenty thousand people and numerous black celebrity performers.[36]

New Yorkers' vigorous response to the Woodard case was conditioned by wartime resentment of police brutality against black servicemen but also by more recent events in and around the city. With the return of many black veterans to the metropolitan area in 1945, more and more incidents of police violence seemed to involve these patriotic native sons. The 1943 Harlem Riot had demonstrated the explosive nature of incidents involving police and black servicemen, and tensions around these symbolically loaded encounters continued in the postwar period. Hoping for a hero's welcome, most black vets returned to high unemployment, a critical housing shortage, and a combative police force determined to control urban disorder fueled by economic adjustment and racial transition. In fact, in the year prior to the blinding of Woodard, the *People's Voice* reported at least six local incidents of alleged brutality involving black servicemen or veterans.[37] The most infamous case occurred in a bus station in nearby Freeport, Long Island, where a white rookie officer fatally shot two black brothers, Charles and Alfonzo Ferguson, while also wounding another brother, Joseph. All three were present or former servicemen (Charles was in uniform at the time) and were unarmed when the officer shot them while making an arrest for disorderly conduct. Despite mass protests and a major legal effort, an all-white Nassau County grand jury declined to indict the officer.[38]

The failure to obtain justice from state and local authorities in the Ferguson and Woodard cases convinced civil rights activists of the need for federal intervention. Police brutality, they argued, was a problem in both the North and the South and constituted a form of state-sanctioned racist violence that was closely related to lynching and mob violence. As in the earlier Tenderloin Riot, black activists equated police brutality with lynching, and now dubbed it "Lynching Northern Style." Like the Scottsboro protesters of the 1930s, Communist and left-wing activists consistently made connections between northern brutality cases and recent incidents of southern mob violence. Both were "part and parcel of the whole postwar wave of reaction designed 'to put the Negro back in his place,'" said Adam Clayton Powell, and both were generally tolerated and covered up by local authorities.

Ultimately, both liberals and radicals took this message to President Harry Truman in September 1946, when they met with him to demand federal protection for civil rights. Although Truman pointedly refused to condemn lynching, he soon convened an executive committee on civil rights that issued a pathbreaking 1947 report, *To Secure These Rights*. Among its many findings and proposals, the report recognized that "improper police practices are still widespread" and recommended that Congress enact a new statute specifically outlawing police use of excessive force and the third degree. Most critically, the committee acknowledged the weakness of the Justice Department's Civil Rights Division (established in 1939) and its poor prosecution record. Acting on the committee's recommendation, Congress in 1948 revised a section of the U.S. criminal code to strengthen federal authority in civil rights cases where state authorities had failed to act. Although the new penalties were weak —a one-thousand-dollar fine and/or a year in prison—civil rights activists could henceforth appeal to federal prosecutors with some hope of getting a hearing outside the often highly politicized local courts.[39]

In general, however, antibrutality activists in New York focused their efforts on the local level. After the 1943 Harlem Riot, Popular Front organizing against police brutality had receded as the Communist party line shifted to stress cooperation between the United States and the Soviet Union in the wake of the Tehran Agreement. Although Powell's Peoples Committee continued to represent brutality victims, Benjamin Davis, Jr., and other Communist activists temporarily withdrew from such work, embracing the accommodationist tendency known as "Browderism." With the end of the war, however, the party line shifted again, becoming overtly anticapitalist and antiracist. Anxious to resume antibrutality organizing, Communist City Council members Ben Davis and Peter Cacchione organized a Citizens' Committee Against Police Brutality (CCAPB) in Harlem and Bedford-Stuyvesant in December 1945 that included local NAACP branches, veterans groups, and CIO unions—thus laying the groundwork for a new broad-based mobilization. As in 1942–43, the committee not only defended alleged victims but protested crime smear campaigns by the New York press.[40]

The CCAPB also condemned official prescriptions for violent and aggressive policing recently issued by Mayor La Guardia and his successor, William O'Dwyer (1946–1950). An Irish-American former police officer and district attorney, O'Dwyer was the last of the old-style Tammany mayors. Republican and reform forces predicted the city would open up to gambling and vice interests under his administration, and O'Dwyer quickly moved to dispel those rumors by ordering stepped up vice raids and aggressive enforcement. O'Dwyer's police commissioner, Arthur Wallander, attempted (with little success) to carry out this program. Wallander was a keen admirer of Valentine's "muss em up" approach and periodically echoed those sentiments to his commanders. In September 1947, for instance, Wallander instructed forty top detectives to

Go out and get the hoodlums off our streets. I mean get the street corner loafers and get the easy money men, the ones who never work, but manage to keep well dressed and have plenty of spending money. Give them the proper treatment. *You know what I mean by that* [emphasis mine].

Once again, official efforts to crack down on crime and corruption served to sanction tough and often illegal police tactics. Furthermore, the return to the muss-em-up style came at a time when thousands of new officers (mainly veterans) were being appointed to the force under accelerated training programs that put rookies on the street prior to graduation from the academy. Concerned with this shift toward strong-arm tactics, the CCAPB passed a resolution in 1945 urging the city council to conduct a formal investigation of police methods, a demand that would be repeated many times over the next decade.[41]

The CCAPB drew support from numerous liberal and left organizations, including the NAACP and the Civil Rights Congress (CRC). The latter was a new left-wing legal defense organization established in 1946 to protect the rights of racial minorities and political dissenters. Although not formally affiliated with the Communist party, the CRC counted many prominent Communists among its leadership and was considered the successor to the now-defunct International Labor Defense. In New York, the local CRC branch, headed by writer Dashiell Hammett, immediately made police brutality its top priority and worked closely with Benjamin Davis on a number of recent cases. As in earlier antibrutality campaigns, the Civil Rights Congress approached police brutality as a political problem that required both legal representation in the courtroom and "mass defense" tactics such as picketing, demonstrations, and petitions to put public pressure on the system.[42] Local branches of the NAACP also represented a growing number of brutality victims in this period and soon embraced the mass action techniques pioneered by the left. While the NAACP and the CRC seldom worked together on individual cases, they sometimes joined forces on neighborhood and citywide coalitions to address police misconduct. Tensions around anti-Communism complicated such coalition efforts, but they did not become fatal until the onset of the Cold War a few years later.

City officials nevertheless tried to exploit such divisions. In August 1946, in the wake of the Ferguson and Woodard cases, a group of prominent Harlem leaders met with Commissioner Wallander and Dan Dodson of the Mayor's Committee on Unity to discuss the brutality problem, including two local cases handled by the CRC. Afterward, Wallander denounced the antibrutality efforts of "certain groups" as a "campaign of calumny" and defended police accounts of events. He vigorously rejected any attempts to compare these cases to those of Isaac Woodard, the Ferguson brothers, or the killings in Monroe, Georgia. The NYPD cases, he insisted, did not involve racial bias and could not be put in the same category "with deplorable incidents of lynching or racial prejudice that have transpired in other sections of the country."[43] Wallander thus sought to distinguish more enlightened forms of northern justice from the racial atrocities taking place in the postwar South, and he attacked the Communist left for inciting racial resentment through such false comparisons.

Many incidents of police violence in New York did, in fact, reflect similar patterns of racial bias and control as those in the South. One of the first cases taken up by the CCAPB, for example, involved Democratic district leader, Guy Brewer, who had been beaten by a police officer at a Harlem polling place in October 1945. Brewer had been arguing with an election official who closed the registration board early, turning away black voters. The officer stationed at the polling place arrested Brewer, kicked him down a flight of stairs, and broke his nose, but he was never brought up on disciplinary charges (despite a recommendation to do so by the district inspector). Just as a dispute over black voting rights lay beneath the Brewer case, the issue of black access to transportation sparked two other incidents. In the summer of 1946, the CRC represented three black defendants, Carlton Powell, Josie Stewart, and Helen Urquhart, who had been physically assaulted by police following disputes with taxi drivers in lower Manhattan. Powell, a musician heading home from a late-night performance in Greenwich Village, argued with a cabbie who refused to take him to Harlem. A couple of weeks later, Stewart and Urquhart had a similar problem trying to get a cab to the Bronx. In both cases, police intervened on behalf of the cab drivers, ignoring city law that barred hack drivers from refusing fares to particular neighborhoods. The NYPD claimed that the officers used justifiable force to subdue the angry passengers—a claim disputed by the complainants. Whether or not the passengers physically resisted, most black New Yorkers saw the officers' refusal to enforce the hack regulations as the key provocation. Beyond the violence itself, police failure to enforce black political or social rights was the critical issue in these cases.

White radicals in Greenwich Village also protested police tolerance of white vigilantism, comparing it to southern-style mob violence. In August 1946 a group of left-wing residents organized the Greenwich Village branch of the Civil Rights Congress to combat what would later be termed "hate crimes" against African Americans and Jews in the city's bohemian center. In response to vigilante attacks on black musicians working at Café Society (an interracial jazz club where Billie Holiday sang the antilynching ballad, "Strange Fruit"), the Village CRC circulated petitions demanding police action against such crimes and presented them to local precinct commanders. Getting no response, the group filed its complaint with NYPD headquarters, listing more than twenty assaults in the Sheridan Square area in the past six months. Protest peaked the following spring after police failed to intervene in a white gang attack on a black painter and his white female friend as they exited a Village restaurant. Following a vocal protest meeting attended by some four hundred people, the Mayor's Committee on Unity met with concerned Village residents to discuss the problem in April 1947. Despite official assurances of improved police response, the CRC continued to monitor a steady stream of hate crimes in the area over the next two years.[44]

Postwar protests over police misconduct also centered on cases involving warrantless searches, a practice that was particularly prevalent in the city's black neighborhoods. Such cases, which had been common in working-class neighborhoods during Prohibition, reemerged in the postwar years as Mayor O'Dwyer ordered crackdowns on the growing network of bookmakers operating in the city. As in the 1920s, payoffs to police sheltered the biggest operators, so raids tended to focus on small-time operators or private individuals suspected of running games in their homes. One of the first cases to come to light involved a Harlem candy-store owner named Samuel Symonette. In October 1947 three plainclothes detectives entered his store looking for policy slips and brutally beat him when he protested the search. Representing Symonette, who was hospitalized with multiple injuries, Ben Davis and the CRC filed assault charges against the officers and demanded a police investigation. Despite testimony by witnesses who saw the officers beat Symonette, the police successfully scuttled the complaint, claiming that the suspect was a "cop fighter" who had resisted arrest. The CRC's protest over the warrantless search was also rejected on the grounds that the Fourth Amendment did not apply in state jurisdictions. The antibrutality movement's challenge to warrantless searches and other unconstitutional procedures in this period contributed to the eventual demise of such procedures in the 1960s.[45]

Other more conventional incidents of street brutality attracted attention because the victims were war veterans. Perhaps the most shocking was the shooting of Lloyd Curtis Jones, a disabled veteran and aspiring musician. On the evening of August 6, 1947, Jones had been singing with friends near the Columbus Circle entrance to Central Park when a rookie officer on his first tour of duty approached them. The officer, Francis LeMaire, demanded to see Jones's identification and then ordered him to leave. When Jones protested, the officer began hitting him with his nightstick until Jones grabbed the baton away. LeMaire then drew his gun and fired three shots into Jones's stomach. Despite the legal efforts of the New York NAACP, the NYPD refused to discipline LeMaire. The Jones case was one of more than two dozen postwar brutality cases filed by black New Yorkers—many of them veterans—in which local authorities took no legal or disciplinary action.[46]

Amid growing community outrage over the city's inaction, Mayor O'Dwyer made a stunning statement denouncing alleged police brutality in two recent cases—both of them involving white motorists. In one case, that of Associated Press photographer Murray Becker, O'Dwyer personally intervened with the district attorney to press for a grand jury hearing and met with police officials to reiterate his policy on excessive force. Commissioner Wallander quickly filed disciplinary charges against the accused officer, explaining "Our policy is to be kind to good people and rough with bums and gangsters." Contrasting the department's aggressive response to the Becker case with its passivity in African-American cases, black New Yorkers could only conclude that the NYPD regarded them all as "bums and gangsters."[47] The following week, when the cases of Samuel Symonette and two other black brutality victims came to light, Ben Davis and Guy Brewer organized a community conference on police brutality in Harlem.

On October 24, more than two hundred citizens gathered at the Harlem YMCA to discuss recent cases and hammer out a series of resolutions. As in earlier antibrutality campaigns, the conference brought together a number of progressive groups including the NAACP, the CRC, local churches, CIO unions, and left-wing political parties. They reiterated their demands for action on twenty-six brutality cases, the withdrawal of NYPD "muss em up" orders, and support for Davis's council resolution on police practices. Reflecting the more recent efforts of the Civil Rights Congress, the group also lent support to the CRC's campaign on behalf of Symonette and the fight against vigilante violence in Greenwich Village. Echoing the priorities of the NAACP, they passed a resolution demanding the appointment of a black police captain in Harlem and the further integration of blacks into all levels of the NYPD hierarchy. The group prevailed on Rev. John H. Johnson, a black police chaplain, to arrange a meeting with Commissioner Wallander to deliver these demands.[48]

On November 12, eighteen conference representatives met with Commissioner Wallander and convinced him to appoint a special committee to review the cases of Samuel Symonette, Lloyd Curtis Jones, and several other recent Harlem cases. Headed by Reverend Johnson, the committee included Walter White of the NAACP, Edward Lewis of the National Urban League, Dan Dodson of the MCU, Samuel Battle (now parole commissioner), and *New York Age* editor C. B. Powell. Perhaps remembering the furor over the 1935 Harlem Riot commission hearings, Wallander soon informed the committee that it would have no investigatory powers and would function as a closed-door advisory body reporting directly to him. He also added several white police officials to the committee who effectively shut down any attempts at independent oversight of department procedures. By early 1948, the committee was in disarray. According to Guy Brewer, chair John Johnson had "sabotaged" the committee by allowing Wallander to restrict its powers since it "would not be a rubber stamp and submit to his attempts to whitewash the police department." In early March, Johnson officially disbanded the ineffectual committee, saying its review of cases had been completed and that all had been appropriately handled by the courts.[49]

The police review committee was an insincere effort to deal with racial injustice and the growing social tensions it provoked. Limiting its membership to moderate black leaders, the police commissioner used the committee as a political buffer between the department and a more militant Harlem movement. But while the committee's deliberations gave the appearance that the city was doing something about the brutality problem, the NYPD in fact stymied serious investigative efforts. By limiting the committee to a mere review of public court records, police obscured some of the key problems in such cases: police intimidation and perjury, a biased and inefficient NYPD disciplinary system, and the unwillingness of district attorneys to pursue indictments against police. At the same time, city officials pointed to the board's exoneration of police as prima facie evidence that brutality was a bogus issue fabricated by Communists. In a well-publicized speech at Riverside Church two days after the disbanding of the board, MCU chair Dan Dodson —the only white civilian member of the police review committee —praised the group's work and described antibrutality efforts as "studied attempts" to discredit the police. Warning against the "sweep of totalitarianism from the East," he condemned those at home who "traffic in human prejudice, and use our prejudices as an instrument to stir us up, create mistrust, divide and ultimately conquer us."[50]

The city administration's dismissal of antibrutality organizing as a Communist plot enraged many black activists. Convinced that city officials were disingenuous about curbing police abuses, the New York and Brooklyn branches of the NAACP decided to make police brutality their top priority and organized vigorous campaigns in 1948–49. At the same time, under the impact of Cold War anti-Communism, the left-wing Civil Rights Congress found its leaders and allies under attack by anti-Communists and had to divert many of its financial and legal resources toward political defense. Moving into the vacuum, local NAACP branches quickly became the leading force in antibrutality work in Harlem and Bedford-Stuyvesant. However, unlike the national NAACP, whose leaders grew increasingly wary of cooperating with Communists, the local branches remained more open to radical influences and strategies until the end of the 1940s.[51]

In Manhattan, the New York NAACP branch announced the formation of a Committee for Action Against Police Brutality, which would receive, investigate, and act upon brutality complaints. Led by civil rights and labor activist Herbert Hill, the committee established an office in Harlem open three nights a week. There, Hill recorded complaints from citizens, collected evidence, interviewed witnesses, and arranged legal advice and representation by NAACP lawyers. Reflecting the left's approach to antibrutality organizing, the committee also used "mass action," a strategy of grassroots community organizing designed to build public support and pressure for governmental action.[52]

A similar campaign by the Brooklyn branch began in early 1949 in response to several fatal police shootings in Bedford-Stuyvesant. The first occurred in February when two police detectives acting on a gambling tip forced their way into the apartment of George Waddell and his family. When Waddell protested the invasion, police beat him with a blackjack and then shot him three times (twice in the back). According to Waddell's wife, police discovered a toy gun in the apartment; the detectives later claimed that Waddell had pointed it at them, forcing them to fire in self defense. A Kings County grand jury refused to indict the officers, ruling that they had acted in the line of duty and therefore had immunity from prosecution under state law. NAACP activists challenged this law as a license for abusive police behavior and called for its repeal. As in the earlier Symonette case, they also challenged the right of police to break into private dwellings and use evidence collected during warrantless searches. Their protests were taken up by Harlem state assembly members Hulan Jack and Elijah Crump, who sponsored legislation barring the admissibility of evidence obtained from unlawful searches.[53]

An equally egregious incident occurred a few months later on Memorial Day 1949. While stopped at an intersection in Bedford-Stuyvesant that evening, Herman Newton became engaged in an argument and fistfight with another motorist, an off-duty police officer (in civilian clothes) named Donald Mullen. According to numerous eyewitnesses, Mullen drew his gun and fired a shot at Newton, who then fled. Pursued by Mullen, Newton tried to hide in a doorway, but the officer chased him out and shot him several more times. Although witnesses described Newton as unarmed, Mullen claimed that Newton attacked him with a jackknife and that he had shot in self-defense. Brooklyn district attorney Miles McDonald, however, reported that he could not locate any witnesses to the incident, and his presentation to the grand jury brought no indictment. Mullen, meanwhile, was never suspended or even transferred out of the area. In a subsequent civil suit filed on behalf of Newton's

widow, however, NAACP attorney Samuel Korb had no trouble locating eight eyewitnesses. Using their testimony to demonstrate
that Newton's shooting was unjustified, he won a surprising victory
from an all-white Brooklyn jury. The state appealed the decision, but
the New York State Court of Appeals upheld it, awarding a fifty-
two-thousand-dollar judgment in 1952. The suit was one of several
successful civil cases involving black brutality victims in this period,
suggesting that civil rights activism was beginning to have some impact on public opinion, even among whites.[54]

Nevertheless, the Brooklyn NAACP was irate over the district attorney's failure to win criminal indictments against officers in the
Newton, Waddell, and other recent cases. Seeking to bypass the
city's uncooperative criminal justice system, the Brooklyn and New
York branches launched petition campaigns directed at Republican
governor Thomas Dewey, calling on him to conduct an investigation of recent brutality cases. Dewey wrote to Mayor O'Dwyer urging him to look into the matter, and O'Dwyer promptly dispatched
Milton Stewart of the Mayor's Committee on Unity to confer with
the NAACP. Meeting for several hours on June 17, Samuel Korb of
the Brooklyn branch, Charles Levy of the New York branch, and
Franklin Williams of the national office detailed the many obstacles
involved in prosecuting police officers. Among the most common
problems, they said, were police perjury and frame-ups, attempts to
intimidate or confuse witnesses, the reluctance of district attorneys
to pursue indictments, and the long delays in investigating and
bringing cases to trial. They also objected to illegal entries and
searches and the immunity enjoyed by police officers in the line of
duty. In the end, however, the meeting brought no real changes in
policy or procedure.[55]

The Brooklyn branch thus redoubled its efforts on the state level,
registering a litany of complaints against the mayor, the police commissioner, and the Brooklyn district attorney. In an accompanying
deposition, the Brooklyn branch president, James Powers, stated
that it was harder "to secure an indictment against police officials
who have victimized Negro citizens in Kings County than it is in
some of the most lynch-ridden places of the South." Powers's repeated charges of "police terror" reflected the radical tenor of the

Brooklyn campaign and the wholesale attack it was waging on the city's Democratic establishment. In fact, the CRC and the American Labor Party had closely cooperated with the Brooklyn branch in organizing efforts around the Waddell and Newton cases. Moreover, when the branch sponsored a metro-area conference on police brutality in June 1949, well-known Communist and CRC national chairman William Patterson and left-wing members of the American Labor Party and CIO were among the featured speakers.[56] As we shall see, the participation of Communists and other leftists in the Brooklyn and New York branches was a source of growing concern to the national office and to other liberal groups in the antibrutality coalition.

Although anti-Communism had a long history in the NAACP, it became particularly virulent in 1949. Longtime leaders of the national NAACP remained bitter over what they saw as an inconsistent party commitment to black civil rights. Citing the CP's complacency on racial issues during the war years, NAACP leaders like Roger Wilkins insisted that Communists' primary loyalties were to the Soviet Union and that their participation in the NAACP would damage the association's credibility during the Cold War. Moreover, with the rise of anti-Communist hysteria, left-wing groups like the CRC increasingly linked the fight against police brutality to police repression of radicals under the Smith Act. While this was consistent with the party's broadly conceived understanding of state repression, many liberals saw this stance as self-serving and accused Communists of using police brutality to embarrass the United States and advance the party's own agenda. At the same time, radicals were challenging the local Democratic establishment through third-party campaigns on the American Labor Party ticket in 1949, vowing to fight police brutality and other forms of racial bias. For many on the left, supporting candidates who pledged to tackle police problems made good sense; many national NAACP leaders, however, believed that radicals were simply exploiting police brutality as a campaign issue.[57]

These growing tensions came to the surface in the summer of 1949. At the NAACP national convention in July, there was serious dissention over resolutions on police brutality introduced by the

Brooklyn branch and other affiliates. NAACP officials tabled the resolutions, claiming that police behavior was not a central focus of the NAACP program but only one facet of the larger civil rights struggle. Concerned about the role of Communists and leftists in local affiliates, the national office sought to distance itself from their organizing efforts. Other liberal groups followed suit. A few days later, representatives of the Protestant and Jewish Community Councils of Brooklyn, who had earlier pledged to join the branch's antibrutality campaign, announced that they were withdrawing because they were unwilling to work with the "groups who are working with them." Catholic liberals also shied away, charging that Communists in the Brooklyn branch "use this issue as a means for attracting and arousing a crowd."[58] The most serious breach, though, began in August when Mayor O'Dwyer announced the appointment of a three-member committee to investigate police brutality in Brooklyn.

At first glance, the creation of the committee seemed to be a victory for antibrutality forces. The committee, headed by Rev. J. M. Coleman of St. Philip's Protestant Episcopal Church in Bedford-Stuyvesant, was instructed to review the cases of George Waddell, Herman Newton, and six other black complainants. Local activists quickly realized, however, that this committee, like the earlier one in 1947, was a political holding action. Meeting quietly behind closed doors for months, the committee was designed to muffle the antibrutality campaign until after the fall election. When the committee indicated that it would not hold open proceedings, the presidents of the New York and Brooklyn NAACP branches wired O'Dwyer and the committee chair demanding public hearings. When the committee refused, the local branches decided not to cooperate with its requests for material and testimony. On October 10, roughly a hundred members of the Brooklyn, Jamaica, and New York branches picketed city hall to protest the "concerted plan to prevent public knowledge of the facts of recent murders and assaults of Negroes by police officers." The NAACP national office, while also urging open meetings, continued working with the committee, hoping that it would hold public hearings after the election.[59]

The committee, however, never did conduct hearings and did not release its findings until more than a year later. In a December 1950 report, the committee exonerated police in all eight cases, essentially reiterating the findings of the district attorney and grand jury that "criminal action was not warranted or was impossible due to lack of identification." The report did recommend departmental disciplinary hearings for officers involved in four of the cases, but the police commissioner rejected the proposal. In the end, the committee sought to downplay the entire brutality issue, noting that the NYPD "makes thousand of arrests yearly. The relatively small number of complaints...does not support the charge of widespread police brutality." Civil rights leaders were enraged at this latest "whitewashing," but antibrutality forces were now in disarray and unable to formulate an effective response.[60]

Bitter infighting over anti-Communism in the NAACP had taken its toll on the antibrutality movement. Concerned about Communist infiltration of the New York area branches and other large urban affiliates, national NAACP leaders tightened their control over local branches. Beginning in late 1949, the NAACP took a firm stand against working with the left-wing CRC. This policy was also extended to the branches, where attempts to form joint defense committees for police brutality victims were strongly discouraged. At its 1950 national convention in Boston, the NAACP took more extreme measures: It prohibited membership to Communists and empowered the national office to revoke the charters of local affiliates and reorganize them. The threat of such action from above resulted in a rash of purges at the local level and a major turnover in leadership, including that of the New York branches.[61] These upheavals did not bode well for the prospects of community-based antibrutality campaigns in which radicals had taken leading roles.

One of the first tests came in December 1950, when two Harlem patrolmen shot and killed John Derrick, a disabled and recently discharged Korean war veteran. According to several witnesses, Derrick was unarmed and in uniform and was shot while lined up with his hands above his head. As in the 1946 Ferguson brothers case, police claimed that Derrick was drunk and had reached for a gun (no gun was found during an initial search, but one was then "discovered" during a second search). To make matters worse, more than a thousand dollars in take-home pay that Derrick had been carrying disappeared. Despite the testimony of dozens of Harlem residents, an all-white grand jury refused to indict the officers, and the latter were fully exonerated by the department. But organizing protests in this staunchly anti-Communist climate proved difficult. Herbert Hill, the former head of the New York branch's antibrutality committee, was sent to Harlem by the national office to help coordinate local action. His report was discouraging. Only a handful of people attended the meetings, many of whom were "not at all convinced of their own position on the Derrick case and cannot therefore function in a forthright manner." They objected to Hill's use of the term "police brutality" on one of the leaflets and showed little enthusiasm for carrying out the necessary organizing tasks. Hill concluded that they were "organizing a fiasco" and expressed his desire to disassociate himself from this "course of action that I believe to be shameful in the light of all the facts of the case." Ultimately, the protest movement fragmented, with a variety of Communist and anti-Communist groups holding separate meetings and rallies.[62]

Hill faced a similar dilemma in Brooklyn when he was sent there in 1951 following the fatal shooting of Henry Fields. A twenty-seven-year-old father of four and resident of Brownsville's growing African-American community, Fields had been pulled over by a patrolman following a minor traffic accident. The officer claimed that Fields refused a direct order to halt and that he shot him to prevent his escape. Witnesses, however, claimed that Fields was not trying to escape and posed no threat to the officer's safety. Once again, an all-white grand jury declined to indict. Protests by Brooklyn's antibrutality forces, however, were disjointed and ineffective. Refusing any cooperation with organizations open to Communists, the Brooklyn NAACP launched its own support committee with the help of the American Jewish Committee and other liberal groups. Much to Hill's dismay, these groups firmly rejected any form of mass action or community organizing, fearing association with Communist tactics. Instead, the committee limited its activities to legal defense work, believing that quiet legal reform and political negotiation would reap more benefits than "meaningless agitation." This reformist approach soon took hold on a citywide basis with the formation of the Committee on Police Practices in 1951, a coalition of liberal organizations led by the NAACP and ACLU that emphasized legal, legislative, and administrative reform. Without a groundswell of grassroots support, however, this approach would bear little fruit for the remainder of the decade.[63]

The Civil Rights Congress, meanwhile, established its own committee to protest the Fields shooting. In this case and others, the CRC reverted to the old ILD practice of holding a "people's" trial to demonstrate popular outrage over the shooting. They also conducted a petition campaign calling for the arrest and suspension of the accused officer, indemnity for Field's widow and children, and an end to police brutality against black and Puerto Rican New Yorkers. Despite constant police surveillance and harassment, the local CRC affiliates in Brooklyn, Queens, Manhattan, and the Bronx continued to agitate and organize against cases of police violence, forming citizen support committees with local community and church groups. In the 1950s, however, they had almost no contact or cooperation with the liberal reformers of the NAACP and the Committee on Police Practices.[64]

During these years, the CRC also shifted its focus to the international arena, drawing on its local files to compile a detailed exposé of racial violence in the United States. Submitted to the United Nations in 1951, the CRC's 240-page petition, *We Charge Genocide,* identified American racism as a violation of international human rights under the UN's antigenocide convention of 1948. The petition reflected the CRC's view that lynching, mob violence, and police brutality were part of a homegrown fascist movement to oppress black Americans and protect capitalist profits. Noting the spread of racial violence to northern cities, the CRC argued that police bullets were replacing the lynch rope and that "the killing of Negroes has become police policy in the United States." The study went on to document hundreds of cases of racial violence from 1945 to 1950, including eleven police killings and more than forty police assaults of African Americans in New York City. Though generally dismissed in the United States as Communist propaganda, *We Charge Genocide* dealt a serious blow to America's image in Europe, Africa, and Asia, and forced U.S. policymakers to defend the nation's commitment to civil rights. At home, however, the petition did little to curb racial violence and reinforced popular perceptions that brutality was merely a Communist propaganda issue.[65]

The following year, however, a leading police reformer lent tacit support to the CRC's findings on police violence. Hired by Mayor Vincent Impellitteri to survey police operations, management specialist Bruce Smith produced a lengthy report that criticized the NYPD for—among other things—inadequate discipline. Police disciplinary proceedings, Smith noted, had declined precipitously since the late 1920s. During the 1930s and 1940s, in fact, roughly 80 percent of all charges subject to disciplinary hearings were either dismissed, handled with a reprimand, or penalized with a fine of one day's pay or less. Among these cases were more than two hundred assaults on citizens, many of them by intoxicated officers. This abysmal record, Smith commented, was the worst he had encountered in his many studies of the world's police forces. Like the Lexow Committee in the 1890s, Smith pointed out the woefully lenient punishments in such cases and the prevalence of repeat offenders. In one case, a fatal shooting by a drunken officer drew only a five-day fine. Another officer, who was tried for seventeen cases of assault in twelve years, was found guilty twelve times but fined a total of only nine days' pay. Such weak penalties, Smith maintained, did not deter misconduct and allowed unsuitable individuals to remain on the force.[66]

Poor police disciplinary practices, coupled with the city's dismal record in prosecuting police officers in the criminal courts, prompted civil rights activists to pursue alternate strategies. Abandoning mass action because of its association with Communist-style organizing, the NAACP now concentrated its energy on civil litigation. In the early 1950s, antibrutality activists filed a steady stream of civil suits, hoping to use negative publicity and financial penalties to pressure the city to reign in abusive police. During the fiscal year 1951–52, for example, New Yorkers filed ten civil suits against the city for police brutality. About half of these cases were successful, requiring the city to pay out more than two hundred thousand dollars in damages. As the NAACP discovered, civil cases were easier to win than criminal ones because of the lower burden of proof required and because they could be tried by the plaintiff's own attorney, rather than by a reluctant or even hostile district attorney. Since state law permitted suits against both the city and the officer, plaintiffs in brutality cases were soon collecting settlements as high as sixty thousand dollars. Under this system, which would become the main recourse for brutality complainants, city taxpayers footed the bill for abusive cops, who remained on the job and rarely faced criminal or disciplinary sanctions. It was not, therefore, a particularly effective tool for police reform.[67]

The other legal option pursued by the NAACP was the filing of federal civil rights charges with the Department of Justice, whose mandate had been strengthened by Congress in 1948. Even with the new mandate, however, civil rights activists found federal authorities unreliable. Despite appeals to the attorney general in the cases of Newton, Derrick, Fields, and others, the Justice Department either declined to intervene or failed to win indictments. The feds' indifference frustrated and perplexed New York civil rights activists until February 1953, when the *World-Telegram and Sun* made a startling revelation. For the past seven months, the Justice Department had deferred its investigations of civil rights complaints against the NYPD and had instead allowed the department to conduct its own inquiries.[68] These revelations resulted in a major public scandal that would plague the NYPD for several months.

Justice Denied: The 1953 Scandal

As in the past, this latest brutality scandal was related to the perennial problem of police corruption. While police departments around the country expressed opposition to increased federal intervention in civil rights cases after 1948, the NYPD's reaction was particularly hostile. The department's bitter resentment of outside scrutiny stemmed from a prolonged and intensive probe into a major gambling syndicate and the police who protected it. In early 1950, a Kings County grand jury launched an investigation that led to the indictment of gambling kingpin Harry Gross and dozens of police officers on his payroll. Over the next three years, the city would fire forty-seven officers, including Police Commissioner

William O'Brien (1949–50) and several high-ranking commanders; another one hundred and fifty police implicated in the affair either resigned or retired. In the wake of the investigation, the new commissioner, George Monaghan, struggled to rebuild the damaged reputation and morale of the force. When FBI agents turned up around the same time to interrogate NYPD officers about brutality complaints, Monaghan appealed to the Justice Department to ease off in the interest of preserving police morale. On July 11, 1952 Monaghan dispatched two of his subordinates to meet with Assistant Attorney General James McInerney and U.S. Attorney Myles Lane in Manhattan. According to McInerney, the four men agreed to give the NYPD "an opportunity to conduct its own investigations and launder its own linen without loss of morale."[69]

This secret agreement came to light several months later following a brutality case involving Jacob Jackson, a black truck driver from Hell's Kitchen. In August 1952, patrolman William Brennan and his partner arrested Jackson, his wife, and another black neighbor, Samuel Crawford, after they challenged the officers' treatment of neighborhood boys who were shooting dice on the sidewalk along West Fifty-fourth Street. The conflict quickly escalated as angry black residents surrounded the officers who then locked themselves and the suspects in the patrol car. Once backup arrived, the officers were able to transport their prisoners to the West Fifty-fourth Street station house, where Brennan allegedly announced that they were "cop fighters." According to the NAACP, police then descended on Jackson and Crawford (who were handcuffed together) and beat them severely. Both men were subsequently hospitalized, and Jackson underwent two operations in which metal plates were inserted in his skull. Police charged both men with assault, while NAACP attorney Edward Jacko filed assault charges and a civil suit against police on Jackson's behalf. As in most brutality cases, the criminal case against the officer was unsuccessful, so the NAACP filed a civil rights complaint with the Justice Department.[70]

Assistant U.S. Attorney Daniel Greenberg, who was assigned to head the Jackson investigation, was apparently not aware of the earlier agreement with the NYPD. When Greenberg attempted to have FBI agents interview police officers about the Jackson case, Commissioner Monaghan refused and instead promised to forward him a copy of the department's own investigation. When the report arrived in December, Greenberg found it to be "virtually worthless . . . a complete whitewash" that omitted any mention of Jackson's injuries and hospitalization. In the weeks that followed, Monaghan again refused to allow FBI agents access to NYPD officers, claiming that federal civil rights statutes were intended "for that section of the country south of the Mason-Dixon Line." When word of Monaghan's remarks filtered up the Justice Department's chain of command, Attorney General James McGranery abrogated the agreement. Monaghan, however, continued to block the FBI's investigation of the Jackson incident, even as a federal grand jury convened to hear evidence in the case. In a last-ditch effort in mid-February, Monaghan traveled to Washington to meet with the new Eisenhower appointees in the Justice Department in hopes of reviving the agreement. The Justice Department rejected Monaghan's request, and the *World-Telegram*'s story of the secret agreement broke the following day.[71]

The revelations produced a firestorm of protest among civil rights groups in the city. The NAACP immediately telegrammed Mayor Impellitteri demanding Monaghan's dismissal and called a citywide meeting attended by representatives of nineteen organizations, including the National Urban League, the AFL, the American Jewish Congress, the ACLU, and a recently formed Citizens Committee on Police Practices headed by Community Church pastor Donald Harrington. The group called for the dismissal of Monaghan and McInerney, a mandatory FBI review of all recent brutality cases, an investigation of all substantiated cases by a federal grand jury, and the formation of an independent citizens' review board. In addition, participants also voiced strong support for a resolution by city council member Earl Brown reviving plans for a citywide investigation of police practices.[72]

The implications of the secret agreement, however, went well beyond city boundaries. New York's attempts to stymie federal oversight threatened to undermine the entire system of civil rights enforcement emanating from the 1947 Truman Commission report. As NAACP secretary Walter White wrote from Birmingham,

Alabama, white authorities in southern cities were watching New York carefully to see if such agreements might be offered to them. If that happened, White noted, the results would be devastating, since the FBI was the sole vehicle for challenging Klan violence and police terror in the South.[73] For this reason, Adam Clayton Powell, Jr.— now a member of Congress representing the Harlem district—convinced the House Judiciary Committee to establish a subcommittee to investigate the agreement.

Convening in Manhattan in early March, the House Judiciary Subcommittee interviewed more than a dozen witnesses, uncovering substantial evidence of the controversial agreement. Justice Department officials acknowledged that an "experimental" arrangement had been made, and local FBI agents and federal prosecutors testified about Monaghan's obstruction of their investigations and his references to the agreement. Monaghan and other NYPD officials, however, flatly denied making any agreements and insisted that their only request was that they be allowed to submit a report on pending cases *before* the FBI launched its own investigation. Moreover, Monaghan defended his refusal to allow FBI questioning of his officers, arguing that "police have civil rights too."[74]

This line of argument, casting the police as aggrieved victims of ill-advised civil rights enforcement, was echoed by the Patrolmen's Benevolent Association (PBA) and other police line organizations. Charging that police were "the target of communistic and other radical groups," PBA President John Carton sent a telegram to the subcommittee reminding it that "policemen also have civil rights." In a subsequent forty-two-page statement to the subcommittee, the police line organizations used strident anti-Communist rhetoric to try to discredit antibrutality forces. Posing as defenders of human rights, Communists were using Negro and civil rights groups as pawns in "a full-scale attack" designed to turn the populace against the police. This strategy, the report said, reflected the Communist belief that police "must be annihilated or at least immobilized before any country may be successfully communized." Conservative newspaper columnists, the NYPD's Catholic chaplain, and other New York state police organizations echoed these accusations. The NAACP vigorously denied this argument and charged the police organizations with "conceal[ing] their misdeeds behind a smoke-screen of Communism." In refuting the PBA, however, Walter White conspicuously denounced Communist subversion and insisted that the NAACP, not the CP, had waged "the most consistent fight against police brutality." White's attempt to minimize the role of the Communist left—which had played an important role in the antibrutality struggle in the black community since the 1930s—fueled a revisionist view of civil rights history that persists to this day.[75]

Despite the politically moderate tone of the antibrutality campaign and the damaging revelations and publicity generated by the hearings, the results were deeply disappointing for civil rights groups. Throughout the hearings, Mayor Impellitteri never wavered in his support of the police commissioner, calling those who demanded his resignation "un-American." Jacob Jackson, whose beating case led to the uncovering of the agreement, was found guilty of assault, and a federal grand jury refused to indict the officer accused of beating him. The same grand jury also declined to review the dozens of earlier brutality cases filed while the secret agreement was in effect.[76]

Meanwhile, the final report of the House Judiciary Subcommittee was held up for more than a year as Monaghan's supporters in Congress attempted to suppress it. A rather tepid document was finally released in July 1954. Although the subcommittee rebuked Monaghan for "attempting" to make such an agreement, it commended him for "fighting for his men" like a good administrator. The report offered praise for federal officials who called attention to and ultimately revoked the improper agreement. In the end, the report concluded, "little practical harm seems to have flowed from the episode." The subcommittee thus downplayed the violation of federal civil rights procedure and reduced the whole affair to one of administrative misjudgment and misunderstanding.[77]

The NYPD's ordeal with the secret agreement, however, did induce the department to introduce some administrative reforms. First, the NYPD finally agreed to long-standing requests by the Mayor's Committee on Unity to institute officer training in human relations. Within two months of the subcommittee's hearings, the New York police academy began offering training to all recruits on intergroup relations and the problems of minority groups. Around the same time, the department also appointed its first black deputy commissioner, George Redding.

Equally significant was the department's creation of a Civilian Complaint Review Board (CCRB) in May 1953. Unlike the city's present CCRB, the original board had no civilian members and was staffed by three police officials who reported directly to the commissioner. Although the board was an internal body that continued to protect the department from outside scrutiny, it soon established some guidelines that the New York Civil Liberties Union had recommended, including time limits for the investigation of complaints, penalties for those who deliberately delayed or obstructed investigations, and the right to legal representation for both officers and complainants. The 1950s CCRB did not noticeably improve the department's disciplinary record in brutality cases, prompting city council member Earl Brown to call it "the same old system with a new coat of whitewash."[78] It did, however, institutionalize and standardize the complaint process and create an administrative entity that civil rights reformers could work to reformulate in later years.

The reforms of 1953, combined with the devastating impact of Cold War anti-Communism, effectively derailed the antibrutality movement for the remainder of the decade. The demise of the left and its grassroots organizing networks left the movement without a community base, and the NAACP fearing association with left-wing groups retreated to a narrower strategy of courtroom litigation and negotiation with political elites. The NAACP thus returned to a more cautious approach to police violence, similar to its stance prior to the Depression. On the left, continuing anti-Communist repression took its toll on the antibrutality movement. Ben Davis, the city council member who had played a leading role in the Harlem antibrutality campaign, was convicted of violating the Smith Act in 1949 and was sentenced to five years in prison. William Patterson and other leaders of the Civil Rights Congress were also convicted for refusing to cooperate with anti-Communist investigators and were jailed in the early 1950s. When the Justice Department forced the CRC to register as a Communist front group in 1956, the organization finally collapsed.[79]

The efforts of civil rights advocates in the postwar era, however, were not in vain. The hard-hitting campaign against police brutality and racial violence in 1946–47 helped strengthen the role of the federal government in enforcing civil rights, a tool that would be used more effectively by later antibrutality activists. Moreover, the struggle against police violence in the postwar period laid the groundwork for the due process revolution of the 1960s by identifying and challenging common police abuses such as warrantless searches and the misuse of deadly force.[80]

The connections between the legal reforms of the 1960s and the protests of the 1940s have been obscured by the disruptive influence of anti-Communism and the revisionist tendencies of civil rights activists who sought to distance themselves from the Communist left. Although NAACP activists in the 1950s downplayed the Communists' role in the antibrutality struggle, the party's efforts to bring police brutality to public attention in the 1930s and 1940s were undeniable. Rooted in the CP's experience with police repression in Harlem during the 1930s, Communists made police brutality a priority and later joined with non-Communist black leaders who framed police brutality as a distinctly racial issue. Fueled by antifascist ideology and wartime struggles for racial equality, their campaigns to monitor and protest police violence intensified during and after World War II until the debilitating effects of anti-Communism took their toll. NYPD officials and their supporters, however, would continue to view police brutality as a Communist issue and would try to discredit a new generation of activists in the 1960s based on the movement's militant "red" past.

7. STORMING THE BARRICADES: THE 1960S

After the creation of the Civilian Complaint Review Board (CCRB) in the mid-1950s, public debate over police misconduct died down considerably. Although the NAACP and the New York Civil Liberties Union (NYCLU) continued to represent brutality complainants, there were few public protests in this period and a general sense among white liberals that the new system was working. In 1961, when the U.S. Commission on Civil Rights issued a report citing police misconduct as a "serious problem throughout the United States," the NYCLU made it clear that the NYPD was not among those departments included in the study. Praising the CCRB and improvements in departmental recruitment and training practices, the NYCLU credited these reforms for an apparent decline in the number of excessive force complaints.[1]

As in the rest of the country, the quiescence of New York in the late 1950s was shattered by the dramatic events of the southern civil rights movement. The heroic example of the student lunch counter sit-ins, the Freedom Rides, and other forms of nonviolent direct action in the early 1960s made a deep impression on Americans and inspired many young people to join the struggle. In New York and other northern cities, much of this new activism was centered in local chapters of the Congress of Racial Equality (CORE). Following CORE's sponsorship of the Freedom Rides in 1961, the group's funding and membership increased markedly, and the number of CORE affiliates in the New York area grew from three to nine. In order to increase CORE's membership among the black poor, the Manhattan chapter moved its office to Harlem in 1961 and began a community-oriented organizing campaign to win better jobs, housing, schools, and services for the black community. The even more radical Brooklyn affiliate, located in Bedford-Stuyvesant, pioneered in developing militant direct action tactics on behalf of the urban poor.[2]

Beginning in 1963, CORE also expressed a growing concern with police brutality. There were several reasons for this new emphasis. First, CORE's growing involvement in ghetto organizing made activists keenly aware of the salience of the police issue in the city's African-American neighborhoods. Like Communists in the 1930s, CORE activists working in these areas witnessed police harassment and abuse on a firsthand basis and came to realize the power of police brutality as a grassroots organizing issue. At the same time, events in the deep South reinforced black grievances against the police. The brutal attacks on civil rights activists by white mobs and the passivity—or even participation—of southern authorities in many of these attacks was a forceful reminder of the partisanship and ruthlessness of police. The most shocking scenes of police violence came in May 1963 when millions of Americans watched on TV as Birmingham police unleashed clubs, attack dogs, and fire hoses on black children protesting racial segregation.

As a national symbol of police brutality and white resistance, Birmingham became a rallying point for more militant civil rights organizing. In the summer of 1963, New York CORE chapters launched a series of direct action campaigns that included rent strikes, school boycotts, and equal employment protests. The latter targeted the all-white building trades and brought hundreds of CORE and NAACP supporters to public construction sites where they laid down in front of trucks and bulldozers and chained themselves to doorways and cranes in an effort to get black workers hired. That summer the NYPD carted off more than eight hundred protesters from construction sites around the city. The Patrolmen's Benevolent Association (PBA) said that officers exercised "the patience of Job," but on a few occasions, tired and annoyed patrolmen dragged or roughly handled the noncooperative protesters. Although CORE instructed its followers to remain nonviolent, scuffles with police broke out at the Downstate Medical Center site in Brooklyn and at a subsequent sit-in at city hall. On these occasions, police used clubs and horses against the demonstrators, drawing vocal complaints from the CORE chapters. More brutality complaints came in the fall when CORE staged a sit-in at ABC studios during the appearance of Alabama governor George Wallace. This time, CORE expressed its disapproval by rallying more than a hundred people to picket the office of the police commissioner, whom it dubbed "Bull Murphy" (after Birmingham's police chief, Eugene "Bull" Connor). Calling CORE's brutality charges "mass libel," Commissioner Michael Murphy angrily accused the group of engaging in "hate-rousing of the lowest type."

As the relationship between CORE and the NYPD deteriorated, civil rights activists became more attentive to black citizens' long-standing grievances against the police. In March 1964, a group of CORE leaders met with police officials to protest police inaction in the case of Jesse Roberts, a black auto repair shop owner who claimed he had been beaten in a Bronx station house. According to Roberts, three detectives had hit him repeatedly in the chest and stomach and thrown hot coffee on him during a five-hour interrogation. Roberts, who had come to the precinct voluntarily to report the theft of his car, had been falsely implicated in a narcotics case involving his vehicle. The CCRB, however, had taken no action on the case and was unresponsive to CORE's latest appeal. Following the meeting, three of the activists handcuffed themselves to a grille outside the commissioner's office and were promptly arrested. Joined by additional supporters, they repeated this act of civil disobedience outside Mayor Robert F. Wagner's office a few weeks later.[5]

Antibrutality sentiment in Harlem that spring was particularly intense. On April 17, police responded to a minor disturbance at a fruit stand on Lenox Avenue that escalated into what residents called "the fruit stand riot." The incident resulted in injuries to several civilians and police and the arrest of three black teenagers who had intervened, they said, to protect younger black children from police blows. The three teens, Wallace Baker, Daniel Hamm, and Frederick Frazier, charged that they were beaten by police during a subsequent interrogation (police later took them to Harlem Hospital for treatment of injuries). Ten days later, Baker and Hamm were rearrested, interrogated, and charged—along with three other Harlem teens—in the murders of two white women in the neighborhood.

231

Three of the teens claimed that police beat them during interrogations at the Twenty-eighth Precinct, the central Harlem station house that locals dubbed "the meat grinder." Police and press reports claimed that the five youth were part of an antiwhite gang influenced by Malcolm X and other dissident Black Muslims. Most Harlem residents, however, dismissed these claims as ridiculous, and the families began a lengthy campaign to defend the youth and to expose police brutality in Harlem.[4]

Public outrage over police violence was also evident in the Puerto Rican community. Conflicts with the police were particularly tense in East Harlem, where thousands of Puerto Rican migrants had settled in the postwar era. Dotted with bodegas and botanicas, El Barrio—as it was commonly known—was also home to a host of activist Protestant churches and Puerto Rican antipoverty and civil rights groups. In February 1964 these organizations mobilized more than 250 people to picket the East 104th Street precinct house following the fatal shooting of eighteen-year-old Francisco Rodriguez by an off-duty Bronx patrolman. Rodriguez, who had been named "Boy of the Year" by the local Boys Clubs, was shot in the back of the head as he fled from a knife fight a few days earlier. Protesters also denounced the earlier slaying of two Puerto Rican men, Victor Rodriguez and Maximo Solero, who had been shot dead in a police patrol car following their arrest in a West Side disturbance in November 1963. Gilberto Gerena-Valentin, a leader of the newly formed National Association for Puerto Rican Civil Rights, charged that police in the barrio violated residents' rights and acted "like they were running a plantation."[5]

The proliferation of brutality complaints and protests in minority communities convinced many liberals of the need for an independent civilian review board. Advocates noted that two such boards were already in existence in other cities. The Philadelphia ACLU had been instrumental in getting the mayor to create the nation's first independent review board in that city back in 1958. More recently, the city council in Rochester, New York, had passed an ordinance establishing a civilian review board following a series of racially charged brutality cases in 1963. Arguing that civilian review would help restore public confidence in the NYPD, Manhattan City

Council member Ted Weiss joined with other liberals in drafting legislation to establish a new all-civilian board that spring.[6]

Commissioner Murphy responded quickly and negatively to the review board proposal. Denying there was any pattern of brutality in the NYPD, Murphy presented police officers as the victims of "unfair abuse and undeserved criticism . . . part of a planned pattern of attack to destroy their effectiveness and leave the city open to confusion." While acknowledging the importance of the civil rights struggle, he appropriated its rhetoric to defend police officers as another minority group "also subject to stereotyping and mass attack."[7]

The Patrolmen's Benevolent Association took an even more hostile stance. PBA president John Cassese, a Brooklyn-born son of Italian immigrants and a twenty-seven-year veteran of the NYPD, was the chief spokesman for the rank and file. Defeating the PBA old guard in 1958, Cassese had introduced a new brand of activism to the organization, winning a dues check-off (an automatic deduction from union members' paychecks) and recognition of the PBA as a certified bargaining agent. By the early 1960s, the PBA had become a powerful voice on behalf of police pay, benefits, and working conditions. With the emergence of the review board issue, it would also become a major player in political controversies involving the police. Arguing that civilian review would immobilize the police force, Cassese charged that civil rights groups had been infiltrated by Communists who sought to undermine the American way of life. Reminiscent of PBA president John Carton's attacks on the NAACP in 1953, Cassese's statements reflected a strong undercurrent of police anti-Communism that dated back to the conflicts of the 1920s and 1930s and which had intensified during the Cold War. That tendency was now encouraged by a nascent right-wing movement centered around the John Birch Society and other ultraconservative groups. On May 17, 1964, roughly one hundred flag-waving demonstrators rallied around police headquarters chanting "Fight the Reds, Support the Blue." The protesters were members of the Committee to Support Your Local Police, a new group founded by the John Birch Society in the wake of the Birmingham violence. Depicting the proposed review board as a Communist plot, the group would soon be recruiting white officers from within the NYPD itself.[8]

In reality, Communists played little role in the drive for civilian review. The new generation of civil rights activists had deliberately distanced themselves from the sectarian battles of the past. Instead, CORE and other civil rights groups found their allies among left-liberal groups such as the NYCLU, the Liberal party (the anti-Communist successor to the American Labor party), the Human Rights Committee of the Democratic party, the Workers Defense League (a Socialist organization), and the Unitarian-Universalist Church. Like earlier antibrutality coalitions, these groups decided to organize an unofficial citizens review board to gather information on recent brutality cases and dramatize the need for independent oversight. They also sponsored pro-review-board demonstrations at each of the precincts where the incidents took place. When Ted Weiss was presenting his bill to the city council in June, they sponsored a march from police headquarters to city hall in support of the bill.[9]

These activities, however, were overshadowed by a massive show of opposition by the PBA. Using a direct mail campaign, the PBA mobilized twelve hundred off-duty police officers to picket outside city hall while the City Affairs Committee held hearings on the Weiss bill. Inside, Commissioner Murphy delivered a lengthy attack on the review board proposal, arguing that it would "create situations where police officers would hesitate to act, fearful of the second guessers and Monday morning quarterbacks." Calling for further investigation, a deeply divided City Affairs Committee shelved the bill indefinitely.[10] Within a month, however, a fateful encounter between an off-duty policeman and a fifteen-year-old boy would propel the review board issue back to the center of public debate.

The Harlem Riot of 1964

On the morning of July 16, 1964, a group of African-American summer school students had gathered on East Seventy-sixth Street, across from Robert F. Wagner Jr. High School. The newly created summer program brought a daily influx of black and Latino teenagers into this affluent white neighborhood, a development that did not sit well with some of its residents. The superintendent of the apartment building across from the school was a case in point. In an attempt to disperse the youths that persistently hung out on the sidewalk, he reportedly used racial epithets and sprayed them with a garden hose. Perhaps unaware of the potent symbolism of spraying school children with a water hose when images of Birmingham were still painfully fresh, the superintendent was soon pelted with soda bottles and garbage can lids. As he fled into the apartment building, fifteen-year-old James Powell pursued him. At this point an off-duty police lieutenant, Thomas Gilligan, emerged from an adjacent store, drew his gun, and called for Powell to halt.

What happened next is less clear. Some witnesses (mainly white adults) said Powell had a knife and lunged repeatedly at Gilligan. Others (mainly black teenagers) said they saw no knife and that Powell had not advanced on the officer. In any event, Gilligan fired three shots that killed Powell. Before long, an angry crowd of three hundred black teenagers began throwing bottles and cans at Gilligan and other police who arrived on the scene, yelling "This is worse than Mississippi" and "Come on, shoot another nigger." As the disorder spread, seventy-five police officers were sent in and had restored calm in about two hours.[11]

But the calm would not last long. Within hours, CORE and the NAACP called for an investigation of the incident and began organizing protest events. The next day, CORE led a march of Powell's schoolmates through the Upper East Side neighborhood where the shooting had occurred. CORE assembled an even larger crowd in Harlem the following night. At the conclusion of the rally, a local minister called on the crowd to march to the local precinct on 123rd Street and demand the suspension and arrest of Gilligan. As the marchers converged on the police station, officers attempted to move them behind barricades across the street. Scuffles broke out, with police using their batons and protesters hurling bricks and bottles. CORE organizers' pleas to remain nonviolent were ignored, and the first major ghetto uprising of the 1960s was underway.

The violence lasted six days, spreading out over large areas of upper Manhattan and Brooklyn. Rioters started fires, looted stores, fought with police, and in a few cases, assaulted white reporters and motorists. On July 19, a second round of rioting broke out during Powell's funeral in Harlem. The next night the disorder spread to Bedford-Stuyvesant, where crowds fought with police following a CORE protest meeting over the Gilligan shooting. Sporadic outbreaks of violence continued for three more nights. All told, the riots resulted in 465 arrests and left one person dead and more than a hundred injured (mainly African Americans). Although the NYPD avoided using fire hoses, tear gas, or other tactics employed in Birmingham, CORE and the NAACP criticized the widespread use of warning shots and the aggressiveness of the city's Tactical Patrol Force (an emergency unit that handled civil disorder). Scoring the widespread reports of reckless shootings and beatings, CORE leader James Farmer called July 18 "New York's night of Birmingham horror." Police, who were often the target of angry rioters and who sustained several injuries, dismissed these criticisms as ridiculous. "They'd scream brutality over anything," said one detective. Residents of Harlem felt differently. In a poll conducted after the riots, 43 percent of Harlem respondents affirmed that police brutality was a serious problem. As in the 1930s and 1940s, local cases of police abuse took on an ominous significance in a national context of racial repression and violence.[12]

Viewing police brutality as a critical cause of the uprising, a coalition known as the Unity Council of Harlem formed in the wake of the riot to propose remedies and spearhead negotiations with the city. The council represented a diverse assortment of black organizations, including the NAACP, the Nation of Islam, several black nationalist groups, as well as African-American churches, labor groups, and small business organizations. Calling for the immediate suspension of Lieutenant Gilligan, the Unity Council also demanded increased recruitment and promotion of black police officers. Seeking to open lines of communication with these black leaders, the police department created a new Community Affairs Committee in which NYPD officials met regularly with minority leaders to assess the status of local police-community relations. The department also announced the formation of a new cadet training program for fifteen hundred minority youth under one of the city's federally funded antipoverty programs. In a historic move, Commissioner Murphy appointed Lloyd Sealey, a Brooklyn-born officer of Afro-Caribbean descent, as captain of Harlem's Twenty-eighth Precinct, where the riots had first broken out. Fulfilling a community demand dating back to the 1935 riot, the new appointment made Sealey the city's first black precinct commander.[13]

Like earlier attempts to recruit black officers, the affirmative action measures of 1964 were important and necessary, but they did not succeed in transforming police culture. Most of the new black and Latino police cadets were funneled into low-level positions in motor vehicle operations, department store security, and bank guard duty. Some were assigned as patrol officers in black and Puerto Rican neighborhoods, but conflicting loyalties to the blue brotherhood and the black or Latino community made such work a difficult balancing act. Sealey's appointment was an important breakthrough, and his philosophy of "Lock 'em up, don't beat 'em up" seemed to augur a new era in Harlem policing. But the problems of racial bias and brutality were systemic and deeply rooted and thus beyond the control of a single commander.[14] The only way to reform such a system, many rightly believed, was to open the police department to public oversight.

In the weeks following the riot, virtually every Harlem organization, from Malcolm X's Organization for Afro-American Unity to the more moderate *Amsterdam News*, joined white liberals in calling for the creation of an independent civilian review board. The district attorney's announcement in September that a grand jury had cleared Gilligan of any wrongdoing reinforced the black community's belief in the injustice of the current system. The riot, black leaders maintained, was an explosive demonstration of the community's lack of confidence in the police. An independent review board would ensure fair treatment of civilian complaints, give citizens a voice in shaping police policy, and help restore public confidence in the system. Moreover, as white liberals especially liked to point out, a civilian review board would serve as a "safety valve" for community discontent in volatile situations like the recent Powell shooting.[15]

For the opponents of civilian review, however, the riot held a different lesson. False charges of police brutality, Commissioner

Murphy argued, were merely excuses for riots started "out of sheer cussedness or for criminal reasons." Forceful police action, like that of the NYPD in the recent riot, was essential for restoring law and order. Civilian review would undercut the authority of the police commissioner and would hamper the police in times of civil disorder. As for the safety valve theory, NYPD and PBA officials noted that both Philadelphia and Rochester, the two cities with functioning civilian review boards, also experienced riots that summer. According to a recent FBI report, police in those cities had a difficult time restoring order because they had been "virtually paralyzed" by civilian review. Although review board directors in both cities disputed the FBI's claim and noted that their boards had pioneered new more restrained riot control tactics, most police officials chose to ignore this argument (even though such tactics would become common practice by the end of the decade).[16]

The strong police opposition to civilian review made Mayor Wagner hesitant to press the issue, fearful that Commissioner Murphy would resign. Despite personal lobbying by Martin Luther King, Jr., the mayor stalled, hoping to pass the issue back to the city council for reconsideration. In the meantime, Wagner appointed a temporary committee under Deputy Mayor Edward Cavanagh to review the procedures of the police-staffed CCRB and its findings in several recent brutality cases. Like the mayoral review committees of the 1940s, the Cavanagh committee proved to be a holding action, spanning many months and approving CCRB findings in all fourteen cases it examined. One member of the committee, however, found the experience unsettling. John Carro, a Puerto Rican lawyer and aide to Mayor Wagner, told of his arrest and unlawful detainment in the Bronx after attempting to intercede on behalf of two Puerto Rican youths subjected to arbitrary arrest. Despite this incident and a flood of new complaints of police misconduct from the Puerto Rican community, Wagner refused to use his executive power on behalf of civilian review.

In the early months of 1965, Puerto Rican activists joined black leaders in the drive for civilian review following a series of recent brutality cases. The most publicized case involved the near-fatal shooting of Gregorio Cruz, a twenty-two-year-old Puerto

Rican man in September 1964. Mistaking him for a Puerto Rican robbery suspect, Detective John Devlin shot Cruz as he fled from a Chinatown housing project. Puerto Rican outrage intensified in February and March 1965 when four Puerto Rican prisoners were found hanged in their cells in precinct jails. Gilberto Gerena-Valentin, president of the National Association for Puerto Rican Civil Rights, noted that there had been nine deaths and six maimings of Puerto Rican citizens at the hands of police in the past fifteen months. He and other Latino leaders suspended their meetings with police community relations officers, insisting that the mayor act on these complaints. Puerto Rican antibrutality protesters now joined CORE and the NAACP in picketing police headquarters and station houses in support of civilian review.[17]

A rash of third-degree cases, many of them involving black and Puerto Rican murder suspects, also came to light around the same time. In 1965 there were press reports of six New York cases in which district attorneys moved to dismiss murder indictments because of false confessions allegedly induced by third-degree tactics. As four of the suspects were black or Puerto Rican, civil rights activists cited these cases as evidence of the need for civilian review. When the NYPD denied that it used violent interrogation methods, African-American police in the Guardians Association attempted to expose the use of the third degree on black suspects in a Bedford-Stuyvesant precinct. Roger Abel, the whistle-blower who led this effort, charged that he was physically threatened and harassed by fellow officers who threw his locker out the window, smashed his car windshield, and slashed his tires. Such experiences helped convince Abel and other Guardian members to align themselves with black community groups in backing citizen oversight. In June 1965, the thirteen-hundred-member black police organization announced its support for civilian review.[18]

As public support for civilian review increased, the city's political leaders responded with a confounding array of review board proposals. Along with an amended version of the Weiss bill—calling for a nine-member all-civilian board—Democratic hopefuls in the upcoming mayoral primary offered other more conciliatory approaches. These included proposals for a five-member review

239

board composed of city council members, a citizen appeals board staffed by respected lawyers and jurists, and an ombudsman's office that would review misconduct in all branches of city government. Liberal/Republican party candidate John V. Lindsay expressed interest in proposals by two New York bar associations calling for the addition of civilian members to the existing CCRB. Several of these proposals became the basis of legislative bills submitted to the City Affairs Committee for consideration at its June meeting.

Under mounting criticism of police misconduct and growing pressure for civilian review, Commissioner Murphy resigned in May 1965. His replacement, former Deputy Commissioner for Legal Affairs Vincent Broderick, was also firmly opposed to civilian review. It was the PBA, however, that spearheaded the anti-review-board effort. Organizing a grassroots petition campaign led by officers' wives and family members, the PBA collected more than four hundred thousand signatures opposing civilian review. At the June 29 meeting of the City Affairs Committee, roughly five thousand off-duty police—some of them responding to calls issued on police radio—turned out to picket city hall while PBA president Cassese presented the petitions. When the police demonstrators encountered an interracial group of fifty pro-review-board pickets from CORE, they reportedly yelled "Go home, Finks," and "Send 'em to Vietnam." Inside the chambers, a battery of anti-review-board statements by Commissioner Broderick and other police advocates had the desired effect. The City Affairs Committee postponed debate on the bills, none of which ever came to a vote.[19]

Although the review board had gone down to defeat, the campaign did result in some significant reforms. In an effort to stave off civilian review, Commissioner Broderick approved a number of reform measures proposed by the local bar associations. Most importantly, the NYPD agreed to establish a new CCRB office outside of police headquarters and staffed by nonuniformed personnel. This arrangement was far less intimidating to civilian complainants, and the number of complaints filed nearly doubled once the CCRB moved to its new uptown office. Under another provision, attorneys for both police officers and complainants were granted the right to cross-examine witnesses during CCRB hearings—an important right long advocated by the NAACP and the ACLU. The CCRB also agreed to publish statistical summaries of its findings, ending more than a decade of official secrecy. In a move aimed at placating the black community, Broderick also appointed the first African-American member of the CCRB, Deputy Commissioner of Legal Affairs Franklin Thomas, in October 1965.[20] Although civil rights activists criticized these measures as insufficient, they were in fact important developments. As in the 1953 federal investigation, the failure of antibrutality activists to secure their larger objectives overshadowed the incremental but significant concessions they won within the system.

Civilian Review—Round Two

Taking office in 1966, the new administration of Mayor John Lindsay revived the dashed hopes of civilian review advocates. Despite his background as the Republican representative of Manhattan's "silk stocking" district, Lindsay was a youthful, charismatic candidate who offered a liberal antimachine platform. The election had been very close, and many believed that black and Latino voters who backed Lindsay's civilian review and antipoverty proposals had provided the critical margin. Once in office, the new mayor moved to expand the existing three-member CCRB by adding four new civilian appointees. Lindsay viewed this arrangement as a good compromise that combined police expertise with citizen oversight, and every major New York newspaper (with the exception of the *Daily News*) expressed editorial support for the plan. CORE, the NAACP, and other civil rights groups continued to call for a wholly civilian board but supported the mayor's plan as a useful first step. Speaking for the NYPD, however, Commissioner Broderick attacked the plan, calling it "a cruel hoax" and an "administrative travesty."[21]

Facing a wall of police resistance, Lindsay sought to overhaul the department's top leadership to make it more amenable to reform. As his new police commissioner, Lindsay selected Howard Leary, current head of the Philadelphia police—the nation's only big-city department with a functioning civilian review board. Though hardly an enthusiast, Leary had learned to live with the Philadelphia board and pledged to work cooperatively with Lindsay's expanded CCRB. The Lindsay administration also hoped that Leary, who had a good reputation with civil rights groups in Philadelphia, could improve the NYPD's relationship with the city's black and Latino communities.

With Leary at the helm, Lindsay issued an executive order in May 1966 expanding the CCRB to include three police and four civilian appointees. Unlike the old CCRB, which relied on supervisors in the accused officer's command to conduct investigations, the new board had its own staff under a civilian director. The new board also handled a wider variety of citizen complaints and featured a conciliation unit designed to handle minor incidents of harassment and discourtesy. In more serious incidents of misconduct, the board conducted investigations and hearings and made formal recommendations for disciplinary action. Final authority in these decisions, however, remained with the police commissioner, as did the power to select the three police members of the board. As for the civilian members, Lindsay named Algernon Black, a white director of the Ethical Culture Society and vice president of the NAACP, as the new CCRB chair. The other civilian appointees were Thomas Farrell, former president of the Catholic Interracial Council in the Bronx; Walter I. Murray, a black education professor at Brooklyn College; and Manual Diaz, Jr., director of the Puerto Rican Development Project. With these appointments, the mayor fulfilled his pledge to create a review board that was more representative of the citizenry.[22]

The PBA, however, denounced the new board as unnecessary and immediately launched a series of legal challenges and a petition drive for a public referendum on the issue. Racial resentments clearly underlay the PBA's staunch opposition. As the association's president, John Cassese, put it, police were "sick and tired of giving in to minority groups with their whims and their gripes and shouting." Civil rights activists would never be satisfied, he claimed, "unless there were nine Negroes and Puerto Ricans browbeating and finding every policeman who goes before them guilty." Racist appeals by the John Birch Society turned up on precinct bulletin boards, while Birchers and the neo-Nazi National Renaissance party both led counterdemonstrations against civilian review. More ominously, two review board appointees received obscene phone calls and nighttime visits by hecklers who shouted "nigger" and "nigger lover" at them and their families.[23]

Racism alone, however, does not explain the intensity of police opposition. Class-based resentments combined with racial antagonism to produce a strong sense of populist indignation. Feeling pressed between angry ghetto-dwellers on the one hand and "limousine liberals" on the other, many white ethnics harbored resentments that were deeply rooted in the city's postwar experience of economic decline and racial transition. In East New York, Brownsville, the South Bronx, and other formerly white working-class neighborhoods, the influx of impoverished blacks and Puerto Ricans in the 1960s was accompanied by wholesale disinvestment that led to neighborhood deterioration, rising crime rates, and a host of other social and economic problems. Blaming the newcomers for these ills, many older residents fled to the white suburban enclaves of Queens, Staten Island, and Nassau County. Those who stayed behind—particularly Catholic ethnics who owned homes in parish-based neighborhoods—often fought bitterly to "preserve" their communities from racial integration. Both the older defended neighborhoods and the white outer boroughs of Queens and Staten Island would prove hotbeds of anti-review-board sentiment.

As the white urban population declined and as liberals paid greater attention to growing black and Latino constituencies, the traditional base of white ethnic political power in the Democratic party also eroded. As liberals scrambled to address chronic social problems, working-class whites came to resent policies that they believed helped others at their expense. Affirmative action in government employment, higher taxes for antipoverty programs, and state-mandated school integration were all viewed as assaults on the economic and social stability that working-class whites had struggled to build. That the architects of these plans were Manhattan-based elites like Lindsay, whose own families were largely sheltered from the fallout of urban social problems, only fueled this politics of resentment.[24]

For most white police officers, who were mainly Irish American and Italian American and heavily Catholic (over 70 percent in the mid-1960s), Lindsay's new police policies were a prime example of liberalism run amok. The ongoing efforts to hire more black and Latino officers and the breakup of the department's old-boy Irish leadership was viewed as a political assault on a traditional white ethnic employment enclave. Likewise, most white police saw Lindsay's efforts to rein in the use of force and introduce civilian review (by elite WASPs and civil rights activists no less) as an attack on their physical security and occupational autonomy. Encouraged by successful PBA organizing, many rank and file police objected to the growing number of bureaucratic controls instituted by management and saw civilian review as another vehicle for limiting their work autonomy and discretion. Beholden to political pressure groups, civilian review boards would rush to judgment against police whose jobs, pensions, and reputations were on the line. Many police officials concurred with this view. Arguing that police brutality was a fabrication of overly sensitive minority groups, NYPD officials insisted that police were the victims of stereotypes and misdirected hatred. Because civil rights activists falsely equated the NYPD with "redneck sheriffs" down South, wrote Deputy Commissioner Walter Arm, the reputation of the department had suffered unjustly. "Cops are used as the convenient target for every type of grievance," he said, "whether the cause is racial prejudice, slum violence or a needed traffic light." Unable to solve the real problems, Arm said, city hall was "using police as whipping boys and political pawns."[25]

Infused with a sense of populist indignation, PBA members and their families collected more than fifty-one thousand signatures for a voter referendum prohibiting civilian review. The Conservative party, led by William F. Buckley, collected some forty thousand signatures for its own anti-review-board referendum, but soon joined forces with the PBA. Forming the Independent Citizens' Committee against Civilian Review Boards, the PBA campaign also won the support of the American Legion, the Businessmen's Citizens' Committee, the Brooklyn Bar Association, the John Birch Society, and numerous local parents, taxpayers, and homeowners' groups. Like many right-wing issue-oriented campaigns of the 1960s, the anti-review-board drive enjoyed fervent grassroots support and developed an extensive and highly effective organizing network. Borrowing innovations from Lindsay's 1965 mayoral campaign, the Independent Citizens' Committee opened thirty-four neighborhood storefronts where campaign workers—mainly police officers' wives and children—distributed literature, telephoned constituents, and conducted door-to-door canvasses.[26] On the citywide level, the PBA's public relations director, Norman Frank, produced a blitz of expensive advertisements for billboards, newspapers, radio, and television.

Street crime and public safety were the central thrust of the PBA-led campaign. Like most American cities, New York saw its crime rate shoot up in the early 1960s, with the number of homicides jumping from 435 in 1960 to 734 in 1966. Fear of crime was rampant and shared by inner city and outer borough residents alike. The notorious murder of Kitty Genovese in 1964 was emblematic of this fear. Returning from work to the quiet Queens community of Kew Gardens one night, Genovese was followed home by a black assailant who stabbed her repeatedly in front of her home. Although dozens of neighbors heard her screams, no one called the police. The apathy of the citizenry and the spread of crime into previously safe neighborhoods sent a chilling message. The Independent Citizens' Committee played on these racialized fears in a newspaper ad showing a young white woman exiting the subway on a dark street. "Only the policeman stands between your family and the continuous threat of the hooligan, the addict, and the criminal," the ad explained, "The Civilian Review Board must be stopped! Her life . . . your life . . . may depend on it." The ad's racial and gender connotations were clear. As Mayor Lindsay put it, "The only thing it didn't show was a gang of Negroes about to attack her."[27]

Similar racial and gender appeals underlay another ad showing a worried white mother waiting at a darkened window over the caption "All mothers wait up at night! We can't take chances . . . not with our children." Listing the city's violent crime statistics for 1965, the ad highlighted the vulnerability of white women and children amid a city "plagued by crime" where "the policeman is all that stands between you, your family, and the mounting threat of violence." Another ad, showing a rubble-strewn Philadelphia street following the 1964 riot, blamed the destruction on the restraints imposed by that city's civilian review board. Both ads stressed that civilian review would reduce the effectiveness of law enforcement, causing police to hesitate for fear of unjust censure. To ensure public safety, police "must feel free to take swift and direct action when danger strikes." This message, reinforced in the neighborhood "Safety" campaigns run by police officers' wives and family members, reflected the dominant ideology of postwar domesticity and the threats to that system posed by rising urban crime and disorder and the misguided efforts of liberal reformers.[28]

Disgusted by this fear mongering, the advocates of civilian review ran a more sober, rational campaign. Spearheaded by the New York Civil Liberties Union, the Federated Associations for Impartial Review (FAIR) was formed in August 1966 with the support of liberal Protestant and Jewish organizations, the Catholic Interracial Council, the National Maritime Union, and several other labor and civil rights groups. The black members of the Guardians Association not only joined FAIR but filed a lawsuit against the PBA for spending police dues money on the anti-review-board campaign without the approval of its membership. PBA president John Cassese lashed back at the Guardians, accusing them of putting "color ahead of their duty as police officers."[29]

Although Guardians president William Johnson said that he had witnessed numerous incidents of police abusing black suspects, other FAIR members shied away from the brutality issue. Even when FAIR campaign workers were harassed and arrested by police, FAIR remained silent about police misconduct. As NYCLU director Aryeh Neier later explained, "There was little discussion of the varieties of police misconduct since we felt that if we were antagonistic to the police we would throw the whole thing away. Instead, we talked of building confidence in the police." Citing the "safety valve" theory of civilian review, FAIR argued that many New Yorkers had lost confidence in the police disciplinary system and that the new review board was needed to help ease racial tensions. In making this argument, however, FAIR was tacitly accepting the PBA's claim that there was no pattern of police brutality in the NYPD and that the review board was merely a public relations gimmick.[30]

Seeking to reassure voters that civilian review would not handcuff police in fighting crime, FAIR pointed to the new board's moderate track record. In its first few months of existence it recommended disciplinary action in only 3 out of 113 cases. Pointing to this record, Lindsay argued that "the board will defend the policemen as much as it's reputed to defend the individual who goes before it." FAIR also reminded voters of the review board's strictly advisory role and the police commissioner's sole authority to administer discipline. FAIR supporters were thus in the awkward position of urging voters to back the board because it was in fact not very effective.[31]

Midway through the campaign, however, FAIR discovered the time-honored tactic of linking corruption to other forms of police misconduct. Noting the sweeping language of a "sleeper clause" in the PBA referendum, FAIR argued that the measure would preclude *all* civilian oversight of the department, even in cases of graft or corruption. According to FAIR's campaign director, the PBA "is asking the voter to build a wall of immunity around the police of New York—to grant them what is accorded no law enforcement body in the country." The PBA denied the charge, but FAIR quickly rounded up dozens of prominent attorneys and bar associations who shared its assessment. A postelection survey suggested that the corruption issue resonated with the 30 percent of voters who understood the sleeper clause issue, but even among these voters resistance to civilian review remained strong.[32] Unlike earlier police reformers who tied corruption to brutality, FAIR did not argue that their reforms would make law enforcement more efficient. Civilian review might produce better police-community relations in the long run, but for many voters, the PBA's emphasis on aggressive, no-holds-barred policing to combat the current crime epidemic seemed more persuasive.

Burdened with a less-than-compelling message, the FAIR campaign had other problems as well. To begin with, the campaign got off to a late start. Fearing that heated debate about policing might trigger another riot, FAIR waited until the end of the summer to begin campaigning. Money was another handicap. While the Independent Citizens' Committee spent more than half a million dollars on its campaign (much of it coming from the PBA treasury), FAIR raised less than two hundred thousand dollars and could not afford to answer the blitz of media advertising by its opponents. The FAIR campaign also suffered from a kind of political battle fatigue at city hall. Having barely recovered from the bruising mayoral election of 1965, Lindsay's aides proved unenthusiastic about the review-board campaign and provided little organizational assistance. Instead, FAIR relied on its speakers' bureau (primarily NYCLU members) and public addresses by prominent liberal politicians including Mayor Lindsay and New York senators and FAIR cochairs Robert Kennedy and Jacob Javits. In the midst of a rising white working-class backlash, reliance on liberal political elites was not a winning strategy. In the end FAIR's heavy reliance on a top-down campaign was no match for the impassioned grassroots campaign run by its opponents.[33]

Not surprisingly, the civilian review board went down to defeat at the polls in November. The magnitude of the defeat, however, was startling: 1,313,161 votes or 63 percent against civilian review and only 765,468 or 37 percent for it. Opposition was strongest in the predominantly white borough of Queens but was also evident in many parts of Brooklyn, the Bronx, and Staten Island. Only in Manhattan, with its large population of blacks, Puerto Ricans, and wealthy and middle-class white liberals, did a majority of the electorate support the new review board.[34]

White voters' positions on the referendum were shaped by their religious, racial/ethnic, and class identities. According to a postelection voter survey, Italian Americans, Irish Americans, and other non-Hispanic Catholics proved the most ardent opponents of the review board, voting five to one against it. More than half of these respondents had personal ties to the police through a friend or family member. Jews were more evenly divided, with 40 percent supporting the board and 55 percent opposing. More affluent, highly educated Jewish professionals voted heavily in favor of civilian review, while less-educated working-class Jews strongly opposed it. A reflection of the class-based resentments raised by civilian review, this differential was evident to a lesser extent among all white voters. Pro-civilian-review sentiment was strongest among professional and technical workers (51.6 percent) and lowest among blue collar, clerical, and sales workers (20 percent). Interestingly, despite the gendered appeals of PBA advertisements, women were slightly less likely to vote against the review board than were men. White fathers and husbands, in fact, may have been more susceptible to such racially charged appeals, fearing the traditional specter of the black criminal victimizing their wives, children, and neighborhoods.

Without a doubt, race and civil rights were the most significant factors in the defeat of the referendum. As the postelection survey revealed, white voters' attitudes toward the civil rights movement were directly related to their opinion of civilian review. For example, 62 percent of the respondents believed that the civil rights movement was pushing too fast, and 68 percent believed that "the recent actions of Negroes were generally violent." Voters who expressed such views, the study noted, disproportionately opposed civilian review.[35] Speaking for the FAIR campaign a week after the election, Aryeh Neier reached a similar conclusion:

We have proved that when the concept of race or civil rights attaches to a referendum, it cannot win. The review board had become the object of the civil rights movement—having it would be giving in to the minority groups as Mr. Cassese said. Its defeat was a way of teaching the minority groups a lesson. . . . In this case, the campaign was lost on racial grounds.

Given the impossibility of defeating the PBA referendum in this climate, Neier regretted that FAIR had not confronted the issue of police abuses more directly—an approach that would have been at least "educationally valuable."[36]

Although the referendum marked the end of civilian review, some of the innovations of the short-lived 1966 board survived the debacle. A week after the election, Commissioner Leary announced the reorganization of the CCRB and appointed five nonuniformed police officials to serve as board members (including African-American deputy commissioner Franklin Thomas). In an effort to give the board a civilian cast, all of the appointees were attorneys and none had ever worked as uniformed line officers. As for the board's investigative staff, police officers were appointed to replace civilian personnel, but this separate and relatively isolated unit retained responsibility for all hearings and investigations. The old practice of having investigations conducted by supervisors in the accused officer's own command—a system that resulted in official stone-walling and cover-ups—was permanently abandoned. The existence of a separate investigative unit was vital, NYCLU lawyer Paul Chevigny explained, because it at least insured an orderly procedure. In an attempt to clear the backlog of complaints, the CCRB staff (20 percent of whom were black or Latino) was increased from forty-five in the fall of 1966 to more than a hundred by the early 1970s. The new conciliation service of the 1966 board was also retained as was its director Bernard Jackson, a black attorney, former NYPD officer, and former vice president of the Guardians Association. By continuing this service, the NYPD acknowledged the importance of improving police-community relations and of developing new police policies and procedures. The new board thus preserved some of the key organizational reforms of its 1966 predecessor.[37]

In fact, over the next few years, the track record of the police-staffed CCRB proved to be equal or better than that of the mixed civilian-police board of 1966. Interestingly, the substitution of police for civilians does not appear to have damaged the public's confidence in the grievance procedure. The controversy over the PBA referendum may in fact have heightened public awareness of the CCRB. During its four-month existence from July to October 1966, the police-civilian review board received an average of 110 complaints per month. During those same months, the new police CCRB received even more: 122 in 1967, 145 in 1968, 247 in 1969, and 264 in 1970. Once these incidents were investigated and a hearing conducted, the CCRB found a certain number of cases to be "substantiated" and made recommendations for a disciplinary trial. Under the old board, 29 percent of cases were substantiated. Although this rate initially dropped under the new board, the percentage of substantiated cases soon rose to 32 percent in 1969 and to 35 percent in 1970. Of the total complaints received by the board from 1967 to 1970, roughly 5 percent resulted in formal disciplinary charges. This rate compared favorably with the 4 percent of cases in which formal charges resulted under the 1966 board. The number of cases that were conciliated also increased—from 14 percent of cases in 1966 to 29 percent in 1970. These somewhat surprising results were not lost on police officers, many of whom continued to resent the CCRB. "The public was against a civilian review board, but actually Lindsay has put a board in there," one officer complained in the early 1970s. "It's close to what he wanted. And we feel he got just about what he wanted."[38]

Although the new CCRB was tougher than its predecessor, its record was hardly exemplary. That only 5 percent of all CCRB complaints resulted in disciplinary charges was not an impressive statistic. Moreover, the board's recent improvements depended heavily on the mayor and the police commissioner, who were determined to tighten up discipline in the department. There was no guarantee that future administrations would share this commitment. The limitations of review boards—civilian or police-run—were also due to evidentiary problems and the typically high standard of proof required in such proceedings. In many cases, the use of excessive force occurred out of public view and ended in a futile swearing contest between officers and suspects. Sustainable cases required an independent witness (preferably several) who had not been arrested and who was willing to testify at review board hearings. Victims also had to win acquittals on any criminal charges before they could hope to press a complaint successfully. Since very few victims could meet these criteria, NYCLU lawyer Paul Chevigny noted, the review board proved to be "an extremely fine sieve through which relatively few complaints are pure enough to pass." Even if one could satisfy these requirements, it was still difficult to win cases because review board members—even civilians—tended to internalize the police ethic. Although reviewers generally frowned on corrupt or negligent police behavior, Chevigny said, they were likely to tolerate misconduct by overzealous officers who were making a good faith effort to do their jobs. As later critics would put it, "the watchdog becomes a lap dog."[39]

Chevigny's analysis of review boards was part of a larger study of police misconduct that grew out of the NYCLU's Police Practices Project (PPP) which he headed in 1966–67. A veteran of the

1964 Freedom Summer campaign in Mississippi, Chevigny had returned to New York and begun work at a neighborhood law office in Harlem where he heard "gruesome stories about the police." In 1966 he agreed to head the PPP, one of several ACLU storefronts (the others were in Watts and Newark) where lawyers worked with community organizations to locate and represent victims of police abuse. Based on this experience, in 1969 Chevigny published *Police Power,* a comprehensive study of police misconduct in New York City and the most important investigation of its kind since the Wickersham Commission report of 1931. But while the Wickersham Commission focused on the third degree, Chevigny concentrated on the now more common incidents of street brutality and harassment and the particular problems these cases raised.

Based on an analysis of 441 complaints handled by the PPP, Chevigny concluded that most cases of street brutality occurred in response to fighting words or other acts of defiance by civilians. Such acts—which might include arguing, insulting, wisecracking, refusing to speak English, or demanding one's rights—were not violations of law but were perceived by police as challenges to their authority. Usually, an argument ensued that led to an arrest and in some cases a beating. Most police believed that their authority and safety depended on the suppression of such defiant behavior and thus adopted an informal code that sanctioned police lawlessness. Although 60 percent of all PPP misconduct complaints were filed by whites, blacks and Latinos made up roughly two-thirds of those who complained of excessive force. "Anyone who defies the police is likely to be arrested," Chevigny explained, "but a Negro or a Puerto Rican is more likely to be clubbed in the process." Chevigny's data indicated that the racialization of police brutality was not just a perception but a statistical reality.

Police Power also described the legal devices that served to silence complainants and protect abusive officers. In the vast majority of brutality cases, police used a trio of cover charges—disorderly conduct, resisting arrest, and assault—to justify the arrest and beating. A familiar police narrative, the disorderly conduct charge justified the initial arrest while the resisting arrest and assault charges accounted for the officer's use of force (and the defendant's injuries).

Defense lawyers understood that such charges were a bid in a plea bargaining system in which the prosecutor would drop the latter two charges in exchange for a guilty plea to the lesser count of disorderly conduct. Once convicted—even of this minor offense—the suspect's chances of pressing a complaint against the officer were slim. In effect, unless the defendant was acquitted of all charges and had independent witnesses to support his/her account, there was little hope for redress. In cases where acquittal was likely, prosecutors frequently offered to drop all charges in exchange for a waiver of claims for damages—including the right to file a complaint with the CCRB. Except in the most serious cases, Chevigny explained, it was ill-advised to reject such offers because prosecutors and police, fearing a civil lawsuit by the defendant, would redouble their efforts to convict. This legal obstacle course helps explain how a total of 441 citizen complaints filed with the PPP resulted in disciplinary charges against only eight officers.

To Chevigny, the use of these legal devices and the collusion of police and prosecutors in concealing and justifying abuse were more egregious than the violence itself. More importantly, these practices indicated that cases of police violence and abuse were not isolated incidents but an integral part of police culture that was condoned by the legal system. This police ethic, which placed safety and order above due process of law, was generally shared by the public. Indeed, the overwhelming defeat of civilian review at the polls "told us that if we wanted to reform the police, we would have to reform the electorate." The need to do so was imperative, for "the system within which the police work is evil . . . it injures people and destroys their respect for the legal process."[40] Chevigny thus echoed the legal and moral arguments against police violence first articulated in the Wickersham report. It was, however, the pragmatic argument that police violence was counterproductive that had helped reduce police reliance on the third degree and violent mass action policing in the 1930s. Because the public continued to believe that tough and aggressive street policing was the most effective means of fighting crime, the problem of routine street brutality had proved intractable.

Over the years, lawyers and activists had developed a variety of antibrutality strategies and won important legal reforms, but police and prosecutors had been equally adept at circumventing them. The extension of the Fourth Amendment to the states in the 1961 *Mapp* decision, for example, helped protect suspects from police beatings administered during illegal raids. But in 1968, the Supreme Court's decision in *Terry* v. *Ohio* backed away from *Mapp* by allowing police to "stop and frisk" suspicious persons without arresting them. Designed to protect police and facilitate crime prevention, the decision nevertheless opened the door to racial profiling and harassment—practices that fueled citizen resentment and defiance and potential police violence. Similarly, a 1967 New York state penal law limiting police use of deadly force to defend an officer's life or that of another person did not prove to be a panacea. Police soon learned to articulate their *perceptions* that suspects were armed, or in some cases, planted guns or other weapons on the victims. Moreover, the passage of New York's so-called "No Sock" law in 1968 eliminated the common law right of a citizen to resist an unlawful arrest. Under the new law, in cases where there were no other witnesses, police could successfully press assault and resisting arrest charges against an injured suspect, even if there was no lawful reason for the initial stop and beating. The New York law, along with similar no sock laws passed in other states, was part of a growing wave of anticrime legislation designed to curb what conservatives viewed as the judicial "excesses" of the Warren Court.

Just as new laws and judicial precedents were used to expand citizens' rights in the early 1960s, a more restrictive set of statutes and decisions began to chip away at those same rights after 1968. Similarly, a growing wave of support for civil rights and citizen oversight of the police in the early 1960s was effectively defeated by the PBA referendum and the politics of resentment that characterized the late 1960s. The struggle against police brutality was thus not a linear process, but entailed periodic gains and setbacks influenced by changing social and political currents.[41]

Taking It to the Streets

The reemergence of violent mass action policing in the late 1960s is a case in point. After thirty years of relative peace on the streets between the NYPD and political dissidents, growing black activism and antiwar protest tested the police commitment to tolerance and restraint. The racial disorder that wracked the city in 1964 was an ongoing concern through the long hot summers of the late 1960s, when almost any incident of police violence threatened to set off a communal uprising. Moreover, by 1967, young activists concerned with racism, poverty, and especially the Vietnam War were taking to the streets to protest government policies, often engaging in civil disobedience and other unlawful behavior. At the same time, the Lower East Side neighborhood known as the East Village had become a countercultural mecca where young hippies with an antiauthoritarian outlook gathered in growing numbers. For many in the city's white middle and working classes—including most police officers—this disorderly behavior was an affront to their patriotism and their identity as hardworking, law-abiding American citizens.

In the face of these events and the powerful controversy they stirred, the policy of police tolerance toward demonstrators faltered. Torn between liberal calls for tolerance, understanding, and the protection of civil liberties on the one hand, and growing conservative appeals for law and order on the other, police officials used a combination of force and accommodation that drew criticism from both sides. Angered by the growing hostility and violence of young militants, some police officers rebelled against Lindsay's policies of restraint and on several occasions unleashed their wrath indiscriminately against demonstrators.

As in other big cities, the threat of serious civil disorder in urban communities in the mid-1960s led police administrators to turn to new military-style tactics and weaponry. Local police and National Guard units acquired tanks, helicopters, chemical mace, grenade launchers, machine guns, and other combat weapons. Most police departments also organized centralized, specially trained units to respond to riots and other potential disorders. In New York this duty was the responsibility of the Tactical Patrol Force (TPF), an elite corps of young officers, many of whom were former marines or para-troopers. First organized in 1959, the TPF expanded rapidly from seventy-five men to almost a thousand by 1970. Used as roving anticrime units during normal shifts, the TPF was primarily intended as a crowd-control force, and its members were specially trained in martial arts, crowd psychology, and riot control maneuvers recommended by the FBI and the Army. Their military background, training, and appearance prompted antiwar protesters to view them as the domestic equivalent of U.S. forces in Vietnam, while many black and Latino radicals saw them as an "occupying army" in their communities. As with past analogies between the police and the Cossacks or the Gestapo, young radicals viewed the repressive role of police through the lens of contemporary global affairs.[42]

At the same time, however, the Lindsay administration hoped to avert racial and political strife through more liberal initiatives of community outreach, mediation, and tactical restraint. Deputy Chief Inspector Eldridge Waith, the first black commander of the Sixth Division, was deployed as the department's point man for community relations in Harlem and worked to open channels of communication with a variety of groups from churches to street gangs. Fearing a resumption of ghetto violence in the summer of 1967, the mayor organized a sixteen-member Urban Action Task Force to monitor potential trouble spots in thirteen different neighborhoods around the city. Urban Task Force members also served as official monitors at protest marches and demonstrations in an effort to mediate disputes and prevent violence. At the same time, the NYPD issued new orders governing police protocols and the use of force in controlling crowds. In both riots and demonstrations, top police officials emphasized containment and restraint in lieu of violence.[43]

The new policy of tactical restraint was first articulated in the early months of the Lindsay administration in the spring of 1966. In printed instructions issued to all officers assigned to riot areas, Commissioner Leary ordered police to refrain from using racial slurs and provocative language or actions and to avoid unnecessary drawing or discharge of weapons. If an officer had to fire his weapon, he was to contact his commanding officer immediately. In practice, this meant containment rather than dispersal of rioters and less aggressive pursuit of looters in a manner that "traded goods and appliances for human lives." While a tense racial truce endured through the summer of 1966, a series of violent racial clashes the following summer put the new policies to the test.

In late July 1967, the shooting of a knife-wielding Puerto Rican man by an off-duty police officer triggered three nights of violence, looting, and arson in East Harlem and the South Bronx. More than a thousand police, including many TPF officers, were sent to contain the disorder, but their presence only aggravated community resentment. Residents demanded the withdrawal of the TPF, and local youth drew a chalk line across Third Avenue at 110th Street that read "Puerto Rican border. Do not cross flatfoot." During the melee, Commissioner Leary and other commanding officers toured the area ordering the police to hold their fire and holster their weapons. Under a hail of bottles, Molotov cocktails, and sniper fire, however, police sometimes ignored them and responded with baton charges and gunfire directed at nearby roofs. In the end, three civilians were fatally shot and more than thirty people injured, including several police officers. While Lindsay praised the police for their restraint in face of provocation, community activists accused officers of using brutal methods against innocent bystanders and inciting the crowd with racial slurs. For their part, NYPD officials dismissed the brutality charges as ridiculous, and some rank and file police officers expressed anger and frustration with the new restraint policies that they believed endangered their lives.[44]

For the rest of the summer, the Lindsay administration attempted to refine and reinforce its violence prevention and restraint policies. During subsequent outbreaks of violence in Bedford-Stuyvesant and Brownsville, Urban Task Forces worked with local activists to try to avert violence and address community problems. When violence broke out anyway, the NYPD dispatched hundreds of predominantly black police officers to the area and issued fifteen written instructions for handling the disorder. The instructions reiterated restrictions on the use of force and limited the use of firearms to self-defense purposes only, but they also ordered police to "enforce all laws, prevent crime and looting and arrest perpetrators." With a large contingent of African-American officers and commanders, the new orders worked out better. Persistently taunted by black youth who called them "Uncle Toms" and "white man's niggers," the police generally maintained discipline and restored order. While officers made dozens of arrests, there was little use of firearms and no fatalities. Although marred by repeated outbreaks of violence, New York had managed to avoid the more serious disorders that plagued Detroit, Newark, and other cities in the summer of 1967.[45]

The following April, the assassination of Martin Luther King, Jr., brought renewed fears of racial uprisings in New York and other U.S. cities. Once again, Lindsay visited black neighborhoods and community leaders and used the Urban Task Forces to try to avert violence. Despite these efforts, sporadic disorders broke out in Harlem, Bedford-Stuyvesant, and other neighborhoods. Saturating these areas with police reinforcements, the NYPD reiterated its orders concerning the use of force and warned officers against apprehending looters without sufficient backup. All told, there were 373 arrests, 77 injuries, and 2 fatalities (although neither appeared to be a result of police action). The *Times, Newsday,* and the *Amsterdam News* all praised Lindsay's efforts and credited them with preventing the kind of catastrophic violence that had struck other cities.

PBA president John Cassese, however, criticized police policy, saying that officers had been instructed "to keep their hands off, to contain the disturbance, but to take no direct action." Merchants in affected areas echoed these sentiments and charged that police just stood by as stores were looted. Mayor Lindsay quickly rebuffed these criticisms. Unlike Chicago—where Mayor Richard Daley had authorized police to shoot young looters and arsonists—Lindsay argued that "protection of life, particularly innocent life, is more important than property . . . we are not going to shoot children in New York City."[46] Soon, other urban police departments would emulate the more restrained riot control techniques practiced in New York and a handful of other cities.

Just as the NYPD was successfully implementing its riot control policies, it was also facing new challenges from white countercultural groups and antiwar protesters. Unlike the black and Latino communities, such groups were made up largely of middle-class

white youth that were unaccustomed to violent treatment by police.
At the same time, the unorthodox dress, outlandish behavior, and
left-wing political views of many of these youth were anathema to
most white working-class police officers who were not inclined to
tolerate much abuse or resistance from what they saw as "spoiled rich
kids." Riven with class and political resentments, police encounters
with these groups were often very hostile, making discipline and restraint difficult.

The first sign of such problems occurred on Memorial Day weekend in 1967 when about two hundred hippies gathered to chant and
play bongo drums in Tompkins Square. For months the Diggers (an
anarchist street theater troupe), the Hare Krishnas (a Hindu religious sect), and other countercultural groups had been gravitating
to the East Village and its assortment of coffeehouses, theaters,
communes and—at the center of it all—Tompkins Square Park. Tensions between these newcomers and police had been growing recently as the NYPD repeatedly raided the Digger commune on East
Eleventh Street in search of narcotics and runaways. That weekend,
when some longtime residents complained to park authorities
about the hippie gathering, police ordered the group to stop singing
and move off the grass. When some individuals refused and linked
arms in protest, police summoned TPF reinforcements and cleared
the area using nightsticks. One of the hippies was clubbed by several
officers and dragged away by the handcuffs with blood streaming
down his face. A melee ensued as the hippies fought back, leaving
seven people injured and forty under arrest. The arrests for disorderly conduct were later dismissed, and Commissioner Leary con-
ceded that police had overreacted to the situation.[47]

While tensions between police and the counterculture continued
to simmer on the Lower East Side, the growing visibility and militancy of the antiwar movement provoked a more visceral reaction.
Police and antiwar protesters first clashed in October 1967, when
officers used fists and batons to arrest thirty-one students blocking
the Navy recruitment office at Brooklyn College. A few weeks later,
police and antiwar protesters confronted each other in a series of
direct actions known as Stop the Draft Week. Organized by a coalition of peace and student groups, approximately two thousand

anti-war protesters attempted to shut down the Whitehall Induction Center in the financial district. A massive showing of police thwarted such attempts the first few days, but on the fifth day serious violence occurred after frustrated protesters at Whitehall decided to march uptown for an impromptu rally in Union Square. At the last minute, a group of marchers veered off toward Irving Place and rallied in front of a building housing military personnel. Police, who had grown increasingly restive and angry, pinned the crowd against the building and ordered it to disperse. When one of the demonstrators responded with an obscenity, police charged the crowd with their clubs, resulting in several minor injuries and 140 arrests.[48]

A few months later, police animus toward antiwar protesters and their distaste for the counterculture converged when the Yippies held a spring celebration, or "Yip-in," at Grand Central Station. Led by the mercurial Abbie Hoffman, the Youth International Party, or Yippies, were an eccentric band of hippie revolutionaries centered in the East Village. In one of their many outrageous antics, some three thousand Yippies and curiosity seekers converged on Grand Central Station on the night of March 23 to celebrate the "rites of spring" with songs and chants. Warned in advance of the gathering, a force of TPF officers was sent to the scene to patrol the event and keep the station open to commuters. With no agenda or leadership, however, the crowd soon became restless. One man unfurled a banner reading "Up Against the Wall Motherfucker," while another climbed up to the clock above the information booth to spray paint "Peace Now" across its face, breaking the hands of the clock in the process. Visibly angered, TPF officers moved in with nightsticks to disperse the crowd. Seventeen people were arrested and several injured, including a *Village Voice* reporter. Based on film shot at the event, the New York Civil Liberties Union later issued a report charging police with failing to give audible warnings to disperse and the subsequent brutal handling and clubbing of several participants.[49]

As in many parts of the world, the spring of 1968 proved to be one of the most explosive periods in the city's history. Three weeks after the King assassination and racial uprisings, students at Columbia University declared their solidarity with the Harlem community by calling a strike to protest the university's plans to build a new gymnasium in Morningside Park. Reflecting the surge of antiwar sentiment in the wake of the Tet Offensive, the Columbia branch of Students for a Democratic Society (SDS) also demanded that the university withdraw from the Institute for Defense Analyses, a government-sponsored think tank for warfare and weapons development. There had already been three antiwar protests on campus in the past year, but none of them had resulted in violence or police intervention. On Tuesday, April 23, however, a group of approximately three hundred black and white students moved into Hamilton Hall (a university administration building), took a dean hostage, and pledged to hold the building until the university met their demands. Early the next morning, black students and Harlem activists who joined them barricaded the building and asked the white students to leave. They did so but soon began occupying other buildings on campus.

Fearing violence, President Grayson Kirk and the Columbia administration were reluctant to call in the police, hoping instead to negotiate a settlement through a newly formed Ad Hoc Faculty Group. But as protest and negotiations continued over the next week, more and more students became involved in the conflict. By Friday a growing number of students occupied Hamilton, Low, Avery, Fayweather, and Math Halls, but they also attracted a sizeable group of student counterdemonstrators who threatened to end the occupation by force. On Sunday the counterdemonstrators formed a cordon around Low Library to prevent strike supporters from passing food and supplies into the building, while concerned faculty attempted to keep the two sides from clashing. After a final negotiation attempt failed, President Kirk called on the NYPD to clear the occupied buildings.[50]

At 2:30 A.M. on April 30, the police department mobilized roughly fourteen hundred officers around the Columbia campus and began what students called "the bust." Much to the administration's surprise, the evacuation of black students in Hamilton Hall proceeded smoothly. Following consultations with Eldridge Waith, the NYPD's community relations specialist in Harlem, eighty-six students agreed to submit to arrest and accompany police out the building through underground tunnels. The evacuation of Avery, Fayweather, and Math, however, proved more difficult. With no underground access to these buildings, police had to remove student and faculty onlookers outside as well as hundreds of noncooperating protesters inside. When they encountered resistance, police reportedly dragged students from the buildings, pushing, kicking, or clubbing those who got in their way. At Avery Hall, a university representative who accompanied police reported that officers formed a gauntlet and pummeled students as they passed down the stairwell. Those arrested at Low Library reported similar treatment.

The most serious violence, however, occurred after the buildings were cleared as police prepared to roll their vans off the campus. Angered at antipolice taunts by the crowd south of College Walk, a group of police charged the students, causing panic and bedlam as the crowd retreated across South Field. An account by staff at the *Columbia Spectator* described the harrowing scene:

Flailing their clubs, the police chased several hundred students onto the lawn, the glare of the bright [police van] lights at their backs as they charged. The athletes [counterdemonstrators] on the Sundial were overrun with the rest, their pro-police chants disregarded. The students who ran slowest in the stampede were struck with clubs, tripped or kicked. In the darker recesses of the field, plainclothesmen stationed themselves near hedges and pummeled demonstrators who tried to run past them. The students who moved faster found, as they reached the south side of campus, that all of the gates had been closed and locked. With the police sweeping across South Field, they had no place to go but inside the lobbies of the dormitories which were now filling up with the limping, the bruised, and the frightened.

Police were apparently unaware that the south gates had been locked, and it is unclear whether the charge was an authorized operation or a spontaneous breach of discipline. In any case, the commanding officer at the scene, Chief Inspector Sanford Garelik, later acknowledged that police had overreacted and criticized the action as "uncalled for."[51]

Over the course of the operation, more than 700 people had been arrested and 148 injured (132 students, 4 faculty, and 12 police). While there were few serious injuries, more than 100 people sought medical treatment at local hospitals. Over the next few months, the CCRB received 162 complaints of excessive force, the most complaints ever filed around a single police action. As with CCRB complaints generally, most of these cases were found unsubstantiated because of difficulties identifying individual officers or locating cooperative eyewitnesses and victims. In the end, the CCRB filed disciplinary charges against only three officers.[52]

The NYPD admitted that force had been used against demonstrators but insisted that such methods were necessary given the large number of protesters and their provocative behavior toward police. Commissioner Leary maintained that university officials had seriously underestimated the number of protesters on campus, leaving police with insufficient staffing to handle the volatile crowds. Moreover, police argued, the unruly behavior of the demonstrators who threw bottles, shouted obscenities and epithets, and obstructed police operations justified the use of force in many cases. In fact, nearly all accounts of the occupation agree that some students taunted police and occasionally threw bottles and other objects. And there is some evidence that a few protesters may have deliberately sought to provoke a violent response from police through vile personal insults. As some radicals did in the 1930s, a few militant students may have hoped to incite police violence in hopes of getting the "pigs" to reveal their "fascist" nature.[53]

More sympathetic observers, however, noted that such actions were not widespread and that the police response was far out of proportion to the provocation. According to several faculty observers, the use of force was gratuitous and excessive, particularly toward passive resisters who were repeatedly dragged, shoved, and throttled. A subsequent NYCLU report on the Columbia action charged that police used "violent and unnecessary force" without first trying alternative means and that the peaceful evacuation of Hamilton Hall suggested that violence could have been avoided in other buildings as well. Referring to the South Field incident, the report faulted police for not issuing clear instructions before charging and for allowing unidentified plainclothesmen to abuse protesters with impunity. The large number of injuries and low number of arrests stemming from this incident, the NYCLU said, suggested that some

263

police were out to punish demonstrators and used violence indiscriminately. Injuries sustained by medical personnel and counterdemonstrators suggest that this was in fact the case.[54]

The violent behavior of police was a reaction—or overreaction—to a hostile and trying situation, but it was also a product of deepseated political and class antagonisms. First, the antiwar message of the Columbia demonstrators was not likely to endear them to the police, many of whom were veterans themselves or had sons or other family members serving in Vietnam. Police at antiwar demonstrations, explained one officer, "really become outraged and confused when they hear some kid question the guts of those fighting in Vietnam." As this comment suggests, police anger was not so much based on differing views of the war as it was on class-based resentments of a primarily middle-class antiwar movement. While working-class youth were disproportionately represented among Vietnam draftees, most students at Columbia and other elite colleges were draft exempt. Viewing them as spoiled rich kids, many police resented what they saw as wasted privileges and opportunities. As one officer who worked the Columbia protest explained, "Everything I got in life I worked for. It gets me sore when I see these kids, who been handed everything, pissing it away, talking like bums, dressing like pigs. . . . It's some joke, ain't it, a rich kid calling a police officer a pig."

Although they did not realize it, the radicals' use of animalistic epithets to describe police—"pigs," "brutes," etc.—drew on centuryold stereotypes that cast working-class police as crude, subhuman beasts. Such negative images were no doubt part of the collective memory of the Irish-American police fraternity and were sure to cause offense, particularly when uttered by elite college students. The fact that Barnard women sometimes shouted these insults was even more shocking to many police who harbored more conventional gender expectations. "Their idea of a woman," explained one officer, "is a nice quiet Catholic girl from Queens." Another officer recounted how he reacted when a Barnard protester yelled an obscene comment at him, "I hit her good. I made her cry."[55]

NYPD officials sympathized with the rank and file's frustrations, but they also took steps to try to rein in unprofessional outbursts of violence. In its final report on the Columbia disturbances, the CCRB spread the blame around, accusing some protesters of violent provocation and some officers with using unnecessary force. Suggesting that violence often resulted from a breakdown in discipline, the report attributed many of the problems to poor supervision by field commanders who allowed subordinates to vent their anger on protesters. Noting the rough treatment of passive demonstrators, the CCRB also called for better police training in handling civil disobedience. In an attempt to end the anonymity that protected abusive police in mass actions, the CCRB proposed mandatory nameplates for all police and an end to the use of plainclothes officers for crowd control. Although PBA opposition effectively scuttled the nameplate idea, the department did reduce the use of plainclothes officers at demonstrations (though they continued to collect intelligence) and did improve training in handling demonstrations.[56] Nevertheless, the vigilante tendencies of some rank and file officers would prove hard to contain and would continue to make headlines for the next two years.

As for the students, their exposure to violent police action at Columbia served to harden the resolve of protesters and increase student sympathy for their causes. As Columbia president Grayson Kirk noted, "a great many people who had been hitherto unsympathetic with any of the demands of the student strikers experienced such a predictable emotional shock that they began to see more validity in some of the strikers' demands." A university survey conducted a week after the occupation, in fact, found that of those students who had witnessed the violent police action on campus that night, 93 percent believed that it was excessive. Many white students were thus exposed for the first time to the kind of brutal police violence that the black community had been complaining about for years. As campus solidarity with Harlem intensified, the strike continued and became more militant, with several combative encounters between police and demonstrators over the next few weeks.

The growing polarization between police and left-wing demonstrators was not unique to Columbia and was played out on the national level that summer outside the Democratic National Convention. As a horrified nation looked on, a motley antiwar demonstration turned into what an investigating committee called "a police riot." Fed up with the antics and abuse of some protesters, Chicago cops took off their badges and charged into the crowd swinging their clubs, spraying mace, and chanting, "Kill, kill, kill!" The melee—which continued sporadically through the duration of the convention—caused hundreds of injuries, left the Democratic party in a shambles, and marked a crucial shift in public opinion away from activism and liberalism and toward conservative forces calling for law and order.[57]

Backlash

In the wake of the Chicago mayhem, the New Left and the black liberation movement became increasingly fragmented and extremist, while the politics of the city and the nation became ever more polarized. As CORE, Student Nonviolent Coordinating Committee (SNCC), and SDS degenerated into a band of warring sectarian factions, militant groups like the Weather Underground and the Black Panther party made headlines with their more violent revolutionary stance. Both black and white revolutionaries took an aggressive antipolice line, equating domestic police repression with imperialist struggles against third-world revolutionary movements. Alarmed by this strident militancy and ongoing urban and campus unrest, growing segments of the white working and middle classes were attracted to the conservative appeals of segregationist George Wallace and Republican Richard Nixon. Within the NYPD, growing popular support for law and order fueled greater rank and file resistance to Lindsay's restraint policies and encouraged right-wing extremists to organize more openly. All of these issues came to a head in the late summer and fall of 1968.

On the evening of August 2, two white police officers were ambushed and shot during a false domestic dispute call in the Crown Heights section of Brooklyn. Many local police officers believed the Black Panthers, whose headquarters were in nearby Bedford-Stuyvesant, were responsible. Founded in Oakland in 1966, the party had made the fight against police brutality a top priority and organized armed self-defense patrols in black neighborhoods in

Oakland, Seattle, and Los Angeles. In recent months the Panthers had established a new chapter in Brooklyn, and it immediately became a flashpoint for conflict. As the Panthers openly challenged police authority, the NYPD stepped up its surveillance and harassment of the group, leading to repeated clashes during the summer of 1968. Police were thus quick to assume that the party was behind any assaults on its officers, including the latest ambush. Soon after, several white police officers in the Eightieth Precinct (on the edge of Bedford-Stuyvesant) organized the Law Enforcement Group (LEG), an organization of right-wing police and their supporters who vowed to reestablish law and order in Brooklyn.

LEG's first action came in response to the arraignment of two Black Panthers who had been arrested in a scuffle with police outside party headquarters in August. Claiming that the criminal court judge, John Furey, had allowed the suspects to wear berets, smoke, and insult police in his courtroom, LEG members circulated a petition calling for Furey's removal. A few days later, LEG issued new demands calling for the abolition of the CCRB, the removal of all civilians from police precincts, and the convening of a grand jury to investigate the judicial "coddling of criminals." NYCLU director Ira Glasser denounced the LEG demands, accusing the group of trying to make the NYPD into "a separate enclave totally insulated from civilian influence of any kind." The PBA initially withheld judgment, but LEG leaders insisted that the PBA back their petition and warned that its four hundred members would withhold dues from the organization otherwise. Seeing an opportunity to coopt the growing right-wing sentiment of the rank and file, PBA president John Cassese issued a statement condemning Lindsay's restraint policies, saying they "hamstrung" police.[58]

LEG, meanwhile, continued its battle with black militants. Looking to monitor judicial behavior in another assault case involving the Black Panthers, LEG members posted flyers in several precincts urging officers to attend a court hearing on September 4. Several Black Panthers and their white allies, including members of Columbia SDS and the local Peace and Freedom Party, also turned out to protest the high bail ordered by the judge. When more than two hundred people showed up at the courthouse on the day of the hearing, Judge George Rader ordered the overflow crowd out into the hallway and then locked the doors behind them. As the hearing convened in chambers, a group of eight or nine Black Panthers and four white sympathizers moved into the main corridor, where a crowd of roughly one hundred fifty white men surrounded them. According to newspaper reports, many of the men were off-duty police officers and a number were wearing George Wallace campaign buttons. Suddenly, amid chants of "White Power," the crowd attacked the Panther group with fists, kicks, and blackjacks. At least three Panthers were injured in the fray, which was broken up by uniformed police who ushered the victims on to a nearby elevator. None of the assailants were arrested.[59]

Public responses to the courthouse attack were overwhelmingly negative. Both Lindsay and Leary immediately condemned the attack and ordered an investigation of the incident. The New York NAACP demanded a grand jury inquiry, while the Panthers and their supporters staged a protest march in front of police headquarters demanding an end to police harassment and violence. Seeking to distance itself from the LEG action, the PBA passed a resolution condemning individuals or groups who brought discredit on the NYPD through "unlawful, antisocial or violent acts." LEG leaders, meanwhile, denied that their organization had been responsible for the attack and backed off from some of their earlier demands. Perhaps mollified by this retreat, neither the CCRB nor the Kings County grand jury filed any charges against the police assailants.[60]

The right-wing militancy that gave rise to the Law Enforcement Group, however, continued to thrive inside the NYPD. By early 1969, LEG claimed to have more than a thousand police members (mainly in Brooklyn and Queens) and was assigning off-duty officers to monitor the courts in an effort to combat the "coddling" of criminals. The group also pressed unsuccessfully for legislation to punish citizens who filed false complaints against police officers—a tactic that was successfully used in Los Angeles and other cities to intimidate brutality complainants. Although not as militant, the PBA and other police unions also lobbied the state legislature for increased surveillance and infiltration of radical groups, tougher sentencing, and the revival of capital punishment for cop killers.[61]

The rise of right-wing militancy in the NYPD, however, did serve to galvanize resistance to racist police violence among African-American officers. While black cops shared police frustrations over crime and public disorder, they believed that some white officers were "taking the law and order thing to mean anti-Negro." Black police officers uniformly condemned the LEG attack on the Black Panthers, and some even worked with the Nation of Islam and other nationalist organizations to promote the hiring of African-American officers. Moreover, white resistance to affirmative action programs and pervasive on-the-job discrimination radicalized many young black cops and made them more sympathetic to the plight of black prisoners. As Capt. James Francis, Jr., explained, "I have witnessed brutality and unnecessary roughness by white officers many times. Every black cop has seen it." Working with civil rights and community groups, the Guardians Association and the Hispanic Society (a Latino officers' group) assisted citizens in filing CCRB complaints and publicly protested police abuse of minority suspects. Such activities provoked bitter controversy and racial antagonism, as white officers accused nonwhites of putting color ahead of professional loyalties. In 1970, patrolman Walter Smith was subject to harassment and death threats after he stopped the beating of a black prisoner who had been handcuffed to a chair in a Brooklyn station house. Warning of possible armed conflict between black and white officers, Guardians president William Perry demanded an immediate end to "these acts of unprofessionalism and latent bigotry." Similar internal conflicts were reported in police departments in San Francisco, Atlanta, and Chicago as black activism and white reaction met head on in the late 1960s.[62]

As in the 1968 Columbia action, the right-wing backlash in the NYPD was also directed against white middle-class students and antiwar protesters. Violent conflicts between police and antiwar demonstrators had marred a December 1969 protest outside the Waldorf Astoria during a visit by President Richard Nixon. More critically, two of the arrested demonstrators—a high school teacher and a college professor—were beaten and injured while in custody in the Seventeenth Precinct, charges that were substantiated by the CCRB.[63] The following spring, the U.S. invasion of Cambodia triggered a new round of antiwar protests around the country and a nationwide student strike. On May 4, 1970, National Guardsmen fatally shot four student protesters at Kent State University in Ohio, shocking the nation and intensifying the protests. In New York, students at New York University, Pace University, and other local colleges organized a series of antiwar protests and sit-ins in lower Manhattan. Mayor Lindsay, an outspoken opponent of the war, ordered flags at half-mast and declared a citywide "day of reflection" in the wake of the Kent State shootings. Some of the more conservative sectors of the city's white working class, however, took offense at the protests and decided to confront the "unpatriotic" demonstrators on the streets of the financial district.

Working-class reaction centered around the building trades, skilled occupations dominated by white ethnic men engaged in a booming construction industry (the World Trade Center and several other lower Manhattan office complexes were then under construction). During marches and sit-ins on May 6–7, police broke up several scuffles between protesters and workers from nearby construction sites who were heckling the students.[64] Much larger crowds, however, were expected on May 8 (the official day of reflection), and rumors were circulating that some construction workers were planning to start trouble. The evening before, an aide at Rep. Allard Lowenstein's office on Long Island, student strike coordinator Steve Kopitko, and numerous construction workers who were unsympathetic to their coworkers' plans telephoned downtown police precincts to warn of the impending violence. But the NYPD claimed it could not verify these reports and that police resources were already spread too thinly to allow for much additional coverage.

The next day, an antiwar rally in front of Federal Memorial Hall on Wall Street proceeded peacefully until its conclusion just before noon. As the rally was breaking up, a group of roughly two hundred construction workers carrying American flags gathered along the west side of Broad Street. Angered that there was no flag on display at Federal Hall, the construction workers and a growing crowd of supporters—mainly local office workers on their lunch hour—broke through police lines and surged up onto the steps of Federal

Hall singing the National Anthem. Following what police described as a flag desecration incident by one of the protesters, the construction workers began assaulting the demonstrators with their fists, helmets, tools, and flagstaffs. As the students fled into the crowd, the workers chased them through the financial district. Dozens of protesters were beaten and injured, as were several downtown office workers who attempted to break up the attacks.

Just as the turmoil on Wall Street was ending, police at city hall reported that a column of construction workers was marching toward the building chanting "USA All the Way" and "Get Lindsay." As police tried to seal off the building, the gathering crowd of workers demanded that the American and New York flags be raised from half staff (in honor of the Kent State deaths) to full staff. In hopes of pacifying the crowd, the police commander on the scene seconded that request, but the mayor's staff refused. A postal worker in the building then took it upon himself to raise the flags, amid much cheering from the crowd. After further negotiation, the deputy mayor allowed the American flag to remain at full staff, and the crowd responded by saluting and singing the National Anthem. Prodded by the workers, five police officers doffed their helmets during the singing, an act of solidarity that was caught on film. The construction workers reciprocated by periodically switching their chants from "USA All the Way" to "PBA All the Way." The class-based solidarity of police and construction workers was not lost on the student demonstrators who looked on, shouting peace slogans and antipatriotic epithets.

When the anthem concluded, a group of workers took off after the protesters, tackling and beating them in various spots around the park. Police tried to break up some of the fights, but made few arrests. Meanwhile another contingent of workers chased students up to the entrance of nearby Pace College, assaulting several of them and ripping down a peace banner which students had unfurled from the roof. After an administrator locked the doors, angry workers smashed the plate glass windows and stormed the building, attacking several students and faculty inside. At this point, a large number of police reinforcements arrived on the scene. By 3 P.M., the officers had dispersed the crowds and restored order in lower Manhattan.[65]

During the course of the three-hour melee, dozens of people were injured, including seven police officers and twenty-nine civilians who were treated at nearby hospitals. In addition, emergency medical personnel at a makeshift clinic in Trinity Church reported treating at least forty people. Considering the scope of the disorder, the police made very few arrests—only six in all (three protesters and three construction workers). A number of eyewitnesses—both protesters and bystanders—claimed that police had not protected students from attack or that they had intervened but refused to make arrests.[66]

Police inaction during the violence at Pace University drew the most criticism. Deputy Manhattan borough president Leonard Cohen, who witnessed the Pace incident, sent a telegram to the mayor charging police with "gross negligence" in failing to protect students. Another eyewitness, Pace administrator R. F. Spinelli, stated that "police stood there and didn't even attempt to help the students." Speaking for the Pace Faculty Council, Joan Roland denounced police inaction as "an expression of class struggle, where the police tacitly, if not explicitly, encouraged the construction workers to vent their rage" on the students. Mayor Lindsay also condemned police negligence, promising a full investigation. The NYCLU meanwhile obtained a federal court order charging the NYPD to provide protection for future antiwar demonstrations.[67]

Lindsay's sympathy for the protesters and criticism of the police infuriated the PBA. According to PBA president Edward Kiernan, Lindsay's restraint policies and "inconsistent directives" were chiefly responsible. In past disorders, he said, "police have been ordered to remove their helmets and nightsticks and take minimal— or no action. After demonstrations get out of hand . . . the police are then criticized for not taking enough action." The only solution, he insisted, was "to permit those patrolmen to enforce the law firmly, consistently, and equally against all violators." Almost immediately, four other police line organizations backed the PBA's statement and accused Lindsay of "undermining the confidence of the public in its Police Department." Rumors then circulated that Commissioner Leary and other top police officials were planning to resign.[68]

Leary, as it turned out, did not resign, at least not right away. He did take steps to beef up police protection at antiwar protests, a move that convinced a federal appeals court to vacate the earlier order. At the same time, Leary used the pending investigation as an opportunity to rationalize the department's role in what were now dubbed the "Hardhat Riots." In a lengthy report issued in August, the department acknowledged problems with police protection on May 8 but blamed them on a lack of advance information, a shortage of police personnel, and the failure of radio communications equipment. The report provided no clear explanation for the small number of arrests and suggested that pending civil suits against the city had prompted many of the injury reports. Despite numerous complaints of police negligence, the NYPD preferred charges against only two officers. Ultimately, the report made only two recommendations: the purchase of better radio equipment and the relocation of the field command observation posts.[69]

The only tangible policy initiative to come out of the whole affair originated with Mayor Lindsay. Following advice from the CCRB and the NYCLU, he created an eight-member corps of independent civilian observers to monitor and issue reports on police and crowd conduct at public demonstrations. Initially, attorneys from the Association of the Bar of the City of New York, the city's most prestigious lawyers' organization, served as volunteers. Prior to serving, members participated in a two-day training program in both police crowd control tactics and citizen rights. The observer corps thus institutionalized the notion of citizen surveillance and oversight of the police, the same principle that had motivated attempts to create a civilian review board. In later years, the National Lawyers Guild assumed responsibility for this function, and its volunteers continue to monitor demonstrations to this day.[70]

Commissioner Leary, meanwhile, was facing another crisis in the department, one that would ultimately end his career with the NYPD. Two weeks before the May 8 riot, the *New York Times* had published a series of front-page stories exposing widespread police graft and corruption in the gambling and narcotics units. Based on information provided by officers Frank Serpico and David Durk, the exposé led to a major scandal and the appointment of a special investigating commission led by Whitman Knapp. During the two-

and-a-half-year investigation, the Knapp Commission documented widespread corruption in both the plainclothes and uniformed divisions and a cover-up by the Lindsay administration. One of the first casualties of the scandal was Howard Leary, who resigned in September 1970.

Unlike earlier corruption scandals, however, the Knapp investigation did not become a platform for airing public criticism of police brutality. In fact, Lindsay's failure to confront the problem was due in part to his concern with maintaining police cooperation in light of ill will generated by the review board battle and the new restraint policies. According to the Knapp Commission, Durk and Serpico met with Lindsay aides on several occasions in 1967 and 1968 but were told that an investigation would have to wait because it would "upset the cops." Presumably, the Lindsay administration needed the NYPD's cooperation in maintaining peace in the city and did not want to risk further alienating the police over the corruption issue.[71] Moreover, the very public debate about police violence in the 1960s had given New Yorkers numerous opportunities to air their grievances about racism and brutality. Lindsay's attempts to reform the NYPD and curtail its use of excessive force made brutality critics less likely to join in the Knapp Commission's efforts to implicate his administration.

The corruption scandal would preoccupy the NYPD and its critics for the next two years, temporarily overshadowing the concern with brutality. Leary's successor, Commissioner Patrick Murphy, made the fight against corruption his top priority but also quietly continued Lindsay's policies of discipline and restraint. As a native New Yorker, a longtime member of the NYPD, and the son of an Irish-American police family, Murphy had more "insider" credibility than Leary, and his restraint policies do not seem to have stirred as much controversy.[72] Perhaps more importantly, the political climate of the city was changing in the early 1970s, as Nixon deescalated the Vietnam War and left-wing militants became increasingly isolated from the political mainstream. The paucity of mass protests or riots after 1970 no doubt made Murphy's restraint policies more palatable, since they were rarely put to the test.

Left-wing political resistance meanwhile became more extreme, covert, and violent, as groups like the Weather Underground and the Black Liberation Army deliberately targeted police through bombings and sniper attacks. In June 1970, the Weather Underground claimed responsibility for the bombing of NYPD headquarters that damaged the building and injured seven people. Violent attacks on police officers also increased, peaking in 1971 with ten police murders—the highest number since 1930. The department responded by stepping up its covert operations under the Bureau of Special Services, using espionage, disruption, and entrapment to destroy extremist groups. As political extremism went underground, so too did police repression. Some observers claimed that these covert operations were part of a trade-off to appease the Law Enforcement Group and other right-wing elements in the department who felt they had been handcuffed by the Lindsay administration.[73] But even if there was no conspiracy, it is nonetheless true that the violent public handling of radicals and minorities gave way to more covert forms of police repression by the 1970s. As in the 1910s and 1930s, the shift from mass police violence to covert operations was based on the belief that the latter were more effective, less controversial, and less likely to generate public sympathy for radical causes. These red-squad activities raised a host of civil liberties concerns, but they usually did not involve the highly visible and objectionable forms of violence that characterized the 1964 Harlem uprising, the Columbia occupation, or the May 8 riots.

In retrospect, the 1960s proved to be a pivotal era in the history of antibrutality organizing. Under the influence of the civil rights movement, police brutality became a focal point for community activism and moved to the center of urban policy debates. Moreover, in the late 1960s, the NYPD's use of violent tactics against white hippies and antiwar protesters made at least some portion of the white middle-class acutely aware of and concerned about police misconduct. As in the past, however, solving the problem proved more difficult. In many ways, Lindsay's reform efforts were a resumption of the tolerance campaign launched by Fiorello La Guardia in the 1930s. But whereas La Guardia's efforts bore fruit in the late 1930s, Lindsay's remained mired in conflict and acrimony. As his critics have pointed out, Lindsay's brusque management style, his poor relations with the police, and his tendency to alienate the electorate all worked against him. But like other 1960s liberals, he faced an exceedingly complex social and political landscape. In the late 1930s, by contrast, La Guardia pressed his tolerance policy with the federal government's explicit support for labor rights and with a left-liberal political consensus for social reform and the protection of civil liberties. In the late 1960s, however, Lindsay waged his campaign for civilian review and police restraint in the midst of growing political polarization around the Vietnam War and civil rights. The city itself was in economic decline, a situation that fueled class and racial resentments. After 1968, conservative appeals for law and order emboldened the right wing while vilifying student protesters and black and Latino activists—a development that only accelerated the fragmentation and dissipation of the left. Clearly, there was no political consensus for reforming the police.

The increased public awareness and better understanding of the problem of police violence, however, could not be erased. As the political scene quieted in the 1970s, the NYPD would begin to experiment with new programs and policies designed to improve community relations and limit the use of deadly force. The battles over police brutality in New York in the 1960s were not fought in vain but would yield reforms in a piecemeal fashion over the next thirty years.

8. WILL THE CYCLE BE UNBROKEN?

In August 1972, two white patrolmen attempted to pull over three black youths riding in a Pontiac in the New Brighton section of Staten Island. The youths, who had stolen the car for a joy ride, immediately sped away. When two other officers attempted to block their path with a patrol car, the car swerved to the side, nearly hitting one of the patrolmen. His partner responded with his weapon, firing six shots at the vehicle as it pulled away. A few blocks down, the police caught up with the car as it pulled over on a side street. They immediately drew their service revolvers and fired several shots at the fleeing driver who, the officers said, had crouched down as if to fire a weapon. At the same time, Ricky Bodden, a ten-year-old boy who had been riding with the two other youths, burst out of the car into the line of fire. He was struck by a bullet, as were the driver and two other black bystanders who were sitting on a nearby stoop. The Bodden boy died soon after; the fourteen-year old driver—who proved to be unarmed—was also injured.

The next night, the predominantly African-American New Brighton neighborhood erupted in violence as residents took to the streets, beating white pedestrians and pelting police cruisers with rocks and bottles.[1] Two days later the NYPD dispatched Deputy Commissioner Benjamin Ward to Staten Island to meet with four hundred angry residents. Rather than making the usual attempts to justify the officers' actions, Ward announced that the NYPD was issuing new regulations governing the use of deadly force that would hopefully reduce unnecessary injury and deaths. As Police Commissioner Patrick Murphy announced the next day, the new regulations prohibited the use of warning shots and barred police from shooting from or at a moving vehicle unless the occupants themselves were using deadly force (other than the vehicle itself).

Most critically, to ensure compliance with departmental regulations, the NYPD announced the formation of a Firearms Discharge Review Board (FDRB), which would review every instance in which police officers fired their weapons. The creation of this new internal unit put teeth into the new policies as well as the department's 1967 regulations that restricted the use of deadly force to defense-of-life situations or to apprehend violent felons. A year later, following the police shooting of another ten-year-old black boy, the department announced the establishment of an Early Warning System that would use FDRB files to identify officers who had repeatedly and unnecessarily fired their weapons. Such officers would be psychologically evaluated and subject to reassignment, discipline, or dismissal.[2] The NYPD's pioneering role in restricting the use of deadly force stands as one of the department's most significant reform efforts.

As in other American cities, police restrictions on the use of deadly force in New York saved numerous lives. FDRB data shows that the number of police shootings and civilian deaths declined steadily after 1971, from ninety-three fatalities in 1971 to only twenty-five by 1976. With some minor variations, the downward trend continued through the 1980s, reaching a low of eleven fatalities in 1985. Contrary to the dire predictions of the Patrolmen's Benevolent Association, the new regulations did not make police work more dangerous. In fact, the number of NYPD officers who were shot (fatally and nonfatally) also declined, from a high of fifty-eight in 1971 to eleven or twelve in 1976, 1983, and 1985. The positive experience of the NYPD and other departments that adopted such restrictions helped convince the Supreme Court to ban police use of deadly force against unarmed nonviolent suspects in its 1985 decision in *Tennessee* v. *Garner*. Based on Fourth Amendment protections against bodily seizure, the ruling invalidated laws in roughly half the states that permitted police to shoot unarmed, nonviolent felons. The new deadly force policies contributed to a general decline in the number of police shootings nationwide. These reforms became standard police practice not only because they helped protect constitutional rights but because they saved the lives of officers and innocent citizens—thus abetting law enforcement and public safety.[3]

The ongoing efforts to restrict the use of deadly force prompted police agencies to turn to alternative, less lethal weapons and tactics. In the 1970s and 1980s, these innovations ranged from simple martial arts moves to elaborate chemical and electronic shock devices. In many instances, these tactics and devices saved lives by providing less lethal alternatives to shooting or bludgeoning with a nightstick. But the potential for misuse raised new problems and concerns and resulted in new forms of police violence and even torture. The chokehold—a martial arts move designed to temporarily asphyxiate and subdue a violently resisting suspect—is a good example. When done properly, police officers found the chokehold very effective; in other instances, improperly applied chokeholds proved lethal. In 1993, following the suspicious deaths of several suspects from asphyxia, the NYPD issued an outright ban on its use. The sudden surge in asphyxia deaths in this period also prompted the NYPD to prohibit hog-tying—a dangerous practice in which a violent suspect's cuffed hands were tied to their bound feet behind the back. Other problems developed around the use of chemical agents (mace and pepper spray) that proved dangerous to subjects with respiratory or heart ailments. Following the deaths of two prisoners who had been sprayed with pepper by NYPD officers in 1995, the Civilian Complaint Review Board began closer monitoring of such cases, urging greater caution and better training in its use and new department protocols for treating and monitoring associated medical problems.[4]

Among the most technologically sophisticated new weapons were the electronic shock devices known as stun guns and Tasers. Developed in the 1980s, these devices were designed to administer high-voltage electric shocks that would temporarily stun violent or deranged subjects. A few officers, however, devised their own unauthorized uses of the weapon. In April 1985, a black high school student in South Ozone Park, Queens charged that he had been falsely arrested on a marijuana charge and had been subsequently beaten and tortured with an electroshock device while handcuffed in the 106th Precinct. The youth, who had no prior arrest record, had mul-

tiple burn marks on his arms, back, and buttocks. He confessed to
the drug peddling charge, he insisted, after officers threatened to
shock his genitals. Within days, four other drug suspects—all black
and Latino—came forward and charged that they too had been
shocked in the 106th Precinct by the same narcotics officers. In the
months that followed, five top commanders were forced to retire,
and four officers were convicted of assault in subsequent criminal
trials. The negative publicity from the cases prompted the NYPD to
discontinue use of the stun gun.[5]

Some of the controversy surrounding less lethal weapons concerned their use against mentally ill or emotionally disturbed persons. Indeed, a whole range of specialized devices—nets, Y-bars,
body restraints, plastic shields, and fire extinguisher sprays—were
developed for police use in subduing such individuals. While
mental-health specialists debated the wisdom of using such potentially frightening tools, the NYPD desperately sought out new methods for handling what was becoming one of the department's most
critical problems in the late 1970s and 1980s. Under the impact
of deinstitutionalization, state psychiatric hospitals in the city discharged more than 126,000 patients between 1965 and 1977, with
many ending up homeless and destitute on city streets. The social
abandonment of this population meant that police were often called
on to deal with disturbed persons who became a danger to themselves or others. The controversial police shootings of Luis Baez in
1979 and Eleanor Bumpurs in 1984 resulted in the introduction of
less-lethal weapons, improved academy training in psychopathol-
ogy, and new protocols for the Emergency Services Unit, a specially
trained detail that was now assigned to handle all cases involving
emotionally disturbed persons. The new guidelines probably contributed to the reduction in police shootings in the 1980s, but they
did not eliminate them. Emotionally disturbed persons continue to
be disproportionately represented among police-induced fatalities.[6]

Activism Rekindled

While emotionally disturbed persons constituted the most visible
new victims, other social groups also became targets of police abuse.

With new immigration increasing their visibility and political power, Asians and new Latino immigrants began to complain openly about police violence in their communities. Although Puerto Rican groups had been concerned with police violence since the 1950s, Dominicans and other Latino newcomers began organizing around police brutality in the 1980s. Appealing to the city's diverse Spanish-speaking population, the National Congress for Puerto Rican Rights took a leading role in antibrutality activism among Latinos, particularly in the Bronx. A new current of activism also took hold in the city's Asian community, which had grown rapidly since the late 1960s and become the target of a powerful racist backlash in the 1980s. In 1986, in the midst of a growing number of brutality incidents in Manhattan's Chinatown and in Queens, young Asian-American women established the Committee Against Anti-Asian Violence to combat racist violence and police brutality. As the formation of these new ethnic defense groups suggests, older patterns of conflict between native-born police and the city's immigrant poor reemerged with the post-1965 immigration wave. Other long-standing patterns of police abuse became visible for the first time. Propelled by the gay liberation movement, the Gay Activists Alliance began defending homosexual brutality victims and joined other gay groups in the 1970s and 1980s in staging antibrutality protests at precincts in Greenwich Village, Chelsea, and Times Square.[7]

Although police misconduct was directed against a wide range of groups in this period, African Americans still made up the largest percentage of CCRB complainants and continued to play a leading role in the fight against police brutality. Although NYPD restrictions on the use of deadly force had helped reduce police shootings, FDRB data revealed that African Americans made up a disproportionate share of police shooting victims. In a study of NYPD shootings from 1971 to 1975, James Fyfe found that blacks made up 60 percent of all persons shot by police while comprising only 20 percent of the city's population. (A smaller but significant discrepancy affected Latinos, who made up roughly 15 percent of the population but accounted for 22 percent of those shot.) Fyfe noted that the racial breakdown of those shot was roughly consistent with the percentage of arrests for violent crimes for each group. He and other NYPD managers thus concluded that racial bias was not a significant factor in police use of deadly force, arguing that such decisions were "situational" and based on the prevalence of violent crime in particular neighborhoods. Civil rights activists, however, rejected this argument and pointed out that law enforcement patterns and practices were themselves racially biased and produced racially skewed rates of arrest and shooting. Although the term "racial profiling" had not yet been coined, activists were beginning to formulate such an analysis to explain the racial discrepancy in the use of excessive force.[8]

In the 1970s and 1980s, controversial shooting cases involving white police officers and young black males occurred with startling regularity. Victims included ten-year-old Clifford Glover in Jamaica, Queens, in 1973; fourteen-year-old Charles Reese in Brownsville in 1974; and fifteen-year-old Randolph Evans of East New York in 1976. In two of these cases, the grand jury declined to indict the officer.[9] Black discontent was further heightened by the choking death of Arthur Miller, a well-known black construction contractor and community development leader who had struggled with police during a traffic stop in Crown Heights in 1978.[10] It was, however, a nonfatal beating case in 1983—a police assault on a young black theology student—that finally attracted federal attention. Stopped in Harlem for a traffic violation, Rev. Lee Johnson said that police made abusive remarks about his race and religion, struck him with a nightstick and flashlight, and then took him to the Twenty-eighth Precinct and beat him again. Pointedly refusing to file a complaint with the CCRB, Johnson's attorney insisted that the board was "nothing but a rubber stamp to justify police misconduct." Instead, Johnson and his supporters convinced U.S. rep. John Conyers, chair of the House Judiciary Subcommittee on Criminal Justice, to hold public hearings on police brutality that summer and fall.

As in past investigations, hundreds of black citizens turned out to recount their stories of police abuse, expressing bitter disappointment with the ineffectiveness of the CCRB and the police disciplinary system. Some of the most persuasive testimony came from members of the Guardians Association who recounted recent cases of shootings of black plainclothes and off-duty officers by their white colleagues. When the House Subcommittee issued its report the following year, it concluded that "racism appears to be a major factor in alleged police misconduct," and it urged greater hiring of black and Latino officers, improved recruitment and training, and most importantly, the establishment of an *independent* civilian review board to handle complaints of misconduct.[11]

As the committee hearings and report made clear, the black community had little confidence in the police-controlled CCRB. Under the impact of budget cuts and changing organizational priorities, the board's staff and funding levels had fallen precipitously since the mid-1970s. The percentage of cases it substantiated had dropped accordingly, hovering at around 10 percent—down from the 20 to 30 percent rates of the Lindsay-Murphy years. The complaint procedure was also hampered by problems on the precinct level. In field integrity tests conducted in 1978, the department found that seven precincts had ignored or discouraged civilian complaints of excessive force or other abuses.[12]

The PBA, which maintained its firm opposition to civilian review, also threw up a barrage of obstacles that hampered CCRB operations. In 1984, the association announced a new policy of countersuing those who filed unsubstantiated complaints of brutality or corruption against police officers and persuaded the city to file such suits at public expense. In its 1984 collective bargaining agreement, the PBA also got the city to pay seventy-five dollars per officer per year into the association's legal defense fund that provided legal services, officers' salaries, and civil indemnity for officers involved in misconduct cases. The city thus paid the price of police misconduct many times over—in police salaries, in civil awards and settlements, in countersuits against complainants, and in contributions to the PBA defense fund. The PBA also went on the offensive against any form of personnel action based on CCRB records, winning a ruling from the Collective Bargaining Board that barred the city from disclosing these records. All of these practices limited the effectiveness of the CCRB and illustrated how class and occupational concerns were implicated in the brutality problem.[13]

The stun gun scandal of 1985 marked the beginning of the end of the police-controlled review board. With widespread public shock over these revelations of police torture, black and Latino leaders stepped up demands for an independent civilian board. At the same time, public attitudes about civilian review had become more favorable in the wake of the Watergate scandal of the mid-1970s that fueled widespread skepticism of government and demands for increased public accountability. As in many other big cities, rising African-American and Latino political power also helped revitalize campaigns for civilian review.[14] During his reelection campaign in 1985, Mayor Koch bowed to public pressure and announced his support for civilian representation on the CCRB, a move that helped him win the Democratic nomination and retain the mayoralty. The city council then voted to revamp the board in 1986, giving it six civilian members appointed by the mayor and six police representatives appointed by the police commissioner. The new CCRB was thus similar to the mixed board that the PBA referendum had eliminated in 1966.[15]

The hybrid police-civilian board, however, was not a promising solution. A similar board under Lindsay had a disappointing debut in 1966 and had proven susceptible to NYPD influence. The new board was no different. Investigations were conducted almost entirely by NYPD detectives, and critics both inside and outside the board charged that the police department continued to dominate the complaint review process and was unwilling to accept CCRB disciplinary recommendations.[16]

Dissatisfaction with the apparently toothless CCRB culminated in its handling of a raucous protest in Tompkins Square Park in August 1988. Protesting a recently imposed 1 A.M. park curfew, a group of artists, squatters, and anarchists staged an impromptu sit-in that escalated when some protesters began throwing bottles and fireworks at police. As all available NYPD units converged on the park, police charged the protesters and pursued the dispersing crowd on foot and horseback. Ignoring their commanders, officers rampaged through the neighborhood, clubbing and kicking peaceful protesters and bystanders, images that were captured on videotape. The riot left forty-four people injured, including thirteen police. Afterward, more than 120 people filed complaints with the CCRB, which conducted an investigation that strongly condemned police behavior. Despite this critical assessment, the incident resulted in only minimal disciplinary action. Because of difficulties identifying individual officers, the CCRB substantiated only 17 of the 120 complaints. Ultimately, the department disciplined only thirteen officers involved in the incident. The New York Civil Liberties Union condemned the CCRB's inability to win justice for the Tompkins Square victims and issued a call for an independent all-civilian board.[17]

Citing Tompkins Square as evidence of the need for an independent CCRB, activists found a supporter in David Dinkins, an African-American candidate for mayor in 1989. Dinkins's strong stance on civil rights—including support for an independent CCRB—helped him win the votes of blacks, Latinos, and white liberals and become the city's first African-American mayor. Once in office, however, Dinkins and his police commissioner, Lee Brown, stalled on the review board issue, focusing instead on community policing initiatives. Like its predecessor, the Dinkins administration was also preoccupied with the massive wave of crime and violence that accompanied the crack cocaine epidemic, which had been ravaging the city since the mid-1980s.[18] Although aggressive NYPD enforcement tactics had helped fuel minority outcry against the police, there was a widespread belief among police that such tactics were essential to curbing the crack-induced crime wave, a belief that served to dampen official enthusiasm for reform.

Fifty-Six Blows

Once again, events outside the city provided a crucial impetus for change. In March 1991, a bystander videotaped four Los Angeles police officers kicking and bludgeoning black motorist Rodney King while another ten officers looked on. The horrifying footage, which showed police delivering fifty-six blows and several jolts from an electronic Taser gun, sparked public outrage around the country—particularly among African Americans. Not since Bull Connor's 1963 assault on Birmingham civil rights protesters had any single media event had such power to stir outrage over police brutality.

While most New Yorkers reassured themselves that the community-oriented NYPD was not the LAPD, many black and Latino New Yorkers were not so sure. Activists drew parallels between the King incident and the NYPD's treatment of Frederico Pereira, a Puerto Rican man who died of asphyxiation at the hands of five police officers in Queens earlier that year. Al Sharpton, a Pentecostal preacher and activist who had been active in antibrutality organizing in the 1970s, joined with the Pereira family to press for convictions of the five accused officers. Their subsequent acquittal fueled racial tensions in the city's Latino and black communities just weeks before the King verdict was due in Los Angeles.[19]

The acquittal of the four LAPD officers by a predominantly white jury on April 29, 1992, set off a five-day riot in South Central Los Angeles and numerous smaller disturbances in cities around the country. In New York, violent incidents broke out in Harlem and Jamaica, and a protest march from midtown to Tompkins Square left a trail of broken store windows along the way. More important was the rapid mobilization of thousands of New Yorkers in a series of peaceful demonstrations and vigils. Although predominantly black, the protesters also included visible numbers of Asians, Latinos, and whites, revealing the growing power of the antibrutality movement in the wake of the King verdict.[20]

Antipolice sentiment escalated a few weeks later with the arrest of six NYPD officers for selling cocaine in Suffolk County. The incident confirmed the long-standing association of police corruption and brutality, but it also raised serious questions about police accountability. A preliminary investigation into the incident revealed a broader network of drug dealing and corruption across several precincts and an earlier Internal Affairs investigation that had failed to root out the problem. Concerned that the NYPD was unable to police itself, Mayor Dinkins took two critical steps that June: He appointed a five-member committee (known as the Mollen Commission) to investigate the corruption scandal, and he announced his unequivocal support for an all-civilian review board.[21] Dinkins's call for an independent board and other reform measures heightened tensions between the mayor and the police rank and file that exploded in an ugly display that September. As the city council debated the pending CCRB proposal, ten thousand off-duty officers bused in by the PBA gathered at a protest rally nearby. Before long, about four thousand protesters swarmed over the barricades to block the entrances to city hall and then moved onto the Brooklyn Bridge, where they tied up traffic for over an hour. Shouting racial insults at the mayor, the police protesters roughed up reporters, blocked traffic, and trampled cars. On-duty officers seemed to look the other way, while mayoral hopeful Rudolph Giuliani addressed the throng, offering his own attacks on Dinkins.

This vulgar display of police animus did more to help the cause of civilian review than hurt it. The police commissioner called the protest "unruly, mean-spirited and perhaps criminal," and said it "raised serious questions about the department's willingness to discipline itself." The press overwhelmingly condemned the protest, with the *New York Times* calling for a crackdown to ensure "that it is the Mayor and Commissioner who command the police, not a union backed by a mob."[22] Ultimately, public outrage over the PBA protest convinced several reluctant city council members to switch their votes in favor of the new CCRB, and the bill was signed into law in early 1993. The thirteen-member board would be aided by an all-civilian investigative staff and have its own budget and subpoena power. Amid high hopes for reform, the new CCRB began operation in July 1993.[23]

Two months later, the Mollen Commission began soliciting dramatic testimony from key players in the department's widening corruption scandal. As in the Lexow Committee hearings a century earlier, the Mollen Commission uncovered evidence of both pervasive corruption and brutality. The spread of crack cocaine in the late 1980s had produced an epidemic of gang-related violence and corruption. As in the Prohibition era, the potential for illicit profits and the public demands to get tough with drug-dealing criminals made for a volatile and violent police culture in the city's high-crime precincts.

Some of the most sensational testimony came from Bernard Cawley, a former police officer in the South Bronx who emerged as the department's modern-day Clubber Williams. Cawley described how he robbed drug dealers and peddled contraband, but also how he and other police conducted a reign of terror in the drug-infested

287

neighborhoods of the Forty-eighth Precinct. Looking to plunder money, narcotics, and guns, they illegally broke into hundreds of private homes and beat up the occupants. In another incident, Cawley described a raid on a brothel in which he and his partners lined up and raped all the women. Very little of this violence was the conventional type of "excessive force" used in the course of stops and arrests. Instead, as Cawley explained, "We just beat people up in general. . . . It was a show of force. To show who was in charge." Cawley's brutal disposition was well known at the precinct, where he was nicknamed "the mechanic" because he randomly "tuned people up" (beat them). Cawley insisted that his supervising officer was aware of this behavior and rewarded him with choice assignments.[24] His account of the intricate web of corruption and brutality in crime-ridden precincts was confirmed by several other officers.

Arguing that "corruption and brutality are often linked in a variety of ways," the Mollen Commission sought to unravel this relationship. Unlike the Lexow Committee, which blamed both corruption and brutality on a crooked political machine, the Mollen Commission offered more sophisticated and useful explanations. In some cases, the report maintained, police violence was simply used to facilitate the theft of drugs or money. More often, however, it was used to show power, compel respect, punish defiance, or vent hostilities or frustrations. In such cases, brutality could serve "as a rite of passage to other forms of corruption and misconduct." Indeed, some officers stressed that participation in violence was a form of initiation into police culture, a way to prove one's toughness and loyalty. Brutality, the Mollen Commission suggested, often served as the first step into a corrupt police culture that plagued many of the city's high-crime precincts. To document this point, the commission conducted a survey of the records of 240 corruption-prone officers and found that they were five times as likely to have five or more force complaints than were a random sample of officers.[25]

Perhaps the commission's most important insight was how a police culture of silence and lack of accountability facilitated both brutality and corruption. Time and again, corrupt and/or brutal NYPD officers described the sense of impunity with which they had operated. Cawley and others underscored the power of the "blue wall" and explained the term "testilying"—a police expression for giving false testimony in court. Police witnesses seemed to agree that anyone who testified against another cop, in either brutality or corruption cases, would be finished in the profession. More disturbing still was police officers' belief that their supervisors didn't want to know about misconduct, fearing that reports of misconduct would damage their careers and the department's public image. This was particularly true in cases of brutality, since there was a strong consensus on the need for tough and aggressive policing.[26]

The commission argued, however, that its own experience running undercover investigations, compelling police testimony, and winning convictions against dozens of corrupt officers showed that the blue wall was not impenetrable. In its final report, released in July 1994, the commission recommended the establishment of an independent police monitor to ensure accountability, and the creation of a civil rights unit within the department's Internal Affairs Division that would work with the CCRB to help expedite investigations into complaints of excessive force, false arrest, and perjury. The commission also urged the NYPD to institute integrity training to drive home the message that the department would not tolerate brutality, corruption, perjury, or other forms of misconduct.[27]

For the most part, the commission's recommendations were ignored. Mayor Dinkins, who appointed the Mollen Commission, had been defeated in the 1993 election by Rudolph Giuliani. A former federal prosecutor and strong police advocate, Giuliani opposed the creation of a police monitor, as did his new police commissioner, William Bratton. And when the deputy inspector of internal affairs, Walter Mack, proposed creating a special twenty-four-hour unit to handle brutality cases, Bratton dismissed him and replaced him with a department insider.[28]

As the NYPD seemed to abdicate its responsibility for combating brutality, many police critics looked to the CCRB as the one independent voice for change. It soon became apparent, though, that the board was not functioning as its advocates had hoped. In its first three years as an all-civilian agency, the CCRB's record was marred by a large backlog of unprocessed cases, low substantiation rates, and poor disciplinary follow-through. Running a backlog of more than three thousand cases, the CCRB substantiated only about 4 percent of all complaints from 1993 to 1996 (an even lower rate than that of the police-controlled board of the early 1980s). The poor performance was due in part to a sharp increase in the number of complaints filed and a series of organizational problems and delays resulting from the transition to a civilian staff. These delays meant that many cases languished until the eighteen-month statute of limitations effectively closed them. Moreover, inexperienced staff produced inadequate investigations that contributed to the low substantiation rate. With growing pressure to expedite cases and improve basic investigations, there was little time left for community outreach, policy analysis, or other forms of oversight that policing experts see as essential.

Perhaps most critically, the new political climate of the Giuliani administration hampered the agency. The mayor effectively shrunk the CCRB staff and budget at a time when the size of the police force was growing (seven thousand Housing and Transit police were merged into the NYPD in 1995) and the number of complaints was skyrocketing. He also replaced Dinkins's CCRB appointees—mostly community advocates—with prosecutors who had spent their careers working closely with police. The new board members often rejected the findings of the investigative staff, leading to political infighting and further staff turnover. Giuliani's police commissioners, William Bratton and Howard Safir, were even less disposed to take action on citizens' complaints and frequently rejected the recommendations of the CCRB. According to a study of police disciplinary records conducted by the public advocate's office, less than 2 percent of officers with CCRB complaints were being disciplined. Despite its strength and independence on paper, the CCRB was largely undermined by a political administration that had opposed its creation and had little interest in furthering its mission.[29]

The city's dismal record handling CCRB cases came at a time when citizen complaints of excessive force were rising sharply, from 2,175 in 1993 to 3,516 in 1996.[30] While there are several factors that contributed to this trend, civil libertarians noted that the increase coincided with the beginning of the Giuliani administration and its new, more aggressive style of policing. Commonly known as "zero tolerance," the new brand of policing was derived from a 1982 *Atlantic Monthly* article by James Q. Wilson and George Kelling called "Broken Windows." According to their theory, police could reduce crime by adopting a tough enforcement stance that includes minor "quality of life" offenses such as public drinking and urination, panhandling, street peddling, truancy, turnstile jumping, squeegee washing, etc. Arresting such violators prevents them from committing more serious offenses, allows police to apprehend those with illegal weapons, drugs, or outstanding warrants, and sends a message that the streets are under control. At the same time, the NYPD also adopted a highly targeted approach based on COMP STAT, a system in which weekly computer crime statistics were mapped out on a block-by-block basis and commanders held accountable for their status. The Street Crime Unit (SCU), a mobile plainclothes operation, was expanded and dispatched to make sweeps of drug and crime-infested areas identified by COMP STAT.[31]

Like the old strong-arm squads and other specialized anticrime units, the SCU swept through the city's poor neighborhoods in an effort to retake the streets. But instead of just beating people up as the strong-arm squads had done, the quality of life strategy provided a thin legal pretext for stopping, frisking, and arresting large numbers of people in poor, nonwhite neighborhoods. In more affluent districts, quality of life policing had the added political benefit of sanitizing the streets by reducing the city's visible population of panhandlers, street vendors, and homeless persons, and by eliminating the broken liquor bottles, loud radio playing, and urine smells which often annoyed local residents. For many prosperous white New Yorkers, quality of life policing was a welcome policy that seemed to revive and reclaim a decaying urban core.

The Giuliani administration credited the new policing with a dramatic drop in crime, citing a more than 50 percent reduction in major felony crimes between 1990 and 1997. Although the falling crime rate was a nationwide trend and began before the new policing policies were put into effect, the decrease was more pronounced in New York and resulted—its proponents argued—from the aggressive zero tolerance approach.[32] The city's experiment was widely heralded in the press and was emulated by other municipal police forces.

But not everyone was so sanguine about the NYPD's new initiatives. Critics noted there was no proven correlation between quality of life policing and crime reduction. Several big cities, including San Diego and Boston, showed equally sharp drops in violent crime in the 1990s without quality of life programs. In New York, while violent crime had dropped, misdemeanors increased 50 percent, clogging the courts and producing large numbers of flawed arrests. The biggest criticism of zero tolerance policing, however, was that by increasing officer discretion to execute stops and arrests, it had expanded the potential for brutality, harassment, and racial and sexual profiling. Activists in the city's African-American, Latino, Asian-American, gay, and homeless communities insisted that police used quality of life policing to target and abuse the city's poor, nonwhite, and socially stigmatized residents. For these citizens, city streets had become *less* safe, and the quality of life had deteriorated.[33]

Protests against police brutality were initially most intense in the Bronx, where several high-profile police killings galvanized the Latino community. In December 1994, Officer Francis Livoti arrested twenty-nine-year-old Anthony Baez after his football hit Livoti's parked patrol car. When Baez resisted handcuffing, Livoti used an illegal chokehold that killed the asthmatic Baez. Less than a week later, two police detectives—one of whom was a former bodyguard for Mayor Giuliani—fatally shot eighteen-year-old Anthony Rosario and twenty-two-year-old Hilton Vega. An autopsy conducted by a pathologist hired by the family indicated that they were shot while laying face down, and a CCRB investigation concluded that the officers had used excessive force.

The three killings sparked a series of community protests and meetings led by the National Congress for Puerto Rican Rights and the birth of a new organization, Parents Against Police Brutality, founded by Iris Baez and Margarita Rosario, the mothers of two of the victims. In October, after the judge acquitted Livoti of criminally negligent homicide, Baez and a dozen supporters from Parents Against Police Brutality occupied the office of the Bronx district attorney, who later announced that Livoti would be reindicted for perjury. The group also kept up pressure on the police department, which dismissed Livoti from the force for using a chokehold in violation of regulations banning the practice. In subsequent police killings, the group provided critical support to victims' families while pressuring public officials for redress. Led by victims' mothers and family members, the new multiracial antibrutality movement would become one of the city's most dynamic grassroots movements of the 1990s.[34]

The local campaign attracted national and international attention to the police brutality problem. The United States' ratification of the International Covenant on Civil and Political Rights and the Convention Against Torture in the early 1990s—both of which barred "torture or cruel, inhuman or degrading treatment or punishment" by the state—made police brutality an international concern. After examining cases in New York and Los Angeles, including the Baez and Rosario/Vega deaths, the United Nations Human Rights Committee expressed concern over police abuses in the United States. The following year, Amnesty International published a critical report on police brutality in New York that concluded that "international standards as well as U.S. law and police guidelines prohibiting torture or other cruel, inhuman or degrading treatment appear to have been violated with impunity."[35]

Although Giuliani's new police commissioner, Howard Safir, dismissed the report as "anecdotal," he quickly announced a new initiative to promote better police-community relations. Called Courtesy, Professionalism, and Respect (CPR), the program established a citizens' advisory committee, new training programs in courtesy and "verbal judo" (mediation strategies), and a public relations campaign to improve the NYPD's image. More importantly, Safir began using COMP STAT to track citizen complaints by precinct and to hold commanders accountable for complaints in their areas. When CCRB complaints declined somewhat in 1996, Safir credited the new system. Others, however, pointed out that citizen complaints filed at precincts (but *not* those filed at the CCRB) had dropped dramatically right after the CPR program started, suggesting that police commanders were discouraging citizens from filing complaints. Two years later, not much had changed. In 1998, NBC's *Dateline* secretly taped an African-American man as he visited thirty different New York precincts trying to file a complaint. In about half the precincts, the desk sergeant refused to give him the form, demanding to know what the complaint was about. In one case, a belligerent sergeant physically ejected the complainant from the station house.[36] The CPR program revealed one of the fundamental contradictions in the battle for police accountability: Even the department's deliberate efforts to hold commanders responsible for abuses could fuel efforts to cover them up. As with other efforts to reduce excessive force, this latest reform had unintended and unanticipated consequences.

Louima, Diallo, and Mass Mobilization

CPR notwithstanding, most antibrutality activists put little faith in the department's new kinder, gentler image. Their worst fears were confirmed on August 9, 1997, when a thirty-year-old Haitian immigrant, Abner Louima, was arrested following a fracas outside a Brooklyn nightclub. Charged with disorderly conduct and resisting arrest, Louima was apparently mistaken for another Haitian man who had punched Officer Justin Volpe at the scene. According to Louima, the four officers who accompanied him in the patrol car beat him twice en route to the Seventieth Precinct. Then, after being strip searched in the station, two officers led him to the bathroom, where one held him down while another shouted racial slurs and sodomized him with a broomstick and then forced the stick into his mouth. Left to bleed in a cell for several hours, he was later taken to the hospital where he was found to have a ruptured bladder, a perforated colon, several broken teeth, and a number of other injuries. In an extreme and horrifying way, Louima had become the target of the special wrath that police harbor toward "cop fighters."

When news of Louima's torture surfaced a few days later, the city reacted with shock and outrage and an outpouring of sympathy for Louima. The Haitian community in Brooklyn offered moral and legal support to Louima and his family and joined with other community groups to sponsor vigils and protests at the Seventieth

Precinct. Mayor Giuliani, who usually stood by police officers accused of misconduct, visited Louima and in the hospital and met with Haitian civic leaders to discuss their concerns. In the meantime, the Brooklyn district attorney's officer brought indictments against four police officers involved in the incident. Later, the Brooklyn district attorney turned the case over to the FBI and federal prosecutors in hopes of winning stiffer sentences under federal civil rights laws. The U.S. attorney in Brooklyn also announced that he would commence a federal inquiry into whether there was a broader pattern of police cover-ups of brutality in the city. It was the first stage in a federal investigation of the NYPD made possible under the 1994 Violent Crime and Control Act, which empowered the Justice Department to file suit against law enforcement agencies that engaged in "patterns or practices" that violated civil rights.[37]

Determined to keep up public pressure on the Giuliani administration, Parents Against Police Brutality and a coalition of other community and civil rights groups launched a mass protest march on August 30. Starting at Grand Army Plaza in Brooklyn, some ten thousand protesters marched over the Brooklyn Bridge and assembled outside city hall. Leading the march was Louima's family and the Rev. Al Sharpton, who was seeking the Democratic nomination for mayor in hopes of a run against Giuliani. Antipolice and anti-Giuliani sentiment was widespread, with some protesters carrying placards reading "Brutaliani" or "Criminals, Perverts, and Racists" —a slap at the police department's CPR campaign. Nevertheless, the scene remained orderly until the remaining crowd returned to Brooklyn that night, where police arrested 110 protesters who attempted to block traffic. The march helped keep media attention focused on the Louima case.[38]

Mayor Giuliani, who was up for reelection in the fall, made a number of concessions. First, he announced a $1.5-million budget increase for the CCRB, allowing it to hire a dozen senior investigators to try to improve the pace and quality of investigations. Within the police department, Commissioner Safir overhauled the Seventieth Precinct, recruiting more African-American officers, including a black captain and several Afro-Caribbean officers who lived in the neighborhood. The criminal prosecution of Louima's assailant,

Officer Justin Volpe, also bore fruit, as four fellow officers agreed to testify against him in court. Facing overwhelming evidence, Volpe pled guilty to assault and violating Louima's civil rights and was sentenced to thirty years imprisonment. Another officer, Charles Schwartz, was convicted of holding Louima down during the attack and was sentenced to fifteen years. In addition, Schwartz and two other officers, Thomas Wiese and Thomas Bruder, were convicted of obstruction of justice for fabricating a story to protect Schwartz. The convictions, Giuliani claimed, showed that the blue wall could be breached and that the Louima case was a tragic aberration in an otherwise well-run police department.[39]

Antibrutality activists rightly disagreed. The torture of Louima was an extreme case of police sadism that shocked the conscience and violated the norms of police culture. Roughing up suspects on the street was one thing; sexually assaulting them in the station house was something else. The blue wall had fallen around Justin Volpe, but it ultimately protected the other officers involved in the case. In 2002, the convictions of Schwartz, Wiese, and Bruder were overturned by a federal appeals court. Schwartz was retried and convicted on a perjury charge, but Volpe's accomplice in the assault would never be conclusively identified or punished.[40] Moreover, subsequent brutality cases of a more conventional nature revealed that the police code of silence was as strong as ever.

Antibrutality activists insisted that police accountability and independent oversight had to be strengthened. In 1998, Human Rights Watch lent support for this view when it published *Shielded from Justice*, a lengthy report on police brutality in New York and thirteen other U.S. cities. Like the Mollen Commission, the report emphasized the culpability of police organizations that failed to discipline and deter police misconduct. "Those who claim that each high-profile human rights abuse is an aberration, committed by a 'rogue officer,' are missing the point," the report argued. "Human rights violations persist in large part because the accountability systems are so defective." Rather than fix those systems, most police departments continue with "business as usual" until the next scandal occurs.[41]

Eight months later, the NYPD's next scandal arrived when four officers from the Street Crime Unit opened fire on Amadou Diallo in the hallway of his Bronx home. A twenty-two-year-old Guinean immigrant, Diallo was a devout Muslim who worked as a street vendor and had no criminal record. Around midnight on February 4, 1999, Diallo was approached by four white officers in plainclothes as he stood by the door of his building. Perhaps assuming he was being robbed, Diallo reached into his pocket and pulled out his wallet. The officers, who suspected him of being a rape or robbery suspect, apparently mistook the wallet for a gun and fired a total of forty-one shots, nineteen of which hit the unarmed Diallo. The killing, and the barrage of semiautomatic firepower that caused it, set off immediate and widespread outrage in the city's black and Latino communities.[42]

As the investigation of the incident proceeded slowly and cautiously, the four officers involved were placed on administrative leave but were not arrested. Demanding the immediate arrest and indictment of the officers, more than a thousand antibrutality protesters led by Al Sharpton gathered on Wall Street on the one-month anniversary of the shooting. Twenty-eight demonstrators, including Sharpton, were arrested when they staged a sit-in outside the World Financial Center. Soon after, Sharpton met with Rev. Herbert Daughtry and other black political activists to make plans for an extended campaign of civil disobedience modeled on the antiapartheid movement. The first demonstration on March 9 attracted about fifty protesters, including many of the mothers from Parents Against Police Brutality, who gathered in front of police headquarters in lower Manhattan. Twelve protesters staged a sit-in outside the main doors and were arrested. Sharpton vowed to return with another dozen protesters each day until the officers were arrested.

Building on the antibrutality network that had been growing since the Baez case, the protests succeeded beyond anyone's expectations. The sit-ins and arrests continued, and after former mayor David Dinkins was arrested a week later, the protests mushroomed. During the last two weeks of March, hundreds of demonstrators representing a diverse racial and ethnic cross section of the city were arrested at Police Plaza everyday. The arrest of such notables as Jesse

Jackson, Ossie Davis, Susan Sarandon, Ruby Dee, and most of the city's prominent Democrats brought intense media attention. All told, more than twelve hundred people were arrested during three weeks of protests, which ended on April 1, when the Bronx district attorney indicted the four officers on second-degree murder charges. The momentum of the protests, however, continued to build. In April, more than twenty-five thousand people marched on Washington, D.C., to protest police brutality, and another ten thousand turned out for a march across the Brooklyn Bridge. Although the mass marches were marred by political squabbles, they brought national attention to the problem of police brutality.[43]

The protests did not, however, have much impact on the outcome of the Diallo case. Fearing the four officers would not get a fair hearing in the Bronx, the judge ordered the trial moved to Albany, a predominantly white county in upstate New York (the Bronx, by contrast, was more than 80 percent nonwhite). On February 25, 2000, a racially mixed jury acquitted the police of all charges, accepting the defense argument that the shooting had been a tragic but understandable error. Unlike the antibrutality protesters in the street, the Bronx prosecutor deliberately downplayed race as a factor in the shooting and said little about the aggressive policing practices of the SCU. The trial focused on the final moments of the incident rather than the underlying patterns and practices of local law enforcement. Tried in a distant city where jurors had little knowledge of NYPD practices, the verdict was decided on narrow, technical grounds. As critics of the prosecution pointed out, the crucial issues of racial profiling and zero tolerance policing were never addressed.[44]

Following the acquittals, antibrutality protests resumed, and activists called on the federal government to file civil rights charges. The Justice Department declined to do so, but Attorney General Janet Reno agreed to expand the ongoing pattern or practice investigation to include a study of the NYPD's stop-and-frisk policy. The state attorney general, the city's public advocate, and other public and private organizations also launched investigations of policing and disciplinary practices in the city in the wake of the Louima and Diallo cases. Most notably, the U.S. Civil Rights Commission announced in May 1999 that it would conduct a major investigation of police practices and their impact on civil rights in the city. Antibrutality advocates hoped that the continued public scrutiny and publicity would help to force changes in the NYPD.[45]

Following a yearlong investigation, the Civil Rights Commission released its final report in August 2000. The report offered a detailed critique and recommendations on everything from recruitment and training to policing policies and discipline. For starters, the report underscored the failure of the department's affirmative action programs and recommended more aggressive recruiting to make the NYPD more representative of the city.[46] In its chapter on civilian complaints, the commission reviewed the poor track record of the CCRB in the mid 1990s, but also noted the improvement in substantiation and discipline rates since 1997. With more funds and staff, the board was able to investigate and substantiate more cases and had undertaken new policy initiatives to monitor recidivist officers. While the commission noted ongoing and serious problems, it recognized that recent improvements had come about as a result of greater public scrutiny and urged that an independent monitor be appointed to provide permanent oversight of the disciplinary process.[47]

Its most important and controversial findings concerned the NYPD's stop-and-frisk practices. Analyzing the department's stop-and-frisk reports, the Civil Rights Commission found a dramatic racial disparity among those stopped by the NYPD. Blacks and Latinos made up 84 percent of people stopped by police, while comprising only 52 percent of the city's population. While the NYPD argued that stops were based on victims' descriptions of criminal suspects, some NYPD officers testified that most stops were based merely on officers' observations or instincts, and that most of the targets were black or Latino males. "The NYPD's data," the commission concluded, "strongly suggest that racial profiling plays some role in the stop and frisk practices of the overall department, and particularly in the Street Crime Unit."[48]

As in the other studies, the commission emphasized the larger social costs of this policy. The reports cited testimony from numerous citizens recounting their humiliation, fear, and resentment when

299

police stopped and searched them for no apparent reason. "I now believe that, for the most part, police officers in my community do not care about the citizens," said one Afro-Caribbean teacher in the Bronx who was stopped, searched, and falsely arrested by police on his way to school. "They treat the area like a war zone, and brutalize people who challenge them or get in their way." This man and other citizens concluded that the aggressive crime-fighting tactics of the NYPD had come at the price of their civil rights and individual freedom. On a larger scale, the commission pointed out, such practices damaged the public's attitude toward police and race relations in the city generally.

The Civil Rights Commission, the public advocate, and some police reformers insisted that effective, aggressive policing could be practiced without trampling on civil rights and individual liberties. Plenty of officers, they pointed out, had good arrest records without accumulating any complaints. The key was better police training, monitoring, and accountability to make it clear that abusive behavior was unacceptable. Citing a 1999 study of two precincts in the South Bronx, these critics argued that commanders who had high standards, firm disciplinary practices, and good community outreach could reduce complaints without compromising their effectiveness in fighting crime. Adopting the tough zero-tolerance language of the NYPD, public advocate Mark Green suggested that the NYPD "use a broken windows approach not only to keep crime going lower but also to strictly punish even small acts of misconduct in order to keep larger abuses from ever occurring."[49]

Most police officials, however, believed that such reform was unnecessary. Throughout the police crises of the 1990s, the NYPD had been reluctant to cooperate with investigating committees and had sometimes refused to turn over documents except under court order. When the reports were published, the Giuliani administration then attacked them as inaccurate and biased and scored them for failing to recognize the department's great accomplishments in crime reduction. The department's response to the Civil Rights Commission report was particularly scathing. Calling it "shoddy reporting" and "an embarrassment to the US government," the NYPD charged that the commission set out "to publicly defame the reputation of the department." For his part, Mayor Giuliani dismissed the report as a political ploy by his Democratic rivals in the Clinton administration.[50]

This is not to say, however, that the report—or those that preceded it—had no impact. In the glare of the Mollen investigation, the NYPD had rooted out and prosecuted dozens of corrupt and brutal cops. Following further investigations after the Louima case, the mayor boosted the funding and staff of the CCRB and the police commissioner began disciplining more misconduct cases. In fact, the department's disciplinary rate for CCRB-substantiated cases continued to rise, reaching 74 percent in 2000, a more than twofold increase over the 1994 rate.[51] As public advocate Mark Green noted, "when the police department felt the heat, they saw the light." This pattern of exposure and reform—both in the 1990s and in earlier periods—constitutes strong evidence of the effectiveness of citizen oversight and the need for a permanent and independent monitor for the police. The Mollen Commission, the public advocate, and the U.S. Civil Rights Commission all recommended such a monitoring system, and for good reason. Without it, the reforms inspired by their work were destined to succumb to departmental retrenchment and backsliding as the crisis receded from memory.

The likelihood of a permanent independent monitor for the NYPD, however, was already dwindling. Although Mayor Giuliani had taken tentative steps toward strengthening the CCRB by granting it power to prosecute misconduct cases, he did so to deter the threat of a federal pattern or practice lawsuit and the possible imposition of a federal monitor. The transfer of prosecutorial power to the CCRB, however, was soon challenged by the PBA and other police unions and remained tied up in court. Meanwhile, the election of Republican President George Bush convinced the mayor that further concessions were unnecessary. Henceforth, the city refused to cooperate in the ongoing federal investigation into the department's stop-and-frisk practices, dismissing any pattern or practice lawsuits as baseless.[52] Ultimately, the Giuliani administration staved off the imposition of a federal monitor while making little if any changes in the way the NYPD operated. As in the 1930s, the involvement of the federal government in the 1990s was a powerful lever for change, but the return of a more conservative administration in Washington in 2000 meant that the potential for federal civil rights enforcement would be seriously diminished.

Police and Civil Rights at Ground Zero

The events of September 11, 2001, stunned and horrified Americans everywhere, but no more so than in New York City, the scene of the worst terrorist attack in the nation's history. The destruction of the World Trade Center in lower Manhattan killed an estimated three thousand people, including more than three hundred police and fire department personnel who died in the rescue effort. As the city suffered through the prolonged search efforts, daily funerals, and ongoing fears of air disasters and anthrax infection, the problem of police violence dropped off the city's agenda.

Police officers had become heroes, the press noted, even to young residents of poor, nonwhite neighborhoods. NYPD officials reported an increased public respect for police officers, and complaints of police misconduct plummeted by 18 percent in the two months following the attack. Moreover, with the need to prevent acts of terrorism, Clyde Haberman of the *New York Times* observed, New Yorkers of all backgrounds were more likely to tolerate racial and ethnic profiling. A *Times* poll conducted a month after the attack indicated that half of all city residents—including 24 percent of African Americans and 31 percent of Latinos—believed that racial profiling might be justified under certain circumstances. The September 11 tragedy, many argued, had united both the country and the city.[53]

The changing public mood, however, was not a straightforward reflection of new priorities as much as it was a temporary moratorium on criticism of the police. Declining complaint rates, for example, were no doubt partially due to the closing down of the CCRB for six weeks following the disaster (the board's officers were located on Rector Street adjacent to Ground Zero). Furthermore, for several months after the attack, police resources were disproportionately channeled into security measures—guarding bridges, closing streets, patrolling Ground Zero, etc.—that resulted in fewer violent confrontations with the public. Moreover, in the midst of the city's prolonged mourning, New Yorkers were understandably hesitant to speak out against the police and imposed a form of voluntary self-censorship.[54]

As the September 11 crisis receded, a new climate of war and heightened terrorist alerts has resulted in a wholesale shift in the resources and priorities of the NYPD. As of this writing, the department has spent more than $150 million on counterterrorism operations and assigned more than a thousand officers to these duties, including 120 detectives working with a joint FBI-NYPD task force and five detectives posted in foreign countries. Periodic terror alerts have also brought increased security patrols and checkpoints, purchases of chemical protective gear and detection equipment, and associated training and overtime expenses. The funding and personnel required for such activities has effectively shifted the department's mandate away from the ruthless anti-street-crime emphasis of the 1990s to a more high-tech, intelligence-oriented campaign against terrorism. The shift was clear as early as the spring of 2002, when newly elected mayor Michael Bloomberg and his police commissioner Raymond Kelly closed down the Street Crime Unit.[55]

As in the past, the growing reliance on clandestine police operations has reduced public outcry over police violence but has increased the potential for other forms of repression. Most notably, civil libertarians have expressed a growing concern over the ethnic profiling and illegal detentions of Muslim and Arab immigrants. The NYPD has also petitioned a federal court to ease restrictions on police surveillance of political groups, regulations that were instituted in the 1970s in response to red-squad abuses. At the same time, it is unclear whether incidents of police violence have actually declined. After a temporary drop in CCRB complaints after September 11, the number of complaints in 2002 increased by 8 percent over the previous year. Some black and Latino activists expressed skepticism that police behavior had changed much after September 11, but a February 2002 poll showed that most New Yorkers—including a majority of black and Latinos—approved of the way police were doing their job. NYCLU director Donna Lieberman agreed that the NYPD was now less hostile and defensive, noting "the public posture regarding police accountability and race relations has certainly changed."[56]

Although we cannot be sure about the current levels of police violence, we can be certain that public controversy over it will eventually reemerge. September 11 marked the end of another cycle of scandal and reform, but the historical record suggests that the latest round of reform efforts will eventually slip away. As we gain greater distance from the crises of the 1990s, new police commissioners with different challenges and priorities will undoubtedly reassess the balance between public safety and civil rights. And though the CCRB is considerably stronger today than it was in 1992, the Giuliani years demonstrated that a lack of political will could easily undercut its effectiveness.

Indeed, one of the key insights of recent inquiries, from the Mollen investigation through the Civil Rights Commission, is the vital importance of consistent citizen oversight and police accountability. In confronting either corruption or brutality, the historic forms of oversight—police beat journalism, investigative committees, and film and video recordings—have been sporadic in nature and produced short-term results that tended to unravel when the glare of publicity died down. Finding ways to open up a historically secretive department and institutionalize the public monitoring of police policies and practices to ensure departmental accountability and CCRB effectiveness remains the fundamental challenge for those seeking more humane and just law enforcement.

One of the main obstacles to such change is the persistent belief that effective law enforcement requires tough, ruthless tactics, and that abusive behavior must be tolerated as the accepted cost of fighting crime. As this study has shown, antibrutality reforms have been successfully implemented and institutionalized when police, prosecutors, judges, and the public at large have been convinced that violent and abusive practices are not only violations of civil rights, but are in fact counterproductive for law enforcement. While we have come to accept this view in regards to the third degree, violent mass action policing, and certain uses of deadly force, more routine forms of street brutality continue despite their obvious toll on urban race relations and public attitudes toward law enforcement in poor and nonwhite communities. The ill will engendered toward police and a racist criminal justice system ultimately makes police work more difficult and further aggravates racial and class resentments that fuel police-community conflict.

Although antibrutality reformers have been making this point for some time, they have not been able to persuade the police and the public, in part because it is so difficult to prove. Moreover, as police brutality has come to be understood as a racial issue, antibrutality activists have made their case mainly on the grounds of civil rights and individual liberties. These issues are enormously important, but they are often seen as antithetical to effective law enforcement—a kind of luxury we can afford only when public safety is not at risk. Contemporary reformers and activists, therefore, must step up their efforts to identify successful experiments and alternatives— such as the two precincts in the South Bronx mentioned earlier— that offer new strategies and concrete evidence that policing can be both effective and respectful. As with affirmative action and other civil rights reforms, reducing police brutality will not only benefit racial minorities, it will improve law enforcement and enhance public safety for all of us.

NOTES

Introduction

1. Historians and other scholars who argue that police violence has decreased include James Richardson, *The New York Police* (New York: Oxford University Press, 1970), 262; Jerome Skolnick and James Fyfe, *Above the Law* (New York: Free Press, 1993), 18–19; and Paul Chevigny, *Edge of the Knife* (New York: New Press, 1995), 138–39.

2. My definition of citizen oversight is premised on the work of Samuel Walker, *Police Accountability: The Role of Citizen Oversight* (Belmont, Calif.: Wadsworth, 2001).

Chapter One

1. *Times*, 28 June 1881.

2. Lincoln Steffens, *The Autobiography of Lincoln Steffens* (New York: Harcourt Brace, 1931). See especially his chapter "Clubs, Clubbers, and Clubbed."

3. James F. Richardson, *The New York Police* (New York: Oxford University Press, 1970), 54–58; Samuel Walker, *A Critical History of Police Reform* (Lexington, Mass.: Lexington Books, 1970), 8–9; Miller, *Cops and Bobbies* (Chicago: University of Chicago Press, 1973), 29.

4. Miller, *Cops and Bobbies*, 29, 43; Walker, *A Critical History of Police Reform*, 27–28; Richardson, *The New York Police*, 68, 76–80, 82–123.

5. "Complaints Against Policemen," January–July and July–December 1846, Papers of the City Clerk, Municipal Archives of the City of New York; Herbert Asbury, *The Gangs of New York* (New York: Blue Ribbon Books, 1939), 49, 104–05; Miller, *Cops and Bobbies*, 19–22, 51–52; Richardson, *The New York Police*, 68, 191–92.

6. Richardson, *The New York Police*, 157; Miller, *Cops and Bobbies*, 96–97; George Walling, *Recollections of a New York Chief of Police* (New York: Caxton Book Concern, 1887), 600; Cornelius W. Willemse, *Behind the Green Lights* (New York: Alfred A. Knopf, 1931), 37.

7. Miller, *Cops and Bobbies*, 51–52, 146; Richardson, *The New York Police*, 113.

8. On the Draft riots, see Iver Bernstein, *The New York City Draft Riots* (New York: Oxford University Press, 1990), 38; Paul Gilje, *Rioting in America* (Bloomington: Indiana University Press, 1996), 92–93; Richardson, *The New York Police,* 137–42. On the Orange riots, see Michael A. Gordon, *The Orange Riots* (Ithaca, N.Y.: Cornell University Press, 1993), 100–01, 113–26.

9. Matthew Hale Smith, *Sunshine and Shadow in New York* (Hartford, Conn.: J. B. Burr and Co., 1869), 300–01, 305–07; for editorials on police violence in this period, see *Times,* 20 April, 30 June, 20 July, and 25 August 1865; 21, 24 August 1866; and 26, 30 May 1867.

10. Richardson, *The New York Police,* 162–63; for examples of the *Times*' more combative attitude toward the Democratic-controlled municipal police, see editorials on 20 February 1872, 19 March, 31 May 1874, and 16 July 1876.

11. For background on judicial reform, see articles on magistrates James T. Kilbreth and Benjamin Wandell, *Times,* 20 June 1873, 7 November 1892, 24 June 1897.

12. Like other daily papers, the *Times* covered only those brutality cases it considered most sensational or newsworthy. There were no doubt many routine cases that were not publicized, and certain types of incidents may have been omitted altogether. As an elite Republican paper, the *Times* was eager to chronicle the abuses of a Tammany-controlled police department, particularly when they involved upper or middle-class citizens like those of its readership. Similarly, abuses against women, children, the sick, the elderly, and other vulnerable individuals received special attention because of their dramatic value in vilifying the police. It is thus likely that brutality complaints brought by poor immigrants and ordinary working men and women were underrepresented in the *Times*' pages.

13. Only 7 percent of *Times* cases took place in private spaces. This is not to say that police beatings did not occur in these areas but may reflect the reduced likelihood of eyewitnesses, whose testimony was imperative for proving claims against the police. Moreover, there were no reported cases of violent police tactics during station house interrogations.

14. Data on officer nativity is taken from the 1887 NYPD Annual Report (the only year for which such numbers are available). By contrast, the ethnicity of suspects and officers was determined through identifiable surname origins. Consequently, the ethnic categories in the NYPD data include only the foreign-born, while the same categories in the brutality data also include a number of second generation (or later) ethnic Americans. For this reason, precise comparisons of the two data sets are impossible, but the discrepancies are large enough to be suggestive.

15. Peddlers were especially likely targets, making up 7 percent of alleged victims. Often recent immigrants who spoke little English, street vendors were regarded as unfair competition by local merchants and were subject to antipushcart legislation. They thus became easy marks for police graft, harassment, and violence. John Higham, *Send These to Me* (New York: Atheneum, 1975), 135; Leonard Dinnerstein, *Uneasy at Home* (New York: Columbia University Press, 1987), 151–52.

16. On the difficulty in getting convictions in police assault cases, see Miller, *Cops and Bobbies*, 43; Smith, *Sunshine and Shadow in New York*, 305; Willemse, *Behind the Green Lights*, 106; *Times*, 24 August 1866; 19 September 1892. On bribes and intimidation, see *Times*, 15 February 1889. For incidents of crowd attacks on police, see Miller, *Cops and Bobbies*, 19; *Times*, 19 April 1871, 16 June, 1 July 1876.

17. *Tribune*, 17, 25 June 1872; *Herald*,17, 22, 25 June 1872; *Times*, 25 June 1872.

18. Herbert G. Gutman, "The Tompkins Square 'Riot' in New York City on January 13, 1874: A Re-examination of Its Causes and Aftermath," *Labor History*, 6 (Winter 1965): 44–55; Samuel Gompers, *Seventy Years of Life and Labor* (Ithaca, N.Y.: Cornell University Press, 1984), 34–35.

19. *Times*, 12, 13, 14, 20 October 1894.

20. *Oxford English Dictionary*, 2nd ed., vol. 10, p. 1032; John Swinton, *The Tompkins Square Outrage* (n.p., 1874), 7; Samuel Gompers, *Seventy Years*, 34; Gutman, "The Tompkins Square Riot," 57. For other comparisons between police actions and tyranny, see *Times*, 22 June 1872; 12 October 1894.

21. Swinton, *The Tompkins Square Outrage*, 5–6; *Times*, 4 April 1890; *Herald*, 17, 22 June 1872.

22. *Herald*, 17 June 1872. On ties between police and employers, see *Herald*, 22 June 1872; *Times*, 22 June 1872, 2 March 1889, 4 April 1890; Richard K. Lieberman, *Steinway and Sons* (New Haven: Yale University Press, 1995), 95. On intraclass tensions between police and organized labor, see Miller, *Cops and Bobbies*, 154–55; Richardson, *The New York Police*, 201; *Sun*, 17 June 1872.

23. Gutman, "The Tompkins Square Riot," 64–66; *Times*, 22 June 1872, 13 October 1894; *Herald*, 22 June 1872.

24. Gutman, "The Tompkins Square Riot," 63–65.

25. Gutman, "The Tompkins Square Riot," 56–57; *Times*, 13, 14 January 1874, 31 January, 6 February 1889; Steffens, *Autobiography*, 207, 211–12.

26. James Turner, *Reckoning with the Beast* (Baltimore: Johns Hopkins University Press, 1980), 79–81.

27. William Browne, *Stop That Clubbing!* (New York: 1887).

28. *Times*, 30 June, 20 July, 25 August 1865, 21 August 1866, 7 September 1880, 20 August 1882 (quote); Browne, *Stop That Clubbing!*, 5.

29. *Times*, 27, 30 June 1877; *World*, 27, 30 June 1877.

30. The beating of intoxicated men was a common police practice in the late nineteenth

century, according to the muckraking journalist Lincoln Steffens. In his autobiography, Steffens recalled that officers frequently practiced baton swinging techniques on sleeping drunks. Steffens, *Autobiography*, 208. Quotes on police beatings of drunks are from the *Times*, 19 December 1874 and 17 April 1874.

31. *Times*, 19 March, 9, 10 April 1874, 10 August 1882.

32. *Times*, 26 May 1867, 20 February 1872, 19 March, 31 May 1874, 16 July 1876.

33. Browne, *Stop that Clubbing!*, 9–10; *Times*, 19 March 1874.

34. *Times*, 14 December 1894, 26 March 1917; *Herald*, 23 April 1879.

35. Herbert Asbury, *The Gangs of New York*, 235–37; Richardson, *The New York Police*, 204–05; *Times*, 26 March 1917, 17 December 1886.

36. *Times*, 18, 21 March, 4, 23 April 1879; *Sun*, 18 March, 4, 23 April 1879; and *Herald*, 4, 23 April 1879.

37. *Times*, 17, 19 October, 19, 21 November 1879; *Sun*, 17, 30 October, 21 November 1879.

38. *Times*, 17, 21, 22 October 1879; *Herald*, 19 October 1879.

39. *Herald*, 19 October 1879; *Sun*, 22 October 1879; *National Police Gazette*, 1 November 1879.

40. *Sun*, 19, 22 October 1879; *Times*, 24 October 1879; *Tribune*, 30 October 1879.

41. *Times*, 30 October 1879; *Sun*, 30 October, 7, 19, 20 November 1879; *Tribune*, 7 November 1879.

42. *Times*, 21 November, 6 December 1879, 18 June, 18 November 1881, 26 March 1917; Richardson, *The New York Police*, 205–06.

43. Richardson, *The New York Police*, 205–06; Asbury, *The Gangs of New York*, 236–37, 248–49; New York, State Legislature, Senate, Committee Appointed to Investigate the Police Department of the City of New York, "Report and Proceedings," [hereafter cited as Lexow Report] vol. 3, (Albany: James B. Lyon, 1895), 2827–28, 2913–31; *Times*, 4 November 1893; Frank Moss, *The American Metropolis from Knickerbocker Days to the Present Time*, vol. 3 (New York: Peter Fenelon Colliers, 1897), 237–39.

44. *National Police Gazette*, 1 November 1879; *Sun*, 30 October 1879.

45. *Times*, 30, 31 January 1889, 4 April 1890, 13, 14 October 1894; *Sun*, 4 April 1890; *Herald*, 4 April 1890; Steffens, *Autobiography*, 207.

46. *Times*, 27 April 1885; *Sun*, 27 April 1885; *Tribune*, 27 April 1885; *Herald*, 27 April 1885.

47. *Times,* 27 April 1885; *Sun,* 27 April 1885; *Tribune,* 16 May 1885; *Herald,* 5, 12 May 1885.

48. *Herald,* 12, 13, 16 May 1885; *Times,* 12 May 1885; *Tribune,* 15 May 1885.

49. *Herald,* 5, 15 May 1885; *Tribune,* 15, 16 May 1885.

50. *Times,* 17 May 1885; *Herald,* 13, 16 May 1885.

51. *Tribune,* 16, 20 May 1885; *Herald,* 16, 19 May 1885; *Times,* 19, 20 May 1885.

52. *Herald,* 2, 16 May 1885; *Sun,* 27, 28 April 1885; *Times,* 3 September 1897.

53. Lexow Report, vol. 3, 2825.

54. Lexow Report, vol. 1, 30; vol. 3, 2826, 2863.

55. Richardson, *The New York Police,* 238–40; Walker, *A Critical History of Police Reform,* 43–44.

56. Lexow Report, vol. 3: 2827–28; Moss, *The American Metropolis,* 237–39.

57. Lexow Report, vol. 4: 3593–96, 4485–87.

58. Lexow Report, vol. 3: 2871–74, 4: 4518–4530.

59. Lexow Report, vol. 3: 3276, 3485, vol. 5: 4848.

60. Lexow Report, vol 3: 2874–78, 2898–2900.

61. Lexow Report, vol. 1: 25, 27, 32.

62. On October 14, about a week and a half after the Clubbers Brigade, the *Times* reported that a young African-American man, John Rowls, was allegedly beaten by police and had vowed to take his case before the Lexow Committee. There is no record of his appearance. *Times,* 15 October 1894.

63. Lexow Report, vol. 1: 30.

64. Richardson, *The New York Police,* 240–45, 262-63.

Chapter Two

1. Gilbert Osofsky, "Race Riot of 1900: A Study of Ethnic Violence," *Journal of Negro Education,* 32 (1963), 16–24.

2. Ibid., 19–20; *Times,* 16 August 1900; *World,* 16 August 1900; *Tribune,* 16 August 1900; *Sun,* 16 August 1900; *Herald,* 16 August 1900.

3. *World,* 16 August 1900; *Evening Telegram,* 16 August 1900; *Commercial Advertiser,* 16 August 1900; Citizens' Protective League (CPL), *Story of the Riot* (New York: Arno Press, 1969, repr. 1900); Seth M. Scheiner, *Negro Mecca* (New York: New York University Press, 1965), 122.

4. CPL, *Story of the Riot,* 14–15.

5. *Tribune,* 17 August 1900; *Evening Post,* 16 August 1900; *Herald,* 16 August 1900; CPL, *Story of the Riot,* 6, 11, 13, 14–20, 22–23, 28–30, 34–35, 37–38, 40, 66–67, 73, 76–77.

6. David R. Roediger, *The Wages of Whiteness: Race and the Making of the American Working Class* (London: Verso, 1991); Noel Ignatiev, *How the Irish Became White* (New York: Routledge, 1995).

7. Report by acting captain John Cooney to Inspector Walter Thompson, August 20, 1900, Police Department—1900 folder, box VWRA 9, Papers of Mayor Robert Van Wyck, Municipal Archives of the City of New York (MACNY); CPL, *Story of the Riot,* 35–36, 40, 42–43, 50–54, 68–73; *Times,* 17 August 1900; *Herald,* 17 August 1900.

8. *Tribune,* 16, 27 August 1900; *Times,* 27 August 1900; *Sun,* 17 August 1900; CPL, *Story of the Riot,* 2, 50–54.

9. *Herald,* 17 August 1900; *Tribune,* 17, 18, 19 August 1900; *Sun,* 17 August 1900; *Commercial Advertiser,* 18 August 1900; CPL, *Story of the Riot,* 1; Scheiner, *Negro Mecca,* 123.

10. *Herald,* 17, 19 August 1900; *Tribune,* 17, 19 August 1900; *Commercial Advertiser,* 16 August 1900; *Evening Post,* 17 August 1900.

11. *Commercial Advertiser,* 16, 18 August 1900; *Herald,* 17, 18 August 1900; *Evening Telegram,* 17, 25 August 1900; *Times,* 17 August 1900; *Evening Post,* 17 August 1900; *Tribune,* 17 August 1900.

12. Report by Inspector Walter Thompson to Chief William S. Devery, August 21, 1900, Police Department—1900 folder, box VWRA 9, Van Wyck Papers; *Times,* 17, 20, 26 August 1900; *Commercial Advertiser,* 16 August 1900; *Sun* 17 August 1900; *Tribune,* 18 August 1900; *Evening Post,* 25 August 1900.

13. *Commercial Advertiser,* 16 August 1900; *Times,* 20, 27 August 1900; *World,* 20, 27 August 1900; *Herald,* 25 August 1900; Michael L. Goldstein, "Preface to the Rise of Booker T. Washington: A View from New York City of the Demise of Independent Black Politics, 1839-1902," *Journal of Negro History,* 62 (January 1977), 92.

14. CPL, *Story of the Riot,* 4; Letter from Rev. W. H. Brooks, president of Citizens' Protective League, to Mayor Robert Van Wyck, November 1900, Citizens' Protective League Papers, Schomburg Library; Goldstein, "Preface to the Rise of Booker T. Washington," 95; *Times,* 30 August 1900; *Sun,* 30, 31 August 1900; *Herald,* 30 August 1900.

15. *Times,* 27 August 1900; *Tribune,* 27 August 1900; Letter from Rev. W. H. Brooks to

Mayor Robert Van Wyck, September 12, 1900, in CPL, *Story of the Riot; Sun,* 30 August 1900.

16. *Times,* 20, 27 August 1900; *Tribune,* 20 August 1900; *World,* 20 August 1900.

17. CPL, *Story of the Riot,* 23–24, 56–58, 68–73, 76–77; Notes of D. Mason Webster for a speech made at a meeting of the Citizens' Protective League, September 12, 1900, Citizens' Protective League Papers.

18. *Times,* 20 August 1900; *Tribune,* 20 August 1900.

19. *Times,* 27 August 1900; *Tribune,* 20 August 1900; Notes of D. Mason Webster, September, 12, 1900, CPL Papers. For an examination of the relationship between black manhood and political power, see Martha Hodes, "The Sexualization of Reconstruction Politics," *American Sexual Politics* (Chicago: University of Chicago Press, 1993), 59–74.

20. Letter [second] from Rev. W. H. Brooks to Mayor Robert Van Wyck, November 1900, and Notes of D. Mason Webster, September 12, 1900, both in CPL Papers; Frank Moss, "Persecution of Negroes by Roughs and Policemen, in the City of New York, August 1900," in CPL, *Story of the Riot,* 5.

21. *Times,* 8 September 1900; *Tribune,* 8, 9 September 1900; *Herald,* 8 September 1900; *Evening Post,* 8 September 1900; Moss, "Persecution of Negroes," 3–4; Committee on Rules and Discipline, New York Police Department, [1900], 7, Police Department–1900 folder, box 9, Van Wyck Papers.

22. Report of Police Commissioner Bernard J. York, 3; *Times,* 8 September 1900; *Herald,* 8 September 1900.

23. Report of Commissioner Bernard J. York, 4–6; *John Hains v. Herman A. Ohm,* and *George L. Myers v. John J. Cleary,* First Division, City Magistrate's Court, Seventh District, October 26, 1900, all in Police Department– 1900 folder, box 9, Van Wyck Papers; *Times,* 22 September 1900; *Tribune,* 25 September 1900.

24. *Times,* 22 September 1900; *World,* 22 September 1900; *Evening Post,* 22 September 1900; *Evening Telegram,* 21 September 1900.

25. Goldstein, "Preface to the Rise of Booker T. Washington," 95–96; Leonard Dinnerstein, *Uneasy at Home* (New York: Columbia University Press, 1987), 149, 163–64.

26. Dinnerstein, *Uneasy at Home,* 150– 52; James F. Richardson, *The New York Police* (New York: Oxford University Press, 1970), 167; *Times,* 13 August 1902.

27. Dinnerstein, *Uneasy at Home,* 155–56; *Times,* 31 July, 16 September 1902; *Evening Post,* 30, 31 July 1902.

28. Dinnerstein, *Uneasy at Home,* 155–61; *Times,* 31 July, 16 September 1902; *Herald,* 31 July 1902.

29. *Commercial Advertiser,* 31 July 1902; *Herald,* 31 July 1902; Dinnerstein, *Uneasy at Home,* 162–63.

30. *Times,* 31 July, 1, 2, 3, 5 August 1902; *Herald,* 1 August 1902; *Evening Post,* 1 August 1902; *Jewish Daily Forward,* 1 August 1902.

31. Dinnerstein, *Uneasy at Home,* 162; *Times,* 31 July, 1, 2, August 1902; *Forward,* 31 July, 3, 13 August 1902.

32. *Forward,* 30 July 1902; *Times,* 2 August 1902.

33. *Times,* 2 August 1902.

34. *Evening Post,* 2 August 1902; *Herald,* 5 August 1902; *Times,* 3, 6 August 1902; *Forward,* 6 August 1902.

35. *Jewish World* quoted in the *Tribune,* 3 August 1902; *Tribune,* 6 August 1902.

36. *Times,* 2, 5 August 1902.

37. *Herald,* 3, 5 August 1902; *Times,* 5, 9 August 1902; *Forward,* 5, 6 August 1902.

38. Dinnerstein, *Uneasy at Home,* 166; *Times,* 7, 9 August 1902; *Forward,* 7 August 1902. For the history of riot commissions, see Anthony Platt, ed., *The Politics of Riot Commissions, 1917–1970* (New York: MacMillan, 1971).

39. Dinnerstein, *Uneasy at Home,* 167–68; *Times,* 13, 14, 19 August 1902; *Herald,* 14 August 1902.

40. Dinnerstein, *Uneasy at Home,* 167; *Times,* 14 August, 16 September 1902; *Herald,* 14 August 1902; *Evening Post,* 8 September 1902; *Forward,* 8 September 1902.

41. For the full text of the report, see *Times,* 16 September 1902.

42. Ibid.

43. *Times,* 16 September 1902; *Evening Post,* 16 September 1902; Dinnerstein, *Uneasy at Home,* 169–70.

44. Dinnerstein, *Uneasy at Home,* 170; *Times,* 21 August, 1 October 1902.

45. *Times,* 25 October, 25 December 1902; Gerald Kurland, *Seth Low* (New York: Twayne Publishers, 1971), 159–60; Dinnerstein, *Uneasy at Home,* 170–72; *Forward,* 26 October 1902.

46. Stuart Swonkin, *Jews Against Prejudice* (New York: Columbia University Press, 1997), 12–13.

47. *Times,* 13, 14 July 1903, 29 December 1904, 18, 19, 21 January 1905.

48. *Times,* 16, 17, 18, 19 July 1905; *New York Age,* 13, 20, 27 July 1905; Frazier quote from *New York Age,* 27 July 1905.

49. *New York Age,* 27 July 1905; *Times,* 20, 21, 25 July 1905.

50. *New York Age,* 27 July, 3, 10 August 1905; CCPL quote from *New York Age,* 10 August 1905.

51. *Crisis,* 2 (August 1911): 152–53; *New York Age,* 5 August 1909; James Alexander, *Blue Coats, Black Skin* (Hicksville, N.Y.: Exposition Press, 1978), 30–33.

52. The defense leagues became part of what Philip Ethington calls pluralist liberalism—a politics of social groups and their needs that came to characterize American urban life during the Progressive Era. Philip J. Ethington, *The Public City* (New York: Cambridge University Press, 1994), 8–9.

Chapter Three

1. James F. Richardson, *The New York Police* (New York: Oxford University Press, 1970), 240–45, 250–53, 262–63; Jay Stuart Berman, *Police Administration and Progressive Reform* (Westport, Conn.: Greenwood Press, 1987), 60.

2. *Times,* 29, 30 October, 15 November, 1892.

3. John J. Hickey, *Our Police Guardians* (New York: 1925), 70.

4. *Times,* 22 December 1892.

5. *Times,* 26 June, 24 September, 2 October 1895.

6. *Times,* 19, 23 December 1897, 18 August 1899.

7. Gerald Astor, *The New York Cops* (New York: Scribner's Sons, 1971), 198; Richardson, *The New York Police,* 263; Berman, *Police Administration and Progressive Reform,* 77–79.

8. *Times,* 21, 22 September 1896, 26, 27 November 1897, 12, 19, 22 January 1899.

9. George B. McClellan, *The Gentleman and the Tiger* (Philadelphia: J. B. Lippincott Company, 1956), 234–35, 295–96; Lately Thomas, *The Mayor Who Mastered New York: The Life and Opinions of William J. Gaynor* (New York: William Morrow and Company, 1969), 145.

10. Richardson, *The New York Police,* 280–81; *Times,* 23 December 1908; 7 September 1934 (Bingham's obituary); Thomas, *The Mayor Who Mastered New York,* 260.

11. *Sun,* 29 March 1908; *Times,* 29, 30 March 1908; *New York Socialist,* 4 April 1908.

12. *New York Socialist,* 4, 11 April 1908; *Sun,* 1, 5, 13 April 1908.

13. *Times,* 23 July 1906; 14, 27 January, 31 March, 5 April, 3 May, 18 June 1909; Astor, *The New York Cops,* 107; Daniel Czitrom, "Underworlds and Underdogs: Big Tim Sullivan and Metropolitan Politics in New York, 1889–1913," *Journal of American History,* 78 (September 1991), 536–58.

14. *Times,* 30 April 1909.

15. *Times,* 8 December 1908, 20 February, 20 September 1909. See also Bingham's obituary in the *Times,* 7 September 1934.

16. Thomas, *The Mayor Who Mastered New York,* 82–93; *Times,* 28 February 1905.

17. Thomas, *The Mayor Who Mastered New York,* 145–49; McClellan, *The Gentleman and the Tiger,* 296; *Times,* 2 June 1909.

18. McClellan, *The Gentleman and the Tiger,* 296–98; Thomas, *The Mayor Who Mastered New York,* 149–50; *Times,* 3, 4, 5 June 1909.

19. Thomas, *The Mayor Who Mastered New York,* 150–51; McClellan, *The Gentleman and the Tiger,* 296–98; *Times,* 1, 2 July 1909.

20. Gaynor's letter quoted in the *Times,* 14 January 1910. See also *Times,* 12, 13, 15 January 1909; and Thomas, *The Mayor Who Mastered New York,* 254–56.

21. Thomas, *The Mayor Who Mastered New York,* 255–57; *Times,* 15, 16, 18, 19, 20, 21, 22, 23, 25, 28 January, 8, 9, 11, 12, 13, 14, 18, 24 February, 3, 24 March 1910; *Herald,* 20, 21 January, 18 February 1910; *Tribune,* 21 January 1910; *Evening Post,* 8, 10 February 1910; *World,* 2 March 1910; see also records of brutality complaints in Police Department Correspondence files, boxes 14, 15, 16, 17, 33, 34, 35, 36, 37, 53, 54, 55, 56, 57, and Subject files, Complaints, 1910–1913, box 82, Gaynor Papers, Municipal Archives of the City of New York (MACNY).

22. Thomas, *The Mayor Who Mastered New York,* 260–61, 347, 373; *Times,* 10 December 1909, 28 January, 4 February 1910.

23. NYPD, Annual Report, 1909, 3; Annual Report, 1910, 9; *Times,* 27 October 1911; Thomas, *The Mayor Who Mastered New York,* 260–67, 444–46.

24. Joseph E. Corrigan, "Magnates of Crime," *McClure's,* November 1912, 8; *Times,* 18 February, 5 September 1910, 23 March 1911; *Brooklyn Eagle,* 31 January 1910.

25. *Times,* 10 February 1911; 18 January 1914; *World,* 19 February 1910.

26. *Times,* 9 August 1910, 13, 18 January 1914; *Brooklyn Eagle,* 29 January 1910.

27. *Times,* 5 September 1910; 24, 25 March, 27 April 1911; Thomas, *The Mayor Who Mastered New York,* 344.

28. *Times,* 30 March, 1 April 1911.

29. *Times,* 29 April, 5, 18 May, 3 June 1911.

30. *Times,* 18, 19 May 1911; Thomas, *The Mayor Who Mastered New York,* 310–12, 340, 353.

31. Records of brutality complaints in Police Department Correspondence files, boxes 14, 15, 16, 17, 33, 34, 35, 36, 37, 53, 54, 55, 56, 57, and Subject files, Complaints, 1910–1913, box 82, Gaynor Papers.

32. *Times,* 13 August 1911; Corrigan, "Magnates of Crime," 10; NYPD, Annual Report, 1911–1913.

33. *Times,* 6, 13 January 1914.

34. *Times,* 18 January, 24 December 1914, 2, 3 January, 14 February 1915; 28 December 1917; Herbert Asbury, *The Gangs of New York: An Informal History of the Underworld* (New York: Blue Ribbon Books, Inc., 1939), 367–69.

35. NYPD, Annual Report, 1914–1917, 18–20.

36. Edward R. Lewinson, *John Purroy Mitchel: Boy Mayor of New York* (New York: Astra Books, 1965), 132–37; Frank Donner, *Protectors of Privilege: Red Squads and Police Repression in Urban America* (Berkeley: University of California Press, 1990), 30–31.

37. NYPD, Annual Report, 1914–1917, 13–15; Lewinson, *John Purroy Mitchel,* 120; Astor, *The New York Cops,* 198.

Chapter Four

1. *Roland West's Alibi* (New York: Kino International, 1998). Third-degree sequences were common in films of the late 1920s and early 1930s, see for example *The Vice Squad, Paid, The Secret Six, Beast of the City,* and *Penthouse.* Carlos Clarens, *Crime Movies* (New York: W. W. Norton, 1980), 73.

2. Herbert Asbury, *The Great Illusion,* repr. 1950 ed. (Westport, Conn.: Greenwood Press, 1968); Gerald Astor, *The New York Cops* (New York: Scribners, 1971), 121–22.

3. *Times,* 29, 30 July, 1, 8, 15 August 1921, 29 January, 11 March 1922. For other citizen complaints stemming from liquor raids, see *Times,* 11, 20 February, 17 August 1926, 26 January 1930, 21 July 1931.

4. For a more detailed account of NYPD corruption during Prohibition, see Michael Lerner, "Dry Manhattan: Class, Culture and Politics in Prohibition-Era New York City, 1919–1933" (Ph.D. dissertation, New York University, 1999), 167–70; *Times,* 15, 16 March 1924; New York State, Legislature, Joint Committee on Affairs of the City of New York, *Final Report of Samuel Seabury,* New York, 1932, 87–89. For other cases involving police shakedowns, see *Times,* 29 August 1921, 6 August 1925, 15 February 1932.

5. *Times,* 14 October 1927, 28 March 1931.

6. *Times,* 7, 8 August 1922.

7. *Times,* 6, 7, 9, 28 January 1926. The department brought neglect of duty charges against three of Brennan's fellow officers for failing to prevent the shooting, but it carefully avoided any suggestion of police tolerance for drinking or speakeasies.

8. *Times,* 16, 20, 21 June, 3, 10, 12, 20 July 1923; letters to Mayor John Hylan from Police Commissioner Richard Enright, 2, 31 July 1923, Departmental Letters Received—Police Department, July–September 1923 folder, box 137, Hylan Papers, Municipal Archives of the City of New York (MACNY).

9. Asbury, *The Great Illusion,* 200–03, 209; Andrew Sinclair, *Era of Excess* (New York: Harper Colophon Books, 1964), 221–23. For homicide rates, see Eric Monkkonen, *Murder in New York* (Berkeley: University of California Press, 2001), 9.

10. *Times,* 24, 25, 26 March, 7, 8 July 1925, 21, 24, 25, 27, 28, 29 December 1928, 3, 4, 21 January, 26 February 1929; letter to Police Commissioner Grover A. Whalen from Arthur Garfield Hays, 23 February 1929, reel 68, vol. 374, ACLU Papers (Wilmington, Del: Scholarly Resources, 1996).

11. Letter to Whalen from Hays, 23 February 1929; Memorandum to Police Commissioner Whalen from ACLU, 23 May 1929, reel 68, vol. 374, ACLU Papers; Ernest Jerome Hopkins, *Our Lawless Police* (New York: Viking Press, 1931), 45, 49; *Times,* 2, 3 April, 24 May 1929, 23 February, 31 July 1931.

12. *Times,* 27 November 1934; *Herald-Tribune,* 27 November 1934; *World-Telegram,* 26 November 1934; Lewis J. Valentine, *Night Stick* (New York: Dial Press, 1947), 188–92.

13. Richard Sylvester, "The Treatment of the Accused," *Annals of the American Academy of Political and Social Science,* 36 (July 1910): 17; *Times,* 24 July 1932.

14. *Times,* 30 August 1931.

15. Quote is from Confidential Memorandum of Interview with Daniel E. Costigan by Carl S. Stern, 15 April 1930, File 9B—Alphabetical Interviews (2), box 243, Record Group 10, Wickersham Commission Papers, National Archives, Suitland, Maryland; *Times,* 23 July 1932; James F. Richardson, *The New York Police* (New York: Oxford University Press, 1970), 193.

16. Association of the Bar of the City of New York (ABCNY), "Annual Report of the Committee on Criminal Courts, Law, and Procedure," (New York, 1927–28), 237–43.

17. *Times,* 16, 17 April 1910; William F. Baker, "The Sweating or Third Degree System," 9; Theodore A. Bingham, "Administration of Criminal Law—Third Degree System," 13, both in *Annals of the American Academy of Political and Social Science,* 36 (July 1910);

Samuel Walker, *A Critical History of Police Reform* (Lexington, Mass.: Lexington Books, 1977), 58.

18. *Times,* 21 January, 5 August 1911; Walker, *A Critical History of Police Reform,* 58; Interview with Daniel E. Costigan, 15 April 1930; Charles J. V. Murphy, "The Third Degree: Another Side of Our Crime Problem," *Outlook and Independent,* 151 (3 April 1929): 526.

19. Hopkins, *Our Lawless Police,* 2–13, 45–49.

20. Fred D. Pasley, *Not Guilty! The Story of Samuel Leibowitz* (New York: G. P. Putnams Sons, 1933); Ogden Chisolm and Hastings H. Hart, *Methods of Obtaining Confessions and Information from Persons Accused of Crime* (New York: Russell Sage Foundation, 1922); Walker, *A Critical History of Police Reform,* 47.

21. In 1920, the VDC merged with the Legal Aid Society of New York, which had worked mainly on civil cases. John MacArthur Maguire, *The Lance of Justice* (Cambridge, Mass.: Harvard University Press, 1928), 270–73, 276.

22. McLaughlin quote from *World,* 29 May 1926; *Times,* 19 May 1926; Murphy, "The Third Degree," 526; Oswald Garrison Villard, "Official Lawlessness: The Third Degree and the Crime Wave," *Harpers Monthly,* 160 (27 October 1927), 608–09; Statement of Louis Fabricant, 21 February 1930, File 9B—Alphabetical Interviews (2), box 243, Wickersham Papers.

23. *World,* 29 May 1926.

24. ABCNY Annual Report: 1927–28, 235–37, 251; *World,* 29 October 1929.

25. Edgar W. Camp, Andrew A. Bruce, and Oscar Hallam, *Report of Committee on Law less Enforcement of Law Made to the Section of Criminal Law and Criminology of the American Bar Association,* Chicago, 19 August 1930, 1, 10–17.

26. ABCNY Annual Report: 1927–28, 236; *Times,* 11, 12 August 1926; Murphy, "The Third Degree," 525. Interestingly, the protesting juror was a chiropractor who claimed that the police had unfairly harassed him and others in his profession.

27. Reformer quote from Hopkins, *Our Lawless Police,* 285–86; Murphy, "The Third Degree," 526, 534–35; Villard, "Official Lawlessness," 610; Memo by Carl S. Stern of Conference with William Dean Embree and Timothy N. Pfeiffer, 19 February 1930, file 9B—Alphabetical Interviews (2), box 243, Wickersham Papers.

28. *Times,* 9 February 1922; Murphy, "The Third Degree," 526; Villard, "Official Lawlessness," 610; Zechariah Chafee, Jr., et al., *The Third Degree* (New York: Arno Press, 1969; repr. 1931), 91 (Note: This is a reprint of the Wickersham Commission's 1931 *Report on Lawlessness in Law Enforcement*); Memorandum of Conference with Magistrate Joseph Corrigan, 7 May 1930, file 9B—Alphabetical Interviews (2), box 243, Wickersham Papers.

29. *People* v. *Doran,* 246 N.Y. 409; 159 N.E. 379 (1927); *People* v. *Weiner,* 248 N.Y. 118; 161 N.E. 441 (1928).

30. *People* v. *Barbato,* 254 N.Y. 170; 172 N.E. 458 (1930); *Times,* 18 September 1929; *Telegram,* 20, 23 September, 10 July 1929, 21 October 1930; *Evening Post,* 29 November 1930; Hopkins, *Our Lawless Police,* 245–49.

31. *World,* 8 December 1930; *Times,* 24 May 1931.

32. Murphy, "The Third Degree," 525; Emanuel H. Lavine, *The Third Degree: A Detailed and Appalling Exposé of Police Brutality* (New York: Vanguard Press, 1930), v–viii, 3–4, 247–48 (quotes). For editorials opposing the third degree, see *Times,* 2 November 1925, 11 February 1932; *Telegram,* 20, 23 September 1929, 19 January 1931; *Bronx Home News,* 10 July 1930.

33. Lavine, *The Third Degree,* v, 3–4, 61–65, 247–48; A. C. Sedgwick, "The Third Degree and Crime," *Nation,* 124 (15 June 1927): 666–67; Murphy, "The Third Degree," 523–26, 534 – 35; *World,* 16 October 1930.

34. Samuel Walker, *Popular Justice* (New York: Oxford University Press, 1998), 154–55; Samuel Walker, *In Defense of American Liberties* (New York: Oxford University Press, 1990), 87; "Ernest Jerome Hopkins," in *National Cyclopedia of American Biography,* vol. 58 (Clifton, N.J.: James T. White & Co., 1979), 74–75.

35. The two-thirds estimate is based on 255 VDC cases in 1930 for which the location of the alleged brutality incident was recorded. See Chafee, *The Third Degree,* 100; Hopkins, *Our Lawless Police,* 215.

36. Chafee, *The Third Degree,* 92–93, 99; Hopkins, *Our Lawless Police,* 208; Villard, "Official Lawlessness," 610; Lavine, *The Third Degree,* 51–52; Confidential Interview Number 9, June 5, 1930, File 9B—Numerical Interviews, and Interview with Emanuel Lavine, 16 February 1931, File 9B—Alphabetical Interviews (2), both in box 243, Wickersham Papers.

37. Chafee, *The Third Degree,* 157–58; Hopkins, *Our Lawless Police,* 215–16; Lavine, *The Third Degree,* 151–52.

38. Lavine, *The Third Degree,* 6; Hopkins, *Our Lawless Police,* 205; Chafee, *The Third Degree,* 101, 159; George C. Henderson, *Keys to Crookdom* (New York: D. Appleton and Company, 1924), 367.

39. The percentage of brutality complaints by African Americans was calculated from VDC third-degree cases listed in Appendix IV of *Lawlessness in Law Enforcement,* 225–32. Unfortunately, there are no racial breakdowns of NYPD arrests for these years; instead I have used black population figures from Kenneth T. Jackson, ed., *The Encyclopedia of New York City* (New Haven, Conn.: Yale University Press, 1995), 920. Ernest Jerome Hopkins, "The Police and the Immigrant," in *National Conference of Social Work,* Proceedings of the National Conference of Social Work

(University of Chicago Press, 1932), 509–19; Hopkins, *Our Lawless Police*, 254–57.

40. Calculations of criminal charges against VDC clients are based on cases listed in Appendix IV of *Lawlessness in Law Enforcement*, 225–32. Hopkins, *Our Lawless Police*, 214–15.

41. *Lawlessness in Law Enforcement*, 156; Lavine, *The Third Degree*, 53; A. C. Sedgwick, "The Third Degree and Crime," 666–67; Letter from Charles Sylvester to Carl Stern, 20 November 1929, Correspondence on Third Degree file, box 240, both in Wickersham Papers; Interview with Jack Black, October 17, 1930, File 9B—Alphabetical Interviews (2), box 243, Wickersham Papers.

42. Michael Fiaschetti, *You Gotta Be Rough* (New York: A. L. Burt Co., 1930), 233–42; Cornelius W. Willemse, *Behind the Green Lights* (New York: Alfred A. Knopf, 1931), 286; *World*, 12 September 1930.

43. Hopkins, *Our Lawless Police*, 57–58, 205; Lavine, *The Third Degree*, 70–84; *World-Telegram*, 18 July 1932; *Times*, 18, 21, 24 July 1932.

44. Fiaschetti, *You Gotta Be Rough*, 233–42; Lavine, *The Third Degree*, 109–112; *World*, 12 September 1930.

45. Chafee, *The Third Degree*, 87, 91, 92; Hopkins, *Our Lawless Police*, 213, 284–85; Murphy, "The Third Degree," 524; *World*, 17 October 1930; Willemse, *Behind the Green Lights*, 292–93; Interview with Mr. Cobb, 27 May 1930, and Interview with Felix B. DeMartini by Carl Stern, 12 May 1930, both in file 9B—Alphabetical Interviews (2), box 243, Wickersham Papers.

46. *Times*, 11 August 1931; Chafee, *The Third Degree*, 173–80; Willemse, *Behind the Green Lights*, 354–55; *World-Telegram*, 20 July 1932; Interview with Felix B. De Martini, 12 May 1930; Interview with Arthur A. Carey, 20 June 1930; Interviews with Daniel E. Costigan, 15 April and 11 June 1930; Interview with Michael Fiaschetti, 16 June 1930; all in file 9B—Alphabetical Interviews (2), box 243, Wickersham Papers

47. Barnes quoted in *World-Telegram*, 30 July 1932; Wickersham quoted in Hopkins, "The Police and the Immigrant," 519; Hopkins, *Our Lawless Police*, 6, 12–13, 59, 205, 320–21. On the Luther Boddy case, see *Times*, 6, 12, 21 January 1922; Murphy, "The Third Degree," 534; Villard, "Official Lawlessness," 611.

48. Hopkins, *Our Lawless Police*, 7–8, 12–13, 284; Chafee, *The Third Degree*, 189–90; *Times*, 28 August 1932; Lavine, *The Third Degree*, 144.

49. Chafee, *The Third Degree*, 125, 187–88; Hopkins, *Our Lawless Police*, 201–02; Confidential Interview Number 9, 5 June 1930, Wickersham Papers.

50. Chafee, *The Third Degree*, 125–26; Hopkins, *Our Lawless Police*, 167; Murphy, "The Third Degree," 534.

51. Chafee, *The Third Degree*, 104–10, 113–18; Hopkins, *Our Lawless Police*, 24, 210–11, 229–35; Villard, "Official Lawlessness," 605–14, 613; *World-Telegram*, 30 July 1930; "Notes: The Third Degree," *Harvard Law Review* (February 1930): 618.

52. Hopkins, *Our Lawless Police*, xii, 349–52, 354–57, 359; ACLU, "Methods of Combating the Third Degree," September 1935, 2–3; ABCNY Annual Report: 1927–28, 253; *World-Telegram*, 30 July 1932; *Times*, 28 August 1932; Confidential Interview Number 9, 5 June 1930, Wickersham Papers.

53. Hopkins, *Our Lawless Police*, 349, 352–53; ACLU, "Methods of Combating the Third Degree," ABCNY Annual Report: 1927–1928, 242–43; *World-Telegram*, 30 July 1932.

54. Hopkins, *Our Lawless Police*, 353–54; ACLU, "Methods of Combating the Third Degree," 4–5; *World-Telegram*, 21 July 1932; ACLU, Annual Report, 1934–35, 35; Memorandum of Conference with Magistrate Joseph Corrigan, 7 May 1930, Wickersham Papers.

55. ACLU, "Methods of Combating the Third Degree," 5–6; Hopkins, *Our Lawless Police*, xii; Letter from Ernest Hopkins to Forrest Bailey, 4 February 1932, vol. 626, 87–89, and letter to Allen Wardwell from unknown author, 24 September 1932, vol. 626, 109–112, both in ACLU Papers, Mudd Library, Princeton University (hereafter referred to as ACLU archives).

56. ACLU, "Methods of Combating the Third Degree," 4–5; Samuel Walker, *In Defense of American Liberties*, 88.

57. ACLU, Annual Report, 1936, 57; letter from Roger Baldwin to Fiorello La Guardia, 17 December 1937, vol. 2005, 191, ACLU archives; *Times*, 4, 15, 16, 19, 23 April 1937. On the Gedeon case, see *Times*, 3, 4, 11, 22 April 1937.

58. Letter from unknown ACLU staff member to Samuel Slaff, 16 February 1938, vol. 2005, 140; and letter to newspaper editors from Theodore Irwin, 3 March 1938, vol. 2005, 144, both in ACLU archives; *Times*, 12 March 1939.

59. Walker, *A Critical History of Police Reform*, 159–60; Walker, *In Defense of American Liberties*, 88; *Post*, 23 March 1936; *Times*, 28 July 1938; W. R. Kidd, *Police Interrogation* (New York: R. V. Basuino, 1940), 48.

60. *Times*, 27, 28 November 1934; "Muss Up the Gangsters," *American City*, 50 (January 1935): 15; ACLU press release, 27 November 1934, v. 712, 190, ACLU archives.

61. *Brown v. Mississippi*, 297 U.S. 278; 56 S. Ct. 461 (1936); Richard A. Leo, "From Coercion to Deception: The Changing Nature of Police Interrogation in America," in *The Miranda Debate: Law, Justice, and Policing*, ed. Richard A. Leo and George C. Thomas (Boston: Northeastern University Press, 1998), 71; Lawrence Herman, "The Supreme Court, the Attorney General, and the Good Old Days of Police Interrogation" in *The Miranda Debate*, 132; Jerome H. Skolnick and James J. Fyfe, *Above the Law: Police and the Excessive Use of Force* (New York: Free Press, 1993), 48–49.

62. Leo, "From Coercion to Deception," 71; Skolnick and Fyfe, *Above the Law*, 48–49; *Jackson* v. *Denno*, 378 U.S. 368; 84 S. Ct. 1774 (1964); *People* v. *Huntley*, 15 N.Y. 2d 72; 204 N.E. 2d 179 (1965).

Chapter Five

1. Frank Donner, *Protectors of Privilege* (Berkeley: University of California Press, 1990), 30–31; Julian F. Jaffe, *Crusade against Radicalism: New York during the Red Scare, 1914–1924* (Port Washington, N.Y.: Kennikat Press, 1972), 67.

2. Donner, *Protectors of Privilege*, 40; Jaffe, *Crusade Against Radicalism*, 80, 84–85, 96; "Russian Pogroms in America," clipping from reel 15, vol. 109, frame 225, ACLU Papers (Wilmington, Del.: Scholarly Resources, 1996).

3. Affidavits from Nathan Birnzweig, Carl Yachuk, et al., reel 15, volume 109, frames 240–56; and reel 18, vol. 132, frame 60, ACLU Papers.

4. Donner, *Protectors of Privilege*, 41; *Times*, 1 August 1927. For details on women strikers' complaints, see affidavits by members of Dress and Waistmakers Union, March 1919; and letter to Mayor John F. Hylan from Police Commissioner Richard Enright, 30 April 1919, Departmental Letters Received—Police Department, 1919 folder, box 44, Hylan Papers, Municipal Archives of the City of New York (MACNY).

5. *Times*, 21 November 1921, 3 April 1925, 7, 15 January, 9 March, 24, 25 July, 2, 11 December 1926, 23 March 1927, 21 September 1929; and 18 January 1966 (obituary for John J. Broderick); ACLU, Annual Report, 1926, 16–17.

6. *World*, 21 May 1930; Donner, *Protectors of Privilege*, 48.

7. *World*, 28 February, 20 May 1929; *Times*, 9 April, 12, 19 May 1929, *Telegram*, 20 May 1929; letter to Grover A. Whalen from ACLU Counsel, 16 April 1929, and letter to Grover Whalen from Roger Baldwin, 13 June 1929, both on reel 68, vol. 374, ACLU Papers.

8. Letter to Jacques Buitenkant, Esq., from Forrest Bailey, 29 April 1929, reel 68, vol. 374, ACLU Papers.

9. Mark Naison, *Communists in Harlem During the Depression* (Urbana: University of Illinois Press, 1983), 22, 38; "Police Club Negro Workers of Harlem," Crusader News Service press release, 16 September 1929, reel 65, vol. 366, ACLU Papers.

10. *Telegram*, 20 May 1929. In the latter months of 1929, police violently broke up CP protests against British imperialism and U.S. repression of Haiti; see *Daily Worker*, 5 October and 16 December 1929.

11. *Times*, 18, 20 January 1930; *Telegram*, 25 January 1930.

12. *Telegram*, 25 January 1930; *World*, 26, 27 January 1930; *Times*, 26 January 1930.

13. *Telegram,* 27 January, 1 February 1930; *World,* 27 January 1930. See also *Evening Post,* 27 January 1930; *Advance,* 1 February 1930; and *Nation,* 5 February 1930.

14. *World,* 26 January 1930; *Telegram,* 27 January 1930; *New Leader,* 1 February 1930.

15. *World,* 27 February 1930; *Times,* 10 February 1930; *New Leader,* 1 February 1930; *Open Forum,* 15, 22 February 1930, reel 74, vols. 400–401, ACLU Papers.

16. *Herald-Tribune,* 26 February, 8 March 1930; *Telegram,* 27 February 1930; *World,* 2, 6 March 1930; *Times,* 7 March 1930; *Sun,* 7 March 1930; American Civil Liberties Union, *Police Lawlessness Against Communists in New York* (New York: 1930), 4–5; Grover A. Whalen, *Mr. New York* (New York: G. Putnam's Sons, 1955), 154.

17. *Telegram,* 10 March 1930; *Times,* 7 March 1930; *Sun,* 7 March 1930; *Daily Worker,* 12 March 1930; ACLU, *Police Lawlessness against Communists,* 5, 7; *Open Forum,* 10 May 1930. The Workers International Relief, a Communist cultural organization and forerunner of the New York Film and Photo League, later released the contested newsreel—along with footage of Steve Katovis's funeral—in a film called *Fighting Workers of New York.* Much of this footage has been incorporated into a recent compilation, *The Film and Photo League, Program 1* (New York: Museum of Modern Art, 2003).

18. *World,* 8 March 1930; *Telegram,* 7 March 1930; *Herald-Tribune,* 7 March 1930; *News,* 7 March 1930; *Times,* 8 March 1930.

19. Whalen quote is from the *Times,* 9 March 1930. Additional coverage of Whalen's anti-Communist campaign can be found in the *World,* 11 March 1930; *Herald-Tribune,* 8 March 1930; *Telegram,* 10 March 1930.

20. *Times,* 12 March 1930; *World,* 12, 17 March 1930; Letter to Mayor James Walker from Marx Lewis, 11 March 1930, Folder 4: Protests Against Police Commissioner Whalen, 1930, box 259, Subject files, Walker Papers, MACNY.

21. Letter to Mayor James Walker from Harry F. Ward, et al., ACLU, 11 March 1930; letter to Walker from Morris Ernst, et al., ACLU, both in Folder 4: Protests against Police Commissioner Whalen, 1930, box 259, Subject Files, Walker Papers; Resolution adopted at the Luncheon Meeting of ACLU, New York, 22 March 1930, reel 77, vol. 428, ACLU Papers; ACLU, *Police Lawlessness Against Communists;* "Whalenism," *Nation,* 26 March 1930; *Times,* 12 March 1930; *World,* 12, 24, 25 March, 9 April 1930; *Herald-Tribune,* 23 March 1930.

22. Exactly what the Workers Defense Corps did is unclear. Former Police Commissioner Grover Whalen claimed it was a group organized "by Moscow" that trained Communists to disarm and disable police officers by taking their clubs and sticking pins into the legs of police horses; Whalen, *Mr. New York,* 150. CP references to the corps are infrequent and vague, see for example, ILD press release, New York, 9 August 1930; reel 77, vol. 428, ACLU Papers; and CP press release quoted in the *Times,* 3 August 1930.

23. Letter to Edward Mulrooney from Roger Baldwin, 1 July 1930, reel 77, vol. 428

(Baldwin quote), ACLU Papers; Ronald Bayor, *Neighbors in Conflict,* 2nd ed. (Urbana: University of Illinois Press, 1988), 19–25, 87. According to a 1931 NYPD survey, Irish immigrants and their children made up roughly a third of the force. With a large but indeterminate number of third and fourth generation Irish officers, we can reasonably assume that officers of Irish descent made up a majority of the force. NYPD memo, 6 April 1931, List of Nationality of Parents, Foreign-born Members folder, box 4504, Fiorello La Guardia Papers, MACNY.

24. *Labor News,* 5 July 1930 (CP quote); letter to Mulrooney from Baldwin, 1 July 1930; letter to Roger Baldwin from Joseph A. Durkin, 2 July 1930, reel 78, vol. 429, ACLU Papers; *World,* 1 July 1930; *Times,* 1, 2 July 1930; *Herald-Tribune,* 1, 2, July 1930.

25. For accounts of consulate protests, see letter to Mulrooney from Baldwin, 30 June 1930; *Telegram* and *Evening Post,* 13 December 1930. For complaints against police brutality in dressmakers' strike, see *Times,* 4 September, 2 October 1930. The Union Square antiwar protest is covered in the *Times,* 2, 3, 6, 8 August 1930; *Evening Post,* 8 August 1930; *World,* 20 August 1930; ILD press release, 9 August 1930, and letter to Edward Mulrooney from Roger Baldwin, 15 August 1930, both on reel 77, vol. 428, ACLU Papers. Unfortunately, I have not been able to locate any extant copies of the Labor Jury pamphlet.

26. *Times,* 17, 18 October 1930; *Telegram,* 17, 18 October 1930; *World,* 17 October 1930; *Mirror,* 17 October 1930; *Sun,* 30 October 1930.

27. *Times,* 17, 18 October, 10 November 1930; *Telegraph,* 18 October 1930; *Telegram,* 17 October 1930; *Sun,* 30 October 1930; *Evening Post,* 10 November 1930; letter to Police Commissioner Edward Mulrooney from Harry Ward, Forrest Bailey and Roger Baldwin, 17 October 1930; and letter to Mulrooney from Harry Elmer Barnes, et al., 7 November 1930, both on reel 77, vol. 428, ACLU Papers; ACLU Annual Report, 1930–1931, 19–20.

28. Irving Howe, *The American Communist Party* (New York: Frederick A. Praeger, Inc., 1962), 193–94; Robert Fisher, *Let the People Decide* (Boston: Twayne Publishers, 1984), 37–38. For instances of clashes between police and Unemployed Councils, see *Daily Worker,* 14 January, 9, 21, 22, 25 April 1932; *Hunger Fighter,* January 1933, reel 2, frames 351–53, International Labor Defense (ILD) Papers (Frederick, Md.: University Publications of America, 1987); ACLU Annual Report, 1932–33, 51–52.

29. Thomas Kessner, *Fiorello H. La Guardia and the Making of Modern New York* (New York: McGraw Hill, 1989), 38–40, 186–89, 242–44, 275.

30. Kessner, *Fiorello La Guardia,* 350–351, 354; Walter Wilson, "Commissioner O'Ryan: Terrorist," *Nation,* 15 August 1934, 181–82. As Kessner explains, O'Ryan was one of La Guardia's Republican challengers in the 1933 mayoral race. He agreed to step aside in exchange for his appointment as police commissioner in the La Guardia administration.

31. *Herald-Tribune,* 15 February 1934; *Times,* 15, 20 February 1934; *Daily Worker,* 15, 16

February 1934; letter to Police Commissioner John O'Ryan from Roger Baldwin and Harry Ward, 15 February 1934, reel 109, vol. 711, ACLU Papers.

32. Herbert Shapiro, *White Violence and Black Response* (Amherst: University of Massachusetts Press, 1988), 210, 213–14; Naison, *Communists in Harlem,* 82, 116; *Times,* 11 April 1933, 19 March 1934; *Daily Worker,* 19 March 1934; letter to Police Commissioner O'Ryan from Chief Inspector Lewis Valentine, 26 March 1934, reel 77, frames 2116–2121, La Guardia Papers.

33. In subsequent disciplinary hearings, however, all of the officers were exonerated. *Times,* 20, 21, 22 March 1934; ACLU, Annual Report, 1933–34, 38–39; letter to John O'Ryan from Lewis Valentine, 26 March 1934, reel 77, frames 2116–2121; and letter to La Guardia from O'Ryan, 2 May 1934, reel 77, frames 2180–81, both in La Guardia Papers. For a full transcript of the investigation, see "Investigation Conducted by Chief Inspector Lewis J. Valentine, re: Alleged Disturbance at 126th Street and Lenox Avenue," reel 77, frames 2208–69, La Guardia Papers; letter to Lewis Valentine from A. L. Wirin, 3 May 1934, vol. 712; and letter to La Guardia from Florine Lasker, 21 June 1934, vol. 712, 162, both in ACLU Papers (hereafter referred to as ACLU archives), Mudd Library, Princeton University.

34. ILD handbill, "Mass Scottsboro Protest Meeting, March 25," reel 77, frame 2201, La Guardia Papers; *Times,* 20, 21, 25 March 1934; *Daily Worker,* 23, 25 March 1934.

35. *Times,* 23, 28 March, 12 April 1934; *City News,* 23 March 1934; Kessner, *Fiorello La Guardia,* 353–54; "Presentment from March Additional Grand Jury to Honorable John J. Freschi, Court of General Sessions," reel 230, frames 2169–75; and Mayor's Office Press Release, 12 April 1934, reel 230, frames 2176–78, both in La Guardia Papers.

36. Daniel Walkowitz, *Working with Class* (Chapel Hill: University of North Carolina Press, 1999), 133; *Times,* 27, 28 May 1934; *Post,* 28 May 1934; ACLU, *What Rights for the Unemployed?* (New York: 1935), 12–14.

37. *NYC Journal,* 1 June 1934; *Times,* 2 June 1934; *World,* 2 June 1934; *Mirror,* 2 June 1934; *Sun,* 2 June 1934; *Daily Worker,* 2 June 1934; *Post,* 4, 21 June 1934; ACLU, *What Rights for the Unemployed?,* 3–5. Letter to La Guardia from Alexander Taylor, Associated Office and Professional Emergency Employees, 26 May 1934; AOPEE flyer, "Blackjacks or Relief?" n.d.; letter to Alderman John J. Cashmore from Helen O'Lochlainn Crowe, 24 June 1934, all in vol. 712, 131–32, 202, ACLU archives. See also the numerous letters to La Guardia from citizens and groups protesting the beating of Rose and James Lechay outside the Tombs Court, reel 22, La Guardia Papers.

38. *Times,* 29 May, 2 June 1934; *Post,* 11, 12, 20 June 1934.

39. Wilson, "Commissioner O'Ryan: Terrorist," 181–82; Kessner, *Fiorello La Guardia,* 355; letter to O'Ryan from La Guardia, 6 July 1934, reel 7, frame 2539, La Guardia Papers. Although O'Ryan was blamed for instituting the photo/credential system, it was in fact ordered by La Guardia at the suggestion of several non-Communist labor leaders. The abuses of the Criminal Alien Squad were particularly evident in the Angelo Blanco and

Patsy Augustine cases; see letters and affidavits from these cases in vols. 711–712, ACLU archives.

40. *Post,* 3 August 1934 (SP quote); *Daily Worker,* 21 June 1934; Wilson, "Commissioner O'Ryan: Terrorist," 181–82.

41. *Times,* 25 August 1934; Kessner, *Fiorello La Guardia,* 355.

42. James Lardner and Thomas Reppetto, *NYPD: A City and its Police* (New York: Henry Holt and Company, 2000), 192–93, 201–06, 212; Lewis J. Valentine, *Night Stick* (New York: Dial Press, 1947), 35–38, 102–03, 118–21, 188–92; *Times,* 26 September, 20 December 1934.

43. James Green, *The World of the Worker* (New York: Hill and Wang, 1980), 150, 162–63; Naison, *Communists in Harlem,* 169–71.

44. ACLU, Annual Report, 1934–35, 62–63.

45. On labor cases, see *Times,* 12, 17, 18, 29 May, 27 July 1936; *Labor Defender,* July 1936. National Committee for Defense of Political Prisoners press release, 19 May 1936, and ACLU Bulletin #715, both on reel 132, vol. 896, ACLU Papers; letter to Florine Lasker from Victor Gettner, 27 April 1937, vol. 2252A, ACLU archives. In the La Guardia Papers, see letter to La Guardia from ILD, et al., 7 March 1935, reel 22, frame 1673; Petition to the Mayor, 20 December 1935, reel 230, frame 483; memo to Valentine from Inspector Harry Lobdell, 14 February 1936, reel 230, frames 312–15; memo to La Guardia from Stone, 18 May 1936, reel 230, frames 1375–77; see also dozens of statements and telegrams from labor and left groups protesting police violence in Seamens' strike, reel 230, frames 1363–1491. On violence at Home Relief Bureaus, see, *Daily Worker,* 13 November 1935, 1 July 1936, 27 January 1937. Memo from CCR, vol. 712, 181; Precinct 18 Employees flyer, vol. 712, 180; open letter from 53rd St. Locals of Unemployed Councils, vol. 712, 182; letter to Valentine from Florine Lasker, vol. 797, 174, all in ACLU archives. Letter to La Guardia from Chelsea and 33rd St. Unemployed Councils, 7 September 1934, reel 22, frame 1572; letter to La Guardia from Sol Berkowitz, Workers Alliance Local 22, 17 September 1936, reel 22, frame 1865, both in La Guardia Papers.

46. *Times,* 16 February, 1, 3, 27 March 1936; ACLU press release, 21 February 1936, and Citizens' Jury press release, 27 March 1936, both on reel 132, vol. 896, ACLU Papers; "Let Them Eat Clubs!" Association of Workers in Public Relief Agencies flyer, reel 22, frame 1823; and letter to La Guardia from Harry Maurer, American League Against War and Fascism, 17 February 1936, reel 22, frame 1759, both in La Guardia Papers.

47. *World-Telegram,* 26 April 1937.

48. "Proposed Police Regulations Relating to Crowds," vol. 2252A, ACLU archives.

49. William J. McMahon, "Mobs, Riots and Disorders," *Spring 3100,* October 1935, 8–9, 26.

50. Valentine, "Our Police Policy Concerning Labor Disturbances," *Spring 3100,* December 1937, 1–3.

51. *Times,* 3 June 1937; *Herald-Tribune,* 3 June 1937; *Post,* 27 July 1937.

52. Samuel Walker, *In Defense of American Liberties: A History of the* ACLU (New York: Oxford University Press, 1990), 106, 111.

53. ACLU, Annual Report, 1937–38, 23; *Civil Liberties Quarterly,* March 1938; Bernard G. Walpin, "Report on Police Attitudes and Actions at Street Assemblages," October 1941, reel 215, frames 126–141, ACLU Papers. For Criminal Alien Squad reports, see Subject Files for "Organizations, Communist Party," reel 150, frames 213-584, and reel 212, frames 1859-1904, La Guardia Papers.

54. Coming just a couple of months after the Memorial Day Massacre, the Brooklyn shipyard strike violence seriously concerned La Guardia. In response, he bypassed the usual police disciplinary channels and ordered an independent investigation by the Commissioner of Accounts. See, *Times,* 5, 11 August 1937; *Herald-Tribune,* 21 July, 8, 10 August 1937; *Post,* 17 August 1937; *Sun,* 16 August 1937. Paul Blanshard, Commissioner of Accounts, "Report to the Mayor on Alleged Police Brutality in Shipyard Strike," 9 August 1937; letter to La Guardia from Osmund K. Fraenkel, 11 August 1937, reel 117, frame 290, La Guardia Papers; letter to Valentine from Florine Lasker, 21 July 1937; Herbert A. Fierst, "Investigation of Police Brutality," 27 July 1937; letter to Paul Blanshard from Herbert D. David, 6 August 1937; and Herbert D. David and Herbert A. Fierst, "Final Report to Mayor: Inquiry into Police Brutality in Brooklyn," n.d., all on reel 146, vol. 998, ACLU Papers. On the WPA protest, see *Times,* 19 July, 3, 20 October 1941; *Daily Worker,* 19, 23, 28 July, 3 October, 18, 21 November 1941; WPA Teachers Union, "Statement of the Facts in the Case of Herbert Newton," 1 November 1941, reel 195, frame 91, ACLU Papers.

Chapter Six

1. James Alexander, *Blue Coat, Black Skin* (Hicksville, N.Y.: Exposition Press, 1978), 30–39, 56; W. Marvin Dulaney, *Black Police in America* (Bloomington: Indiana University Press, 1996), 22; James Lardner and Thomas Reppetto, *NYPD: A City and its Police* (New York: Henry Holt and Company, 2000), 240–43.

2. For excessive force cases involving black suspects, see *Times,* 28 July 1919, 11 April 1922, 20 February, 6, 8 March, 4 June, and 30 August 1926. On the 1928 Harlem disorder, see *Times,* 23 July 1928.

3. For brutality cases involving black police, see *Times,* 29, 31 December 1924; 15 January, 10, 14 March 1925. On Officer Benjamin Wallace, see Dulaney, *Black Police in America,* 106–07; Lardner and Reppetto, *NYPD,* 248; Lewis J. Valentine, *Night Stick* (New York: Dial Press, 1947), 266.

4. Mark Naison, *Communists in Harlem During the Depression* (Urbana: University of Illinois Press, 1983), 9, 59. The best example of the NAACP's conservative approach to

police brutality was its handling of the case of Ralph Baker, a black medical student shot by an off-duty police officer in Brooklyn in 1929. For more on this case, see the extensive documentation on reel 3, frames 376–702, and reel 4, frames 1–46, NAACP Papers, Part 8A (Frederick, Md.: University Publications of America, 1982).

5. Naison, *Communists in Harlem,* 3–11.

6. Ibid., 82, 85, 116; Cheryl Lynn Greenberg, *"Or Does It Explode?": Black Harlem in the Great Depression* (New York: Oxford, 1991), 42–43, 79, 156–58; *Times,* 19 March 1934; *Daily Worker,* 19 March 1934; *Amsterdam News,* 24 March 1934; letter to Police Commissioner O'Ryan from Chief Inspector Lewis Valentine, 26 March 1934, reel 77, frames 2116–2121, La Guardia Papers, Municipal Archives of the City of New York (MACNY).

7. Crusader News Agency press release, 22 July 1933; and "Police Activity in Harlem," 16 August 1933, both in vol. 517, ACLU Papers (hereafter referred to as ACLU archives), Mudd Library, Princeton University; *Hunger Fighter,* January 1933, reel 2, frame 353, International Labor Defense (ILD) Papers (Frederick, Md.: University Publications of America, 1987); "Unemployment and Discrimination on Relief and Works Jobs in Harlem, Testimony of James W. Ford before the Mayor's Commission on Conditions in Harlem," 13 April 1935, reel 77, frame 641, La Guardia Papers.

8. *Hunger Fighter,* March 1933, reel 2, frame 367, ILD Papers.

9. Greenberg, *Or Does It Explode?,* 3–5; Naison, *Communists in Harlem,* 140–41; Mayor's Commission on Conditions in Harlem, *The Complete Report of Mayor La Guardia's Commission on the Harlem Riot of March 19, 1935* (New York: Arno Press, 1969), 7–11 [hereafter cited as La Guardia Commission Report].

10. Naison, *Communists in Harlem,* 140–42.

11. Ibid., 143, La Guardia Commission Report, 8–9, 15–16, 113–21, letter to La Guardia from Adam Clayton Powell, Jr., 28 March 1935, reel 76, frame 792; letter to Mayor's Committee from James Ford, 25 March 1935, reel 76, frame 754; Statement by Lloyd Hobbs, March 1935, reel 76, frame 680, all in La Guardia Papers; *Times,* 21 April 1935; *Amsterdam News,* 27 April 1935.

12. La Guardia Commission Report, 115, 121 (quotes), 133–35.

13. Letter to La Guardia from Lewis Valentine, 30 April 1935, reel 76, frames 1505–10; letter to La Guardia from Uptown Chamber of Commerce, 14 August 1935, reel 76, frames 1075–79, La Guardia Papers; Thomas Kessner, *Fiorello H. La Guardia and the Making of Modern New York* (New York: McGraw Hill, 1989), 375.

14. Naison, *Communists in Harlem,* xviii, 145–46, 148, 169–72.

15. ACLU, Annual Report, June 1936, 57-58; *Daily Worker,* 15 April, 28 May, 17 June, 24 July, 12 August, 4 September 1936; 9, 10 March 1937; letter to La Guardia from Charles Romney, 8 June 1936, reel 76, frame 1592-93, La Guardia Papers.

16. Mario A. Charles, "Bedford-Stuyvesant," in Kenneth T. Jackson, ed., *The Encyclopedia of New York City* (New Haven, Conn.: Yale University Press, 1995), 94–95; *Times,* 17 December 1936; *Daily Worker,* 28 July, 15 August 1936; 17 December 1937; Petition to Mayor from Sixth Assembly District Communist Party, 25 June 1936, reel 22, frame 1859; and letter to La Guardia from CP Stuyvesant Heights Branch, 5 August 1936, reel 22, frame 1865, both in La Guardia Papers.

17. John B. Streater, Jr., "The National Negro Congress, 1936–47" (Ph.D. dissertation, University of Cincinnati, 1981) 169–71; Herbert Shapiro, *White Violence and Black Response* (Amherst: University of Massachusetts Press, 1988), 261; John Lovell, Jr., "Washington Fights," *The Crisis,* 46 (September 1939): 276–77.

18. Martha Biondi, "The Struggle for Black Equality in New York City" (Ph.D. dissertation, Columbia University, 1997), 15.

19. For background on African Americans on the New York homefront, see Dominic Joseph Capeci, Jr., *The Harlem Race Riot of 1943* (Philadelphia: Temple University Press, 1977); and Nat Brandt, *Harlem at War* (Syracuse, N.Y.: Syracuse University Press, 1996). On the rise of youth gang violence during the war, see Eric Schneider, *Vampires, Dragons, and Egyptian Kings* (Princeton, N.J.: Princeton University Press, 1999).

20. On the killings of black soldiers in the South, see Brandt, *Harlem at War,* 129–30; Walter White, "Behind the Harlem Riot," *New Republic,* 16 August 1943, 221. On the Camp Stewart situation, see Brandt, 136–37; *People's Voice,* 15, 22 May, 5, 12 19 June 1943.

21. *Times,* 13 May 1942; *People's Voice,* 14, 16, 23 May 1942; *Amsterdam News,* 16, 23 May 1942; *Daily Worker,* 14 May 1942. There are also several documents related to the Armstrong case in the La Guardia Papers; see memo to Lewis Valentine from Edward Butler, 12 May 1942, reel 77, frames 790–91; letter (and attached handbill) to La Guardia from Lewis Valentine, 15 May 1942, reel 77, frames 794–95; and report to Commanding Officer of the Criminal Alien Squad from Acting Lieutenant Schilbersky, 17 May 1942, reel 77, frames 805–09.

22. *People's Voice,* 18 July, 24 October, 14, 21, 28 November 1942; letter to Lewis Valentine from Lionel C. Barrow, 13 May 1942, reel 18, frame 754, and letter to NAACP from Ethel Blae, 5 November 1942, reel 20, frame 867, both in Part 8B, NAACP Papers.

23. *People's Voice,* 12 December 1942.

24. Gerald Horne, *Black Liberation/Red Scare* (Newark: University of Delaware Press, 1994), 103; *Times,* 19, 20 March 1943; *People's Voice,* 5 September, 21 November, 12 December 1942, 20, 27 March, 10, 17, 24 April, 8 May, 24 July 1943.

25. Capeci, *The Harlem Riot of 1943,* 100–08; Walter White, "Behind the Harlem Riot," 221.

26. Capeci, *The Harlem Riot of 1943,* 100–08; Walter White, "Behind the Harlem Riot," 221; *Times,* 3 August 1943; *People's Voice,* 7 August 1943; Harold Orlansky, *The Harlem*

Riot: A Study in Mass Frustration, Social Analysis Report No. 1 (New York: Social Analysis, 1943), 1–5.

27. Adam Clayton Powell, Sr., *Riots and Ruins* (New York: Richard R. Smith, 1945), 47; *People's Voice,* 7 August 1943; "Statement by Walter White re Harlem Riot, August 1, 1943," and "Harlem Riot Showed Resentment to Soldier Treatment, August 6, 1943," in Racial Tension, Harlem 1943 file, box A506, Group II, NAACP Papers, Library of Congress (LOC); Patricia Turner, *I Heard It Through the Grape Vine* (Berkeley: University of California Press, 1993), 44; Orlansky, *The Harlem Riot,* 19.

28. Winifred Raushenbush, *How to Prevent a Race Riot in Your Hometown,* (New York: ACLU, 1943), 7–8; Capeci, *The Harlem Riot of 1943,* 102–08, 116–118; White, "Behind the Harlem Riot," 222.

29. *World-Telegram,* 4 August 1943; Capeci, *The Harlem Riot of 1943,* 143.

30. *Times,* 16 November 1943; "Presentment of the August 1943 Grand Jury of Kings County in the Investigation of Crime and Disorderly Conditions of the Bedford-Stuyvesant Area of Brooklyn," Crime—NYC—Bedford-Stuyvesant 1943-44 folder, box A220, Part II, NAACP Papers, LOC.

31. Ibid.; *Times,* 18, 24 November 1943; *Daily Worker,* 27 November 1943; Statement by Walter White regarding Kings County Grand Jury, 17 November 1943, Crime—NYC—Bedford-Stuyvesant, 1943-44 folder, box A220, Part II, NAACP Papers.

32. *Times,* 16, 17, 18, 20, 22, 24 November 1943; *People's Voice,* 27 November 1943; Kessner, *La Guardia and the Making of Modern New York,* 533–34.

33. Citizens' Committee on Better Race Relations, *Recommendations for Action,* Racial Tension—Harlem 1944, August-December folder, box A506, Part IIA, NAACP Papers; Capeci, *The Harlem Riot of 1943,* 143–44; *People's Voice,* 4, 11 September 1943; *Times,* 1 May 1944; Andrew Darien, "Patrolling the Borders," (Ph.D. dissertation, New York University, 2000), 51, 53.

34. Darien, "Patrolling the Borders," 53–54, 59, 63–64.

35. Shapiro, *White Violence and Black Response,* 355, 362–65; President's Committee on Civil Rights, *To Secure These Rights* (New York: Simon and Schuster, 1947); Biondi, "The Struggle for Black Equality," 237–40.

36. *Times,* 25 July, 18, 19 August, 18 September 1946; *Post,* 17 July 1946; *People's Voice,* 20 July 1946; Shapiro, *White Violence and Black Response,* 373. For extensive documentation on the NAACP's handling of the Isaac Woodard case, see the Part 8B, reels 28 and 29, NAACP Papers.

37. *People's Voice,* 23 June 1945, 2, 23 February, 13 April, 4 May 1946.

38. *Times,* 6, 22 February, 9 March, 10, 16, April, 3 May, 6, 8, 18, 20, 24 July, 4 August

1946; *People's Voice,* 23 February, 2, 9, 16 March, 27 July 1946; Biondi, "The Struggle for Black Equality," 223–36.

39. Biondi, "The Struggle for Black Equality," 240–42; President's Committee on Civil Rights, *To Secure These Rights,* 25, 114, 155–57. For a good example of the Popular Front's attempts to connect lynching and police brutality, see Horace Marshall, *Police Brutality: Lynching Northern Style,* Part I, reel 12, frames 869–81, Civil Rights Congress Papers (Frederick, Md.: University Publications of America, 1988).

40. Horne, *Black Liberation/Red Scare,* 137-43, 161; *People's Voice,* 15 December 1945.

41. *Times,* 2 December 1945, 4 April 1946, 9 September 1947 (quote); *Post,* 9 September 1947; *People's Voice,* 21 December 1946; "Reminiscences of Arthur Wallander," April 1950, 39, Oral History Collection of Columbia University. In September 1946, the NYPD appointed 2,090 new officers, the largest number of rookies ever added to the department at one time. Although they underwent the usual three-month academy program, they were part of a new on-the-job training system in which they did field duty each week under veteran officers. "A History of Police Training in New York City," *Spring 3100,* 36 (January 1965): 12–16. On CCAPB resolution, see *People's Voice,* 15 December 1945.

42. "Introduction," to *Civil Rights Congress Papers Index,* (Frederick, MD: University Publications of America, 1989), v–vi.

43. *Times,* 8, 10 August 1946; *Herald-Tribune,* 8 August 1946.

44. *Times,* 8 December 1946, 29 April 1947; *People's Voice,* 2 November 1946, 19, 26 April, 19 July, 20 September 1947; New York State Civil Rights Congress, "Police Brutality," reel 36, frame 548–56, Part II: Files of William L. Patterson, CRC Papers.

45. *Times,* 20 October, 25 November, 31 December 1947; *People's Voice,* 25 October, 20 December 1947; Marshall, *Lynching Northern Style*; Biondi, "The Struggle for Black Equality," 221, 250–51.

46. *People's Voice,* 27 September 1947; Marshall, *Lynching Northern Style.* Letter to Arthur Wallander from NAACP assistant secretary, 14 August 1947, reel 20, frames 248–49; NAACP press release, 15 August 1947, reel 20, frame 250; and memo to files from Marian Wynn Perry, 13 September 1947, reel 20, frame 261, all in Part 8B, NAACP Papers.

47. *Times,* 10, 11 October, 11 November 1947; *People's Voice,* 18 October, 1 November 1947.

48. Marshall, *Lynching Northern Style.*

49. *Times,* 13 November 1947, 15 February, 6, 8 March 1948; *People's Voice,* 22 November 1947, 21 February, 20 March 1948; Citizens Committee to End Police Brutality, press release, 14 February 1949, reel 22, frames 460–61, Part 8B, NAACP Papers.

50. *Times,* 8 March 1948; Dan Dodson, "Speech at Riverside Church," 7 March 1948, MCU folder, box A455, Part II, NAACP Papers, LOC.

51. Biondi, "The Struggle for Black Equality," 253.

52. *People's Voice,* 27 March 1948; *Amsterdam News,* 22 March 1948.

53. *Brooklyn NAACP Spotlight,* June 1949, box 118C, Brooklyn Branch folder VI, Group II, NAACP Papers, LOC; letter to James Powers from Samuel Korb, 2 May 1949, and deposition of Samuel Korb, 12 April 1949, both on reel 45313, frames 843–54 and 863–65, Subject Files, Vincent Impellitteri Papers, Municipal Archives of the City of New York (MACNY); Biondi, "The Struggle for Black Equality," 256–57.

54. *Brooklyn NAACP Spotlight,* July 1949, box 118C, Brooklyn branch folder VI, Part II, NAACP Papers, LOC. Letter to Franklin Williams from James Powers, 4 June 1949, reel 21, frames 984–85; Conference with Members of the NAACP, 17 June 1949, reel 21, frames 1022–25; deposition by Lottie Newton, 21 June 1949, reel 22, frames 26–28; deposition by James Powers, 25 July 1949, reel 22, frames 13–21, all in Part 8B, NAACP Papers. For civil court decision, see 303 N.Y. 936, 105 N.E.2d 628, 1952.

55. "Conference with Members of the NAACP," 17 June 1949; Petition to Hon. Thomas E. Dewey presented by Brooklyn Branch NAACP, 22 April 1949, reel 21, frames 954–58, Part 8B, NAACP Papers.

56. Memorandum to Gloster B. Current from Herbert Hill, 28 June 1949, reel 21, frames 1062–63; Petition to Thomas Dewey from James A. Powers, 8 July 1949, reel 22, frames 3–5; Deposition of James Powers, 25 July 1949, reel 22, frames 13–21, all from Part 8B, NAACP Papers.

57. For a good summary of the national NAACP view, see the open letter to William Patterson from Roy Wilkins, 23 November 1949, box 369, Part IIA, NAACP Papers, LOC; and Wilson Record, *Race and Radicalism* (Ithaca, N.Y.: Cornell University Press, 1964), 132–68. For an overview of the CRC's approach, see William L. Patterson, ed., *We Charge Genocide: The Historic Petition to the United Nations for Relief from a Crime of the United States Government Against the Negro People* (New York: Civil Rights Congress, 1951), 3–28. On the 1949 elections, see Memorandum to Gloster B. Current from Herbert Hill, 28 June 1949; memo to Thurgood Marshall from Constance Baker Motley, 25 August 1949, reel 22, frames 49–50, Part 8B, NAACP Papers; and Biondi, "The Struggle for Black Equality," 262.

58. Quote from *Catholic Interracialist,* November 1949; *Times,* 13 July 1949; letters to Madison Jones from J. Henry Carpenter, 14 and 18 July 1949, reel 22, frames 7 and 491, Part 8B, NAACP Papers.

59. *Times,* 9 August, 19 September, 11 October, 1949. Letter to John Coleman, John Murtagh, and Jacob Grumet from James Powers, 22 August 1949, frame 47; memo to Thurgood Marshall from Constance Baker Motley, 25 August 1949, frames 49–50; Resolution adopted by the Executive Board of Brooklyn Branch NAACP, 1 September

1949, frame 71; Brooklyn Branch NAACP Press Release, "Mayor's Committee Refuses to Allow Open Hearings," frames 64–65; letter to John Murtagh from Robert L. Carter, 19 September 1949, frames 76–77; memo to Thurgood Marshall from Constance Baker Motley, 3 October 1949, frames 80–81; Joint Committee of NYC Branches Press Release, 10 October 1949, frames 82–83, all on reel 22, Part 8B, NAACP Papers.

60. Report to Vincent Impellitteri from John Coleman, John Murtagh, and Jacob Grumet, 26 December 1950, reel 45313, frames 954–60; and letter to Charles Horowitz from Thomas Murphy, 18 January 1951, reel 45313, frame 977, both in Subject Files, Impellitteri Papers.

61. Record, *Race and Radicalism,* 146, 154–56, 160–64.

62. *Times,* 10, 15 December 1949; *Amsterdam News,* 16, 23, 30 December 1950; Biondi, "The Struggle for Black Equality," 263–65; "Some Case Histories of Police Brutality in New York City," reel 268, box 1075, Folder 12, ACLU Papers, 1950 — 1990 (Wilmington, Del.: Scholarly Resources, 1996). Memo to Gloster Current from Herbert Hill, 28 December 1950, box 126, New York Branch files, Group IIC, NAACP Papers, LOC.

63. Biondi, "The Struggle for Black Equality," 269–73; telegram to Vincent Impellitteri from Citizens Committee on Police Practices, 16 March 1951, reel 45313, frame 1011, Subject Files, Impellitteri Papers.

64. Biondi, "The Struggle for Black Equality," 273–75; for more on CRC organizing in the 1950s, see CRC case files, reels 36 and 37, Part II, CRC Papers.

65. Patterson, *We Charge Genocide,* 8–9 (quote), 58–121; Gerald Horne, *Communist Front? The Civil Rights Congress, 1946–1956* (Cranbury, N.J.: Fairleigh Dickinson University Press, 1988), 167–76. For more on the impact of foreign relations on U.S. civil rights rhetoric and policy, see Mary Dudziak, *Cold War Civil Rights* (Princeton, N.J.: Princeton University Press, 2000).

66. Bruce Smith, *The New York Police Survey* (New York: Institute of Public Administration, 1952), 7–10; *Times,* 23 February 1953.

67. *Times,* 19 February, 28 April 1953. The city's assumption of liability for police misconduct happened earlier in New York than most other cities where governments did not become liable for civil rights violations until the Monell decision by the Supreme Court in 1978; see Skolnick and Fyfe, *Above the Law,* 201–05.

68. *World-Telegram and Sun,* 16 February 1953.

69. Ibid. (quote); Lardner and Reppetto, *NYPD,* 263–64; *Times,* 25, 28 February 1953.

70. *Times,* 17, 18 February 1953; editorial in *Crisis,* 60 (March 1953).

71. *Times,* 17, 28 February, 6 March 1953; *Amsterdam News,* 21 February, 7 March 1953.

72. *Times,* 17, 19, 20 February 1953; *Amsterdam News,* 28 February 1953; letter to Vincent Impellitteri from Ella Baker and Edward Jacko, 16 February 1953; and press release, 19 February 1953, both in NYC Police Brutality 1953–54 folder, box 456, Part IIA, NAACP Papers, LOC; New York City Council, Resolution No. 753, 24 February 1953, reel 31, frame 381, Part 8B, NAACP Papers.

73. Walter White, press release, 26 February 1953, Subject files, Discrimination, January–June 1953 folder, reel 45313, frames 1333-34, Impellitteri Papers.

74. *Times,* 19, 28, February, 1, 3, 6 March 1953; *Amsterdam News,* 7 March 1953.

75. *Times,* 2, 16, 23 March 1953; *Amsterdam News,* 21 March 1953; Association of Former New York State Troopers, Resolution, 24 March 1953, Subject Files, Discrimination, January–July 1953 folder, reel 45313, frame 1349, Impellitteri Papers; Biondi, "The Struggle for Black Equality," 286–88; Statement by Walter White, 15 March 1953, NYC Police Brutality 1950–52 folder, box 456, Part IIA, NAACP Papers, LOC.

76. *Times,* 27 February, 7, 21 March, 4, 18, 20 June 1953, 6 July 1954.

77. *Times,* 6, 7 July 1954; Biondi, "The Struggle for Black Equality," 289–90.

78. *Times,* 23 May, 17 October 1953, 16 May 1955; Edith M. Alexander, *Ten Years along the Path of Unity in New York City,* 12 July 1954, Subject files, Mayor's Committee on Unity folder, reel 40102, frame 1199, Robert F. Wagner Papers, MACNY; Darien, "Patrolling the Borders," 65; ACLU Annual Report, 1951–1953, 94–95; *Times,* 2, 23 May 1953; NYCLU, Recommendations to Police Department for Investigating Complaints of Civil Rights Violations, NYC Police Brutality 1953–54 folder, box 456, Part IIA, NAACP Papers, LOC; NYPD, Press Release No. 44, 16 May 1955, in Police-Civilian Complaint Review Board—Pre-1960 folder, vertical files, MACNY; Biondi, "The Struggle for Black Equality," 291.

79. Horne, *Black Liberation/Red Scare,* 208, 244; Horne, *Communist Front,* 354–58.

80. Biondi, "The Struggle for Black Equality," 292.

Chapter Seven

1. Letter to Spenser Coxe from George Rundquist, Folder 12: Police Practices, box 1074, reel 267; and Press Statement on Federal Civil Rights Commission Report on Police Lawlessness, Folder 13—Police Practices, box 1077, reel 269, both in Subject Files, ACLU Papers, 1950—1990 (Wilmington, Del.: Scholarly Resources, 1996); *Times,* 18 November 1961.

2. August Meier and Elliot Rudwick, *CORE* (New York: Oxford University Press, 1973), 150, 198–99.

3. Ibid., 228, 230, 237, 250–51; *Times,* 9, 20 November 1963, 7 March, 5 June 1964; Vincent Cannato, *The Ungovernable City* (New York: Basic Books, 2001), 157.

4. In the wake of the Harlem Riot of 1964, the case was passionately described in a book by a sympathetic white author. See Truman Nelson, *The Torture of Mothers* (Boston: Beacon Press, 1968).

5. *Times,* 24, 28 February, 7 May 1964.

6. *Times,* 7 April 1964; Samuel Walker, *In Defense of American Liberties* (New York: Oxford University Press, 1990), 248; *Civil Liberties Quarterly,* September 1966, 4–5.

7. *Times,* 28, 29 April 1964; Michael J. Murphy, *Civil Rights and the Police* (New York: NYPD, 1964), 11–12, in Municipal Archives of New York City (MACNY) vertical files.

8. Thomas Brooks, "25,000 Police Against the Review Board," *New York Times Magazine,* 16 October 1966, 128–31; *Times,* 11, 17 May, 17 June 1964; Paul Hoffman, "Police Birchites: The Blue Backlash," *The Nation,* 7 December 1964, 425, 448.

9. *Times,* 19, 22, 23 May; 5, 10 June 1964.

10. *Times,* 17, 19 June 1964.

11. *Times,* 17, 18 July, 2, 3 September 1964; Meier and Rudwick, *CORE,* 301–02; James Lardner and Thomas Reppetto, *NYPD* (New York: Henry Holt, 2000), 253.

12. *Times,* 18, 19, 20, 21, 22, 23, 24 July 1964; *Amsterdam News,* 25 July 1964; Andrew Darien, "Patrolling the Borders," (Ph.D. dissertation, New York University, 2000), 156–57; Lardner and Reppetto, *NYPD,* 254–55; M. Douglas Haywoode, "Statement and Recommendation of New York Branch NAACP Regarding July Social Unrest in Harlem Area," New York Branch folder, box 103C, Group III, NAACP Papers, Library of Congress (LOC); President's Commission on Law Enforcement and the Administration of Justice, *Task Force Report: The Police* (Washington, D.C., 1967), 147–48.

13. *Times,* 22 July, 1 August, 7 August 1964 ; Darien, "Patrolling the Borders," 157–58, 161; Lardner and Reppetto, *NYPD,* 252–53.

14. Darien, "Patrolling the Borders," 161, 164–65.

15. *Times,* 21, 22 July, 1, 7 August, 2 September 1964; Gertrude Samuels, "Who Shall Judge a Policeman?" *New York Times Magazine,* 2 August 1964, 8; Committee on Civil Rights, New York County Lawyers Association (NYCLA), "Civilian Complaints Against the Police," 1965, 12, 16. CORE issued its own report disputing many of the findings of the grand jury report. While conceding that Powell was carrying a knife, CORE noted that many witnesses testified that he did not use it and that Gilligan could have resolved the standoff without firing his weapon. Foreshadowing policies that the NYPD would adopt a few years later, CORE argued that "The right to use deadly force is not a license to kill." *Times,* 3 September 1964.

16. *Times,* 27, 28, 29 September, 7 October 1964; NYCLA, "Civilian Complaints Against the Police," 16.

17. *Times,* 24 July, 1 August 1964, 26, 30, 31 January; 23 March; 7, 8, 10 April 1965.

18. For third-degree cases see, *Times,* 6, 12, 26 March, 1, 3 April, 25, 26 August, 9 November 1965; NYCLU News Releases, 9 November 1965, 8 February 1966, Folder 2: New York City Review Board, box 1083, reel 273, Subject files, ACLU Papers. On Roger Abel and the Guardians, see Darien, "Patrolling the Borders," 151–52; *Times,* 15 June 1965, *Amsterdam News,* June 1965.

19. *Times,* 20 May, 21, 28, 29, 30 June; 14, 15, 16 July 1965.

20. *Times,* 30 June, 18, 26 July, 26 October 1965; Thomas Brooks, "Necessary Force—or Police Brutality?" *Times,* 5 December 1965.

21. *Times,* 14 January, 9 February 1966; Cannato, *The Ungovernable City,* 160–61. 169; David Abbott, Louis H. Gold, and Edward T. Rogowsky, et al., *Police, Politics, and Race* (Cambridge, Mass.: Harvard University Press, 1969), 5–6.

22. *Times,* 16 February, 3 May, 11, 12 July 1966; Cannato, *The Ungovernable City,* 167, 169; Darien, "Patrolling the Borders," 185–89.

23. *Times,* 21 February, 9 May, 24 June, 20 July, 16 August, 10 September 1966.

24. Cannato, *The Ungovernable City,* 172. The "politics of resentment" is discussed by Alan Crawford in *Thunder on the Right* (New York: Pantheon, 1980). In *The Populist Persuasion* (New York: Basic Books, 1995), Michael Kazin argues that this white backlash was part of a deeply rooted populist impulse in American history. On the particular role of white Catholic ethnics, see John McGreevy, *Parish Boundaries* (Chicago: University of Chicago Press, 1996).

25. Nicholas Alex, *New York Cops Talk Back* (New York: John Wiley and Sons, 1976), 56; Walter Arm, "Speaking Out: Civilians Shouldn't Judge Cops," *Saturday Evening Post,* 7 May 1966, 12; *Times,* 5 February 1966; Joseph P. Viteritti, *Police, Politics, and Pluralism* (Beverly Hills, CA: Sage Publications, 1973), 20–21; Darien, "Patrolling the Borders," 162.

26. *Times,* 8 July, 15 September, 6 November 1966; Brooks, "25,000 Police Against the Review Board," 126–27; Cannato, *The Ungovernable City,* 168-69. The referendum was just one of many grassroots, single-issue campaigns of the 1960s that targeted civil rights. See Lisa McGirr, *Suburban Warriors* (Princeton, N.J.: Princeton University Press, 2001), 185, 225–26.

27. Homicide statistics are listed in Robert Snyder, "Crime," *The Encyclopedia of New York City* (New Haven, Conn.: Yale University Press, 1995), 298. On the Genovese murder case, see A.M. Rosenthal, *Thirty-eight Witnesses* (New York: McGraw Hill, 1964). The subway ad appeared in the *Times* and other daily papers on 26 September 1966. Lindsay's comment is cited in Cannato, *The Ungovernable City,* 175.

28. The mother ad appeared in the *Times* and other papers on 4 November 1966; the

Philadelphia riot ad appeared on 3 October 1966. On neighborhood "Safety" campaigns, see *Times,* 15 September 1966.

29. *Times,* 29 August, 4 October, 6 November 1966; Aryeh Neier, *Taking Liberties* (New York: Public Affairs, 2003), 23–24.

30. *Times,* 29 August, 12 October 1966; Minutes of NYCLU Staff Meeting, 14 November 1966; Address of Mayor John V. Lindsay [St. George's Church, 1966], both in Folder 19: Miscellaneous—Police Review Boards 1966, box 1082, reel 273, ACLU Papers. For information on police harassment of FAIR campaign workers, see *Times,* 23 October, 2, 3 November 1966; Chevigny, *Police Power* (New York: Vintage, 1969), 112.

31. *Times,* 3 July, 17, 28 October 1966; Cannato, *The Ungovernable City,* 175.

32. *Times,* 18, 25, 27 (FAIR quote), 29, 30 October, 5, 7, 8 November 1966; Abbott, *Police, Politics, and Race,* 11.

33. *Times,* 6, 9 October 1966; Minutes of NYCLU Staff Meeting, 14 November 1966; Cannato, *The Ungovernable City,* 176–77; Abbott, *Police, Politics and Race,* 19; Neier, *Taking Liberties,* 24–25.

34. *Times,* 9, 10 November 1966; Cannato, *The Ungovernable City,* 183.

35. Abbott, *Police, Politics and Race,* 13–14, 16, 24, 27, 37.

36. Quoted in NYCLU Staff Meeting Minutes, 14 November 1966.

37. *Times,* 16, 17, 23 November 1966, 24 February 1967; Chevigny, *Police Power,* 56, 265; Viteritti, *Police, Politics and Pluralism,* 51–53. Jackson went on to become the CCRB's executive director in 1967, replacing civilian director Harold Baer.

38. Viteritti, *Police, Politics and Pluralism,* 54–56, 58–60; Alex, *New York Cops Talk Back,* 77.

39. Viteritti, *Police, Politics and Pluralism,* 60–61; Chevigny, *Police Power,* xiv, xv, 56, 82, 261–63; Samuel Walker, *Police Accountability* (Belmont, Calif.: Wadsworth, 2001), 64.

40. Chevigny, *Police Power,* xiii, xix, 25–28, 43, 48, 68–70, 114, 132, 138, 275, 277, 283, 286; Walker, *In Defense of American Liberties,* 274.

41. Chevigny, *Police Power,* 176, 192–94, 237, 246–47, 254; Jerome Skolnick and James Fyfe, *Above the Law* (New York: Free Press, 1993), 98.

42. *Times,* 8 April, 24 July, 1 August 1967, 1 April 1968; Robert Fogelson, *Big-City Police* (Cambridge, Mass.: Harvard University Press, 1977), 220; Lardner and Reppetto, *NYPD,* 254–55.

43. *Times,* 2 October, 1967, 12, 17 April 1968; Cannato, *The Ungovernable City,* 129–30; Chevigny, *Police Power,* 176–78; "Guidelines for Arrest at Scene of Mass Demonstra-

tions," Confidential Subject Files, reel 8, box 14, Folder 174: Police Department (4), John V. Lindsay Papers, Municipal Archives of New York City (MACNY); "The Law and Public Demonstrations," *Spring 3100,* March 1969, 8–19.

44. *Times,* 24, 25, 26 July 1967, 12 April 1968; *Post,* 24, 25 July 1967; Cannato, *The Ungovernable City,* 132–35.

45. *Times,* 30, 31 July, 6, 8 September 1967; Cannato, *The Ungovernable City,* 135–39.

46. *Times,* 6, 12 April 1968; *Newsday,* 8 April 1968; *Amsterdam News,* 13 April 1968; *Daily News,* 17 April 1968; Gloria Steinem and Lloyd Weaver, "The City on the Eve of Destruction," *New York Magazine,* 22 April 1968; Cannato, *The Ungovernable City,* 210–15.

47. *Times,* 1 June 1967; Chevigny, *Police Power,* 173–75; Cannato, *The Ungovernable City,* 143; *Civil Liberties Quarterly,* September 1967.

48. *Times,* 7, 11, 12 December 1967; Cannato, *The Ungovernable City,* 151–52; *Civil Liberties Quarterly,* March-April 1968, 3, and January 1968, 1–2; letter to Lindsay from Conor Cruise O'Brien, 7 December 1967; and letter to O'Brien from Lindsay, 4 January 1968, both in Subject Files, reel 44, box 86, Police Department folder (4), Lindsay Papers.

49. *Times,* 23, 24, 25 March, 5, 20 April 1968; Cannato, *The Ungovernable City,* 222–23.

50. *Times,* 24–27 April 1968; Fact-Finding Commission Appointed to Investigate the Disturbances at Columbia University in April and May 1968 [hereafter cited as Cox Commission] *Crisis at Columbia* (New York: Vintage Books, 1968), 11–13; Jerry L. Avorn, et al., *Up Against the Ivy Wall* (New York: Atheneum, 1970), 15–21, 163–66; Cannato, *The Ungovernable City,* 239–53.

51. *Times,* 30 April, 1 May 1968; Avorn, *Up Against the Ivy Wall,* 186–95 (quote is from page 195); Cannato, *The Ungovernable City,* 253 54; Roger Kahn, *The Battle for Morningside Heights* (New York: William Morrow, 1970), 200–13; Cox Commission, *Crisis at Columbia,* 140–42.

52. *Times,* 1 May 1968; Louis Stutman, R. Harcourt Dodds, Joseph T. McDonough and Benjamin Ward, "CCRB Report on the Disposition of Complaints Arising from the Columbia University Incidents in April and May 1968," 26 March 1970, Subject Files, reel 11, box 21, folder 364: Civilian Review Board 1966–70, Lindsay Papers.

53. *Times,* 7, 27 May 1968; Cannato, *The Ungovernable City,* 258–59; Kahn, *The Battle for Morningside Heights,* 195–96.

54. *Times,* 3 June 1969; Darien, "Patrolling the Borders," 339; Michael Baker, *Police on Campus: The Mass Police Action at Columbia University* (New York: NYCLU, 1969), 70–74, 117–22.

55. *Times,* 7 July 1968 (Vietnam quote); Christian Appy, *Working-Class War* (Chapel Hill: University of North Carolina, 1993), 41; Darien, "Patrolling the Borders," 339–40;

Kahn, *The Battle for Morningside Heights,* 204 (pig quote); Cannato, *The Ungovernable City,* 254–60.

56. *Times,* 28 March 1970; CCRB Report on Columbia Incidents.

57. For a detailed account of the events in Chicago, see Daniel Walker, *Rights in Conflict* (New York: Grosset and Dunlap, 1968).

58. *Times,* 2, 3, 5, 6, 7, 9, 15, 16 August 1968; *Post,* 15 August 1968; Darien, "Patrolling the Borders," 340–41; *Civil Liberties Quarterly,* October 1968, 3.

59. *Times,* 4, 5 September, 11 October 1968; *Post,* 5 September 1968; *Amsterdam News,* 7 September 1968.

60. *Times,* 6, 7, 8, 13 September, 20 October 1968, 28 April 1970; *Amsterdam News,* 14, 21 September 1968.

61. *Post,* 20 February 1969; *Times,* 17 September 1970.

62. *Times,* 6 September 1968, 28 September 1969, 21 June 1970; Darien, "Patrolling the Borders," 296, 301. In 1971, the Guardians also protested the recruitment of black officers by the Bureau of Special Services, the city's "red squad," claiming that BOSS exploited black police to betray black radicals. Frank Donner, *Protectors of Privilege* (Berkeley: University of California Press, 1990), 180.

63. *Times,* 12, 13, 31 December 1969; Donner, *Protectors of Privilege,* 165.

64. *Times,* 7, 8 May 1970; "Report Relating to the Role of the Police in Connection with Disorders which Occurred in Lower Manhattan on May 8, 1970" [hereafter referred to as May 8 Report], 1–6, in Confidential Subject Files, reel 8, box 14, folder 173: Police Department (3), Lindsay Papers.

65. *Times,* 9, 17 May 1970; May 8 Report, 6–16; Cannato, *The Ungovernable City,* 448–51.

66. May 8 Report, 17–18, 20, 27, 42, 44.

67. *Times,* 10 May 1970; May 8 Report, 41–42; Darien, "Patrolling the Borders," 353–54; *Civil Liberties Quarterly,* July 1970.

68. *Times,* 11, 12 May 1970.

69. May 8 Report, 22–25, 42; *Civil Liberties Quarterly,* July 1970.

70. *Times,* 10 May 1970; memo to Lindsay, Richard Aurelio, and Tom Morgan from Jay Kriegel, 17 June 1970, Confidential Subject Files, reel 8, box 14, folder 173: Police Department (3), Lindsay Papers.

71. Commission to Investigate Allegations of Police Corruption and the City's Anti-

Corruption Procedures [Knapp Commission], *Report* (New York: George Braziller, 1972), 200; Lardner and Reppetto, *NYPD,* 267–69; Cannato, *The Ungovernable City,* 466–69.

72. Lardner and Reppetto, *NYPD,* 269; Cannato, *The Ungovernable City,* 471.

73. Cannato, *The Ungovernable City,* 478–79; Donner, *Protectors of Privilege,* 194–95.

Chapter Eight

1. *Times,* 17, 18 August 1972.

2. *Times,* 19 August 1972, 5 May, 14 June 1973; Amnesty International, *Police Brutality and Excessive Force in the New York City Police Department* (New York: June 1996), 37–38; Jerome H. Skolnick and James J. Fyfe, *Above the Law* (New York: Free Press, 1993), 234–35.

3. William A. Geller and Michael A. Scott, *Deadly Force: What We Know* (Washington, DC: Police Executive Research Forum, 1992), 64, 256–67, 516–17, 576; *Times,* 28 March 1985, 25 January 1987.

4. Geller and Scott, *Deadly Force,* 376–79; Amnesty International, *Police Brutality and Excessive Force,* 28; *Times,* 18 July 1980; U.S. Commission on Civil Rights, *Police Practices and Civil Rights in New York City* (August 2000), chapter 4: 23; CCRB, "Report of the Pepper Spray Committee" (New York, May 1997, October 2000).

5. *Times,* 22, 24, 25, 26, 27, 28 April, 3 May 1985, 3 May, 18 July 1986, 10 January, 25 February, 30 May 1988; Geller and Scott, *Deadly Force,* 382.

6. *Times,* 23, 24, 25, 28 August, 21 November 1979, 18 July 1980, 2, 3, 10, 16, 21, 22, 24, 30 November 1984, 5, 6 February 1985, 27 February 1987; New York State Commission on Criminal Justice and the Use of Force, "Report to the Governor," [hereafter cited as Curran Commission Report] vol. 1 (Albany. 1987), 47–50; Geller and Scott, *Deadly Force,* 332; Heather Barr, "Policing Madness," in Andrea McCartle and Tanya Erzen, eds., *Zero Tolerance* (New York: New York University Press, 2000), 50–84.

7. *Times,* 12 November 1972, 10 August 1973, 29 February 1980, 16 October 1982; Amnesty International, *Police Brutality and Excessive Force,* 19, 21; Dayo Folayan Gore, Tamara Jones and Joo-Hyun Kang, "Organizing at the Intersections," in *Zero Tolerance,* 251–53. The records of the New York Mattachine Society, a homophile organization active in the 1950s and 1960s, indicate that police had long targeted gay men for harassment and violence and were often unwilling to protect them from vigilante attacks. For the most part, however, gay men were unwilling to file complaints, for fear of public exposure. Recognizing the importance of curbing police misconduct and providing a confidential procedure for filing complaints, the Mattachine Society had quietly supported the 1966 campaign to preserve Lindsay's civilian review board. See: Untitled typescript, n.d., reel 8, box 3, folder 9: Civilian Review Board; and letter to William Stringfellow and Frank Patton, Jr., from Marjorie Friedlander, 16 August 1965, reel 8,

box 3, folder 7: Civilian Review, both in Mattachine Society Papers, New York Public Library.

8. James J. Fyfe, "Race and Extreme Police-Citizen Violence," in *Readings on Police Use of Deadly Force* (Washington, D.C.: Police Foundation, 1982), 175–78; Geller and Scott, *Deadly Force,* 154, 209–10; Curran Commission Report, 3.

9. On Glover killing, see *Times,* 29, 30 April, 1, 3 May, 14 June 1973; on Reese killing, see *Times,* 16, 17, 19, 20, 21 September, 22 December 1974; on Evans case, see *Times,* 3, 8 December 1976, 1 December 1977.

10. *Times,* 19, 20, 23 June, 17 July 1978; 10, 30 June, 25, 29 August 1979. Sharpton's National Youth Movement was involved in protesting the Claude Reese killing in 1976, see Al Sharpton, *Go and Tell Pharaoh* (New York: Doubleday, 1996), 60.

11. *Times,* 6, 21 May, 20, 24, 25, 28 July, 20, 29, 30 September, 20, 29 October, 29 November 1983; Curran Commission Report, 42–43; Union Theological Seminary press release, 5 May 1983, box 230, folder 4, Edward Koch Papers, Municipal Archives of New York (MACNY).

12. *Times,* 1 January 1973, 9 March 1976, 6 March 1978, 21 September 1983, 28 April, 5 May, 18 July 1985.

13. *Times,* 7 March 1978, 20 February 1985, 15 September 1985; Human Rights Watch, *Shielded from Justice* (New York, 1998), 306.

14. Samuel Walker, *Police Accountability: The Role of Citizen Oversight* (Belmont, Calif.: Wadsworth, 2001), 31, 34; *Times,* 21 April 1975.

15. *Times,* 28 April, 7, 8 June 1985, 22 October, 7 November 1986, 5 September 1987.

16. *Times,* 1, 24 November 1988, 24 May 1989, 15 June 1990.

17. Paul Chevigny, *Edge of the Knife* (New York: New Press, 1995), 74–77; Skolnick and Fyfe, *Above the Law,* 85; *Times,* 14 August 1988, 22 March, 22 April 1989, 15 June 1990.

18. James Lardner and Thomas Reppetto, *NYPD* (New York: Henry Holt, 2000), 292–99.

19. Skolnick and Fyfe, *Above the Law,* 1–3; *Times,* 16, 24, 25, 30 March, 5 April, 28, 30 June, 14 July 1991, 25 March 1992; Sharpton, *Go and Tell Pharaoh,* 185–86.

20. *Times,* 3 May 1992; *Newsday,* 2, 3 May 1992.

21. *Times,* 25, 26, 27 June, 5, 7, 9 July 1992; Geller and Scott, *Deadly Force,* 9; *Newsday,* 5, 7, 8, 9, 12, 14 July 1992.

22. *Newsday,* 14 July, 17 September 1992; *Times,* 17, 18, 20 September 1992;

Amnesty International, *Police Brutality and Excessive Force,* 6, 21–22; Human Rights Watch, *Shielded From Justice,* 276-77; Chevigny, *Edge of the Knife,* 65. The NYPD later disciplined forty-two officers identified in videotape of the protest and dismissed another officer involved in a subsequent assault incident on the subway.

23. *Times,* 22, 25 September, 30 October, 1 December 1992, 3 July 1993.

24. Commission to Investigate Allegations of Police Corruption and the Anti-Corruption Procedures of the Police Department, *Report* [hereafter cited as Mollen Commission Report], 7 July 1994, 47–48; *Times,* 30 September 1993.

25. Mollen Commission Report, 44–48.

26. Ibid., 1, 3, 36, 48–49.

27. Ibid., 6–7, 50, 142 ; *Times,* 7 July 1994.

28. Chevigny, *Edge of the Knife,* 33; Human Rights Watch, *Shielded from Justice,* 274; USCRC, *Police Practices and Civil Rights,* 2. In lieu of the independent police monitor, Giuliani created a blue ribbon Commission to Combat Police Corruption, which reported to the mayor and had no subpoena power. Its major focus, however, was corruption, not brutality. See *Times,* 22 September 1997.

29. *Times,* 23 April, 20 November 1995, 25 July 1996; USCRC, *Police Practices and Civil Rights,* chapter 4: 10–11; Amnesty International, *Police Brutality and Excessive Force,* 57–59; Human Rights Watch, *Shielded From Justice,* 269, 283–85; Samuel Walker, *Police Accountability,* 68, 76, 87; Mark Green, *Investigation of the New York City Police Department's Response to Civilian Complaints of Police Misconduct: Interim Report,* 15 September 1999, i; and *Disciplining the Police,* 27 July 2000, 3.

30. CCRB Status Reports, July–December, 1993, 1994, 1995.

31. James Q. Wilson and George Kelling, "Broken Windows," *Atlantic Monthly,* February 1982; Tanya Erzen, "Turnstile Jumpers and Broken Windows," in Andrea McCartle and Tanya Erzen, eds., *Zero Tolerance,* 19–35; Robert C. Davis, *Respectful and Effective Policing* (New York: Vera Institute of Justice, 1999), 1–2; Amnesty International, *Police Brutality and Excessive Force,* 14–15.

32. Davis, *Respectful and Effective Policing,* 2–3.

33. Erzen, "Turnstile Jumpers and Broken Windows," 23; *Times,* 4 March 2000.

34. Andrew Hsiao, "Mother of Invention," in McCartle and Erzen, eds., *Zero Tolerance,* 179–86. See also the documentary film *Justifiable Homicide,* directed by Jon Osman and Jonathan Stack, Gabriel Films, 2001.

35. Amnesty International, *Police Brutality and Excessive Force,* 2.

36. *Times,* 27 June 1996, 20 June 1997; Human Rights Watch, *Shielded From Justice,* 281–82; Walker, *Police Accountability,* 5–6.

37. *Times,* 13, 14, 15, 16, 19, 22, 24 August, 9 September 1997, 27 February 1998; USCRC, *Police Practices and Civil Rights,* 6; Human Rights Watch, *Shielded from Justice,* 270; Norman Siegel, Michael Meyers, and Margaret Fung, *Deflecting the Blame* (New York: New York Civil Liberties Union, March 1998).

38. *Times,* 30 August 1997.

39. *Times,* 17 September 1997, 10 August 1998, 25, 26 May, 9 June, 14 December 1999, 7 March, 28 June 2000.

40. *Times,* 1 March, 21 July 2002.

41. *Times,* 10 November 1998; Human Rights Watch, *Shielded from Justice,* 2. For views of antibrutality activists in New York, see Siegel, et al., *Deflecting the Blame.*

42. *Times,* 5, 6 February 1999.

43. *Times,* 4, 26 March 1999; Hsiao, "Mothers of Invention," 189–90.

44. *Times,* 26, 27, 28 February 2000.

45. *Times,* 6, 19 March, 1 December 1999, 1 February 2001.

46. USCRC, *Police Practices and Civil Rights,* chapter 2: 2, 4, 25–26.

47. Ibid., chapter 4: 10–15, 28, 49.

48. Ibid., chapter 5: 9–12. The commission's findings of racially skewed stop-and-frisk practices confirmed similar findings by the New York State attorney general and the CCRB. See, Eliot Spitzer, *The New York City Police Department's Stop and Frisk Practices,* New York, 1 December 1999; and CCRB, *Street Stop Encounter Report,* June 2001. Spitzer's report noted that even when the statistics were adjusted to reflect the different arrest rates among racial groups, Latinos were still stopped 39 percent more often than whites, and blacks were stopped 23 percent more often.

49. USCRC, *Police Practices and Civil Rights,* chapter 1: 5; Mark Green, *Disciplining the Police* (New York: Public Advocate's Office, 2000), 5–6; Robert C. Davis, *Respectful and Effective Policing.*

50. *Times,* 16 May 2000. Investigations by Mark Green, Human Rights Watch, and Amnesty International all encountered difficulty getting data from the NYPD.

51. Police Department Dispositions of CCRB Substantiated Cases, 1994–2001, *www.nyc.gov/html/ccrb/html/depdispln.html.*

52. *Times,* 27 January, 27 March, 13 April, 14 July 2001.

53. *Times,* 13 September, 30 November 2001, 1 March 2002.

54. CCRB, Status Report, January–December 2001, 1; and Executive Director's Report, July 2002; *Times,* 30 November 2001; *Village Voice,* 21 November 2001. One example of this self-censorship was the pulling of a new documentary film, *Justifiable Homicide,* about the 1995 Rosario and Vega shooting cases. Slated for release in late September 2001, the film's premier was canceled and would not be seen by audiences for another nine months. *Variety,* 15 July 2002.

55. *Times,* 10 April, 7 September 2002, 14 February, 14 May 2003.

56. *Times,* 23 September 2002, 22 February 2003; *Village Voice,* 12 March, 25 March, 7 August 2002; CCRB, Public Meeting Transcript, 12 February 2003, *www.nyc.gov/ html/ccrb/html/reports.html*; Quinnipiac University Poll, 7 February 2002, *www.quinnipiac.edu/x2743.xml.*

ACKNOWLEDGMENTS

Since I began work on this project nearly a decade ago, I have lived in three states, worked at two academic jobs, and begun raising two children. Needless to say, completing the book proved to be more challenging than I ever imagined. I could not have done it without the help and support of numerous people and institutions.

As every historian knows, dedicated librarians and archivists are critical to the success of historical research. I am particularly indebted to Ken Cobb and the staff of the Municipal Archives of the City of New York who patiently endured my many requests, questions, and visits to that invaluable collection. Randy Boehm, editor of the NAACP Papers, was extremely helpful in introducing me to that collection and its many hidden treasures. I am also very grateful to the professional staffs at Princeton's Mudd Library, the Schomburg Center for Research in Black Culture, the Manuscripts and Archives Division of the New York Public Library, the Library of Congress, and the National Archives at Suitland, Maryland. While at home, the helpful staff at the interlibrary loan office at Boston College processed my countless book and microfilm requests with great courtesy and efficiency.

I could never have surveyed the voluminous newspaper and manuscript resources for this project without the help of my research assistants. Rachel Matson sifted through countless boxes of nineteenth-century mayoral papers, while Chris Samito provided his legal expertise in researching case law on the third degree. My undergraduate research assistants at Boston College—Melissa Lopes, Jennifer Pish, Robin Wheeler, Caroline Vasicek, Lete Childs, and Nicole Spain—canvassed newspapers and other essential sources. Arriving at a critical time in the summer of 2002, Kevin Hoskins expertly collected and distilled hundreds of newspaper and magazine articles published since 1970 as well as conducting last minute mop-up operations in the archives.

Much of this research was subsidized by grants from Boston College, which also provided me with an extended sabbatical in 2001–2002 as well as funds for travel and indexing. I am likewise indebted to the American Council of Learned Societies, which awarded me a research fellowship in 1997–1998. During the year I spent in Seattle in 1994–1995, the History Department at the University of Washington graciously sponsored me as a visiting scholar, while Jim Gregory, Susan Glenn, and Glennys Young made me feel at home in the Northwest. While on the road, Steve Aron and Amy Green put me up at their home in Princeton, as did Murray Rosenblith and Carol Leven in Brooklyn and Claire Potter and Nancy Barnes in Manhattan.

Colleagues around the country have offered much useful feedback and advice over the course of this project. I would like to thank members of the Massachusetts Historical Society's Seminar on Urban and Immigration History, the Columbia Seminar on Twentieth Century Politics and Society, the Gotham Center History Forum, and the Boston College History Department Seminar for listening to my works-in-progress and offering their comments. Many individuals also offered much-needed criticism of earlier versions of this work, including Danny Walkowitz, Ed Escobar, Wilbur Miller, Joanne Klein, Chris Wilson, David Quigley, and Ken Jackson. Bob Fogelson not only read and commented on parts of the manuscript but generously invited me to share his extensive files on urban policing. I also benefited from informal conversations with Herbert Hill and Paul Chevigny, who shared their memories and thoughts about antibrutality organizing over the past fifty years. In the final stages of writing, the members of my writing group—Julie Reuben, Wendy Luttrell, and Deborah Levenson—offered some of the toughest criticism and warmest support a writer could hope for, and I am immensely grateful to them. Finally, at the eleventh hour, Susan Ware read the entire manuscript, delivered her characteristically expert editorial advice, and motivated me as I drudged down the homestretch.

I am very fortunate to have found a home for this book at Beacon Press. Thanks to a fortuitous meeting in a taxicab in Rochester, New York, I discovered a talented and enthusiastic editor in Amy Caldwell, who helped me reshape and improve the manuscript in numerous ways. Timothy Maher provided expert copyediting, and Sara Eisenman worked diligently to create a striking cover.

My family has lived with this project for as long as I have, and my debt to them is greatest of all. My mother-in-law, Meira Zedek, contributed many hours of her retirement retrieving documents and newspaper articles from the Library of Congress. With the help of my father-in-law, Misha Zedek, she also translated dozens of articles from Yiddish to English—helping me understand Jewish attitudes toward police violence in the early twentieth century. Both of them provided countless hours of baby-sitting, meals, and transportation to the archives as I conducted research in Washington, D.C. My parents, Mary and Tom Johnson, have likewise offered emotional support and encouragement and many opportunities for rest and relaxation at their home in Florida. Finally, Dan Zedek has heard more, read more, and viewed more photographs of the New York police than anyone should ever have to. He has—along with our children, Rosa and Jacob—listened to my ideas, endured my research trips, encouraged me through the writing process, and offered the love and support that kept me going. This book is dedicated to them.

INDEX